Contents

Module 1 Learning (p.7)

A Smart learners

Reading	Language development	Vocabulary	Listening	Speaking	Writing
Find specific information; Short-answer questions (pp. 8–9)	Present simple (p. 10)	Studying; Collocations; Skills (p. 11)	Predict answers; Section 1: Notes completion (p. 12)	Introductions; Use a range of vocabulary; Part 1 (p. 13)	Introduce advantages and disadvantages; Task 2: Advantages-disadvantages essay (p. 14)

Module 2 Connecting (p.23)

A Family and friends

Reading	Language development	Vocabulary	Listening	Speaking	Writing
Understand general meaning; Matching headings (pp. 24–25)	Comparatives and superlatives (p. 26)	Family; Other relationships; Phrasal verbs; Talking about relationships (p. 27)	Understand important information; Section 2: Sentence completion (p. 28)	Talk about friends and family; Explain and justify answers; Part 1 (p. 29)	Interpret visual data; Task 1: Bar charts (p. 30)

Module 3 Earning a living (p.39)

A Jobs

Reading	Language development	Vocabulary	Listening	Speaking	Writing
Identify specific detail; *True/False/Not given* (pp. 40–41)	Present continuous; Present continuous and present simple; Stative verbs (p. 42)	Jobs; Adjectives to describe jobs; Activities at work (p. 43)	Understand detailed information; Section 3: Multiple choice (p. 44)	Give your opinion: adjectives; Part 2 (p. 45)	Paragraphing; Express cause and effect; Task 2: Problem-solution essay (p. 46)

Module 4 Well-being (p.55)

A Health

Reading	Language development	Vocabulary	Listening	Speaking	Writing
Understand connections; Matching sentence endings (pp. 56–57)	Past simple; Past continuous; Past simple and past continuous (p. 58)	Illnesses and symptoms; Accidents and injuries; Getting better; Staying healthy (p. 59)	Listen for detail; Section 4: Matching (p. 60)	Agree and disagree; Part 3 (p. 61)	Write an introduction; Paraphrase; Task 2: Opinion essay (p. 62)

Module 5 The world around us (p.71)

A Journeys

Reading	Language development	Vocabulary	Listening	Speaking	Writing
Understand detailed information; Matching information (pp. 72–73)	-*ing* forms and infinitives (p. 74)	Travel and transport; Tourism: compound nouns, phrasal verbs, dependent prepositions (p. 75)	Understand main points; Section 2: Table completion (p. 76)	Structure your answer; Part 2 (p. 77)	Organise information; Describe changes and trends; Task 1: Line graphs (p. 78)

Contents

B Studying at university

Listening	Language development	Vocabulary	Reading	Writing	Speaking
Section 1: Notes completion (p. 15)	Present simple with adverbs of frequency; *can* for ability, possibility and permission (p. 16)	Higher education; Subjects; Collocations (p. 17)	Short-answer questions (pp. 18–19)	Add supporting points; Task 2: Advantages-disadvantages essay (pp. 20–21)	Use a range of vocabulary: adjectives; Give opinions; Part 1 (p. 22)

B Events and celebrations

Listening	Language development	Vocabulary	Reading	Writing	Speaking
Section 2: Sentence completion (p. 31)	Adverbs and adverbial phrases (p. 32)	Countries, nationalities, languages; Celebrations (p. 33)	Matching headings (pp. 34–35)	Identify key features; Task 1: Bar and pie charts (pp. 36–37)	Expand answers; Part 1 (p. 38)

B At work

Listening	Language development	Vocabulary	Reading	Writing	Speaking
Section 3: Multiple choice (p. 47)	*have to* and *must*; *need to*; *should* (p. 48)	Different types of work; Confusing words; Collocations; Job benefits and rewards; Phrasal verbs (p. 49)	*True/False/Not given* (pp. 50–51)	Introduce solutions; Task 2: Problem-solution essay (pp. 52–53)	Prepare your answer; Use grammar accurately; Part 2 (p. 54)

B Nature

Listening	Language development	Vocabulary	Reading	Writing	Speaking
Section 4: Matching (p. 63)	Countable and uncountable nouns; Quantifiers (p. 64)	The animal kingdom; Geographical features; Verbs (p. 65)	Matching sentence endings (pp. 66–67)	Organise ideas; Write topic sentences; Task 2: Opinion essay (pp. 68–69)	Give examples; Speak fluently; Part 3 (p. 70)

B Our environment

Listening	Language development	Vocabulary	Reading	Writing	Speaking
Section 2: Table completion (p. 79)	Prepositions of place, time and movement (p. 80)	Weather; Climate change; Environmental issues (p. 81)	Matching information (pp. 82–83)	Describe changes and trends: adjectives and adverbs; Task 1: Line graphs (pp. 84–85)	Structure your answer: use time phrases; Part 2 (p. 86)

Contents

Module 6 Buying and selling (p.87)

A The food we eat

Reading	Language development	Vocabulary	Listening	Speaking	Writing
Understand paraphrasing; Summary completion (pp. 88–89)	be going to (p. 90)	Food groups; Flavours; Types of food; Diet (p. 91)	Follow a conversation; Section 1: Matching (p. 92)	Say you are not sure; Part 3 (p. 93)	Structure a paragraph; Give examples; Task 2: Opinion essay (p. 94)

Module 7 City life (p.103)

A Communities

Reading	Language development	Vocabulary	Listening	Speaking	Writing
Understand sequencing; Flow chart completion (pp. 104–105)	Zero conditional (p. 106)	Communities; Adjectives; Crime; Verbs (p. 107)	Identify different types of information; Section 3: Short-answer questions (p. 108)	Express opposing ideas; Part 3 (p. 109)	Write an introduction and overview; Describe numbers; Task 1: Tables (p. 110)

Module 8 Activity (p.119)

A Sport

Reading	Language development	Vocabulary	Listening	Speaking	Writing
Understand the difference between detail and general information; Multiple choice (pp. 120–121)	Present perfect (p. 122)	Doing sports; Sporting equipment; People in sport; Phrasal verbs (p. 123)	Follow a talk; Section 4: Summary completion (p. 124)	Balance information; Link ideas; Part 2 (p. 125)	Generate ideas and vocabulary; Introduce reasons and solutions; Task 2: Problem-solution essay (p. 126)

Module 9 Media (p.135)

A The news

Reading	Language development	Vocabulary	Listening	Speaking	Writing
Understand connections; Matching features (pp. 136–137)	Present perfect and past simple (p. 138)	Media; Adjectives; Social media; Phrasal verbs (p. 139)	Locate information; Section 1: Form completion (p. 140)	Express attitude; Part 3 (p. 141)	Compare and contrast data; Task 1: Pie charts (p. 142)

Module 10 Communicating (p.151)

A Being understood

Reading	Language development	Vocabulary	Listening	Speaking	Writing
Identify ideas and opinions; Yes/No/Not given (pp. 152–153)	Relative clauses (p. 154)	Communicating; Spoken communication; Non-verbal communication (p. 155)	Connect information to a visual; Section 4: Label a diagram (p. 156)	Emphasise a point; Part 2 (p. 157)	Write a conclusion; Concluding phrases; Task 2: Opinion essay (p. 158)

IELTS overview (p. 6)
Module reviews 1–10 (p. 168)
Test strategies (p. 178)
Expert grammar (p. 183)
Expert speaking: useful language (p. 193)
Expert speaking (p. 194)
Expert writing (p. 200)
Audio scripts (p. 210)

Contents

B How we buy

Listening	Language development	Vocabulary	Reading	Writing	Speaking
Section 1: Matching (p. 95)	*will*; *will* and *be going to* (p. 96)	Types of shops; Shopping; Verbs and verb phrases; Dependent prepositions (p. 97)	Summary completion (pp. 98–99)	Link ideas; Task 2: Opinion essay (pp. 100–101)	Degrees of certainty; Use a range of vocabulary; Part 3 (p. 102)

B Public services

Listening	Language development	Vocabulary	Reading	Writing	Speaking
Section 3: Multiple choice; Short-answer questions (p. 111)	First conditional (p. 112)	Public buildings; Public services (p. 113)	Flow chart completion; Multiple choice (pp. 114–115)	Introduce and describe information; Task 1: Tables (pp. 116–117)	Give yourself time to think; Part 3 (p. 118)

B Work and play

Listening	Language development	Vocabulary	Reading	Writing	Speaking
Section 4: Multiple choice; Summary completion (p. 127)	Articles (p. 128)	Sporting events; Sports and business; Compound nouns; Collocations (p. 129)	Notes completion; Multiple choice (pp. 130–131)	Add information; Task 2: Problem-solution essay (pp. 132–133)	Develop a topic; Make yourself clear; Part 2 (p. 134)

B Technology

Listening	Language development	Vocabulary	Reading	Writing	Speaking
Section 1: Matching; Form completion (p. 143)	Possessives; Pronouns; Quantifiers (p. 144)	Technology; Word formation; Phrasal verbs (p. 145)	Matching features; Sentence completion (pp. 146–147)	Describe similarities; Task 1: Bar charts and line graphs (pp. 148–149)	Ask for clarification/repetition; Speak fluently; Part 3 (p. 150)

B Understanding others

Listening	Language development	Vocabulary	Reading	Writing	Speaking
Section 4: Label a diagram; Notes completion (p. 159)	*may/might* for possibility and permission; *could* for ability, possibility and requests (p. 160)	Intercultural communication; Attitudes (p. 161)	Short-answer questions; *Yes/No/Not given* (pp. 162–163)	Express certainty; Check your work; Task 2: Opinion essay (pp. 164–165)	Express manner, means and purpose; Use correct stress and intonation; Part 2 (p. 166)

IELTS overview

Listening (30 minutes + 10 minutes transfer time)

Discourse types	Question types	Skills
Section 1: a conversation between two people in an everyday context **Section 2:** a monologue in an everyday context **Section 3:** a conversation between up to four people in an educational setting **Section 4:** a monologue on an academic subject	40 questions, including: • Multiple choice • Short-answer questions • Notes/Table/Form/Flow chart completion • Diagram labelling • Matching • Classification • Sentence completion • Flow chart summary • Plan/Map/Diagram labelling	• Listening for gist • Listening for main ideas • Listening for specific information • Understanding opinions

Academic Reading (60 minutes)

Text types	Question types	Skills
General interest texts taken from journals, newspapers, textbooks and magazines. These non-specialist texts are graded in difficulty and are representative of reading requirements for undergraduate and postgraduate students. Total of 2,000–2,750 words	40 questions, including: • Multiple choice • Short-answer questions • Notes/Table/Form/Flow chart completion • Diagram labelling • Matching • Classification • Sentence completion • Flow chart completion • Matching paragraph headings • Matching lists/phrases • *True/False/Not given*	• Reading for gist • Skimming • Reading for main ideas • Reading for detail • Understanding logical argument • Recognising opinions, attitudes and purpose

General Training Reading (60 minutes)

Texts and extracts taken from books, magazines, newspapers, notices, advertisements, company handbooks and guidelines that you would encounter on a daily basis.

Academic Writing (60 minutes)

Task 1: a minimum of 150 words. A summarising description of graphic or pictorial input. **Task 2:** a minimum of 250 words. An extended piece of discursive writing.	**Task 1:** Describe, summarise or explain information from a graph, table or chart. **Task 2:** Respond to a point of view, argument or problem. Formal register required.	• Using the appropriate writing conventions and register • Describing processes • Describing data • Expressing a point of view • Comparing and contrasting • Analysing problems and solutions

General Training Writing (60 minutes)

Task 1: a minimum of 150 words. Writing a letter or email. **Task 2:** a minimum of 250 words. An extended piece of discursive writing.	**Task 1:** Write a letter or email to someone explaining a situation or requesting information. **Task 2:** Write an essay in response to a point of view, argument or problem. Can be personal in style.	

Speaking (11–14 minutes)

Format	Nature of interaction	Skills
Part 1: Introduction and interview (4–5 minutes) **Part 2:** Individual long turn (3–4 minutes) **Part 3:** Exploring a topic/discussion (4–5 minutes)	**Part 1:** Speaking on familiar topics like home, family, work, studies, interests, etc. **Part 2:** You will be given a card which asks you to talk about a topic. You have one minute to prepare before you speak for two minutes. You will then be asked one or two questions on the same topic. **Part 3:** You will be asked more questions about the topic in Part 2 so you can discuss more abstract ideas.	• Giving personal information • Talking about everyday habits and issues • Expressing opinions • Organising ideas • Understanding the rules of conversation

Total test time: 2 hours and 45 minutes (+10 minutes transfer time for Listening)

1 Learning

1a Training
- **Reading:** Find specific information (Short-answer questions)
- **Language development:** Present simple
- **Vocabulary:** Studying
- **Listening:** Predict answers (Section 1: Notes completion)
- **Speaking:** Introductions; Use a range of vocabulary (Part 1: Introduction and interview)
- **Writing:** Introduce advantages and disadvantages (Task 2: Advantages-disadvantages essay)

1b Testing
- **Listening:** Section 1: Notes completion
- **Language development:** Present simple with adverbs of frequency; *can* for ability, possibility and permission
- **Vocabulary:** Higher education
- **Reading:** Short-answer questions
- **Writing:** Task 2: Advantages-disadvantages essay
- **Speaking:** Part 1: Introduction and interview

Are you an early bird or a night owl?

We asked 100 people, 'At what time of day do you feel most productive? Most creative?'

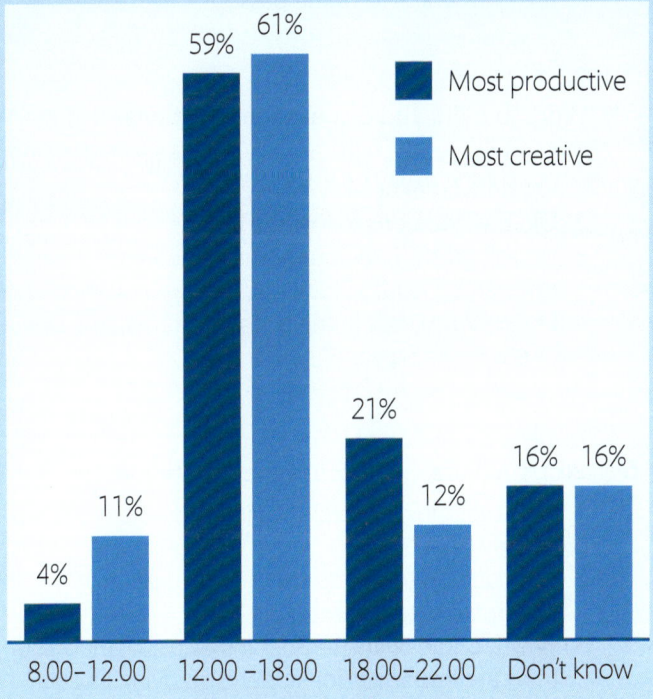

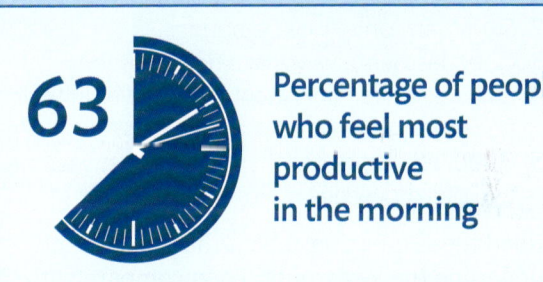

63 — Percentage of people who feel most productive in the morning

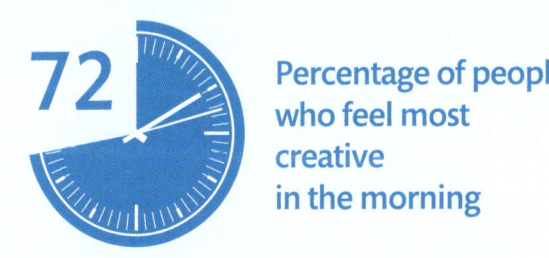

72 — Percentage of people who feel most creative in the morning

productive = making things in large quantities or producing a good result

creative = using imagination to produce new ideas or things

Lead-in

Discuss the questions.

1. Look at the infographic. At what time of day are people:
   - most productive?
   - least productive?
   - most creative?
   - least creative?
2. At what time of day are you most/least productive? Most/Least creative?

1a Smart learners

Reading (Short-answer questions)

Before you read

1 Work in pairs and discuss the questions.
   1 Do you think you are a good learner? Why/Why not?
   2 Do you think good learners share particular characteristics? If so, what characteristics are typical of good learners?

Find specific information

2 Read the passage quickly and choose the correct answers.
   1 What is the purpose of the passage?
      A to give instructions
      B to give an opinion
      C to give advice
   2 Who wrote the passage?
      A a student
      B a psychologist
      C a teacher

3a Read the passage again. Match these key ideas (1–5) with the paragraphs (A–E).
   1 Good language skills are important.
   2 Study can sometimes be boring.
   3 Good learners always have new questions.
   4 Good learners think about their studies in their free time.
   5 Good learners realise there is a link between new and old knowledge.

b Read these questions about the passage and underline the key words. Then compare with a partner.

   1 What do good learners never stop trying to do?
   2 How do good learners feel about their chances of finding the answer to a study problem?
   3 What makes doing boring learning tasks worthwhile?
   4 What do good learners modify as they learn more?
   5 Who can good learners explain new knowledge to in an appropriate way?

c Match each question in Exercise 3b with the kind of information you need to find.
   A a person or people _____
   B an activity or a thing _____ _____ _____
   C a feeling _____

d Work in pairs. Look at question 1 in Exercise 3b and follow these steps to answer it. Use no more than three words in your answer.
   1 Which part of the passage contains the answer?
   2 What is the correct answer?
   3 Which words in the passage reflect the words in the question (*never stop trying to do*)?
   4 Check the number of words. If there are more than three words, what can you leave out?

Test training

4 Answer questions 2–5 in Exercise 3b. Follow the steps in Exercise 3d for each question. Remember that you should:
   • use no more than three words in each answer.
   • use only words from the passage.

Task analysis

5 Work in pairs and discuss the questions.
   1 How did reading the whole passage first help you to find where the answers were?
   2 Did the questions follow the order of the passage?
   3 Which words in the questions helped you understand what to look for?
   4 Do the key words in the questions repeat the words in the passage?

Discussion

6 Work in pairs and discuss the questions.
   1 Which of the characteristics in the passage do you already have?
   2 How do you think you can help yourself to become a better learner?
   3 Which of the characteristics in the passage do you think are important for students studying English? Are there any other characteristics that you think are important?

Who makes a good learner?

An experienced university teacher has put together a list of the psychological characteristics that good learners have.

A Good learners are curious. They wonder about all sorts of things. They love the discovery part of learning. Finding out about something gives them an intense satisfaction. But their curiosity is addictive, so they always want to find out more.

B Good learners work hard. A few things may come easily to learners, but most knowledge requires effort and good learners are willing to put in the time. They talk with others, read more, study more and carry around what they do not understand, thinking about it before they go to sleep, at the gym, on the bus. Good learners are persistent. When they fail, they carry on, confident that they will figure it out eventually. In the meantime, they learn from their mistakes.

C Good learners recognise that learning is not always fun. But that does not change how much they love it. Understanding the topic, when they finally get there, makes it all worth doing. But the journey to understanding is not generally all that exciting. Some learning tasks require boring repetition; others a mind-numbing attention to detail; still others involve periods of intense mental focus.

D Good learners make knowledge their own. This is about making the new knowledge fit with what the learner already knows. Good learners have to change and adapt their knowledge structures in order to make room for what they are learning. In the process, they build a bigger and better knowledge structure. It is not enough to just take in new knowledge. It has to make sense, to connect in meaningful ways with what the learner already knows.

E Good learners share what they have learned. Unless knowledge is passed on, it is lost. Good learners love sharing what they have learned. They write about it and talk about it. Good learners can explain what they know in ways that make sense to others. They are not trapped by specialised language. They can find examples that make what they know meaningful to other learners.

1a Module 1 Learning

Language development

Present simple

➤ EXPERT GRAMMAR page 183

1 Match the sentences (1–3) with what they express (A–C).
   1 We work in teams most of the time.
   2 My brother works in Berlin.
   3 The course lasts three years.

   A a fact that is always true
   B a habit or repeated action
   C a permanent situation/state

2 Complete the sentences with the present simple form of the verbs in brackets.
   1 It _____ (be) sometimes hard to organise your work at university.
   2 They _____ (have got) a lot of reading to do on this course.
   3 We really _____ (enjoy) the lectures on this subject.
   4 She usually _____ (study) in the library.
   5 He always _____ (help) me with my writing.
   6 You _____ (remember) facts very well.
   7 Sam _____ (watch) the lectures online.
   8 He _____ (carry) his laptop with him everywhere.
   9 The university _____ (have got) good sports facilities.
   10 I _____ (be) very good at maths but my sister _____ (be) better at languages.

3a Find and correct the mistakes in seven of the questions.
   1 How you travel to work or college?
   2 How many people there are in your family?
   3 Where does your family lives?
   4 What you like about your home town?
   5 Your house is big or small?
   6 Is there anything about your English course you don't like?
   7 You have any hobbies?
   8 You are good at sport?

b Work in pairs. Take turns to ask and answer the questions in Exercise 3a.

4a Are these sentences true for you? If not, make them true by making the verb negative.
   1 My first language is English.
   2 I'm very good at tennis.
   3 Most of my friends are British.
   4 I've got a very big family.
   5 I enjoy reading in another language.
   6 My best friend lives in Canada.
   7 I study very hard every evening.
   8 My house has got ten bedrooms.

b Work in pairs. Talk to your partner about the sentences in Exercise 4a. Give more information.

   > My first language isn't English – it's Chinese.

5 Complete the text with the present simple form of the verbs in brackets. Use short forms where possible.

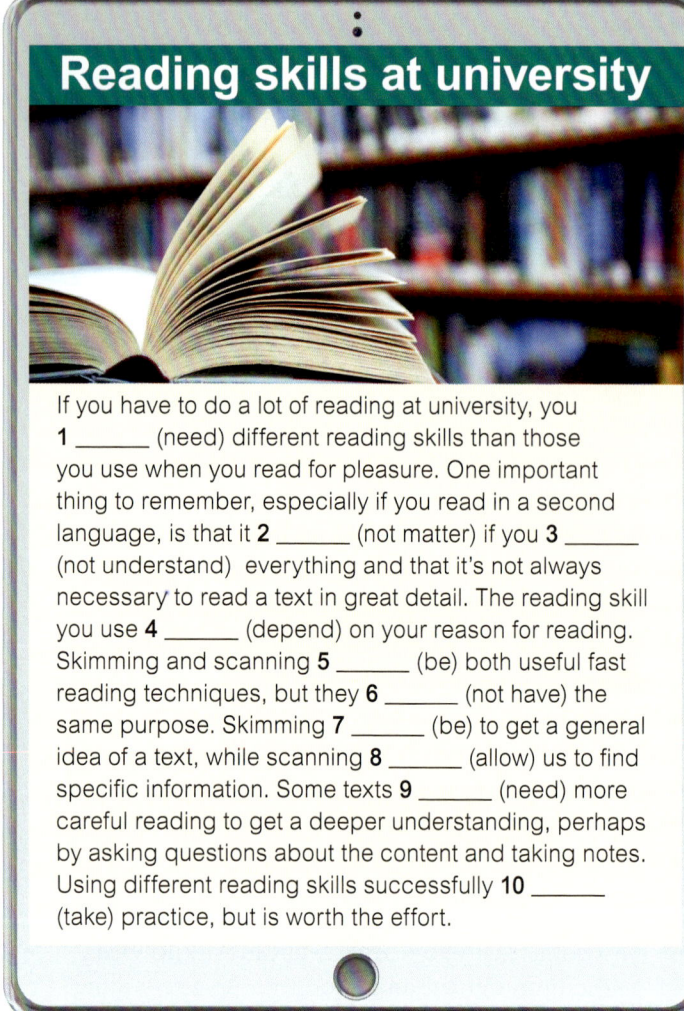

Reading skills at university

If you have to do a lot of reading at university, you 1 _____ (need) different reading skills than those you use when you read for pleasure. One important thing to remember, especially if you read in a second language, is that it 2 _____ (not matter) if you 3 _____ (not understand) everything and that it's not always necessary to read a text in great detail. The reading skill you use 4 _____ (depend) on your reason for reading. Skimming and scanning 5 _____ (be) both useful fast reading techniques, but they 6 _____ (not have) the same purpose. Skimming 7 _____ (be) to get a general idea of a text, while scanning 8 _____ (allow) us to find specific information. Some texts 9 _____ (need) more careful reading to get a deeper understanding, perhaps by asking questions about the content and taking notes. Using different reading skills successfully 10 _____ (take) practice, but is worth the effort.

6 Work in pairs. Tell each other about your typical study day. Use the verbs/phrases in the box to help you. Ask your partner at least three questions about his/her day.

   discuss with friends   do homework   go to classes
   go to lectures   go to the library   read   study
   take a break   use a computer   write

   > Do you study in the library?
   >
   > Sometimes, but I usually study at home.

10 Student's Resource Book > Language development page 8   MyEnglishLab > 1a Language development

Module 1
Learning
1a

Vocabulary

Studying

1a Match the words in the box with their meanings (1–10).

assignment course essay examination grade presentation project report research term

1 a piece of work that someone gives you to do
2 a piece of planned work that is done over a period of time
3 an event at which someone explains an idea to a group of people
4 a piece of writing that gives facts about a situation or event
5 a mark that your teacher or tutor gives you
6 a spoken or written test of knowledge
7 a piece of writing about a particular subject
8 detailed study of a subject to find out new information
9 a set of lessons in a particular subject
10 one of the three parts of a school, college or university year

b Choose the correct options in *italics* to complete the text.

Midlands College International Foundation Course

Academic English Module

The Academic English module aims to prepare students for higher education at an English speaking university. There are four **1** *courses / assignments* over three terms, followed by two final **2** *examinations / grades* of three hours each at the end of Term 3.

Term 1
• Students write a **3** *research / report* based on information collected from a questionnaire and interviews.
• Students write a 1,000-word **4** *essay / research* on a given topic.

Term 2
Students give an academic **5** *essay / presentation* on a subject of their choice.

Terms 2 and 3
• Students complete a group **6** *report / project* by carrying out **7** *examinations / research* into a given academic topic.
• Students will receive their final results and **8** *grades / assignments* at the end of July.

Collocations

2 Choose the options in *italics* which <u>cannot</u> be used with the nouns in bold.

1 For your next piece of work, you need to *write / do / carry out* some **research**.
2 I'm going to *do / make / give* a **presentation** on my home country.
3 How many **exams** do you have to *take / make / do* this year?
4 I need to *get / do / have* very good **grades** to do a medical degree.
5 In the exam, we have to *write / do / carry out* two **essays** before the end of term.
6 Can you *finish / complete / make* your **assignment** by the end of this week?
7 It's difficult to *produce / make / write* the **report** without the necessary information.
8 You need to work together in order to *complete / carry out / have* this **project**.

3 Complete the collocations with the verbs in the box.

ask do give have prepare take

1 _____ revision   4 _____ questions
2 _____ for a test   5 _____ notes
3 _____ a discussion   6 _____ your opinion

4 Complete the sentences with collocations from Exercises 2 and 3.

1 I need to <u>do research</u> for my assignment.
2 Use phrases like *I think* and *I believe* to _____ .
3 I am very nervous because I have to _____ in front of 50 people.
4 I find it difficult to _____ when I listen to a lecture.
5 I can't go out – I have to _____ a maths _____ .
6 After my presentation, I asked the audience if they would like to _____ .

Skills

5a Work in pairs. Match the skills (1–6) with the examples of activities (A–F). Can you think of any more examples?

1 practical skills   A creating reports
2 management skills   B using Excel
3 computer/IT skills   C being a good listener
4 reading/writing skills   D typing
5 people skills   E speaking French
6 language skills   F being a good leader

b Work in groups and discuss the questions about the skills in Exercise 5a.

1 Which three skills do you think are important for success at work today? Why? Put them in order of importance.
2 Which are your three best skills?

1a Module 1
Learning

Listening (Section 1: Notes completion)

Before you listen

1. Work in pairs and discuss the questions.
   1. Which of these do you often have problems with?
      - writing essays
      - preparing for presentations
      - handing work in on time
      - revising for exams
      - managing your study time
   2. Who do you talk to if you have a problem with your studies?
      - a friend
      - a family member
      - your personal tutor
      - somebody else?

Predict answers

2a. Look at the notes. What is the situation? Who are the two people talking?

Record of tutorial

Date: 27 March

Student's name: Rashad Al-Hashimi

Topics discussed:
- presentation
- essay feedback
- advice about 1 _____

Action points:
- attend talk with 2 _____ (Tuesday at 3 _____)
- arrange meeting at 4 _____

Next tutorial: 5 _____ at 10.30 a.m.

b. Decide what kind of information goes in each gap in Exercise 2a. Use the words before and after each gap to help you.
   A a date
   B a time
   C a name
   D a place
   E a topic

c. 🔊 1.1 Complete the notes in Exercise 2a with the words in the box. Then listen and check.

17 April   3.15 p.m.   Dr Green   exams   Student Services

Test training

3a. Read the test task. Think about what kind of information goes in each gap.

Complete the notes below. Write NO MORE THAN TWO WORDS AND/OR A NUMBER for each answer.

Meeting with Student Services Advisor (Lin Wood)
- Organise time: make a 1 _____ for revision.
- Practise past exam papers.
- Start a 2 _____ with other students.
- Take regular study breaks: 3 _____ every hour.
- Make time for 4 _____ , e.g. sport.
- Lin's working hours: every morning and 5 _____ afternoons
- Contact number: 6 _____

b. 🔊 1.2 Complete the test task.

Task analysis

4. Work in pairs and discuss the questions.
   1. Did the questions follow the same order as the recording?
   2. Did you correctly predict the type of information for each gap?
   3. Did you check the number of words you used for each answer?

Discussion

5. Work in pairs and discuss the questions.
   1. Do you think Lin's advice is helpful?
   2. Can you think of any other advice to help a student prepare for exams?

Module 1
Learning
1a

Speaking (Part 1)

Introductions

Pronunciation: connected speech

Use a range of vocabulary

Test training

Task analysis

1a When you first meet someone, what do you like to find out about them?
- their home town
- their family
- their work or studies
- something else?

b 🔊 1.3 Listen to two students meeting each other. Which of the topics in Exercise 1a do they talk about? What other topics do they discuss?

2a 🔊 1.3 Listen again and complete the questions.
1 _____ you like the course so far?
2 _____ do you live?
3 _____ do you travel to classes?
4 _____ do you live with?
5 _____ you do a lot of sport?
6 _____ type of films do you like?

b 🔊 1.4 Listen again to the questions in Exercise 2a. How do the speakers pronounce *do you*?

c Practise saying the questions in Exercise 2b.

3a Look at audio script 1.3 on page 210. Which of the adjectives in the box do the speakers use to describe:
- their course?
- their accommodation?
- meeting people?

boring cheap comfortable convenient difficult easy expensive
fantastic great hard interesting modern quiet small

b Work in pairs. Imagine you are just meeting each other. Take turns to ask and answer the questions in Exercise 2a. Try to use as many of the adjectives in Exercise 3a as possible in your answers.

4a Write some questions to ask your partner about their home town and family. Use the words and phrases below to help you.
- Do you … ?
- What (do you) … ?
- Where (do you) … ?
- How often (do you) … ?
- How many …?
- Why?

b Work in pairs. Take turns to ask and answer your questions from Exercise 4a. Remember to use adjectives in your answers.

5 Work in pairs and discuss the questions.
1 Were some questions more difficult to answer? Which ones? Why?
2 Did you give short answers or did you add extra information?
3 Did you use weak forms of *do you* in your questions?
4 Which adjectives did you use in your answers?

Module 1
1a Learning

Writing (Task 2)

What's in an essay?

1 Choose the correct answers. You must choose more than one option in two questions.
   1 What is an essay?
      A a description of an event or experience, giving a personal view
      B a piece of writing about a particular subject, usually with the writer's own opinions
      C a piece of writing that gives facts and details about a situation or an event
   2 Who might we write an essay for?
      A a friend or relative
      B an unknown audience
      C a tutor or lecturer
   3 Which of the following do you find in an essay?
      A an introduction
      B a conclusion
      C a main idea
      D lots of difficult vocabulary

2a Read the writing task and underline the key words. Then choose the correct answer in the question below.

   Many students work while they are studying.
   What are the advantages and disadvantages of working while you study?

   What do you need to write about?
   A the difficulty of studying
   B how study prepares you for work
   C working and studying at the same time

 b Work in pairs. Follow the steps below.
   1 Think of one advantage and one disadvantage you could include in your essay.
   2 Discuss your ideas with another pair.
   3 Read the model answer. Does it mention any of your ideas? What other advantages and disadvantages does it mention?

Going to university can be very expensive and so many students decide to work while they are studying.

The main advantage of working while studying is earning money. A salary allows students to pay for their living accommodation, their food, their books and their fees. As a result, they do not need to borrow money from the bank or from their parents. Another advantage is that it gives students experience of working. This looks very good on their CV when they leave college.

One disadvantage is that it is hard to work at the same time as studying. Work can make people feel very tired, and this means it is difficult for students to make themselves read a textbook or work on an assignment when they get home after work. Another problem is that having a job means there is simply much less time available for study. Working students may not be able to complete their assignments as well as full-time students and so get poor marks.

Overall, in my opinion, it is a good idea to work and study at the same time. Working gives students valuable experience, which makes it easier for them to find a job afterwards. However, they need to be very good at organising their time so they can still read all the books on their reading list and hand in well-written assignments.

Introduce advantages and disadvantages

3 Look at the phrases in the box for introducing advantages and disadvantages. Which ones does the student use in the model answer?

   One advantage/disadvantage is …
   The main advantage/disadvantage is …
   Another advantage/disadvantage/problem is …

4 Write sentences for the essay about the advantages and disadvantages of working and studying at the same time. Use your ideas from Exercise 2b and the phrases in Exercise 3.

1b Studying at university

Listening (Section 1: Notes completion)

Before you listen

1 Work in groups and discuss the questions.
   1 What decisions do you and/or your family have to make during your education?
   2 How did you choose the course or subject(s) you study? Was it difficult to decide? Who helped you decide?

Test practice

> TEST STRATEGIES page 178

2 Work in pairs. Read the test task and answer the questions.
   1 Who do you think is talking?
   2 How many words should you write in each gap?
   3 What kind of information do you need for each gap?

Questions 1–8
*Complete the notes below. Write **ONLY ONE WORD OR A NUMBER** for each answer.*

Course options
- Engineering: need high grade in 1 _____
- Economics and business studies: need high level of 2 _____
- Business studies course: three days of 3 _____ and two days in a company
- Course organiser has contacts with local 4 _____
- Speak to Professor 5 _____ in Room 6 _____
- Business school talks by guest speakers: ring 7 _____ to book
- Final decision by end of 8 _____

> **HELP**
1 Listen for a subject.
3 Listen for an example of something you might do on a course.
5 Listen for a name.
7 Listen for a telephone number.

3 🔊 1.5 Complete the test task.

Task analysis

4 Work in pairs and discuss the questions.
   1 Did you correctly predict the type of information for each gap? Which answers were easier to predict? Which were more difficult?
   2 Look at audio script 1.5 on page 210 and underline the correct answers. Which key words in the listening helped you find the answers?

Discussion

5 Work in pairs and discuss the questions.
   1 Is it better to make important decisions on your own or is it better to ask other people? Why?
   2 Do the decisions you make about your education have an effect on your future career? In what way?

Student's Resource Book > Listening page 11   MyEnglishLab > 1b Listening

15

Module 1
Learning

Language development

Present simple with adverbs of frequency

▶ EXPERT GRAMMAR page 183

1 Write the adverbs in the box in the correct place on the scale.

~~always~~ ~~never~~ normally/usually occasionally often rarely sometimes

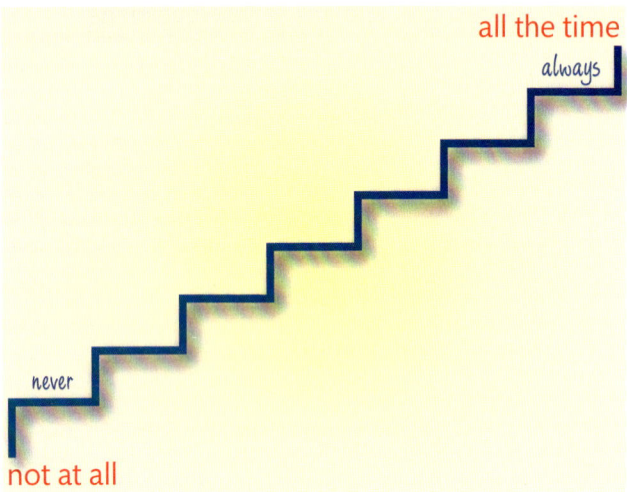

all the time
always

never

not at all

2 Rewrite the sentences putting the adverb in the correct place.
   1 Lectures start at nine. (usually)
      Lectures usually start at nine.
   2 We don't study in the library. (often)
   3 She's late for class. (rarely)
   4 He goes to the library at 8 a.m. (always)
   5 Do you write reports? (often)
   6 I am confused by the lectures. (sometimes)
   7 He doesn't fail exams. (normally)
   8 They have to give presentations. (occasionally)
   9 We write essays. (rarely)
   10 He goes to tutorials. (never)

3a Put the words in the correct order to make sentences.
   1 grades / get / often / for / assignments / I / bad
   2 interesting / lectures / usually / my / are / very
   3 have to / I / give / sometimes / a presentation
   4 at / study / I / rarely / weekends
   5 in / always / library / study / Fridays / on / I / the
   6 have / homework / to / never / I / do / any
   7 exams / do / I / occasionally
   8 research / online / I / do / normally

b Make the sentences in Exercise 3a true for you. Then talk to your partner. Add extra information.

> I rarely get bad grades for assignments but I occasionally get a bad mark for maths – it's very difficult!

can for ability, possibility and permission

4 Look at these sentences with *can/can't*. What does each one express? Write *A* for *ability*, *PO* for *possibility* or *PE* for *permission*.
   1 Can I borrow your laptop? _____
   2 I can't speak French or German. _____
   3 You can ask your tutor for help with references. _____
   4 You can read about the course on our website. _____
   5 I'm sorry, I can't help you with that. _____
   6 Can I come in? _____

5 Rewrite the sentences using *can* or *can't*.
   1 I am not able to speak French very well but I am able to understand it a little.
      I can't speak French very well but I can understand it a little.
   2 We've got permission to leave the lecture early.
   3 Do you think Xi is able to help us with this assignment?
   4 Some people don't have the ability to read quickly.
   5 It's not possible for you to study economics without a good grade in maths.
   6 Are you able to hear what's she's saying?
   7 They haven't got permission to use the computers in the library.
   8 It's not possible for you to see Professor Gibson now. Is it possible for you to come back later?
   9 Some people are not able to work in a team.
   10 Do you have permission to use material from the college website?

6a Look at this list of skills and activities. Add three more ideas of your own.
   - play a sport well
   - give an academic presentation
   - speak another language (apart from English and your first language)
   - write essays in English
   - sing
   - read quickly
   - play a musical instrument
   - use research skills
   - drive
   - _____
   - _____
   - _____

b Work in pairs. Take turns to ask and answer about the skills and activities in Exercise 6a.

> Can you play a sport well?

> I can play basketball quite well, but I can't play many other sports.

Vocabulary

Higher education

1a Write the words in the box in the correct place in the table.

admissions office   advisor   campus   classmate
department   faculty   laboratory   lecturer   library
professor   tutor

Places	People

b Match the words (1–5) with their meanings (A–E).
1 degree
2 undergraduate
3 post-graduate
4 PhD
5 MBA

A a student at university studying for their first degree
B a higher university degree in research in a particular subject
C what you get when you successfully finish any university course
D a higher university degree in business
E a student at university who has already done a degree

c Complete the text with the correct form of words from Exercises 1a and 1b.

About Brindel University

Our **1** _____ is set in a green area outside the city. Each **2** _____ has its own building, but the science departments share a large **3** _____ for research and projects. Please refer to our interactive map. The **4** _____ is in the centre of the campus; it is open every day for borrowing and returning books from 8 a.m. to 9 p.m. but online access is 24 hours.

We offer a range of **5** _____ at undergraduate and post-graduate level. Your personal **6** _____ can help you with your choice. Please contact the **7** _____ with any questions you have about entry requirements.

Subjects

2a Complete the sentences with the words in the box.

accountancy   architecture   business studies
computer science   dentistry   economics   engineering
law   medicine

1 A degree in _____ involves designing and building things like machines, roads and bridges.
2 To study _____ , you need to be creative and good at art and design.
3 A degree in _____ is not just about looking after teeth; you also study general health of the human body.
4 _____ is a difficult degree course and you need to be able to think clearly and be good at essay writing.
5 Many banking, sales and marketing jobs require a degree in _____ or _____ .
6 If you want to get a job keeping financial records, you need to study _____ .
7 In the digital age, when technology is so important, it is usually easy to get a job with a degree in _____ .
8 You need to get excellent grades in science subjects to do a degree in _____ and it can take years to become qualified.

b Work in pairs. Which of the subjects in Exercise 2a do you find interesting? Why?

Collocations

3a Choose the correct options in *italics* to complete the questions.
1 What do you do if you *pass / miss* a lesson?
2 How do you feel when you *make / do* a mistake when speaking English?
3 Would you like to *do / get* a course in a language apart from English? If so, which one?
4 What's the best way to *make / do* progress when learning a language?
5 How many lessons or lectures do you *go / attend* every week?
6 What do you find difficult about *making / doing* assignments?
7 Have you ever *failed / lost* an exam?
8 What was the last exam you *wrote / passed*?

b Work in pairs. Ask and answer the questions in Exercise 3a.

What do you do if you miss a lesson?

I usually call a friend and ask if I can borrow their notes.

1b Module 1
Learning

Reading (Short-answer questions)

Before you listen

1 Work in pairs. What do you think students learn about on a business degree course?

2 You want to carry out a survey of students doing a business course. Which four of the below would you choose to ask about? What questions would you ask?
- their reasons for studying business
- what they study on their course
- whether their course includes any practical work experience
- which part of their course they like best
- what useful skills their course gives them
- their plans for the future

Test practice

▶ TEST STRATEGIES page 179

3a Read the test task and underline the key words.

Questions 1–6

Answer the questions below. Choose **NO MORE THAN TWO WORDS** *from the passage for each answer.*

▶ HELP

2 Look for a phrase which shows that something is necessary.

3 Be careful: the passage mentions two aspects and talks about the one that students do *not* prefer. You need the other one for your answer.

4 Look for a word that has a similar meaning to *usually*.

1 What do most business students expect to get after graduating?
2 What do students on an MBA course need?
3 Which aspect of a business degree do students prefer?
4 How long do most business students usually spend on a work placement?
5 What type of business department do most students plan to work in?
6 Who thinks business graduates have good presentation skills?

b What kind of information do you think the answer to each question will be (e.g. a person, a time, a quality)?

4 Complete the test task.

Task analysis

5 Look at the key words you underlined in the questions. Which words in the passage helped you find your answers? Compare your ideas with a partner.

Discussion

6 Work in pairs and discuss the questions.
1 Which do you think is the most useful part of a business degree: the theory or the practical work? Why?
2 How valuable is practical work experience:
  - for the students?
  - for the company that employs them?
3 Do you think it is better to study business as an undergraduate or as a professional with some years of experience? Why?

Module 1
Learning

International survey of business courses

A recent international survey of business degrees shows that business and related subjects – such as accounting and economics – are among the most popular courses at universities worldwide. Students say that they choose these courses because business has an impact on almost every aspect of modern society. They also believe that a business degree makes it easy to find a job. Business graduates often earn a good salary although very few of the students in the survey give that as their reason for studying business.

The term 'business degrees' includes a wide variety of courses; some are specialised and others are more general; some are very academic and others focus on practical professional development. There are also different levels of degree. Most business students are undergraduates. However, there are also large numbers of business students on post-graduate courses. Professional qualifications such as MBAs are only for people who already have some business experience.

The study shows that all types of business degree look at both theory and practice. Of these two parts of a course, the theoretical aspect is less popular with most students although all agree that it is an essential part of a good degree course. Students look at practice through case studies, problem-solving tasks and project work. They also often have the chance during their course to spend a period of time – typically three months but it can be up to one year – actually working in a company.

The survey also shows that the majority of students plan to go into a career in business. There are, of course, many different types of business career. Only a relatively small percentage of students plan to set up their own business. Some aim to work in finance departments, others in advertising and still more in sales. Human resources and business consultancy are also options which some graduates consider.

A few students who study business decide that it is not after all the career for them. However, their degree is still a very useful qualification. The international survey also reports on interviews with a range of employers. These say they like the fact that business graduates are excellent team workers and can present information well both in writing and in front of an audience. These are valuable skills in all workplaces. The survey concludes that choosing to study business can be a very good decision.

Module 1
Learning

Writing (Task 2)

Lead-in

1 Work in pairs and discuss the questions.
 1 Which of the extra-curricular activities in the photos would you like to get involved in?
 2 What skills do you think these activities might give you?
 3 How could these skills help you in the workplace?

Understand the task

> EXPERT WRITING page 200

2a Read the test task and choose the correct answer in the question below.

Write about the following topic.

Many students like to get involved in extra-curricular activities at university such as social clubs or sports.
What are the advantages and disadvantages of this?

Give reasons for your answer and include any relevant examples from your knowledge or experience. Write at least 250 words.

What do you need to write about?
 A the good and bad points of doing extra activities
 B an extra activity that is good for students
 C an extra activity that is not good for students
 D your experience of doing extra activities at university

b Underline the parts of the essay question that helped you answer the question in Exercise 2a.

Module 1
Learning
1b

Plan your essay

3a Read the model answer. Match the parts of the essay (1–4) with the paragraphs (A–D).
1 the disadvantages
2 introducing the topic
3 the conclusion
4 the advantages

A As well as studying hard at university, there are many opportunities to do extra-curricular activities while you are there. There are all sorts of different clubs that you can join, for example.

B In my view, the main advantage of doing extra-curricular activities is that you make a lot of friends. You get on well with each other because you share the same interest. Another advantage is that you can learn a new skill – how to ski or fly a helicopter, for example – relatively cheaply. Obviously, it is a good idea to make the most of that opportunity.

C There are also disadvantages. One disadvantage is the fact that doing extra-curricular activities can take a lot of time away from your studies. It is easy to take on too many new things and this means you do not have enough time to go to the library or write your assignments. You have to find the right balance between study and fun. Another problem is that doing extra-curricular activities means you do not have the time to do a part-time job. This means that you can finish university with big debts.

D My personal opinion is that taking part in extra-curricular activities is a good thing. It is an opportunity to develop old interests and to take up new ones, and it is one of the best ways of making close friends while you are at university.

b Read the model answer again and answer the questions.
1 Does it answer the question in the task?
2 Which advantages and which disadvantages does it mention?

c Work in pairs. Think of two advantages and two disadvantages you can include in your essay. Make notes in the table.

Advantages	
Disadvantages	

Language and content

4a Look at paragraphs B and C in the model answer. Find the parts where the student explains their answer. Find one point that explains or supports each advantage and disadvantage.

b Work in pairs. Look at your plan in Exercise 3c. Think of one supporting point for each advantage and disadvantage. Add them to your plan.

Write your essay
> TEST STRATEGIES page 181

5 Write two paragraphs for the essay in Exercise 2a: one discussing the advantages and one the disadvantages. Use your plan from Exercise 3c. Remember to:
• introduce each advantage and disadvantage using appropriate phrases.
• include a supporting point for each advantage and disadvantage.
• write about 150 words.

Assess and improve

6 Check your work. Did you do these things in your paragraphs?
1 I included at least two advantages.
2 I included at least two disadvantages.
3 I used phrases to introduce each advantage and disadvantage.
4 I included a supporting point for each advantage and disadvantage.

Student's Resource Book > Writing page 14

Module 1
Learning

Speaking (Part 1)

Use a range of vocabulary

1 a Think about a course or subject you are studying. How many different adjectives can you think of to describe it?

b 🔊 1.6 Listen to a candidate doing Part 1 of the Speaking test and answer the questions.
1 What topic is he talking about?
2 Which sentence best describes the students' answers?
  A He uses the same words all the time to say what he thinks about something.
  B He avoids repeating the same words in his answers by using a range of vocabulary.

c Look at audio script 1.6 on page 211. Find and underline the adjectives the candidate uses.

Give opinions

2 a 🔊 1.6 Listen again and complete the sentences with the phrases the candidate uses to give his opinions.
1 _____ the course is quite exciting.
2 Well, _____ , it's quite hard work.
3 _____ you can ask as many questions as you'd like to.
4 Mainly because _____ I can get a good job when I finish.
5 _____ , it's quite easy to get jobs in engineering.

b Look at audio script 1.6 on page 211. What words and phrases does the student use to give reasons for his opinions?

c Write the phrases from Exercises 2a and 2b in the table.

Giving opinions	Giving reasons for opinions

d Work in pairs. Tell each other what you think about these things. Use phrases from Exercise 2c. Remember to give reasons for your opinions.
- a course you are studying
- a film you like
- a sport you enjoy
- a town or city you like

> I think … is a beautiful and interesting city because it has many historic buildings and lots of green parks.

Test practice

▶ **TEST STRATEGIES** page 182

▶ **EXPERT SPEAKING** page 194

3 Work in pairs. Follow the instructions and complete the test task. Then swap roles.
- Student A: Ask the questions. Listen carefully to help your partner afterwards.
- Student B: Answer the questions.

1 What do you study?
2 Do you enjoy it?
3 Is there anything you don't like about it?
4 What is the most interesting thing about your course?

Assess and improve

4 Work in pairs. Ask your partner to tell you if you did these things in your answers.
1 Did you use a range of vocabulary? Which adjectives did you use?
2 Did you give your opinions? Did you use appropriate phrases to introduce them?
3 Did you give reasons for your opinions? Did you use appropriate phrases to introduce them?

2 Connecting

2a Training
- **Reading:** Understand general meaning (Matching headings)
- **Language development:** Comparatives and superlatives
- **Vocabulary:** Family; Relationships
- **Listening:** Understand important information (Section 2: Sentence completion)
- **Speaking:** Talk about friends and family; Explain and justify answers (Part 1: Introduction and interview)
- **Writing:** Interpret visual data (Task 1: Bar charts)

2b Testing
- **Listening:** Section 2: Sentence completion
- **Language development:** Adverbs and adverbial phrases
- **Vocabulary:** Countries, nationalities, languages; Celebrations
- **Reading:** Matching headings
- **Writing:** Task 1: Bar and pie charts
- **Speaking:** Part 1: Introduction and interview

Lead-in

Discuss the questions.
1 What do you think is the best way to make friends? Why?
2 Where do you make most of your friends?
3 What kind of activities do you do with your friends?

2a Family and friends

Reading (Matching headings)

Before you read

1 Work in pairs and discuss the questions.
   1 Are your friends and family important to you? Why?
   2 Which of these things do you do with family? With friends?
   - get advice on your work or studies
   - talk about your relationships
   - spend leisure and social time

Understand general meaning

2a Read the title of the passage and the introductory sentence. What do you expect to read about?
   A family life in different cultures
   B how families spend their leisure time
   C how individual families have their own way of doing things

b Read the passage quickly and check your answer to Exercise 2.

c Read the passage again and match the topics (1–5) with the paragraphs (A–E).
   1 family size
   2 the individual and society
   3 social change
   4 different sides of the family
   5 roles in the family

d Underline the key words in each paragraph that helped you find your answers in Exercise 2c. Then compare with a partner.

3 Read paragraph A again and look at the paragraph headings in the test task. Follow steps 1–4 to find the heading that matches that paragraph.
   1 Underline the key words in the headings.
   2 Read the first sentence of paragraph A carefully. The first sentence, called the topic sentence, usually introduces the main theme of the paragraph. The rest of the paragraph then explains or says more about the topic sentence.
   3 Read the whole paragraph, looking for key words that match words you underlined in one of the headings.
   4 Think about the meaning of the whole paragraph. Check that it matches the heading you have chosen.

*Choose the correct heading for paragraphs **A–E** from the list of headings below. Write the correct number, i–vi.*

List of headings
i Whose side of the family: the mother's or the father's?
ii How is society changing?
iii Who is more important: the person or the group?
iv Who makes which decisions?
v How well do families get on with each other?
vi Who shares your home?

1 Paragraph A _____
2 Paragraph B _____
3 Paragraph C _____
4 Paragraph D _____
5 Paragraph E _____

Test training

4 Read the rest of the passage and choose the correct headings for paragraphs B–E. There is one extra heading you do not need to use. Follow the same steps as you did for paragraph A in Exercise 3.

Task analysis

5 Work in pairs and discuss the questions.
   1 Are the headings about one part of a paragraph or about the whole paragraph?
   2 Are the words in the headings the same or different from the words in the passage?
   3 Which heading was not needed? Why was this extra heading wrong?

Discussion

6 Work in pairs and discuss the questions.
   1 Do you like the idea of many generations living together? Why/Why not?
   2 How do you make decisions in your family? For example, do you ask one person or many people?
   3 Is family life in your country changing? How?

The meaning of family

We all know that each family is unique and that families differ around the world, but how?

A We are all individual people and we are all members of society too. Cultures differ in the relationship between the individual and the community. Some cultures focus on the significance of each individual; some believe that the interests of the community matter more than those of the individual. This has an impact on attitudes towards family life. Cultures that value individuality focus on the individual's right to independence and a private life. Cultures that give greater value to the community say that individuals must put the wishes of their family and their society before their own individual wishes.

B Many western cultures place a high value on the individual. In these cultures, people live in 'nuclear families'. This means that only the parents and their children live together. In many other cultures people live in 'extended families'. In these families children are not only close to their immediate family; they also have very strong relationships with their grandparents as well as their aunts, uncles and cousins. The different generations of extended families often live together in one house.

C In modern nuclear families the mother and father usually decide together how they want to live and how they will educate their children. In extended families there is often a more traditional sharing of responsibility. The father is usually responsible for life outside the home. He, for example, is responsible for financial or legal decisions. It is usually a woman – the mother or sometimes the grandmother – who has responsibility for life inside the home. She chooses, for instance, what the family will eat and what colour the walls will be.

D Another difference is the relative importance of the man's and the woman's family when a couple marry and have children. In most European cultures children traditionally take their father's surname, but they are not 'more related' to either their father's or their mother's family. This is not always the case in other cultures. In Middle Eastern families, for example, the father's family is often the more important one. However, in some American Indian and African cultures children are, first and foremost, members of their mother's family.

E Nowadays many societies are multicultural. So everyone has to understand that cultural differences affect family relationships. It is important to remember, however, that cultures do not stand still. This means that we cannot know for sure what a person's attitude towards their family is today just because they come from a particular culture.

Module 2
Connecting

Language development

Comparatives and superlatives

▶ EXPERT GRAMMAR page 183

1 Match the sentences (1–5) with what they express (A–C).
   1 My father is the most intelligent person I know.
   2 I'm just as close to my brother as I am to my sister.
   3 I think having a big family is more interesting than having a small one.
   4 I'm not as confident as my sister.
   5 My grandfather is the oldest member of our family.

   A to say two people, things or situations are different (x2)
   B to say two people, things or situations are the same
   C to compare people or things with the group they are in (x2)

2 Complete the sentences with the comparative form of the adjectives in brackets.
   1 I have two _____ (old) brothers and a _____ (young) sister.
   2 My parents are both good at tennis but my mother is _____ (good) than my father.
   3 My brother works very hard now but in the past he was much _____ (lazy).
   4 It's _____ (easy) to make friends in a small town than in a big city.
   5 I'm not very good at keeping my room tidy but my sister is even _____ (bad).

3 Complete the sentences with *more* or *less*.
   1 Which is _____ important for you: friends or family?
   2 I find it _____ difficult to make friends than my sister does – she's very sociable.
   3 These days it's _____ common to be an only child; most people have brothers and sisters.
   4 My brothers are all very confident but I'm quite shy and much _____ sociable than they are.
   5 I prefer eating at home with my family because it's _____ expensive than eating out.

4a Complete the questions with the superlative form of the adjectives in brackets.
   1 Who's your _____ (good) friend?
   2 Which member or your family is _____ (similar) to you?
   3 Who's the _____ (confident) person you know?
   4 Who's the _____ (young) person in your family?
   5 Who's the _____ (interesting) person you know?
   6 Who's your _____ (funny) friend?

  b Work in pairs. Take turns to ask and answer the questions in Exercise 4a. Give more information in your answers.

(*not*) *as … as …*

5 Rewrite the sentences using (*not*) *as … as …* .
   1 My mother is older than my father.
      My father _____ my mother.
   2 My best friend and I are both very sociable.
      I'm just _____ my best friend.
   3 He's got a much bigger family than I have.
      My family _____ his.
   4 I'm less confident than my sister.
      I'm _____ my sister.
   5 My grandparents have busier lives than I do.
      My life _____ my grandparents'.
   6 I'm closer to my father than my mother.
      I'm _____ I am to my father.

Making comparisons with nouns

6a Look at the bar chart below showing the percentage of families who spend time doing different activities together. Choose the correct options in *italics* to complete the sentences.
   1 A *greater / smaller* number of families spend time at the cinema than watching TV at home.
   2 Families spend *more / less* time visiting relatives than going to the cinema.
   3 A *greater / smaller* number of families spend time eating together at home than eating in a restaurant.
   4 *More / Fewer* families spend time eating together at home than watching TV.

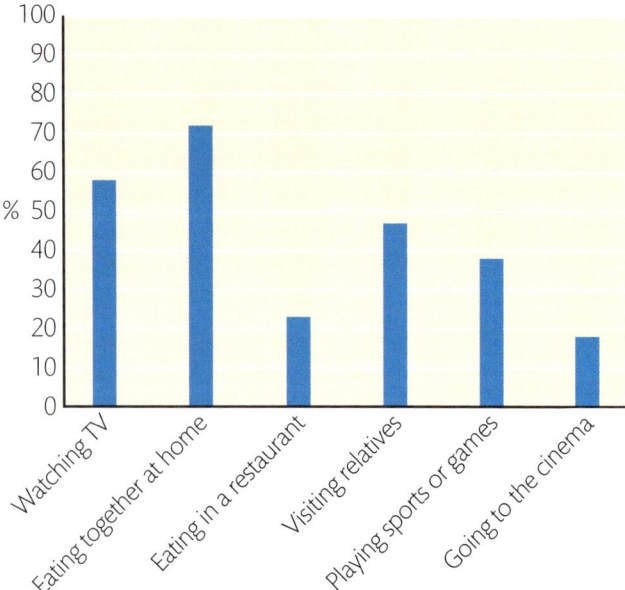

  b Use the information in the chart in Exercise 6a to complete the sentences.
   1 A _____ number of families spend time visiting relatives than going to the cinema.
   2 Families spend _____ time playing sports than eating together at home.
   3 _____ families go to the cinema than watch TV at home.
   4 _____ families play sports or games together than eat in a restaurant.

Vocabulary

Family

1 Match the family words in the box with the descriptions (1–10).

aunt cousin granddaughter ~~grandfather~~ grandson
mother-in-law nephew niece stepfather uncle

1 your mother's father — grandfather
2 your father's sister — _____
3 your aunt's son — _____
4 your mother's brother — _____
5 your mother's new husband — _____
6 your son's daughter — _____
7 your sister's son — _____
8 your brother's daughter — _____
9 your daughter's son — _____
10 your husband's mother — _____

Other relationships

2 Choose the correct options in *italics* to complete the sentences.

1 We have good *acquaintances / neighbours* – they always look after our house when we go on holiday.
2 My *manager / lecturer* always makes the subject interesting and easy to understand.
3 I am doing a group project with some of my *tutors / classmates*.
4 I don't like having *roommates / neighbours*, so I live on my own.
5 I like my *housemates / colleagues* but we never meet outside work.
6 If you have a problem with your studies, it's a good idea to talk to your *tutor / employer*.
7 I work in a very small office with just three other *roommates / co-workers*.
8 I don't know Mr Lawrence very well; he's just a(n) *acquaintance / classmate* of my family.

Phrasal verbs

3a Complete the sentences with the words in the box.

after (x2) on out up (x2)

1 Do you take _____ either of your parents?
2 Do you ever look _____ young members of your family?
3 Which member of your family do you get _____ with best?
4 Is it easy to bring _____ children well?
5 Do you ever fall _____ with your friends?
6 Which member of your family do you look _____ to most?

b Work in pairs. Take turns to ask and answer the questions in Exercise 3a.

Talking about relationships

4a Complete the sentences with the verbs in the box.

be enjoy get have (x2) keep lose

1 It doesn't matter if you _____ touch with school friends when you go to university; you will soon make new ones.
2 It's difficult for brothers and sisters to _____ close to each other if there is a big difference in age.
3 It's important for married couples to _____ a lot in common with each other.
4 It's a good idea for colleagues to _____ together outside work occasionally.
5 These days it's easier to _____ in touch with old friends by email and social networking.
6 It's a good idea to _____ a good relationship with your neighbours in case you need their help.
7 It doesn't matter if you don't _____ spending time with your roommates.

b Work in pairs. Do you agree or disagree with the sentences in Exercise 4a? Give reasons for your answers.

> I think it's important to keep in touch with your school friends so you can see them when you go home from university.

5 Work in pairs. Choose five people from Exercises 1 and 2. Talk about your relationship with them using language from Exercises 3a and 4a.

2a Module 2 Connecting

Listening (Section 2: Sentence completion)

Before you listen

1 Do you think you need to have similar opinions and beliefs to have a good relationship with someone? Why/Why not?

Understand important information

2a Read the sentences summarising information from a radio programme about relationships. Underline the key words.
   1 The idea that we like people who have a different personality to us is not true.
   2 When making friends, it's important for us to concentrate on what is similar about us.
   3 It's wrong to think you can change your friend when you begin a friendship.
   4 If our friends are the same as us, we will not experience new ideas.

b Match these words and phrases with some of the key words you underlined in Exercise 2a.
   1 a mistake
   2 what we have in common
   3 different ideas
   4 enter a relationship
   5 not correct
   6 opposite character
   7 similar to
   8 find attractive

Test training

3a Work in pairs. Read the test task. What aspect of relationships do you think the radio programme is about?

*Complete the sentences below. Write **NO MORE THAN TWO WORDS** for each answer.*

The same or different?
1 Most people believe they are _____ on the topic of relationships.
2 We like people who are similar to us and stay away from those who do not _____ us.
3 Research showed that people in all types of relationship had a lot _____ with each other.
4 A second study showed it's difficult to _____ a friend's opinions.
5 It's better to choose a friend who shares our opinions and our _____ from the start.
6 It's important to connect with people who are _____ us.

b 🔊 2.1 Look at sentence 1 in the test task and follow these steps.
   1 Underline the key words in the sentence.
   2 Decide what type of word is missing (noun, verb, adjective, etc.).
   3 Listen to the first part of the programme and complete sentence 1 with one word.

c Did the speaker use the key words you underlined or did she use different words to say the same thing?

d 🔊 2.2 Complete the rest of the test task.

Task analysis

4 Work in pairs and discuss the questions.
   1 Look at the key words you underlined in sentences 2–6 in the test task. Find words or phrases with a similar meaning in audio script 2.2 on page 211.
   2 Did you correctly predict the type of missing word in each sentence?

Discussion

5 Work in pairs and discuss the questions. Give reasons and examples.
   1 Do you usually agree with your friends on most subjects?
   2 Are there any subjects on which you have different opinions to your friends?
   3 Do you think it is easy or difficult to change a friend's ideas and opinions?

> I usually agree with my best friend on most subjects, but we have different opinions about music; I like classical music and she likes rock.

Module 2
Connecting
2a

Speaking (Part 1)

Talk about friends and family

1 Who are you most similar to in your family? Who are you most different from? How? Think about:
   - your appearance.
   - your personalities.
   - things you like/don't like.
   - your hobbies and interests.

2 🔊 2.3 Listen to two students talking about one of their families and answer the questions.
   1 Why does Ken get on well with his brother?
   2 Why is he not as close to his sister?
   3 How is Ken different from his mother?
   4 Why do Ken and his father sometimes disagree?
   5 Why is his grandmother his favourite person?

Explain and justify answers

3a 🔊 2.3 Complete the sentences Ken uses to explain and justify his answers with the words/phrases in the box. Then listen again and check your answers.

and   as   because   but   in fact   so   that's why

   1 I get on better with my brother _____ we're closer in age.
   2 I'm eight years younger than her, _____ we're not as close _____ we don't have that much in common, really.
   3 We're both confident _____ I'm not as sociable as she is.
   4 We have very different personalities and _____ we sometimes disagree.
   5 We're very close. _____ , she's probably my favourite person _____ although she's in poor health, she's the most cheerful person I know.

b Which of the words/phrases in Exercise 3a does Ken use to:
   1 introduce a reason?
   2 add extra information?
   3 introduce a result?
   4 show a difference?

c Join the beginnings of the sentences (1–7) with the endings (A–G) using words/phrases from Exercise 3a.
   1 My grandparents live a long way from me
   2 I sometimes have to look after my younger sister
   3 My brother is very funny
   4 My best friend lives next door to me
   5 My grandfather is very old;
   6 I look like my mother
   7 My friend is not as close to his brother

A they don't have much in common.
B he makes me laugh.
C he's almost 90!
D it's difficult to visit them very often.
E we have very different personalities.
F she is only eight.
G we see each other every day.

Pronunciation: word stress

4a 🔊 2.4 Write the adjectives in the box in the correct part of the table according to the stress pattern. Listen and check your answers.

attractive   different   favourite   important   interesting   sociable

1 Oo	2 Ooo	3 oOo

b 🔊 2.5 Mark the stress in the words in bold. Then listen and check your answers.
   1 My sister and I have very **similar** ideas and opinions.
   2 It's very **expensive** to bring up children these days.
   3 He's not as **clever** as his sister.
   4 She's the most **popular** girl in the class.
   5 I'm not as **confident** as my mother.
   6 She's always very **cheerful**.

c Work in pairs and practise saying the sentences in Exercise 4b.

Test training

5 Work in pairs. Take turns to ask and answer these questions about your families. Remember to explain and justify your answers.
   1 Do you have a large or small family?
   2 Do you all live together in the same house?
   3 Who do you get on best with in your family?
   4 Are people in your country generally close to their families?
   5 Do you prefer spending time with friends or family?

Task analysis

6 Work in pairs and discuss the questions.
   1 Did you use some of the words/phrases in Exercise 3a to explain and justify your answers?
   2 Did you use adjectives with correct word stress?
   3 Did you make any comparisons?

MyEnglishLab > 2a Speaking

2a Module 2 Connecting

Writing (Task 1)

Interpret visual data

1 Work in groups. How many close relatives do you have? How many close friends do you have?

2a Look at the chart and answer the questions.
   1 Who does the chart give information about?
   2 What do the blue bars show? The orange bars?
   3 Do the numbers on the y axis (the vertical axis) show total numbers or percentages?
   4 Do the numbers on the x axis (the horizontal axis) show total numbers or percentages?

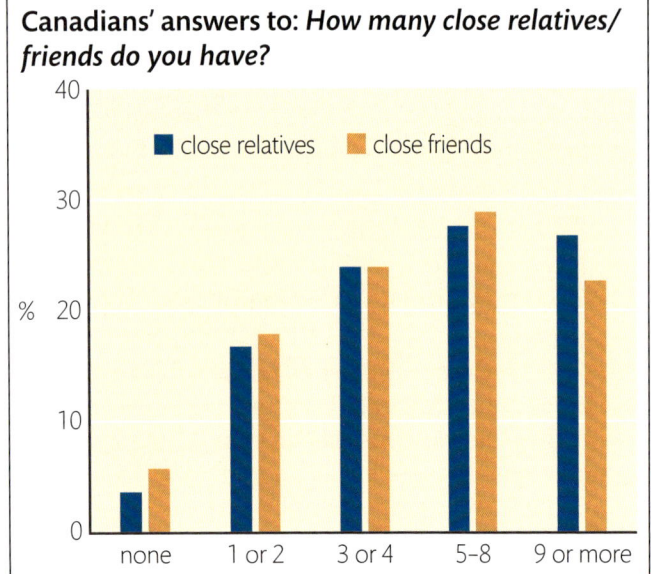

Canadians' answers to: *How many close relatives/friends do you have?*

b The beginning of a summary of a chart introduces what the chart is about. Which of these is the best introduction for the chart in Exercise 2a?
   A Some Canadians say they have very few close relatives or friends while others have many more. Most Canadians have between five and eight close friends and a similar number of relatives.
   B The chart shows that most Canadians say they have more close friends than close relatives. A surprising number of people have no close relatives or close friends.
   C The chart shows the number of close friends and the number of close relatives that Canadians have. It gives the percentage of people with specific numbers of friends and relatives, ranging from none to nine or more.

3a Read the beginning of a student's summary and complete the heading and labels in the chart that follows.

> The chart shows the numbers of close friends that British men and women in their twenties have. It gives the percentages of men and women with specific numbers of close friends, ranging from none or one to eight or more.

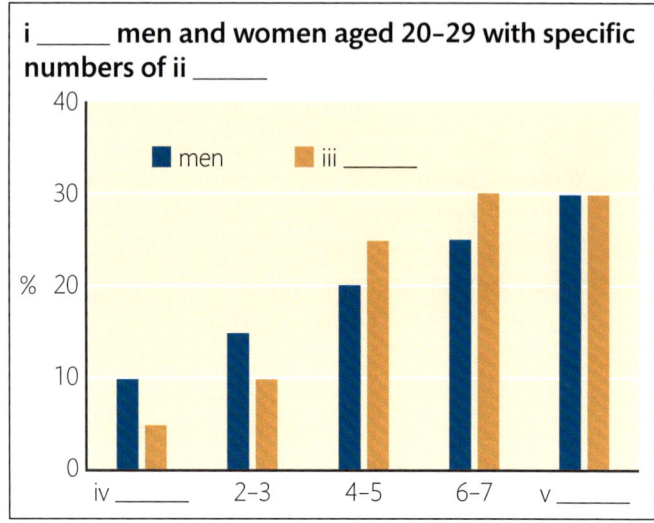

i _____ men and women aged 20–29 with specific numbers of ii _____

b Read part of a student's summary of the chart in Exercise 3a. Complete the introductory sentences with one or two words in each gap.

> The **1** _____ gives information about how British **2** _____ in their twenties answered the question 'How many **3** _____ do you have?' It shows the **4** _____ of men and women giving answers that range **5** _____ none or one to eight or more.
>
> Overall, the chart shows that British women in their twenties have more close friends than men of the same age do. However, nearly one third of both men and women say they have at least eight close friends.
>
> Ten percent of men and five percent of women say they have no more than one close friend. For both genders, the percentages rise as the number of friends increases.

c What does the student do in the later paragraphs?
   A gives an opinion on the main features
   B describes the main features

4 Write the beginning of a summary of the chart below. Write two sentences introducing the main topic.

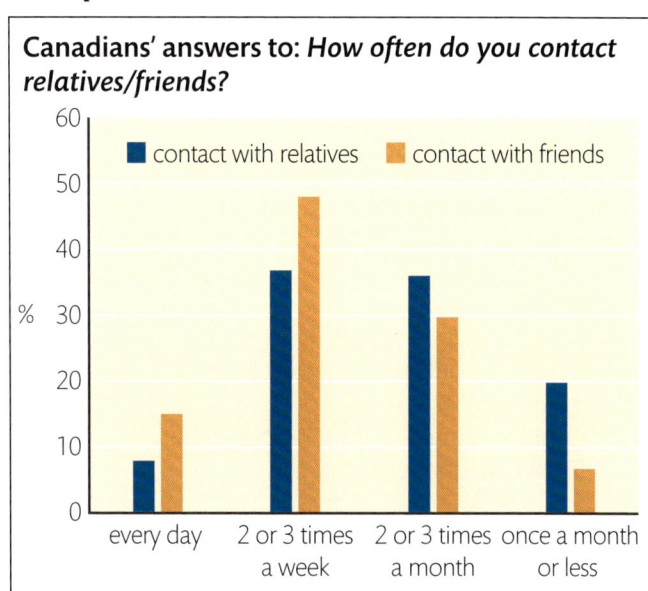

Canadians' answers to: *How often do you contact relatives/friends?*

2b Events and celebrations

Listening (Section 2: Sentence completion)

Before you listen

1 Work in groups and discuss the questions.
  1 Do you have many big celebrations with your family and friends? Who organises them?
  2 Which of these do you typically find at a celebration?
   • special food and drink   • music
   • decorations   • entertainment
   • family and friends   • other?

Test practice

➤ TEST STRATEGIES page 178

2a Read the test task. The sentences summarise information from a talk. Who do you think is giving the talk?

Questions 1–8
Complete the sentences below. Write **NO MORE THAN TWO WORDS** *for each answer.*

Event planning
 1 When you are organising an event for a client, it is important to do everything in the _____ .
 2 Before you start planning, talk about the budget _____ with your client.
 3 You need to book _____ locations early.
 4 When choosing the location, ask the customer what _____ they have in mind.
 5 Make sure that the _____ include all the important information.
 6 You and your client will have to choose food, table decorations and _____ .
 7 Don't worry if you have to _____ some details.
 8 Always keep a _____ so you don't forget anything.

b Work in pairs. Underline the key words in the test task. Can you think of other words/phrases the speaker might use instead of the key words?
  1 *organising = planning*

c Decide what type of word is missing from each sentence (noun, verb, adjective, etc.).

3 🔊 2.6 Complete the test task.

➤ HELP

2 You need a preposition in this answer.
3 Listen for why you should book locations early.
8 Listen for what the speaker says is the most important tip.

Task analysis

4 Work in pairs and discuss the questions.
  1 Look at the key words you underlined in the test task. Find words or phrases with a similar meaning in audio script 2.6 on page 211.
  2 Did you correctly predict the type of missing word in each sentence?

Discussion

5 Work in pairs. What type of event/party do you like best? What is most important for you? Think about these things.
  • the location
  • food and drink
  • entertainment
  • seeing family and friends
  • decorations

> The most important thing for me is seeing my family and friends because I like spending time with them. The location is less important, but I like to have good food.

Student's Resource Book > Listening page 21   MyEnglishLab > 2b Listening

2b Module 2
Connecting

Language development

1 Look at the words in bold in the sentences (1–4). Which of the questions (A–D) does each sentence answer?

1 She plans things very **carefully**.
2 We eat together at a restaurant **on Fridays**.
3 He lives **next door** to us.
4 I **rarely** go to parties.

A How often?   C When?
B How?   D Where?

Adverbs of manner

➤ EXPERT GRAMMAR page 184

2a Match graphs A–C with descriptions 1–3.

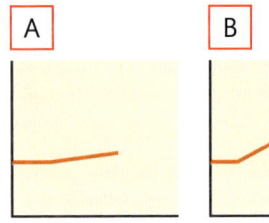 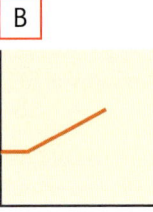 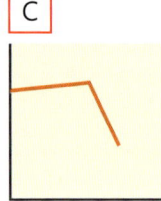

1 a sharp fall   3 a slight rise
2 a steady increase

b Rewrite the phrases in Exercise 2a using adverbs.
1 It is *falling sharply*.   3 It is _____ .
2 It is _____ .

3a Choose the correct options in *italics* to complete the sentences.
1 There is a *sharp / sharply* rise in the number of old people living alone.
2 You can make friends quite *easy / easily*.
3 This answer looks *wrong / wrongly* to me.
4 I don't get on *good / well* with my cousin.
5 My neighbours are very *noisy / noisily*.

b Complete the sentences with adverbs of manner.
1 I can't answer this question _____ (correct).
2 The prices are increasing very _____ (quick).
3 They're bringing up the children very _____ (good).
4 The number of students is falling _____ (steady).
5 The population is rising _____ (slow).

c Complete the sentences so that they are true for you. Use adverbs of manner.
1 I get on _____ with _____ .
2 Family size in my country is increasing/decreasing _____ .
3 I speak _____ very/quite _____ .
4 I make friends _____ .
5 I can _____ very/quite _____ .

d Work in pairs. Talk to your partner about your sentences in Exercise 3c. Give reasons and extra information.

> I get on well with my neighbours – they are very friendly and always help us.

Adverbs and adverbial phrases of frequency

4 Replace the words/phrases in bold with a word/phrase from the box with a similar meaning.

daily   every week   from time to time   hardly ever
once a year   several times a month   three times a year
twice a year

1 We get together for a big family celebration **every December**.
2 My family go on holiday **in March, July and October**.
3 I **rarely** speak to my neighbours.
4 I visit my grandparents **in the summer and again in the winter**.
5 My family only eat together **once in a while**.
6 I go out with my best friend **four or five times each month**.
7 My friends and I meet **every day** and go for a coffee.
8 I invite my friends for a meal **each Sunday**.

Adverbial phrases of place and time

5a Underline the words and phrases that show place or time.
1 I feel very tired today.
2 I like doing things outdoors.
3 I have holidays from June to July.
4 I study best in the evening and at night.
5 I like to go somewhere hot for my holidays.
6 I have to travel far to get here.
7 I can study anywhere.
8 I don't like going abroad.

b Work in pairs. Tell your partner which of the sentences in Exercise 5a are true/not true for you. Give more information in your answers and try to use other phrases of place and time.

> I don't feel very tired today but I feel quite hungry at the moment because it's lunchtime soon.

> I like doing things outdoors. For example, I like going to the park with my friends in the summer.

Vocabulary

Countries, nationalities, languages

1a Complete the sentences with the correct form of the words brackets.

1 An important North _____ (America) festival is Thanksgiving Day.
2 Many people around the world celebrate _____ (China) New Year.
3 _____ (France) people celebrate their National Day in July.
4 Most _____ (Greece) people have a special day to celebrate their name.
5 _____ (Brazil) Independence Day is in September.
6 A popular _____ (Asia) festival is the Mid-Autumn Festival in September.

b Change the country names in the box into adjectives.

Argentina   Australia   Britain   Canada   Egypt   Germany
Ireland   Italy   Japan   South Africa   Spain   Thailand
Turkey   Vietnam

c Work in pairs. What language is spoken in each of the countries in Exercises 1a and 1b? Use a dictionary to help you or look online.

Celebrations

2 Complete the text with the verbs/verb phrases in the box.

celebrate   decorate   dress up   have the day off   hold
invite   make a speech   take part   take place

New Year celebrations around the world

New Year celebrations **1** _____ at different times of year and in different seasons around the world. For many countries New Year is in winter, but Australia and New Zealand **2** _____ their celebrations in summer, and for many southeast Asian countries New Year is in spring.

In Denmark, before people start to **3** _____ New Year on the evening of 31 December, it is traditional to watch the Queen **4** _____ on TV. She talks about events of the old year and wishes everyone a Happy New Year.

At the end of the old year, people in Korea clean their homes to prepare for the coming year and **5** _____ them with red paper lanterns. On New Year's Day they **6** _____ in traditional colourful clothing called Hanbok.

In England and Wales, many people go out with friends on New Year's Eve to **7** _____ in special public events with music and fireworks. Some people prefer to have parties at home and **8** _____ their friends and family. New Year's Day is a public holiday, so most people **9** _____ work.

3a Choose the correct options in *italics* to complete the text.

Festivals in Scotland

The winter **1** *custom / season* is important for Scottish people because there are two big celebrations in December and January. People celebrate New Year, or Hogmanay, on the evening of 31 December. The celebrations continue on 1 and 2 January, which are both **2** *parades / public holidays*, so most people do not have to work. Hogmanay has many different **3** *customs / costumes* and the most important of these is the 'first-foot' – the first person to enter the house after midnight. This **4** *musician / guest* is often a neighbour or friend and they bring **5** *fireworks / gifts* of food and money to bring the home luck for the coming year.

Another Scottish **6** *tradition / party* is the singing of *Auld Lang Syne*. In big cities like Edinburgh and Glasgow, there are street parties and **7** *gifts / parades*, where people walk through the streets in **8** *customs / costumes* and **9** *musicians / guests* entertain the crowds. At midnight everyone enjoys a display of **10** *food / fireworks*, which are beautiful but very noisy.

Another important part of Scottish **11** *culture / season* is Burns Night. People celebrate it on 25 January, the **12** *anniversary / party* of the birthday of Scottish poet Robert Burns. People get together at special Burns Suppers. Everyone eats soup, haggis and other **13** *special food / decorations*, and afterwards different people make **14** *gifts / speeches* about the life of Robert Burns.

b Write five sentences about a celebration or festival in your country. Use words from Exercise 3a. Share your sentences with a partner.

4 Work in pairs. Think of a celebration or festival. Talk to your partner about it using words from the page. Can your partner guess what it is?

> It's a festival where people dress up in traditional costumes and there are parades in the street.

2b Module 2
Connecting

Reading (Matching headings)

Before you read

1 Work in pairs and discuss the questions.
  1 Do you enjoy parties? Why/Why not?
  2 Why do people have parties? What do they celebrate?
  3 What is there to do at a party?

Test practice

▶ TEST STRATEGIES page 179

2a Read the passage and think about the main theme of each paragraph. Which paragraph:
  1 focuses on the food at parties in Ancient Egypt?
  2 describes what happens when guests first arrive at a party?
  3 explains how we know about celebrations in Ancient Egypt?
  4 mentions lots of reasons for parties and other celebrations?
  5 talks particularly about parties when someone dies?
  6 is mainly about music and dancing at parties?

b Read the test task and underline the key words in the headings.

Questions 1–6

Choose the correct heading for paragraphs **A–F** from the list of headings below. Write the correct number, i–viii.

List of headings
  i   The range of celebrations
  ii Parties till the end
  iii The guest list
  iv Learning about the past
  v   The entertainment
  vi The variety of food
  vii What to wear
  viii The party begins

1 Paragraph A _____
2 Paragraph B _____
3 Paragraph C _____
4 Paragraph D _____
5 Paragraph E _____
6 Paragraph F _____

▶ **HELP**

i Look for a paragraph that talks about reasons to celebrate.
ii The word *end* in the heading refers to the end of life. Which paragraph talks about this?
v What do you expect to read about for *entertainment*?

c Complete the test task.

Task analysis

3 Work in pairs and discuss the questions.
  1 Did the title help you to think about what kind of information to expect?
  2 Did you use the topic sentence of each paragraph to help you?
  3 Did you use all the headings?
  4 Can you match words in the headings to similar words in the passage?

Discussion

4 Work in groups and discuss the questions.
  1 What do people usually celebrate in your country?
  2 In what ways are parties today the same as parties in Ancient Egypt? In what ways are they different?

Party time in Ancient Egypt

A Academics often think the ancient Egyptians were obsessed with death. But when we look at the paintings on the tombs of ancient Egypt, we see these ancient Egyptians having fun at big celebrations. The drawings of these events are where we get our information about these special parties that happened so long ago. We see how the guests are enjoying themselves in the company of others. They are eating and drinking as they watch dancers and acrobats.

B It's not hard to imagine most of ancient Egyptian society celebrating throughout the year. The tomb pictures show them marking different events in the farming calendar, as well as marriages, the birth of children and funerals for the dead. And, of course, richer Egyptians invited lots of guests to meals and parties simply for enjoyment. The ancient Egyptians loved a good time. Food, drink and music were clearly a big part of their lives.

C The tomb pictures show, for example, male and female hosts warmly welcoming each of their guests when they arrive at the party. They each receive a necklace of flowers and girls offer plates of food to them as they enter the room. Imagine those delicious dishes of butter and cheese, birds and beef, honey and fruit.

D It is clear that these hosts do not worry about money when they invite guests to a celebration. They are serving beef, duck, goose, goats and fish. There are plates filled with all sorts of different vegetables. The tomb pictures show about 15 different types of bread. The guests eat at their own individual tables and they use attractive bowls, plates and cups with pretty designs of flowers on them.

E Tomb paintings show the importance of music and dance in the lives of the ancient Egyptians. Some pictures show dancers performing for the guests. In other pictures of celebrations musicians are playing the drums and other instruments. The guests are taking part too – they sing, clap their hands and play simple instruments like tambourines or cymbals.

F For poor people, life is sometimes very different from the lives of the rich. But the pictures seem to show poor people also taking part in celebrations to mark a person's death. In these celebrations the Egyptians are preparing for life after death. That is probably because they hope to enjoy the same pleasures after death that they enjoyed in their lives on earth. And clearly, for them, parties are one of the big pleasures of life.

2b Module 2 Connecting

Writing (Task 1)

Lead-in

1 Work in pairs and discuss the questions.
  1 Which foreign languages do you speak?
  2 Which languages do other members of your family or your friends speak?
  3 How often do you practise these things outside the classroom for English or any other foreign languages you speak?
     • reading   • listening   • speaking   • writing

Understand the task

▶ EXPERT WRITING page 201

2a Read the test task and answer the questions.
  1 Do you need to write a summary or a detailed description of what the chart shows?
  2 What does the task ask you to report on?

The chart below gives some information about languages in two countries. Summarise the information by selecting and reporting the main features, and make comparisons where relevant.

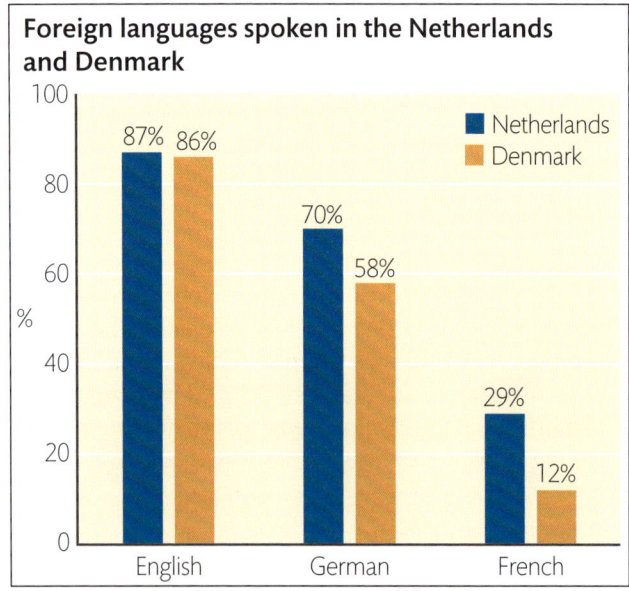

Foreign languages spoken in the Netherlands and Denmark

b Which of these pieces of information should you include in the first part of your summary?
  A the names of the two countries
  B the three languages
  C 87%, 86%, 70%, 58%, 29% and 12%

c Read the first part of a student's summary. Does it include the same information you chose in Exercise 2b?

> The chart gives information about the use of English, German and French as foreign languages in the Netherlands and Denmark. It shows the percentages of the population who can speak these languages in each of these two countries.

3 Now look at some sentences about the information in the chart. Which ones are correct?
  1 A greater number of people speak English in the Netherlands than in Denmark.
  2 More people in Denmark speak French than German.
  3 Fewer people in the Netherlands speak French than German.
  4 A smaller percentage of people speak French in Denmark than in the Netherlands.
  5 English is the most popular foreign language in both the Netherlands and Denmark.
  6 More people speak German in Denmark than in the Netherlands.

Module 2 Connecting — 2b

Plan your summary

4 Read the test task and choose the correct answers in the questions below.

The charts below give some information about Japanese university students' use of English. Summarise the information by selecting and reporting the main features, and make comparisons where relevant.

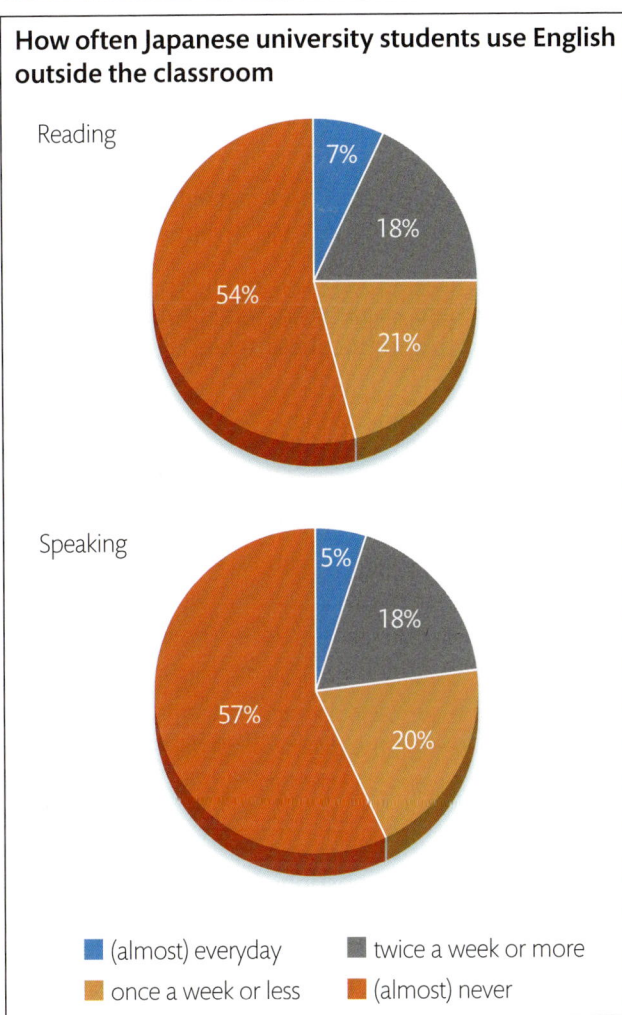

How often Japanese university students use English outside the classroom

Reading: 7%, 18%, 21%, 54%
Speaking: 5%, 18%, 20%, 57%

■ (almost) everyday   ■ twice a week or more
■ once a week or less   ■ (almost) never

1 What is the main topic?
   A how many Japanese university students use English
   B how well Japanese university students use English
   C how frequently Japanese university students use English
2 What do the charts give more detailed information about?
   A different language skills
   B different courses studied
   C different levels of ability

5 Which two of the below do you need to include in your answer?
   A a summary of the main topic
   B some key information from the charts
   C information about all the percentages presented in the charts

Language and content

6a Find these features in the charts in Exercise 4. What does each one represent?
   1 the smallest percentage
      5% – the percentage of students that speak English every day or almost every day
   2 the largest percentage
   3 a percentage that is the same in both charts
   4 the largest percentage in the first chart
   5 two percentages that are almost the same in both charts

b Match these sentence beginnings (A–E) with the features you identified in Exercise 6a (1–5).
   A The largest number of students in the charts …
   B The same proportion of students …
   C Slightly fewer Japanese university students …
   D The smallest percentage of students …
   E Over half of the students in the survey …

Write your summary

▶ **TEST STRATEGIES** page 181

7a Write two sentences introducing the main topic of the charts.

   The charts give information about _____
   _____
   _____
   _____
   _____

b Now write five sentences describing the main features. Use Exercise 6 to help you.

   • The largest number of students in the charts
   • _____
   • _____
   • _____
   • _____

Assess and improve

8 Check your work. Did you do these things in your answer?
   1 I introduced the main topic in the first part.
   2 I checked the information in my sentences against the charts, to make sure it is correct.
   3 I only wrote about the main features.

Student's Resource Book > Writing page 24

2b Module 2 Connecting

Speaking (Part 1)

Expand answers

1 Work in pairs. Why do people enjoy celebrations and festivals? Think of as many reasons as you can.

2a 🔊 2.7 Listen to three candidates doing Part 1 of the Speaking test. Match the candidates (A–C) with the questions they answer (1–3).
   1 What big celebrations are there in your country?
   2 Do you enjoy attending celebrations?
   3 What kind of things do you celebrate with your family?

  b 🔊 2.7 Listen again. What extra information does each candidate give?

  c Look at audio script 2.7 on page 212. Find words/phrases the candidates use to add extra information and give reasons or examples.

3a Work in pairs. You are going to ask and answer the questions in Exercise 2a. Before you do this, think about these things.

   Question 1
   • Think of some celebrations in your country.
   • What do people do?
   • Are there any traditions and customs?
   • Do people eat special food?

   Question 2
   • Think of some celebrations you go to.
   • Think about the reasons you enjoy them (e.g. seeing family and friends, having time off work, eating special food).

   Question 3
   • Think of some events that people celebrate with family (e.g. birthdays, weddings, passing exams).
   • What do people do?
   • Why do you like them?

  b Take turns to ask and answer the questions in Exercise 2a. Remember to give reasons/examples and add extra information.

Test practice

▶ TEST STRATEGIES page 182
▶ EXPERT SPEAKING page 197

4 Work in pairs. Follow the instructions and complete the test task. Then swap roles.
   • Student A: Ask the questions. Listen carefully to help your partner afterwards.
   • Student B: Answer the questions. Make sure you give reasons/examples and add extra information.

   1 What is your favourite family celebration?
   2 What do you celebrate on that day?
   3 Is there anything special that you and your family do on the day?
   4 What do you enjoy most about that day?

Assess and improve

5 Work in pairs and discuss the questions.
   1 Did you expand your answers by giving reasons/examples and adding extra information?
   2 Did you use some of the words/phrases from Exercise 2c?

3 Earning a living

3a Training
- **Reading:** Identify specific detail (*True/False/Not given*)
- **Language development:** Present continuous; Present continuous and present simple; Stative verbs
- **Vocabulary:** Jobs
- **Listening:** Understand detailed information (Section 3: Multiple choice)
- **Speaking:** Give your opinion: adjectives (Part 2: Long turn)
- **Writing:** Paragraphing; Express cause and effect (Task 2: Problem-solution essay)

3b Testing
- **Listening:** Section 3: Multiple choice
- **Language development:** *have to* and *must*; *need to*; *should*
- **Vocabulary:** Working
- **Reading:** *True/False/Not given*
- **Writing:** Task 2: Problem-solution essay
- **Speaking:** Part 2: Long turn

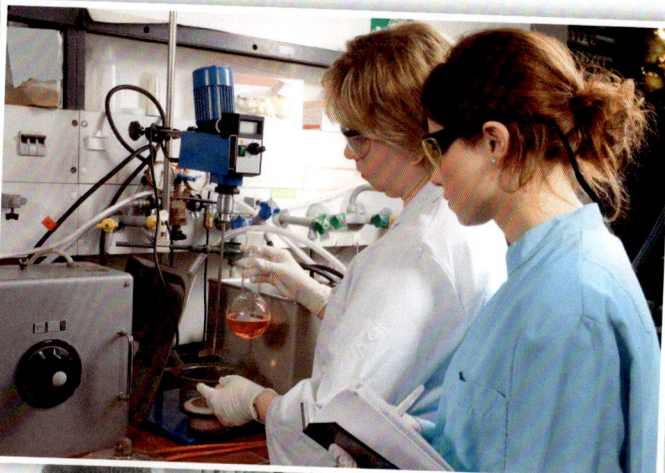

Lead-in

1 Discuss the questions.
  1 Do you think it is a good idea to do a degree which includes work experience? Why/Why not?
  2 How useful do you think an MBA is for your own career? Why?

2 Read the quotes about MBA programmes. Which ones do you agree/disagree with? Why?

An MBA is expensive, but it gives you skills in all business areas so you can progress quickly in a job.

MBAs are only useful if you do one after you've worked for several years.

I think MBAs can help only if you want to change career.

3a Jobs

Reading (*True/False/Not given*)

Before you read

1 Work in pairs and discuss the questions.
   1 What can you do with an electronic map that you can't do with a map on paper?
   2 GPS maps (maps that use global positioning systems) have had a great impact on certain jobs. Which jobs? In what ways are these jobs different now?

Identify specific detail

2 Read the passage quickly. What is it about?
   A how to use Google maps effectively
   B collecting images for Google Street View
   C the growth of Google as a company

3a Look at these sentences from the first paragraph of the passage. Choose the option (A or B) that best describes the meaning of each sentence.
   1 Most people know that Google is creating maps for the entire world.
      A It is generally known that Google's intention is to map every place on earth.
      B Google is becoming the best-known maker of maps in the world.
   2 Google Street View started in 2007, with the aim of providing photographs of the streets on its maps.
      A When Google Street View started, it could provide images for most of the streets on its maps.
      B Google's initial plan was to offer pictures to match all the streets on its maps.

 b Underline the words in the sentences in Exercise 3a that helped you decide.

4a Read this statement about the passage and underline the key words.
   Google Street View uses trekkers to take pictures for them.

 b Now read the second paragraph of the passage and follow these steps.
   1 Find information in the paragraph that answers these questions. Underline the parts of the passage where you find the answers.
      A What is Google Street View's aim?
      B Who or what are trekkers?
      C What is the trekkers' role?
   2 Decide if the statement in Exercise 4a is True or False, according to the information in the passage.

5a Match the options (1–3) with their meanings (A–C).
   1 True   A The statement contradicts the information in the passage.
   2 False   B The statement has information that is not in the passage.
   3 Not given C The statement says the same thing as the passage.

 b Work in pairs. Read three more statements about the second paragraph of the passage and follow these steps.
   1 Underline the key words in the statements.
   2 Decide if each statement is True, False or Not given.
   3 Underline the parts of the passage that helped you decide.

   A Trekkers use cameras fixed to a special kind of hat.
   B Trekkers are experienced photographers.
   C Trekkers go to places that are difficult to reach.

Test training

6 Read the passage again. Decide if the statements are True (T), False (F) or Not given (NG). Remember to follow the same steps as you did in Exercise 5b.

   1 The map project is having a positive effect on other businesses.
   2 The trekkers choose which places to photograph.
   3 The trekkers pay for the equipment they use.
   4 Luis Martin is an Argentinian scientist.
   5 Some people think Google should pay for photos it receives.

Task analysis

7 Work in pairs and discuss the questions.
   1 Look back at your answers. Did underlining key words in the statements help you decide? How?
   2 Did you both find the answers in the same parts of the passage?
   3 If you got an answer wrong, explain to your partner why your answer was not the correct one.

Discussion

8 Work in pairs. Would you be like to be a trekker? Why/Why not?

Mapping the world in photos

Most people know that Google is creating maps for the entire world. Google Street View started in 2007, with the aim of providing photographs of the streets on its maps. So a user in New York, for example, can click on a street on a Google map of Paris, Tokyo or Buenos Aires and see what it actually looks like. The photos are taken by cars which drive down streets capturing images with a 360-degree camera on their roof.

Over time, the project has expanded. Google Street View now aims to include photos of smaller towns and even places where there are no roads. Clearly, this is an enormous task. It is carried out by people who are known as 'trekkers'. Carrying a special backpack holding a 360-degree camera, trekkers go on foot to take photos in different locations. This means trekkers are able to take pictures of a whole new range of interesting places that cars cannot get to.

Google's ultimate aim of creating a complete image of the world on its maps has obvious advantages for individual users. It can help them get to know a place before they travel there; or it can help them find where they are once they are in the area. But the detailed views of beautiful places can also benefit businesses. For example, photos can help to attract tourists – many tourist agencies say that the publicity their area receives from being on the system is bringing in many more visitors.

Google has developed a clever business model. Instead of employing its own trekkers, it finds a local organisation to be a partner and then their employees go out and take photos of an area they know well. This programme currently has more than 200 partners, including tourist agencies and universities. Google lists the exact locations they want photos of and then gives the partner the camera backpack. The system works because the trekkers really care about the locations and know where the best spots are. Luis Martin, a trekker based at a national park in Argentina, one of Google's partner organisations, says, 'The pack is heavy but at the moment I'm enjoying the work – it's demanding but very rewarding.'

With no salaries to pay, Google gets the photos it wants in a very inexpensive way. Some people argue that it is not fair for a major international company to receive such valuable data without paying for it. However, others point out that anyone with access to a computer can use and enjoy Google's maps and photos. It is certainly an interesting and ambitious use of both human and technological resources.

3a Module 3
Earning a living

Language development

Present continuous

> EXPERT GRAMMAR page 184

1. Read the sentences and answer the questions below.

   A I'm waiting for a phone call right now.
   B I'm currently looking for a new job.
   C We're working on our presentation at the moment.
   D Sales aren't doing very well this year.

   1 Which sentences refer to an action happening now?
   2 Which sentences refer to an action happening around now?
   3 Apart from the verbs, what other words tell you when the action is happening?

2. Complete the sentences with the present continuous form of the verbs in brackets.

   1 I'm so busy that I _____ (not spend) much time at home at the moment.
   2 He doesn't like his current job, so he _____ (look for) a new one.
   3 We _____ (not expect) the business to do well this year.
   4 I _____ (hope) to start a new course next year.
   5 The company _____ (not do) very well, so they _____ (not employ) any new staff at present.
   6 We _____ (get) a little nervous about our presentation this week.
   7 I _____ (write) the report now but I _____ (not find) it easy.
   8 She can't speak to you now because she _____ (wait) for an important phone call.

3a. Find and correct the mistakes in four of the questions.

   1 You currently working hard? Why/Why not?
   2 What you're doing to improve your English?
   3 What do you think your best friend is doing right now?
   4 What assignments or projects are you work on this week?
   5 Do you enjoying your work/studies at the moment? Why/Why not?

   b Work in pairs. Take turns to ask and answer the questions in Exercise 3a.

Present continuous and present simple

4. Read the sentences. Which one is about something happening now? Which one is about something that happens regularly? How do you know?

   1 I'm working hard at the moment but I'm enjoying it.
   2 I usually work hard but I enjoy it.

5. Choose the correct ending (i–ii) for each sentence beginning (A–B).

   1 A I'm working in London
      B I work in London
      i but I don't live there.
      ii for a few months.
   2 A Are you learning
      B Do you learn
      i to drive at the moment?
      ii languages easily?
   3 A Sales are slowly increasing
      B Sales usually increase
      i during the winter months.
      ii this winter.

6a. Make questions in the present simple or present continuous.

   1 you / often / stay up / late / to work or study?
   2 you / read / anything good / at the moment?
   3 you / do / any sports / these days?
   4 you / do / some exercise / every day?
   5 how / you / usually / travel / to work or your place of study?

   b Work in pairs. Take turns to ask and answer the questions in Exercise 6a.

Stative verbs

7. Choose the correct options *in italics* to complete the sentences.

   1 *I don't like / I'm not liking* my job at the moment.
   2 *He gives / He's giving* a presentation to the manager today.
   3 This assignment *seems / is seeming* much easier than the last one.
   4 *I want / I'm wanting* to do more training this year.
   5 This course *gets / is getting* more and more difficult.
   6 *I think / I'm thinking* this answer is wrong.

8. Complete the text with the present simple or present continuous form of the verbs in brackets.

   Student jobs

   These days more than half of students 1 _____ (have) a part-time job and this number 2 _____ (steadily / increase). The jobs students usually 3 _____ (take) are unskilled, low-paid ones, for which they 4 _____ (need) little or no special training. It is easy to see why so many students 5 _____ (like) to work alongside their studies these days as student costs are so high, and more and more students 6 _____ (find) it difficult to pay for things. Some students 7 _____ (not need) to work for the money but choose to do so in order to improve their skills. However, some university lecturers 8 _____ (believe) that working can have a negative effect on studies and advise their students to work no more than 16 hours a week.

Module 3
Earning a living
3a

Vocabulary

Jobs

1a Match the jobs (1–10) with what each person does (A–J).

    1 chemist   A looks after people's teeth
    2 accountant   B designs and builds things
    3 engineer   C works with legal agreements
    4 doctor   D prepares medicines in a shop
    5 dentist   E works in films and on TV
    6 actor   F sells things to customers
    7 police officer   G works with numbers
    8 shop assistant   H designs buildings
    9 lawyer   I looks after sick people
   10 architect   J catches criminals

 b Work in pairs. Think of three more jobs you know and write similar phrases describing what this person does. Use a dictionary to help you.

Adjectives to describe jobs

2a Match the adjectives (1–7) with their meanings (A–G).

    1 rewarding   5 well-paid
    2 challenging   6 badly paid
    3 repetitive   7 demanding
    4 stressful

    A boring because you have to do the same thing many times
    B paying a lot of money
    C not paying much money
    D difficult but interesting or enjoyable
    E making you feel happy and satisfied
    F needing a lot of ability, skill or effort to do
    G making you worried and unable to relax

 b Match each job in Exercise 1a with adjectives from Exercise 2a. Compare your answers with a partner. Do you agree or disagree? Give reasons for your opinion.

> I think being a doctor is very rewarding because you help people. It is also stressful because you …

Activities at work

3a Read the first part of an article and underline five more activities.

Job extras – Are you ready?

Most graduates hope to find a job which allows them to use the knowledge and skills they learned during their studies. However, it is often the case that many work activities have nothing to do with things studied at university. For most jobs these days, you need to spend a lot of time <u>doing paperwork</u>, which can seem boring, and some jobs involve meeting customers. For many jobs it is helpful if you are good at giving presentations and writing reports, both of which are skills which students have experience of at university. However, for some jobs you need experience which you do not often get at university, for example, managing teams of people. If you like meeting people, you will probably enjoy attending conferences, which are a good opportunity to share and discuss ideas with colleagues.

 b Complete the sentences with the underlined activities in Exercise 3a.

    1 I get very nervous about _____ , especially when there is a big audience.
    2 The thing I enjoy least about my job is _____ – there is a form to fill in for everything!
    3 To be a good boss, you need to be good at _____ and helping people to do their best.
    4 When _____ , it is important to get the organisation and structure right.
    5 If your job involves selling something, then _____ is an important part of your work.
    6 I enjoy _____ but I don't like spending too long away from home.

 c Work in pairs. Which of the activities in Exercise 3a do you have experience of? Which are you good/not good at? Give reasons and examples.

> I have experience of giving presentations because I do them at university. I'm not very good at it because I get nervous.

 d Work in pairs. Choose one job from Exercise 1a. Think of two advantages and one disadvantage of the job.

> The advantages of being a doctor are that it is a well-paid and rewarding job but you spend a lot of time doing paperwork.

43

3a Module 3
Earning a living

Listening (Section 3: Multiple choice)

Before you listen

1 Work in pairs. Think of three different ways you can find a job. Which way do you think is the most successful? Why?

Understand detailed information

2a 🔊 3.1 You will hear an extract from a conversation between a student and a careers advisor. Look at the question and five options below and follow these steps.
   1 Underline the key words in the question and options.
   2 Try to think of different ways of expressing the options.
   3 Remember that even if you hear the exact words of one of the options, it may not be the correct answer, so listen carefully.
   4 Listen and answer the question.

   Which **TWO** types of job is the student looking for?
   A medical sales
   B in a research laboratory
   C teaching science
   D in the food industry
   E in the drugs industry

b Work in pairs. Look at audio script 3.1 on page 212 and discuss the questions.
   1 Does the student mention all five options?
   2 Why are the incorrect options wrong?
   3 Does the student use the same words as the options or does he express them in a different way?

Test training

3a Read the test task and follow these steps.
   1 Underline the key words in both the questions and the options.
   2 Try to think of other ways of expressing the words you underlined.

   Questions 1 and 2
   Choose **TWO** letters **A–E**.

   Which **TWO** things is the student doing in order to find a job?
   A talking to big companies
   B looking in magazines
   C sending his CV to employers
   D looking online
   E looking at a jobs notice board

   Questions 3 and 4
   Choose **TWO** letters **A–E**.

   Which **TWO** things does the careers advisor say the student needs to do?
   A look in newspapers
   B attend a jobs fair
   C continue using the careers service
   D use social media
   E go to a job agency

b 🔊 3.2 Complete the test task.

Task analysis

4 Work in pairs and discuss the questions.
   1 Were the questions in the same order as the information in the recording?
   2 Were the options in the same order as the information in the recording?
   3 Look at audio script 3.2 on page 212. Why were the incorrect options wrong?

Discussion

5 Think about one advantage and one disadvantage of each of these ways of finding a job. Then work in pairs and discuss your ideas.
   • online advertisements and social media
   • a job agency
   • job fairs

Module 3
Earning a living — 3a

Speaking (Part 2)

Give your opinion: adjectives

1a Work in pairs. What kind of things do you ask people about their job?
- the place they work
- who they work with
- what they like/don't like about it
- what they are doing at the moment
- something else?

b 🔊 3.3 Listen to a man talking to students about his job as an engineer. Which of the things in Exercise 1a does he talk about?

2a 🔊 3.3 Listen again. Which of the adjectives in the box does the speaker use to describe these aspects of his job?

beautiful boring brilliant difficult easy enjoyable exciting fantastic
fascinating interesting rewarding routine surprising terrible unusual

1 meeting people
2 the project he's currently working on
3 working overseas
4 doing paperwork
5 solving problems
6 the easier parts of his job

b Work in pairs. Use the adjectives in Exercise 2a to give your opinion on the things below.
- a book you're reading
- a subject you're studying
- the town or city you live in
- an activity you do

Pronunciation: schwa /ə/

3a 🔊 3.4 Listen and repeat. Notice how the underlined schwa sound is pronounced in each word.

1 lawy<u>er</u>   4 t<u>o</u>day
2 <u>a</u>gain   5 c<u>o</u>ntinu<u>ou</u>s
3 presid<u>e</u>nt

b 🔊 3.5 Listen and underline the schwa sound in each word. Then work in pairs and practise saying the words.

1 doctor   4 problem
2 colour   5 million
3 about   6 museum

Test training

4a You are going to describe a job to your partner. Before you speak, make notes about the points below.
- what the job involves
- positive things about the job
- negative things about the job
- Is the job important? Why/Why not?

b Work in pairs. Take turns to talk about the job you chose. Use your notes to help you.

Task analysis

5 Work in pairs and discuss the questions.
1 Did you talk about all the points?
2 Did you use adjectives to give your opinion?
3 Did you give reasons?

MyEnglishLab > 3a Speaking

45

3a Module 3
Earning a living

Writing (Task 2)

Paragraphing

1a Read the writing task and underline the key words. Then choose the correct answer in the question below.

Many graduates nowadays are finding it difficult to get a job.
Why do you think this is? How can this problem be solved?

What do you need to write about?
A why studying is difficult and what solutions there may be
B why there are not enough jobs nowadays and what solutions there may be
C why graduates cannot find jobs and what solutions there may be

b Work in pairs and follow these steps.
1 Think of one reason and one solution you could include in your essay.
2 Discuss your ideas with another pair.
3 Read the model answer. Does it mention any of your ideas? What other reasons and solutions does it mention?

> A Many students spend a lot of money nowadays on a university education but it is not always easy for them to find a job when they graduate. There are several reasons for this, but there are also solutions.
>
> B The main reason why finding a job is difficult is due to the choice of course that many students make. They choose a subject that does not lead directly to work. So there are, for example, large numbers of students studying history and philosophy and there are very few jobs for graduates in those fields. Another reason is that universities give too much importance to theoretical knowledge and too little to practical skills. Therefore, students do not graduate with skills that are useful in the workplace.
>
> C One solution is that the government should encourage students to study science, engineering, medicine and law because these are subjects which offer better opportunities for employment. As the country will always need more doctors, engineers and lawyers, the state could pay university fees for students in those departments. A further solution is that university arts faculties should offer students the chance to do extra courses in more practical skills. So students could add courses in computing, a foreign language, teaching or business skills to their literature or history degree. This should make it easier for them to find work.
>
> D Both these solutions should do a great deal to help solve the problem. They will mean that burger bars will not have to employ so many disappointed graduates.

c What does each paragraph in the model answer include? Match the descriptions (1–4) with the paragraphs (A–D).
1 describing solutions and saying why they can help
2 explaining the reasons and supporting them with examples or additional information
3 introduction: summarising the task and saying what you're going to write about
4 conclusion: summarising your own point of view

Express cause and effect

2a Look at the words/phrases in the box for expressing cause and effect. Which ones does the student use in the model answer?

as   as a result   because   because of   due to
for this reason   so   therefore

b Write the words/phrases in Exercise 2a in the correct place in the table.

To introduce a cause	To introduce an effect

c Choose the correct options in *italics* to complete the sentences.
1 There are fewer jobs nowadays *due / because* to problems with the economy.
2 *Because / Therefore* there are more graduates, there are more people looking for jobs.
3 There are more universities nowadays. *As a result, / Because* there are more graduates.
4 There are fewer jobs in some countries, *so / due to* people are travelling abroad to find work.
5 Students who study medicine usually find good jobs. For *a result / this reason*, there is a lot of competition for places in medical schools.

3a Work in pairs. Look at the task in Exercise 1a again. Think about the reasons and solutions you discussed in Exercise 1b. Think of one more reason and one more possible solution and make notes in the table.

Paragraph 2	Reason 1	
	Reason 2	
Paragraph 3	Solution 1	
	Solution 2	

b Write the two middle paragraphs of an essay for the task in Exercise 1a: one explaining the reasons and one suggesting solutions. Use your notes to help you. Remember to use some of the words/phrases from Exercise 2.

3b At work

Listening (Section 3: Multiple choice)

Before you listen

1 Work in pairs and discuss the questions.
   1 Do you ever have to give presentations? If so, when and for what reason?
   2 What do you need to do for a presentation? Think about:
      • how to prepare.   • how to speak.   • how to dress.

Test practice

➤ TEST STRATEGIES page 178

2a You will hear a discussion between two students about a presentation they are working on. Read the test task and follow these steps.
   1 Try to predict what the discussion might be about.
   2 Underline the key words in the questions and options.
   3 Try to think of other ways of expressing the words you underlined.

Questions 1 and 2
Choose **TWO** letters **A–E**.

Which **TWO** challenges does this type of business face?
   A doing all the paperwork
   B not having enough money to start the business
   C not having enough space to store the products
   D not having enough products to sell
   E not having enough business experience

Questions 3 and 4
Choose **TWO** letters **A–E**.

Which **TWO** benefits does this type of business have?
   A There are so many customers.
   B It's easy to keep customers satisfied.
   C You can have a wide range of products.
   D It's very rewarding.
   E You don't need much to start the business.

➤ **HELP**

Which student is asking the questions and which student knows the information? Which one of them is more likely to give the correct answers?

1–2   Listen for different words the speakers use to express *challenge*.

3–4   Listen for different words the speakers use to express *benefit*.

b 🔊 3.6 Complete the test task.

Task analysis

3 Work in pairs. Look at audio script 3.6 on page 213 and discuss the questions.
   1 What other words did the speakers use to express *challenges* and *benefits*? Did you spot these words while you were listening? Did this help you find the correct answers?
   2 Why were the incorrect options wrong?

Discussion

4 Work in pairs and discuss the questions.
   1 Do you ever buy or sell anything on online marketplaces?
   2 Do you think selling online like this is a good way to start a business? Why/Why not?

3b Module 3
Earning a living

Language development

have to and must

→ EXPERT GRAMMAR page 185

1 Match the sentences (1–4) with what they express (A–D).
   1 For my job interview next week, I have to give a presentation.
   2 I must work late tonight to prepare for an important meeting tomorrow.
   3 One of the rules is that you mustn't smoke anywhere in the office.
   4 You don't have to wear a suit to work but it's a good idea to dress smartly.

   A something that I think is necessary
   B something that is not necessary
   C something that is not allowed
   D something that somebody else thinks is necessary

2 Complete the sentences with *must* or *have to/has to*.
   1 There are many jobs where you _____ do a lot of paperwork.
   2 I _____ start work at 6 a.m. tomorrow, so I _____ go to bed early tonight.
   3 The worst thing about his job is he _____ write a lot of reports.
   4 I would like to get a job overseas but first I _____ improve my language skills.
   5 Our sales are decreasing this year, so we _____ try to do better.

3 Choose the correct options in *italics* to complete the sentences.
   1 The job is very easy, so he *doesn't have to / mustn't* work very hard.
   2 I don't like public speaking, so it's good that I *don't have to / mustn't* give any presentations.
   3 If you want to do a project well, you *don't have to / mustn't* rush it.
   4 All workplaces have health and safety rules – things the employers *don't have to / mustn't* do.
   5 Finding a new job *doesn't have to / mustn't* be difficult if you work hard and make an effort.

need to

4 Rewrite the sentences using the correct form of *need to*.
   1 It's not necessary for you to attend the meeting tomorrow.
   2 It's important for her to work harder.
   3 Is it necessary for this report to be longer?
   4 You don't have to finish this paperwork tonight.
   5 For this job, it's necessary to have a qualification in maths.

5 Work in pairs. Think of a job and describe the things you need to do and don't need to do. Your partner will try to guess the job.

> You sometimes need to be good at maths but you don't need to go to university. You sometimes need to wear a uniform.

> Is it a shop assistant?

should

6 Match the statements with the advice.
   1 I would like to have some more training at work.
   2 I have an important exam tomorrow.
   3 I'm nervous about attending the conference.
   4 I haven't got much work experience to put on my CV.
   5 I'm not sure what type of job to do.

   A You shouldn't stay up late tonight then.
   B You should speak to a careers advisor.
   C You shouldn't worry – it will be a good experience for you.
   D You should talk to your boss to see if she can organise some for you.
   E You should include any part-time work you're doing – it's better than nothing.

7 Work in pairs. Give advice to someone starting a job in your workplace or on your course of study. Write four sentences using *should* or *shouldn't*.

8 Choose the correct options in *italics* to complete the text.

Tips for job interviews

These days when you apply for a job, there are probably many other candidates, so when you are invited to attend an interview, you **1** *should / don't have to* make sure you spend time preparing for it.

One of the first things you **2** *must / mustn't* do is find out about the company, to show the interviewers that you are interested. Although you **3** *don't need to / mustn't* find out everything about the company, it's a good idea to know something about them.

It's a good idea to know your own application well, so you **4** *should / must* study it in order to be able to answer any questions about it. You can often predict some common interview questions, so you **5** *should / have to* practise answering these with a friend. But you **6** *mustn't / don't have to* learn your answers by heart as this will sound unnatural.

On the day of the interview, you need to be fully prepared. Don't forget to find out the best way to get to the interview – you **7** *mustn't / don't need to* be late as this will make a very bad first impression.

During the interview, try to answer questions in an open and friendly manner. But you **8** *don't have to / shouldn't* sound too confident as this is not attractive for employers.

Vocabulary

Different types of work

1a Match the words/phrases in the box with the sentences. There is one extra word/phrase.

an apprenticeship an internship full-time overtime
part-time shift work voluntary work

1 My mother is a nurse, so she sometimes works days and other times she works nights.
2 I work three evenings a week – I can't do any more because I have to study.
3 My brother is learning how to become an electrician; he's working with an experienced electrician and studying for a qualification.
4 My working hours are generally 8.30 a.m.–5 p.m., five days a week.
5 I work two afternoons a week in a charity shop; I don't get paid for it but it's good experience.
6 I'm spending my summer holiday working in a large company to get experience before my final year at university.

b Which of the words/phrases in Exercise 1a go with *work* and which go with *do*? Which can go with both?

do an apprenticeship

Confusing words

2 Complete the pairs of sentences with the correct word in bold.

1 **employment / unemployment**
  A It is difficult to get a job – _____ is very high.
  B There are many engineering jobs, so graduates in this subject have a good chance of _____ .
2 **employee / employer**
  A The largest _____ in my town is a car manufacturer.
  B Each _____ in the company is allowed six weeks holiday a year.
3 **career / profession**
  A All my family work in the medical _____ .
  B People can change jobs many times throughout their _____ .
4 **interviewers / interviewees**
  A All the _____ have to take part in a group task before an individual interview.
  B There were four different _____ who all asked me questions.
5 **colleagues / partners**
  A My mother and my uncle are business _____ .
  B I get on well with all my _____ and we often go out together after work.
6 **applicants / applications**
  A We are trying to decide which of the _____ to interview for the job.
  B The company receives many job _____ .

Collocations

3 Complete the sentences with the verbs in the box to make collocations.

do earn find go make run work

1 Actors and sports stars _____ *a lot of money* but they _____ *very hard* for it.
2 It's impossible to _____ *work* if you haven't got good qualifications.
3 To be successful these days, you have to _____ *business* with overseas companies and online.
4 It is very stressful to _____ *your own business*.
5 It's hard to _____ *a living* as an artist or writer.
6 All workers should be able to _____ *on strike*, especially if they are unhappy about their pay or working conditions.

Job benefits and rewards

4 Match the words in the box with their meanings.

bonus experience job satisfaction opportunities
pay rise pension promotion salary training
working conditions

1 the money you receive every year or every month for the job you do
2 a move to a more important position in a company
3 learning skills for a particular job or activity
4 an increase in the money you get for your job
5 a feeling of happiness or pleasure because you enjoy your job
6 the situation and environment in which people work, e.g. the place of work, the working hours
7 knowledge or skill that you get from doing a job
8 extra money that you get for good work
9 money that you get from your company or the government when you no longer work
10 chances to do things that are good/positive for you

Phrasal verbs

5a Complete the questions with the words in the box.

down for in up (x2) with

1 What are the advantages and disadvantages of setting _____ your own business?
2 What's the best way of dealing _____ difficult people at work?
3 Why might people turn _____ a job if someone offers it to them?
4 What's the best way to look _____ a job?
5 Why do people give _____ their jobs to go travelling?
6 Can you give some advice about the best way to fill _____ an application form?

b Work in pairs. Ask and answer the questions in Exercise 5a.

3b Module 3
Earning a living

Reading (*True/False/Not given*)

Before you read

1 Work in pairs and discuss the questions.
   1 Is it a good idea to spend time after work with work colleagues? Why/Why not?
   2 Imagine you can work from home as often as you wish. How often will you choose to work from home?

Test practice

▶ TEST STRATEGIES page 179

2a Read the test task and underline the key words in the statements.

Questions 1–6

Do the following statements agree with the information given in the reading passage? Write:

TRUE   *if the statement agrees with the information.*
FALSE   *if the statement contradicts the information.*
NOT GIVEN *if there is no information on this.*

   1 Buffer has its headquarters in the UK.
   2 A distributed team helps Buffer offer good customer service.
   3 Team members contact their managers daily.
   4 The money employees get for their work varies according to where they live.
   5 When they meet face to face, team members give presentations about their work.
   6 Buffer employees focus on the financial benefits of the company's approach.

▶ **HELP**

1 Look for a phrase in the first paragraph that has the same meaning as 'has its headquarters in'.

4 Look for a word that has the same meaning as 'the money employees get for their work'.

b Complete the test task. Remember to:
   • look for the correct part of the passage for each statement.
   • underline the parts that help you decide.

Task analysis

3 Work in pairs and discuss the questions.
   1 Did underlining the key words in the statements help you? How?
   2 Did you identify which part of the passage each statement referred to?
   3 How do the false statements contradict the information in the passage?

Discussion

4 Work in pairs. Would you like to work for a company like Buffer? Why/Why not?

A different way of working

Buffer is a company producing software that allows users to manage their social media accounts effectively. The company originated in the UK and is now officially based in the USA. Many individuals and businesses all around the world find Buffer software extremely useful, but what is most interesting about the company is its relationship with its employees. The unusual aspect of this relationship is that it uses what is known as a distributed team. This means that each employee can choose to work in any part of the world they wish.

Because Buffer has team members in different time zones, it means that someone is available to speak with customers 24 hours a day – which they say is central to their aims as a company. A distributed team is better for their customers and so it is also better for their business.

To keep their remote team happy and productive, Buffer provides staff with all the tools they need to be successful. Tools include laptops, tablets and e-readers. A favourite software application for employees is one that makes video conferencing with management and customers fast and reliable. Another important piece of software allows people to know where other team members are and what time it is where they are. The team also uses software that encourages chat between employees as that helps everyone to feel part of a friendly team.

Keeping an international team happy also means paying people in a way that depends partly on where they are. The price of accommodation, food and transport is very different in different cities. Buffer's system of payment makes it possible for team members to afford the cost of living no matter where they are.

Buffer also brings the team together for one week every five months in different locations. Previous events have, for example, taken place in Thailand, South Africa, the US, Australia and Iceland. These weeks are an opportunity not only to talk about company matters, but also to get to know colleagues as friends.

One of the many things Buffer does better than so many organisations is telling everyone how they encourage a culture where everyone respects and trusts each other. They claim that remote work plays a key role in that. And indeed, many members of the team have written about this and how working remotely with Buffer allows them to live much happier, more fulfilled lives. The quality of life, they say, is far more important to them than having a lot of money in the bank.

3b Module 3
Earning a living

Writing (Task 2)

Lead in

1 Work in pairs and discuss the questions.
1 What are the advantages of working for a large company?
2 What are the advantages of being self-employed?
3 Would you prefer to be self-employed or to work for a large company?

Understand the task

➤ EXPERT WRITING page 202

2a Read the test task and underline the key words. Then choose the correct answer in the question below.

Write about the following topic.

> Many people nowadays decide not to work for a large company but to become self-employed.
> What problems might this decision cause? What can they do to solve these problems?

Give reasons for your answer and include any relevant examples from your knowledge or experience. Write at least 250 words.

What do you need to write about?
A choosing a job
B being self-employed
C working for a large company

b Which of the these do you need to include in your essay?
A problems self-employed people may face
B solutions to the problems
C the advantages of being self-employed
D reasons why people choose to become self-employed

Language and content

3a Work in pairs. Look at two problems self-employed people may face. Think of two more problems to add to the notes.

Problems
- no colleagues – no one to discuss things with
- responsible for success of their business – can mean they have to work very hard = stressful and bad for health
- _____
- _____

b Work in the same pairs. Look at solutions to the problems in Exercise 3a. Add solutions to the problems you thought of.

Solutions
- join a local business club – can discuss problems with others and get useful advice
- make it their rule not to work 7 days a week + exercise daily = reduce stress + good for health
- _____
- _____

c Read the model answer. Does it mention any of the problems and solutions in Exercises 3a and 3b?

Many people nowadays decide it is better to be self-employed than to work for a large company. Self-employment has many advantages, but there are problems as well.

One of the problems is that self-employed people do not have lots of colleagues to discuss work tasks with. As a result, they have to make big decisions on their own and this can be very stressful. It can also be enjoyable to relax with colleagues over lunch and self-employed people often miss this aspect of working. Self-employed people can also have problems because the success of their business depends totally on them. For this reason, they often have to work very long hours. Many work most evenings and weekends and their health may suffer because of this.

So what are the solutions to these problems? One solution to the lack of colleagues is for the self-employed business person to join a club for business people. Most towns have such clubs and they organise a wide variety of enjoyable and useful events. These give the self-employed the chance to discuss their problems with others and to receive useful advice from them. One way to solve the problem of working too much is for self-employed people to make it their rule not to work at least one day a week. They can also go for a run every day. Both these solutions will have a very beneficial impact on their health.

In my view, choosing to become self-employed can be a very positive step. Anyone who takes the decision to work for themselves will experience some problems, but it is important to remember that there are solutions to all these problems.

Module 3
Earning a living
3b

4a Look at the phrases in the box for introducing solutions. Which ones does the student use in the model answer?

One solution is to …   Another solution is to …
One way to solve the problem is to …
Another way to solve the problem is to …
To solve this, …   (They) can …   (They) can also …

b What words/phrases does the student use to describe cause and effect?

c Read about two more problems self-employed people may face. Follow these steps.
1 Underline the words/phrases that introduce cause and effect.
2 Write full sentences introducing the suggested solutions for each problem. Use phrases from Exercise 4a.

A

Problem: Because self-employed people are responsible for every aspect of their business, they need to have a very wide range of skills. So, for example, they need to know about book-keeping, marketing and customer service. Not many people have these skills.

Solutions: (take courses in skills they need but do not have; pay an expert to do specialist tasks – e.g. an accountant)

B

Problem: Many self-employed people work from home. As a result, they do not have much working space. Their office may perhaps be in their bedroom or their kitchen and this can cause all sorts of difficulties for them.

Solutions: (learn to be very well organised – e.g. keep good records, always put things in the correct place; rent some storage space)

Plan your essay

5a Work in pairs. Read the model answer again and answer the questions.
1 How many paragraphs are there?
2 What does each paragraph include?
3 How many problems and solutions does the writer mention?

b You are going to write the two middle paragraphs of an essay for the test task in Exercise 2a. In pairs, follow these steps.
1 Decide on two problems to include in paragraph 2. You can use your ideas from Exercise 3a.
2 Decide on at least one solution for each problem for paragraph 3. You can use your ideas from Exercise 3b.
3 Plan your paragraphs. Make notes in the table.

Paragraph 2	Problem 1	
	Problem 2	
Paragraph 3	Solution(s) to problem 1	
	Solution(s) to problem 2	

Write your essay

▶ **TEST STRATEGIES** page 181

6 Write your paragraphs. Use your plan from Exercise 5b. Remember to:
- explain each problem clearly.
- suggest at least one solution for each problem.
- use words/phrases for describing cause and effect and for introducing solutions.

Assess and improve

7 Work in pairs. Read each other's paragraphs and make notes in the table. Then use your notes to tell your partner what you think.

Was the content of each paragraph clear (paragraph 2: problems, paragraph 3: solutions)?	
Did your partner explain each problem clearly?	
Did your partner suggest at least one solution for each problem?	
Did your partner use words/phrases for describing cause and effect?	
Did your partner use phrases for introducing solutions?	

Student's Resource Book > Writing page 34

3b Module 3
Earning a living

Speaking (Part 2)

Prepare your answer

1 a Think of a job. In one minute, write down as many words and phrases as you can think of related to this job.

teacher: school, students, learn, subject, teach, mark homework, tests, exams, reports, qualifications

b Read the test task and the notes a candidate made to prepare for the task. Do the notes include all the points in the task?

Describe a job that you think is important.
You should say:
  what the job is
  what the job involves
  what training or qualifications you need for this job
and explain why you think this job is important.

> *teacher – schools, universities*
> *different subjects, preparation, marking, paperwork, meetings*
> *degree: 3–4 years? other teaching qualifications/training*
> *important for students, not just academic subjects, rewarding*

c 🔊 3.7 Listen to the candidate doing the task and answer the questions.
1 Does the candidate mention all the points she made in her notes?
2 Does she add any extra information not in the notes? If so, what?
3 Does she use adjectives to give her opinion? Does she give reasons for her opinions?

Use grammar accurately

2 Look at these extracts from different students' answers to the task in Exercise 1b. Find and correct grammar mistakes in five of the sentences.
1 Nurses are usually working in a hospital.
2 They have to spending a lot of time doing paperwork.
3 I think the training is more easy now than in the past.
4 I don't think it's as difficult as working in a school.
5 You mustn't have any special qualifications to do this job.
6 At the moment he is work on a project in India.

Test practice

▶ **TEST STRATEGIES** page 182
▶ **EXPERT SPEAKING** page 195

3 a Read the test task. How is it different from the task in Exercise 1b?

Describe a job that someone you know does.
You should say:
  what the job is
  what the job involves
  what training or qualifications you need for this job
and explain why this person likes or doesn't like their job.

b Prepare to do the task in Exercise 3a. Spend one minute making notes. Write down key words and ideas for each point.

c Work in pairs. Follow the instructions and complete the test task. Then swap roles.
• Student A: Use your notes from Exercise 3b and talk about the topic. Try to speak for at least one minute.
• Student B: Listen and make notes in the table.

	Notes/Examples
Did your partner talk about all the points in the task?	
Did your partner use a range of adjectives to give his/her opinion?	
Did your partner give reasons for his/her opinions?	
Did you hear any mistakes?	

Assess and improve

4 a Work in the same pairs. How well did your partner do? Use your notes from Exercise 3c to give him/her feedback.

b How did making notes help you?

4 Well-being

4a Training
- **Reading:** Understand connections (Matching sentence endings)
- **Language development:** Past simple and past continuous
- **Vocabulary:** Health
- **Listening:** Listen for detail (Section 4: Matching)
- **Speaking:** Agree and disagree (Part 3: Discussion)
- **Writing:** Write an introduction; Paraphrase (Task 2: Opinion essay)

4b Testing
- **Listening:** Section 4: Matching
- **Language development:** Countable and uncountable nouns; Quantifiers
- **Vocabulary:** The natural world
- **Reading:** Matching sentence endings
- **Writing:** Task 2: Opinion essay
- **Speaking:** Part 3: Discussion

Lead-in

Discuss the questions.
1 What examples of healthy living do the photos show? Can you think of any others?
2 How often do you do the things in the photos?
3 Which of these do you think is the best way to stay healthy? Why?

4a Health

Reading (Matching sentence endings)

Before you read

1 Work in pairs and discuss the questions.
   1 What apps and electronic devices are there to help people improve their health or fitness?
   2 Can you think of one advantage and one disadvantage of using such apps or devices?

Understand connections

2a What is the connection between the two parts of these sentences? Match the sentences (1–6) with what they express (A–F).
   1 I'll do my research project on developing a new fitness app if my supervisor agrees.
   2 Some people would like the forest to become a conservation area while others think the land should be used for agriculture.
   3 Jack went to Australia last summer because he wanted to attend a conference on sports science.
   4 Due to cutting down large areas of rainforest, we have now lost many medicinal plants.
   5 Kennedy published a series of articles on electronics and fitness soon after he started teaching at this college.
   6 International action is essential if we want to slow down the process of climate change.

   A cause and effect
   B problem and solution
   C two contrasting ideas
   D two time-related events
   E action and purpose
   F plan and condition

b Work in pairs. Read these sentence beginnings. What kind of information do you think can complete each sentence? Choose from the options in *italics*.
   1 Climate change is becoming more rapid as …
      a condition / a cause
   2 All countries need to do more to protect endangered species because …
      a reason / a result
   3 Schools need to raise students' awareness of the importance of healthy eating so that …
      a purpose / a plan
   4 I am interested in doing a research project on exercising at high altitudes because …
      an action / an explanation
   5 If you would like to specialise in sports science, …
      an example / a suggestion
   6 Many people believe in the medicinal powers of natural products whereas …
      a contrasting opinion / a cause

c Match the sentence endings (A–F) with the beginnings in Exercise 2b (1–6).
   A others prefer to rely on antibiotics.
   B there is still so much to learn about that.
   C air travel is becoming more frequent.
   D our society's future citizens can lead healthier lives.
   E not doing so could have very serious results.
   F there is a good course at the university I went to.

Test training

3a Read the passage quickly. Is the writer's opinion of fitness apps positive or negative, or does he refer to both positive and negative aspects?

b Underline the key words in these sentence beginnings. What kind of information do you think can complete each sentence?
   1 Sports scientists approve of the decision to use fitness apps because …
   2 People have reported that when their fitness apps stop working …
   3 It is not sensible to rely too much on fitness apps because …
   4 Sports psychologists recommend that …
   5 Writing a fitness diary is helpful when …

c Look at sentence 1 in Exercise 3b and follow these steps.
   1 Find the part of the passage the sentence refers to.
   2 Read that part of the passage carefully.
   3 Read the sentence endings below. Which one matches what the passage says?
   4 Underline the part of the passage where you found the answer.

   A they can give an unrealistic impression of a person's level of fitness.
   B people become very attached to their electronic devices.
   C anyone interested in becoming fitter should pay more attention to their appearance.
   D it shows that the user wishes to develop better fitness practices.
   E someone wants to lose weight.
   F they lose the motivation to be active.
   G they won't help you achieve your goals.

d Match the rest of the sentence beginnings in Exercise 3b with the endings in Exercise 3c. There are two extra endings you do not need to use. Remember to follow the same steps as you did in Exercise 3c.

Monitoring fitness

Do fitness apps really work? Are they helpful? Or do they drown out the conversation people should be having with their bodies?

Technology has become an important aspect of life for people who want to get and stay fit. They use apps on their smartphone or other devices, for example, to count the number of steps they take every day, to measure their heart rate, to record their sleep patterns and to work out how many calories they consume.

Sports scientists recognise that deciding to use a fitness tracker or app is good because it means a person is curious about health and keen to improve their habits. If the attractive design of a device or app encourages an interest in keeping fit, its impact is clearly positive. After all, many people have reported that fitness devices have motivated them to get off the sofa and go for a walk after dinner.

Unfortunately, however, many of those after-dinner walkers have added that when their devices broke and they no longer knew how many steps they had taken, there seemed little point in heading out for that walk. Consequently, sports scientists agree that people need to be aware of the fact that apps alone are not enough.

One of the problems with fitness trackers is that they usually measure very limited pieces of information – steps taken, movements when asleep or heart rate, for example – and this does not give a clear overall picture of a person's health. They may record that someone worked out for two hours on a rowing machine, but not that they then spent the rest of the day eating pizza and watching DVDs. In other words, fitness apps can help people to deceive themselves about how healthy their lifestyle is.

What sports psychologists recommend users of electronic fitness devices to do is raise their awareness of how their body looks. No one actually needs an app to tell them that they have had a bad night's sleep; the bags under their eyes can do that just as well. And if people want to lose weight, they may find it more effective to take a regular look at themselves in the mirror rather than try to motivate themselves to diet by checking everything they eat against a calorie counting app. Unfortunately, tracking the calories is also ineffective because the body metabolises* calories from sugar differently than those from fat.

Keeping a fitness diary is also useful. In it, people should record what they ate and what their mood was two or three hours later. Tracking calories in a food app after eating a large tub of ice cream is not going to solve anyone's problems. Reflecting on how bad they felt after eating it will. Keeping a fitness diary helps people to eat well and exercise not for the sake of meeting the app's artificial targets, but because exercise makes everyone feel, look and be better.

*metabolise: change food in the body into energy and new cells

Task analysis

4 Work in pairs and discuss the questions.
  1 Did you think about what kind of information completes each sentence? Did this help you?
  2 Did you underline the parts of the passage where you found the answers?

Discussion

5 Work in pairs and discuss the questions.
  1 Do you use fitness apps? If so, what for and how often?
  2 How do you motivate yourself to take exercise and to eat healthily?

4a Module 4
Well-being

Language development

Past simple

➤ EXPERT GRAMMAR page 185

1 Read the sentences. Are the actions complete? How do you know? Do you know when the actions happened?
1 I lost weight last year when I started exercising.
2 Al didn't go to work yesterday because he was ill.

2a Complete the sentences with the past simple form of the verbs in brackets.
1 Last year the number of people buying apps to help them get fit _____ (increase) dramatically.
2 Two years ago I _____ (go) on a diet but I _____ (not lose) much weight.
3 They _____ (do) various tests last month and the results _____ (be) very surprising.
4 During the winter, the students _____ (not be) very healthy and _____ (not do) any exercise.
5 150 years ago people _____ (not have) some of the medicines we do now, so more people _____ (die) of minor illnesses.
6 In the past, people generally _____ (have) more active jobs than they do now, so they _____ (be) fitter.

b Underline the time expressions in Exercise 2a. Write three sentences about yourself using some of the time expressions.

3a Complete the questions using *you* and the past simple form of the verbs in brackets.
1 _____ (eat) any fruit or vegetables yesterday?
2 How much coffee _____ (drink) yesterday?
3 How many meals _____ (have) yesterday?
4 _____ (do) any exercise last week?
5 How much sleep _____ (get) last night?
6 When _____ (last/take) a day off because you were ill?

b Work in pairs. Take turns to ask and answer the questions in Exercise 3a.

Past continuous

4 Match the sentences (1–3) with the explanations (A–C).
1 I was waiting to see the doctor at 5 p.m.
2 They were using up a lot of energy while they were running.
3 The sun was just rising and it was starting to get warm.

A two actions happening at the same time
B an action in progress at a specific time
C two or more actions setting the scene at the beginning of a story

5 Complete the sentences with the past continuous form of the verbs in brackets.
1 At 8 o'clock this morning I _____ (work out) at the gym.
2 They _____ (not follow) a very healthy lifestyle at that time.
3 All last year his health _____ (slow/get) worse.
4 _____ (she/try) to lose weight before the holiday?
5 I _____ (not feel) well, so I didn't go for a run.
6 It _____ (become) more difficult for them to follow a healthy lifestyle.

Past simple and past continuous

6 Choose the correct options in *italics* to complete the sentences.
1 While I *grew up / was growing up*, I *ate / was eating* a lot of sweets and biscuits.
2 Ten years ago I *had / was having* a healthier diet than I do now.
3 When I *was / was being* younger, I *went / was going* swimming regularly.
4 At 10 p.m. last night I *watched / was watching* TV and at 11 p.m. I *went / was going* to bed.
5 Last year I *did / was doing* no exercise and I *ate / was eating* lots of fast food.
6 I *stayed / was staying* at home on Sunday because it *rained / was raining*.

7 Complete the text with the words in the box.

ago   did   didn't   last   was   were   weren't (x2)
when   while

Changes in lifestyle

Over the years our ideas and habits regarding health can change dramatically. For example, in the middle of the **1** _____ century many people didn't realise the dangers of smoking. By the 1960s scientists **2** _____ just starting to realise that smoking can affect health, but it **3** _____ only later that the public really began to understand the dangers.

Our habits regarding diet and exercise were also very different in the past. People now eat much more sugar than they **4** _____ in the past. This is because 150 years **5** _____ sugar was a luxury food, so many people **6** _____ eat a great deal of it. At that time most people had a diet high in bread, vegetables, fruit and fish, which **7** _____ as expensive as meat. They usually had physical jobs and were very active **8** _____ they were working, so they didn't have to worry about exercise. It was only **9** _____ people started to do less active jobs and eat more sugar that they started to have weight problems. Therefore, it's easy to see why people at that time **10** _____ always trying to lose weight like they are now and why they didn't need to go to the gym.

Vocabulary

Illnesses and symptoms

1 Complete the sentences with the words in the box.

allergy   asthma   cold   flu   food poisoning
heart attack   infection   stress

1 Many people have a food _____ , which means they have to be careful about what they eat.
2 To avoid having a(n) _____ , you should eat a healthy diet and do regular exercise.
3 Modern life can make people worry a lot, which can lead to _____ .
4 _____ is a serious illness which is caused by bacteria in something you eat.
5 People with _____ often have difficulty breathing.
6 To avoid getting a(n) _____ in harsh winter weather, you should dress warmly and stay dry.
7 If you are ill, wash your hands frequently to stop the _____ spreading to other people.
8 _____ is a common illness which makes you feel very tired and weak.

2 Complete the sentences with the words in the box.

cough   headache   pain   runny nose   sore throat
stomachache   temperature   toothache

1 If you eat too much, you could get a _____ and feel sick.
2 I'm finding it very painful to speak at the moment because I have a _____ .
3 I saw an emergency dentist because I had _____ .
4 Have you got any tissues? I have a _____ .
5 Normal body _____ is around 37°C.
6 Working at a computer for too long is bad for your eyes and can give you a _____ .
7 My flatmate has a bad _____ – I couldn't sleep last night because the noise was so loud!
8 If you have a _____ in your chest, see a doctor immediately – it could be something serious.

Accidents and injuries

3 Choose the correct options in *italics* to complete the sentences.

1 He suffered a serious *injury / bruise* to his back and was in hospital for two weeks.
2 She survived the explosion but they took her to hospital with serious *burns / stings*.
3 I have a big purple *cut / bruise* on my arm where I fell over.
4 Mosquito *bites / stings* can be dangerous.
5 He *broke / burnt* his leg playing football.
6 You should keep knives away from children in case they *burn / cut* themselves.
7 Bee *bites / stings* can be very painful.

Getting better

4 Match the words in the box with their meanings.

antibiotics   cure   prescription   prevention   surgery
treatment   vaccination

1 a piece of paper where a doctor writes the medicine you should have
2 a medical operation in which a doctor cuts open your body to repair or remove something inside
3 drugs that are used to kill bacteria and infections
4 something given to a person to protect them from a disease
5 something that is done to make an ill person better
6 a medicine or medical treatment that makes an illness go away completely
7 an action that can stop something happening

5a Cross out the option in *italics* that is not possible.

1 *have / get / need* surgery
2 *have / take / get* treatment
3 *make / find / develop* a cure
4 *write / give / make* a prescription
5 *give / take / do* antibiotics or medicine
6 *take / give / have* a vaccination
7 *prevent / treat / make* an illness
8 *make / get / feel* better after an illness

b Complete the questions with verbs from Exercise 5a. More than one answer may be possible.

1 What is the best way to _____ a cold?
2 What's the best way to recover after you _____ surgery?
3 Do you think doctors _____ too many prescriptions?
4 Do you usually _____ traditional or alternative treatments when you are ill?
5 Do you think it's possible to _____ a cure for all diseases?
6 What makes you _____ better when you are stressed?

c Work in pairs. Take turns to ask and answer the questions in Exercise 5b.

Staying healthy

6a Choose the correct options in *italics* to complete the sentences.

1 I try to *have / do / make* a balanced diet, with a little meat and plenty of fruit and vegetables.
2 I don't always *take / get / put* enough sleep.
3 I don't often *do / go / visit* for medical check-ups.
4 I find it easy to *stay in / keep on / work on* shape because I go to the gym every week.
5 I don't *make / do / practise* regular exercise – I'm very lazy and I hate sport.

b Work in pairs. Are any of the sentences in Exercise 6a true for you?

4a Module 4
Well-being

Listening (Section 4: Matching)

Before you listen

1 What do you think are the most important medical inventions and discoveries?
- vaccinations to prevent diseases
- anaesthetics (to make people sleep during surgery)
- the discovery of what causes disease
- antibiotics to treat diseases
- something else?

Listen for detail

2a You will hear the first part of a lecture about medical discoveries. Read the test task and follow these steps.
1 Underline the key words in the instructions. Do you need to listen for the main idea or for specific points?
2 Look at options A–C. Can you think of different ways of saying these things?
3 What do options A–C tell you? What do you need to listen for?
4 Underline the key words in questions 1–4. Can you think of different ways of saying the words in bold?

When does the speaker say the following medical discoveries took place? Choose your answers from the box and write the correct letter A–C next to questions 1–4. You may choose any letter more than once.

| A before 1800 |
| B 19th century |
| C early 20th century |

1 the discovery of something that can help in **surgery** _____
2 the discovery of something that causes **illness** _____
3 the discovery of something that can **prevent** disease _____
4 the understanding of the importance of keeping **clean** _____

b 🔊 4.1 Complete the test task.

c Work in pairs and discuss the questions.
1 Was there any information in the recording that sounded like the correct answer but wasn't?
2 Look at audio script 4.1 on page 213. How does the speaker express:
   A the dates in options A–C?
   B the words in bold in questions 1–4?

Test training

3 🔊 4.2 You will hear the second part of the lecture. Complete the test task. Remember to:
- underline the key words in the instructions and options.
- think about different ways of expressing options A–C.
- think about what you need to listen for.

Which description matches each scientist? Choose your answers from the box and write the correct letter A–C next to questions 1–4. You may choose any letter more than once.

| A He investigated how diet affects health. |
| B His work won an award. |
| C His work was important for medical education. |

1 Henry Gray _____
2 Jan Purkinje _____
3 Robert Koch _____
4 Casimir Funk _____

Task analysis

4 Work in pairs and discuss the questions.
1 Were questions 1–4 in the same order as the information in the recording?
2 Were options A–C in the same order as the information in the recording?
3 Did listening for the names of the scientists help you follow the lecture?
4 Did the speaker use the same words as options A–C? Look at audio script 4.2 on page 213. How does the speaker express the options?

Discussion

5 Which of the medical breakthroughs in the recording do you think was the most important? Why? Discuss in groups.

Module 4
Well-being
4a

Speaking (Part 3)

Agree and disagree

1a Which of these do you think is the most important factor in keeping healthy? Which is the least important? Number them 1–7 (1 = most important, 7 = least important).
- having a healthy diet
- doing regular exercise
- having friends and family around you
- having a job you enjoy
- sleeping well
- keeping your brain active

b Compare your ideas with a partner. Do you agree or disagree?

2a 🔊 4.3 Listen to two students having a discussion about the factors in Exercise 1a. Who thinks that:
1 smoking is bad for you?
 the man / the woman / both
2 having a job you enjoy is important?
 the man / the woman / both
3 keeping your brain active is important?
 the man / the woman / both

b Look at audio script 4.3 on page 214. What phrases do the speakers use to agree or disagree? Write them in the correct place in the table.

Agreement	Partial agreement	Disagreement
I totally agree (with that).	I agree up to a point.	I'm not so sure about …

c Work with a different partner. Talk about the factors in Exercise 1a. Use phrases from Exercise 2b and give reasons for your opinions.

Pronunciation: sentence stress

3 Choose the correct options in *italics* to complete the sentences.
1 We usually stress *all / some* of the words in a sentence.
2 The *stressed / unstressed* words are the words that are more important because they carry the meaning of the sentence.

4a 🔊 4.4 Listen to the same sentence with the stress on different words. Underline the stressed word each time.
1 I think exercise is really important.
2 I think exercise is really important.
3 I think exercise is really important.

b Match the sentences in Exercise 4a (1–3) with their meanings (A–C). Why does the meaning change?
A I think so – not somebody else.
B Exercise is important – not one of the other things we are discussing.
C Exercise is very important.

5 🔊 4.5 Listen and underline the stressed words. Then work in pairs and practise saying the sentences. Try putting the stress on different words. How does the meaning change?
1 I think it's true but he doesn't agree.
2 I suppose you might be right.
3 Diet is much more important than exercise.

Test training

6a Look at the question below and make notes.
- Think of two or three unhealthy habits you can talk about.
- Think of some reasons to support your opinions.

What habits do you think are unhealthy?

b Work in pairs. Discuss the question in Exercise 6a. Do you agree or disagree with your partner? Remember to use phrases for agreeing and disagreeing and give reasons for your opinions.

Task analysis

7 Work in pairs and discuss the questions.
1 Did you use phrases for agreeing and disagreeing?
2 Did you give reasons for your opinions?

4a Module 4
Well-being

Writing (Task 2)

Write an introduction

1 Read the writing task and underline the key words. Then answer the questions.
   1 What does the first sentence in the task do?
   2 Where is the instruction telling you exactly what you need to write about?

Some people choose to keep fit by joining a gym but gyms can be crowded and expensive.
Do you think the advantages of joining a gym outweigh the disadvantages?

2a What is the best way to start an essay?
   A You repeat the words in the question and state your point of view.
   B You give the main reasons for your opinion.
   C You explain the focus of the question in your own words.

b Work in pairs. Read an introduction for the writing task in Exercise 1 and discuss the questions.
   1 Does the student copy the question or paraphrase it (put it in their own words)?
   2 Does the student give a reason why it is important to think about this topic?
   3 How many sentences are there?
   4 Does the student say whether they think the advantages outweigh the disadvantages?

> Many people nowadays decide that taking out a gym membership will be an ideal way for them to stay healthy. However, belonging to a gym has both positive and negative aspects and although some people are happy with this decision, others quickly regret it. It is, therefore, sensible to consider what these aspects are before paying membership fees.
>
> In my view, ...

c Match the three sentences in the introduction in Exercise 2b with their descriptions.
   A a sentence suggesting how opinions on the topic may differ
   B a sentence introducing the topic area in the writer's own words
   C a sentence suggesting the approach the writer is going to take

Paraphrase

3 Read some statements from writing tasks and some paraphrases. Which is a better paraphrase for each statement, A or B?
   1 Some people believe that all children should have to do some kind of organised physical activity every day.
      A Many people argue that some form of physical exercise should be a daily part of every child's life.
      B Some people believe that teachers need to give all children regular lessons in how to play sports well.
   2 Many universities encourage students to walk and cycle by not allowing them to bring cars to the campus.
      A The majority of students prefer not to drive to their place of study but to use public transport or ride a bicycle to get there.
      B It is common for students to have to go to their university on foot or by bicycle because they are forbidden to drive there.
   3 Competitive sports are bad for children because they put too much emphasis on the importance of winning.
      A Some people believe that competitive sports have a negative effect on young people because they encourage them to feel that coming first is all-important.
      B Some people say that competitive sports are harmful because they make some young people believe that sport is as important as their academic studies.

4 Read the writing task. Which words/phrases in the task do the phrases below paraphrase?

Some people believe that schoolchildren of all ages should have a sports lesson every day to help improve their fitness.
Do you think the advantages of having a sports lesson every day outweigh the disadvantages?

   1 aged from five to eighteen
   2 make them fitter and healthier
   3 daily
   4 pupils
   5 physical education

5a Write an introduction for the writing task in Exercise 4.

b Check your introduction with a partner.
   1 Did you use three sentences?
   2 Do they cover the points in Exercise 2c?
   3 Did you use your own words or did you copy the words from the task?

4b Nature

Listening (Section 4: Matching)

Before you listen

1 Work in pairs and discuss the questions.
  1 What do you do when you have a minor illness like a cold or a stomachache?
     • go to the hospital
     • go to the doctor
     • buy some medicine from a chemist
     • something else?
  2 What do animals in the wild do when they are ill?

Test practice

▸ TEST STRATEGIES page 178

2a Read the test task and follow these steps.
  1 Underline the key words in the instructions.
  2 Underline the key words in options A–C.
  3 Try to think of different ways of expressing options A–C.

Questions 1–6

*Why does the speaker say the following animals self-medicate? Choose your answers from the box and write the correct letter **A–C** next to questions 1–6. You may choose any letter more than once.*

A to get rid of parasites*
B to relieve an upset stomach
C to help them give birth

1 dogs and cats _____   4 elephants _____
2 the macaw _____   5 many birds _____
3 chimpanzees _____   6 the brown bear _____

* small animals that live on or inside another animal

▸ **HELP**

A Listen for examples of different parasites.
B Listen for symptoms of an upset stomach.
C Listen for words connected to birth.

b 🔊 4.6 Complete the test task.

Task analysis

3 Work in pairs and discuss the questions.
  1 Did listening for the names of the animals help you follow the lecture?
  2 Look at audio script 4.6 on page 214. In what different ways does the speaker express options A–C?

Discussion

4 Work in pairs and discuss the questions.
  1 What can humans learn from animal self-medication?
  2 Are home-made medicines from natural products like plants popular in your country?

Student's Resource Book > Listening page 41   MyEnglishLab > 4b Listening

63

4b Module 4 Well-being

Language development

Countable and uncountable nouns

➤ EXPERT GRAMMAR page 186

1 Are these nouns countable (C) or uncountable (UC)?

  1 air   5 bird   8 advice
  2 meat   6 research   9 fact
  3 flower   7 rain   10 information
  4 vegetable

2 Choose the correct options in *italics* to complete the sentences.

  1 It's very dry this year, so there *isn't a lot of water / aren't a lot of waters* in the river.
  2 People like visiting the mountains because the *air is / airs are* very clean.
  3 The lecture was boring and I didn't learn *one / some* interesting fact.
  4 *A / Some* very rare flower grows in this forest.
  5 We're expecting *a / some* rain this afternoon.
  6 If you go walking in the mountains, you should take *some / one* advice from the locals.
  7 They did *a / some* research into animal behaviour.
  8 There was *a / some* very unusual bird in the garden this morning.
  9 Have you got *any / an* information about when we can go fishing in the lake?
  10 I love spending time in the *countryside / countrysides*.

a few/ a little

3 Complete the sentences with *a few* or *a little*.

  1 We need _____ more time to finish.
  2 Only _____ people visit this beach.
  3 Could you give me _____ more information?
  4 There are only _____ places where you can see these elephants in the wild.
  5 _____ students understood the lecture but most of them found it too difficult.
  6 The weather was generally good but we had _____ rain too.
  7 We had _____ minutes to make a decision.
  8 Some animals can survive with only _____ water.

how much/ how many

4a Complete the questions with *how much* or *how many*.

  1 Do you know _____ people live in your town or city?
  2 _____ natural tourist attractions are there in your local area?
  3 _____ traffic do you have in your town or city?
  4 Approximately _____ kilometres do you live from the sea?
  5 _____ parks or green spaces are there in your town or city?
  6 _____ time do you spend outdoors every day?
  7 _____ money do you think we should spend on protecting the natural world?
  8 Are there any rivers in your town or city? _____?

b Work in pairs. Take turns to ask and answer the questions in Exercise 4a.

too much/ many and (not) enough

5a Rewrite the sentences using *too much*, *too many* or *(not) enough*.

  1 We should do less research on animals.
     We do too much research on animals.
  2 We should spend more time visiting natural places.
     We don't _____.
  3 The world has more forests than it needs.
     The world has _____.
  4 We need to care more about the countryside.
  5 People should spend less time indoors.
  6 There should be more green spaces in cities.
  7 Governments should spend more money on protecting animals.
  8 There should be fewer zoos.

b Tick the sentences in Exercise 5a that you agree with. Compare your answers with a partner.

6a Find and correct the mistakes in six of the sentences.

  1 I visit the countryside only a little times a year.
  2 There are too much people living in my town.
  3 My country doesn't get enough sun.
  4 There aren't much tourist attractions in my country.
  5 I don't spend a lot of times outdoors.
  6 I only eat meats once or twice a week.
  7 The traffics are terrible in my town.
  8 There are a lot of green spaces in my town.

b Work in pairs. Are any of the sentences in Exercise 6a true for you? Give reasons and/or examples.

> I visit the countryside quite a few times a year – I love spending time outdoors.

Vocabulary

The animal kingdom

1a Write the words in the box in the correct place in the table. Then think of one more animal to add in each category.

alligator   ant   butterfly   eagle   gorilla   lizard   lobster   octopus   owl   sheep

Reptiles	Mammals	Insects	Sea creatures	Birds

b Which of the animals in Exercise 1a are domestic animals? Which are wild animals? Do you know if any of these animals are endangered?

2 Complete the sentences with the words in the box.

colouring   feathers   fur   habitat   life cycle   nest   species   wings

1. Some _____ of animal are dying out because humans are destroying their natural _____ , so they no longer have a place to live.
2. This diagram shows the _____ of a salmon from the egg stage to adulthood.
3. Many people are against the _____ trade – that is, the buying and selling of animal's coats.
4. Penguins are an example of a bird that uses its _____ to swim instead of fly.
5. It is illegal in some countries to steal eggs from a bird's _____ in the wild.
6. The _____ of a horse can be anything from black or white to brown and grey.
7. Male and female birds often have different coloured _____ .

Geographical features

3a Look at the words in the box and answer the questions. You can use the words more than once.

beach   coast   desert   forest   hill   island   lake   mountain   ocean   rainforest   river   sea   waterfall   wood

1. Which of the features contain water?
2. Which are next to or surrounded by water?
3. Which contain many trees and plants?
4. Which contain sand?
5. Which are high?

b Complete the descriptions with the correct form of the words in bold.

1. **beach / coast / ocean / island**
   My country is a(n) _____ in the Indian _____ . It has a long _____ with many beautiful _____ .
2. **hill / mountain**
   The area where I live is quite flat; there aren't any _____ – just a few _____ , which aren't very high.
3. **rainforest / river**
   Many tourists to my country visit the _____ , where they can see all sorts of plants and animals. The best way to get there is on a three-hour boat trip up the _____ .
4. **sea / waterfall**
   An important natural attraction in my country is a _____ which is over 200 metres high and empties into the _____ .
5. **desert / forest**
   Much of my country is _____ and it is very dry. You rarely see trees except in the city, and we do not have any _____ .
6. **wood / lake**
   A popular tourist attraction in my country is a beautiful _____ where you can do water sports. It is next to a(n) _____ where people often camp.

c Work in pairs and discuss the questions.

1. Which of the geographical features in Exercise 3b do you have in your country? Which do you not have?
2. Can you name an example of each geographical feature which is not in your country?

Verbs

4a Choose the correct options in *italics* to complete the sentences.

1. You should never *pick / plant* flowers from the wild – they're better left where they are.
2. People should be allowed to *hunt / fish* in any lake and river.
3. It's impossible to *protect / farm* all endangered plants and animals.
4. The government should give more help and money to people who *farm / grow* the land.
5. I think *growing / hunting* animals is cruel and should be forbidden.
6. If they have a garden, people should *pick / grow* their own vegetables.
7. Farmers should only *plant / pick* crops in a way which is good for the environment.

b Work in pairs. Do you agree or disagree with the statements in Exercise 4a? Give reasons for your answers.

4b Module 4 Well-being

Reading (Matching sentence endings)

Before you read

1 Work in groups and discuss the questions.
  1 What plants do you know of that can help when someone is not well?
  2 What animals can you think of that have provided people with things that have a medical value?

Test practice

▶ TEST STRATEGIES page 179

2a Read the test task. What do you need to do? Number steps A–E in the best order (1–5).
  A Find where the first part of each sentence is mentioned in the passage.
  B Read the passage quickly.
  C Match the sentence beginnings with the endings.
  D Read the sentence beginnings, underline the key words and think about what kind of information is needed to finish each sentence.
  E Look in the passage for the information that completes each sentence.

Questions 1–6.
Complete each sentence with the correct ending **A–G** below.

1 It is many thousands of years since
2 People are often very surprised to learn that
3 Scientists estimate that
4 Destroying different ecosystems means that
5 What is making the problem worse is the fact that
6 The writer thinks the situation will improve if

A many potential cures will disappear forever.
B some of the most medically valuable species do not seem very attractive.
C natural medicines can be more effective than modern drugs.
D medical students learn more about the development of treatments.
E people discovered how powerful natural substances can be.
F researching new treatments takes considerable time.
G many possible medicines from the natural world are still unknown.
H medical knowledge is not growing quickly enough to fight new diseases.
I modern medicine still makes so much use of nature.

▶ **HELP**

1 'Many thousands of years since' tells you that you are looking for something that happened a long time ago.
2 Find a word in the passage that means 'very surprised'.

b Complete the test task.

Task analysis

3 Work in pairs and discuss the questions.
  1 Did you follow the steps in Exercise 2a? If not, what steps did you follow?
  2 Did you underline the parts of the passage where you found the answers?

Discussion

4 What do you think we need to do to make sure that nature continues to help medical science?

66 MyEnglishLab > 4b Reading

Remedies from nature

In all the discussions about saving the world's biodiversity from extinction, people often forget one point: the world's species provide people with a large number of life-saving medicines.

Animal and plant species have given people important medicines such as quinine and aspirin, as well as many cancer and HIV-fighting drugs. People have used plants and animals as sources of medicine for thousands of years. For example, medicinal plants that people used over 60,000 years ago were found in an Iraqi cave site. A fur strap found on the arm of a 5,000 year-old Ice Man from the Alps contained a type of *fungus which is able to kill bacteria.

Most people are amazed to discover that our dependence on nature for health has not reduced. Over the past quarter century, more than half of all the products that drug companies have developed actually use, or copy, substances from the natural world. Moreover, the World Health Organization estimates that in many developing countries, 80 percent of the population relies on traditional medicines from natural sources.

However, scientists generally believe that researchers have fully examined less than one percent of all species in order to discover their possible uses in medical treatments. They believe that nature still holds many valuable cures for research to discover. In particular, they point to the importance of tropical rainforests as a potential source of new medicines. Although rainforests cover only six percent of the earth's land surface, they contain over half of its *biodiversity.

Unfortunately, the ecosystems that provide some of the world's most important drugs, such as rainforests and coral reefs, are also the ecosystems that are most at risk today. There are concerns that warming temperatures mean that few coral reefs will remain by the end of the century. Meanwhile, agriculture and various major development projects are making the world's rainforests vanish at an alarming rate – the world is losing more than 320 km^2 every day. The inevitable result is that many species with important medicinal powers will become extinct.

Another problem is that most of nature's medicines do not come from big and beautiful mammals, such as tigers and elephants. Instead, they come from the least popular of the world's ecosystems: plants, fungi and *invertebrates. Some particularly valuable species are often either poisonous or so small that we cannot see them without a microscope. This makes campaigning for their *preservation much more difficult.

An additional problem is the fact that medical schools teach their students very little about the discovery of new treatments. Few young doctors, for example, know that the blood pressure medicine captopril, one of the best-selling drugs of all time, comes from the poison of a Brazilian snake. Antibiotics, most of which come from nature, are a miracle drug but doctors use far too many of them. This is partly because they do not realise the dangers involved or how closely connected these drugs are with the natural world.

Nature and medicine are closely connected. We must protect nature. If we don't, we not only risk losing many plant and animal species but we are also risking our own health.

*fungus: a simple type of plant that has no leaves or flowers and grows on plants or other surfaces
*biodiversity: the variety of plants and animals in a particular place
*invertebrate: an animal that does not have a backbone
*preservation: when you keep something in its original state or in good condition

4b Module 4
Well-being

Writing (Task 2)

Lead-in

1 Work in pairs and discuss the questions.
1 Why is it important to test new medicines before people use them?
2 Why do pharmaceutical companies often test new medicines on animals first?

Understand the task

▶ EXPERT WRITING page 203

2a Read the test task and underline the key words. Then choose the correct answer in the question below.

Write about the following topic.

Some people believe that it is wrong to test new medicines on animals.
Do you think the advantages of testing new medicines on animals outweigh the disadvantages?

Give reasons for your answer and include any relevant examples from your knowledge or experience. Write at least 250 words.

What do you need to write about?
A the good and bad points of using animals to test medicines
B the advantages of developing new medicines
C suggestions for how best to test new medicines

b What is the difference between these two essay questions? Choose the statements that are true for each question.
1 Do you think the advantages of … outweigh the disadvantages?
2 What are the advantages and disadvantages of … ?

A This question only asks you to discuss the advantages and disadvantages.
B This question asks if there are more advantages or disadvantages.
C You need to decide which side is stronger and explain your opinion.

Language and content

3a Read the model answer and match the descriptions (1–4) with the paragraphs (A–D).
1 the stronger side
2 the conclusion, with the writer's opinion
3 the introduction
4 the weaker side

68

A Many people think that using animals is the best way to find out if new medicines work. Others, however, disagree, saying that it is not right to make use of animals in this way. Let us consider both sides of the argument.

B <u>It is certainly true that there are disadvantages to using animals to test new medicines.</u> Firstly, it is cruel. Is an animal's life worth less than that of a human? Animals are living creatures too and we should respect them. Secondly, a new medicine may not work in the same way on an animal as it does on a person. So the conclusions the researchers come to may be wrong.

C <u>However, it is very important to test new medicines.</u> Scientists need to develop new medicines so that doctors can improve the quality of life for millions of people all over the world. Giving new medicines to animals will show that they work well. These experiments are also necessary to make sure that the new medicines pharmaceutical companies develop do not have any serious side effects. It is too risky to experiment with new drugs on humans but if chemists are not able to test them, then sick children and adults will not be able to benefit from new treatments.

D I would therefore argue that although it is not good if animals suffer, the advantages of using them to test new medicines outweigh the disadvantages. It is very important for the future of medical science.

b Work in pairs and choose the correct answers.
  1 Why does the student make more points about the advantages?
    A to show that they think the advantages outweigh the disadvantages
    B because it is usually a good idea to include more points about the advantages
  2 Why does the writer put the disadvantages first?
    A because they think it's the most important point and so needs to come first
    B to make their argument for advantages stronger and to connect with the conclusion

4a Work in pairs. Look at the underlined sentences in paragraphs B and C. These are called topic sentences. Choose the correct options in *italics* to describe their role.
  1 Topic sentences *introduce the main idea of / give supporting details for* the paragraph.
  2 They usually come at the *beginning / end* of the paragraph.

b Number the sentences in the best order (1–4) to make a paragraph. Which sentence is the topic sentence?
  A Poor people may decide to take part in a drugs experiment because pharmaceutical companies usually pay participants.
  B As a result, they may even become seriously ill themselves.
  C This may encourage them to agree to do things that they know are not good for their bodies.
  D Testing new medicines on people can have serious consequences.

Plan your essay

5a Read the test task in Exercise 2a again and follow these steps.
  1 Decide what your point of view is: do you think there are more advantages or disadvantages?
  2 Think of two ideas to support the side you think is stronger.
  3 Think of one idea to support the side you think is weaker.

b Make notes for your essay in the table. For paragraphs 2 and 3, use your ideas from Exercise 5a. Remember to:
  • use your own words in the introduction.
  • include topic sentences for paragraphs 2 and 3.

Paragraph	Focus	Notes
1	Introduction	
2	Idea for weaker side	
3	Ideas for stronger side	
4	Conclusion	

Write your essay

▶ TEST STRATEGIES page 181

6 Write your essay. Use your plan from Exercise 5b.

Assess and improve

7 Check your work. Did you do these things in your essay?
  1 I used three sentences in the introduction.
  2 I used my own words in the introduction.
  3 I included one point about the side I feel is weaker (paragraph 2).
  4 I included at least two points about the stronger side (paragraph 3).
  5 I used topic sentences for paragraphs 2 and 3.

Module 4
Well-being

Speaking (Part 3)

Give examples

1a Read three questions from Part 3 of a Speaking test. For each question, write down as many ideas as you can think of.

1 Why do people like visiting natural attractions?
2 How can people who live in the city enjoy the natural world?
3 What can we teach children about the natural world?

b Work in pairs and compare your ideas from Exercise 1a.

c Match each of these points (A–E) with one of the questions in Exercise 1a (1–3).
 A to do activities and water sports
 B to keep the countryside clean and tidy
 C by using green spaces to enjoy nature
 D to see wildlife
 E to protect animals

d 🔊 4.7 Listen to a candidate answering the questions and check your answers to Exercise 1b.

2a 🔊 4.7 Listen again. Match the points in Exercise 1c (A–E) with the examples the candidate uses (1–5).
 1 tigers and pandas
 2 parks and rivers
 3 picking up rubbish, cleaning up after themselves
 4 fishing and sailing
 5 birds, trees and plants

b Look at audio script 4.7 on page 214. What words/phrases does the candidate use to introduce her examples?
 1 _____
 2 _____
 3 _____
 4 _____
 5 _____

3 Work in pairs. Look at these answers to the questions in Exercise 1a. Give examples to support each point. Try to use words/phrases from Exercise 2b.
 1 People enjoy visiting beautiful places.
 2 People who live in cities can experience nature by going on holiday.
 3 We need to teach children about where food comes from.

Speak fluently

4 🔊 4.7 Listen to the candidate's answers again. Which of these things does she do in order to speak fluently?
 1 repeat phrases
 2 stop to think about the right word
 3 talk without too many silences
 4 use plenty of examples to support her points

Test practice

▸ TEST STRATEGIES page 182
▸ EXPERT SPEAKING page 196

5a Read the test task. Think about what you can say for each question.

 1 What are the benefits of visiting natural attractions?
 2 How can we protect the natural world?
 3 Where can you see wildlife in a city?

b Work in groups of three. Follow the instructions and complete the test task. Then swap roles.
 • Student A: Ask the questions.
 • Student B: Answer the questions. Remember to give reasons and examples. Avoid too many pauses.
 • Student C: Listen and make notes in the table.

Did your partner:	Notes/Examples
answer each question?	
pause a lot?	
give examples?	
use phrases to introduce the examples?	

Assess and improve

6 Work in the same groups. How well did your partner do? Use your notes from Exercise 5b to give him/her feedback.

5 The world around us

5a Training
- **Reading:** Understand detailed information (Matching information)
- **Language development:** *-ing* forms and infinitives
- **Vocabulary:** Travel and transport; Tourism
- **Listening:** Understand main points (Section 2: Table completion)
- **Speaking:** Structure your answer (Part 2: Long turn)
- **Writing:** Organise information; Describe changes and trends (Task 1: Line graphs)

5b Testing
- **Listening:** Section 2: Table completion
- **Language development:** Prepositions
- **Vocabulary:** Weather; Environmental issues
- **Reading:** Matching information
- **Writing:** Task 1: Line graphs
- **Speaking:** Part 2: Long turn

Lead-in

Discuss the questions.
1 What is most important to you when you book a holiday? Why?
- the cost
- the accommodation
- the sights/places to visit
- the activities/things to do
- the weather
- shopping
- something else?

2 What do you like to do on a holiday? Why?

71

5a Journeys

Reading (Matching information)

Before you read

1 Work in pairs and discuss the questions.
   1 What do you think is the most enjoyable way to travel?
   2 Would you like to travel abroad for a long period? Why/Why not?

Understand detailed information

2 Read the passage about Mark Beaumont, a cyclist who travelled round the world. Where has he been on his bike?

3a Read the sentences from the passage (1–4). What different types of information do they give? Match them with the functions (A–D).
   1 When I look back now, it was one of my favourite times.
   2 In Europe, North America and Australia, cycling is a sport which people do mainly to keep fit and have fun.
   3 Even in the poorest countries, I never had to ask a second person for a place to stay.
   4 I was in the middle of this enormous desert and all I could hear was the sound of animals calling.

   A an example of people's character
   B reasons for doing something
   C a comment on an experience
   D a description of a situation

b Read the question about the passage. Underline the key words and then answer the questions below.

Which paragraph contains examples of different attitudes towards the bicycle?

   1 Is the question about the general idea of the passage or about a specific part of the passage?
   2 Is the question about the general idea of a paragraph or do you need to look for specific information in the paragraph?
   3 What type of information are you looking for?

c Read the question in Exercise 3b again. Follow these steps to answer it.
   1 Look at the key words you underlined. Think about:
      A the type of information your are looking for (examples).
      B the details you are looking for (different attitudes).
   2 As you read the passage, look out for the paragraph with information that matches the question.
   3 Be careful: do not just pick a paragraph because it has some words that are the same as words in the question. The paragraph must contain the necessary information.
   4 Find and underline the specific information the question asks for.

Test training

4 Complete the test task. Remember to underline the key words and then follow the same steps as you did in Exercise 3c.

The passage has seven paragraphs labelled A–G. Which paragraphs contain the following information?

   1 an example of a place where Mark felt bored
   2 a comment on the expense of organising a cycle trip
   3 a description of the extent of Mark's travels
   4 a reference to how cold the weather was
   5 some reasons why making progress can be difficult

Task analysis

5 Work in pairs and discuss the questions.
   1 Did all the paragraphs contain an answer?
   2 Did each question refer to details or the main idea of a paragraph?
   3 Did you and your partner underline the same parts of the passage?

Discussion

6 Work in pairs. Would you like to go on a long cycle trip like one of Mark's? Why/Why not?

A different way to see the world

Mark Beaumont found that many countries look different from a bicycle. Our reporter writes about Mark's experience of cycling round the world.

A An extraordinary cyclist, Mark Beaumont, has completed a number of amazing long-distance trips on his bike. In 2008, for example, he rode for 18,296 miles around the world. Two years later he made a 13,080-mile journey through the Americas. In 2015 he cycled 6,762 miles from Cairo to Cape Town.

B On that last journey Mark succeeded in breaking – by as much as 17 days – the world record for cycling across Africa. To do this, he rode 160 miles a day. He explains that it was certainly not easy to keep up this speed. There were, for example, long delays at border crossings and queues of traffic often stopped him from travelling fast. Broken roads caused problems and the weather also affected how fast he could go.

C On all his journeys Mark has been interested by the landscapes he has seen. He says these often differ from what he expected. 'When people think about Patagonia, for instance, they imagine the beautiful mountains and lakes you see in holiday brochures; but when I cycled there, I realised that large parts of it are just miles and miles of grassland. What is romantic and exciting for most holidaymakers can become very boring when you see nothing else for several days.'

D Of all the landscapes he has seen, Mark has particularly enjoyed some of the wild parts of Texas and the Deep South of the USA. 'I remember waking before daylight. I had to remove the ice from my tent when it was still dark. Then I set out on roads with absolutely no one else around. I was in the middle of this enormous desert and all I could hear was the sound of animals calling. When I look back now, it was one of my favourite times: to be totally alone in that environment.'

E His travels have also taught Mark about how differently people around the world view cycling. In Europe, North America and Australia, cycling is a sport which people do mainly to keep fit and have fun. But in many places Mark visited, a bicycle is something rather different. It is a type of transport that many people dream of getting one day. People who are used to walking everywhere wish they had enough money to buy a bike in order to get from A to B much more quickly and easily. People who see a bicycle that way often found it hard to understand why Mark wanted to cycle such long distances for no obvious reason.

F But for Mark, cycling is by far the best way to see the world. 'It's never boring when you're cycling. You notice everything, especially when riding alone. When you cycle, you get a wonderful view of the world. It is amazing to see how the people and cultures change from one place to the next.' The kindness of the people Mark met was what impressed him most. 'Even in the poorest countries, I never had to ask a second person for a place to stay.'

G So how does Mark feel at the end of one of his big adventures? He says that, because the projects involve huge effort, time and costs, his main emotion is relief that he has completed the trip successfully. 'It is not until later that you have time to think about what the journey meant, the landscapes you saw and the people you met. And then you start thinking about where you might go next.'

5a Module 5
The world around us

Language development

-ing forms and infinitives

▸ EXPERT GRAMMAR page 187

1 Look at the words in bold and match the sentences (1–7) with the explanations (A–G).
   1 I **like going** somewhere where I can relax on a beach.
   2 I find it **difficult to sleep** on a plane.
   3 Last year we **decided to go** on a walking holiday in the mountains.
   4 I think **travelling** by train is more comfortable than flying.
   5 When I was young, my parents always **made me go** camping with them.
   6 Last year I went to Egypt **to see** the pyramids.
   7 I always feel sad **after returning** from holiday.

   A Use the -ing form after prepositions.
   B Use the infinitive with to to express purpose.
   C Use the infinitive without to after certain verbs.
   D Use the -ing form after certain verbs.
   E Use the infinitive with to after certain verbs.
   F Use the -ing form as a noun or subject of a sentence.
   G Use the infinitive with to after certain adjectives.

-ing forms

2a Write sentences using -ing forms.
   1 walk / around a town / is / the best way to find interesting places
   2 I can't stand / fly / because there's so little space
   3 I hate / visit / hot countries
   4 I don't enjoy / visit / tourist attractions in my own country
   5 travel / alone / can be very hard
   6 I'm good at / learn / new languages when I travel

b Tick the sentences in Exercise 2a that you agree with. Discuss your ideas with a partner.

Infinitives

3 Choose the correct options in *italics* to complete the sentences.
   1 Some countries refuse *let / to let* you in without a visa.
   2 It can be difficult *decide / to decide* where to go on holiday.
   3 I usually call a travel agent *book / to book* my holiday rather than doing it online.
   4 We might *visit / to visit* the museums or art galleries.
   5 They let us *walk / to walk* round the site for a couple of hours.
   6 My family prefers me *go / to go* on holiday with them.

-ing forms and infinitives

4a Complete the questions with the correct form of the verbs in brackets.
   1 Can you imagine _____ (sail) round the world on a yacht?
   2 What would you choose _____ (do) on holiday – riding or walking? Why?
   3 Are you good at _____ (find) your way round in a new place?
   4 Do you think it's a good idea to read guidebooks _____ (decide) what to do?
   5 Do you think _____ (speak) the local language is necessary?
   6 Do you find it hard _____ (save) money for holidays?

b Work in pairs. Take turns to ask and answer the questions in Exercise 4a.

5 Complete the text with the correct form of the verbs in brackets.

Travel differences

The travel industry groups people by their different stages in life and each group has different demands. For example, **1** _____ (travel) with young children can be difficult, so this type of family often want **2** _____ (stay) closer to home. They also generally prefer **3** _____ (stay) in accommodation that has many facilities like swimming pools and play areas. It can be difficult **4** _____ (entertain) young children, so kids clubs that look after and provide activities for children are very popular with parents. Families with teenage children are also looking for activities that can **5** _____ (keep) their kids busy, and swimming pools and water sports are popular with this age group. Young adults, particularly students, often can't afford **6** _____ (stay) in luxurious accommodation but they are generally quite adventurous and enjoy **7** _____ (visit) more remote and unusual places. Older people often have more time **8** _____ (spend) travelling and are becoming more adventurous nowadays. Instead of **9** _____ (lie) on a beach, they are now choosing **10** _____ (visit) faraway places and go on more active holidays. People who work in tourism have to be able to cater to all these different demands and understand why they are important to the customers.

6 Make notes about your holidays using some of these verbs/phrases. Then discuss with a partner.
   • enjoy
   • don't mind
   • hate
   • can't afford
   • insist on
   • would rather
   • hope
   • find it difficult
   • prefer

Vocabulary

Travel and transport

1 Write the words in the box in the correct place in the table.

activity adventure beach bike bus camping city coach cottage cruise driving ferry flying guesthouse hostel hotel package ship sightseeing tent train

Types of holiday	Transport/ Ways of travelling	Accommodation

2 Complete the sentences with the correct form of the words in brackets.
1 Our _____ (fly) was late and so we missed the connecting train.
2 We had a _____ (reserve) for three nights but we decided to stay an extra day.
3 The _____ (depart) time was very early in the morning, so we took a taxi.
4 When we arrived at the hotel, there was no one at the _____ (receive) desk.
5 The hotel staff were very friendly and welcoming on our _____ (arrive).

3 Choose the correct options in *italics* to complete the questions.
1 Do you think plane *fares / costs* are too expensive nowadays?
2 Do you prefer to be a *passenger / guest* or to drive?
3 What do you think can be done to improve *waiting rooms / departure lounges* in airports?
4 How do you think *traffic / distance* is affecting some historical cities?
5 What is your favourite part of a(n) *journey / arrival*?

Compound nouns

4a Match words 1–8 with words A–H to make compound nouns.

1 public   A trip
2 information B flight
3 one-way   C break
4 round   D desk
5 five-star   E attendant
6 direct   F ticket
7 flight   G transport
8 city   H hotel

b Complete the sentences with compound nouns from Exercise 4a.
1 Many people think the job of a(n) _____ is exciting but in fact, it's hard work.
2 The best way to travel in my town is by _____ because it's cheap and reliable.
3 The train station has a(n) _____ where you can get a map of the city.
4 We're going all the way to Melbourne and back – it's a 400-kilometre _____ .
5 My brother has to travel a lot for his work and often gets to stay in a luxury _____ .
6 There isn't a(n) _____ from here – you have to change in Dubai.
7 We have a few days holiday next month, so we're planning on having a(n) _____ in Paris.
8 I only need a(n) _____ because my friend is driving me home on Sunday.

Phrasal verbs

5 Replace the words/phrases in bold with the correct form of the phrasal verbs in the box.

check in eat out get around look around
look forward to set off show (someone) around take off

1 My favourite thing about visiting different countries is **going to restaurants** and trying new food.
2 When I'm visiting a new city, I prefer to have a local to **take me to different places**.
3 Although I enjoy myself on holiday, I always **feel excited about** coming home.
4 I don't mind flying but I don't like it when the plane **leaves the ground**.
5 When I fly somewhere, I prefer to **register** online rather than at the airport.
6 I always plan my journey carefully before I **leave**.
7 The best way to **travel** in London is by underground.
8 I don't like **visiting places in** a city on my own.

Dependent prepositions

6 Choose the correct options in *italics* to complete the text.

Austria is a popular destination both for travellers **1** *on / for* business and with tourists. It is best known **2** *for / as* a winter destination, when its mountains are crowded **3** *with / by* tourists enjoying winter sports. However, it is a country rich **4** *on / in* history and culture and so it is equally popular in the summer, when tourists from **5** *in / around* the world enjoy its historic cities and go walking in the lakes and mountains. It is possible to get around **6** *with / by* public transport and you can go **7** *on / by* train between most big towns and cities. However, you can only get **8** *to / by* some of its most beautiful mountain attractions **9** *in / by* car and some of them you can only reach on skis in winter or **10** *in / on* foot in summer. Vienna, the capital, is a beautiful city, famous **11** *with / for* its architecture and cafés and is definitely worth visiting.

5a Module 5
The world around us

Listening (Section 2: Table completion)

Before you listen

1 Work in groups and discuss the questions. Do you prefer:
  1 a beach holiday or an adventure holiday? Why?
  2 to explore new places or to go to a place that is familiar? Why?

Understand main points

2a You will hear the first part of a talk. Look at the headings in the table below. Work in pairs and discuss the questions.
  1 What do you think the talk will be about?
  2 What main points will the speaker discuss?

Borneo trip			
Destination	Activities	Details of activities	Advice
Day 1: Kota Kinabalu	visit Mari-Mari Cultural Village	• see how the 1 _____ live • includes lunch	don't eat a 2 _____
	A _____	see birds and 3 _____	take sunscreen and swimsuit
	tour of 4 _____	B _____	• C _____ • take lots of 5 _____

b Match these main points with the headings in the table. Then write them in gaps A–C in the table.
  • wear suitable shoes
  • Gaya Island jungle trek
  • museum visit included

c Look at gaps 1–5 in the table above and the words around the gaps. What type of information do you need to listen for in each case?

d 🔊 5.1 Listen and complete gaps 1–5 in the table. Use no more than two words for each answer. Remember to check:
  • that the words make sense with the words before and after each gap.
  • that you have used the correct number of words.
  • your spelling.

Test training

3a Work in pairs. Look at the table below with notes from the rest of the talk. Work in pairs and discuss the questions.
  1 How can the information in the left-hand column help you follow the talk?
  2 Look at the words around each gap. What type of information is missing?

Borneo trip			
Destination	Activities	Details of activities	Advice
Day 2: Kinabalu National Park	• park walk with guide • visit 1 _____	see rare species of plant	go to talk on history, 2 _____ and ecology of park
Days 3–4: Mount Kinabalu	climb mountain	• overnight on mountain • see sunrise at 3 _____	• bring snacks • bring 4 _____ for last part of climb
Days 5–7: Mantanani Islands	• diving and snorkelling • sea kayaking	• see different types of 5 _____ • good for finding quiet beaches	• no equipment needed • buy 6 _____ before you go

b 🔊 5.2 Listen and complete gaps 1–6 in the table. Use no more than two words for each answer.

Task analysis

4 Work in pairs and discuss the questions.
  1 Did you use the headings and the information in the left-hand column to follow the talk? Did this help you?
  2 Look at the list in Exercise 2d. Did you check these things?

Discussion

5 Work in pairs. Which part of this holiday would you enjoy? Are there any parts you wouldn't like? Why?

Module 5
The world around us — 5a

Speaking (Part 2)

Structure your answer

1a When you ask someone about their holidays, which of these things do you usually ask about?
- the accommodation
- how they travel
- the activities they do
- the sights they see
- the food
- the weather
- who they go with
- what they buy
- what books they read
- something else?

b Think about a type of holiday you often go on and choose three things from the list in Exercise 1a. What kind of things could you talk about for each point? Make notes.

the accommodation – what kind of accommodation, the cost

c Work in pairs. Use your notes from Exercise 1b to tell your partner about your holidays.

2 🔊 5.3 Listen to a candidate doing Part 2 of the Speaking test. Which things from the list in Exercise 1a does she talk about?

3a Look at the underlined words/phrases in audio script 5.3 on page 215. Why does the candidate use them? Write them in the correct place in the table.

Make generalisations	Sequence ideas	Add another idea

b Choose the correct options in *italics* to complete another candidate's answer.

> I don't **1** *first of all / generally* go on many holidays, but **2** *to start with / overall*, my favourite type of holiday is going somewhere where I can do something active. I don't like going to a city for my holiday, **3** *on the whole / firstly* because I live in a big city, so I prefer to go somewhere different, but **4** *also / as well* because I like to go somewhere more peaceful with clean air, like the mountains. **5** *On the whole / To start with*, I like holidays where I can meet people and try something new, like a sport. For example, two years ago I went waterskiing for the first time and I **6** *also / as well* tried snorkelling, which was great. **7** *Generally / Another thing* I like doing on holiday is eating out and trying new food. **8** *Lastly / Firstly*, I love going somewhere where the weather is very hot – the hotter, the better, in fact!

c Work in pairs. Tell your partner about your favourite type of holiday. Use words/phrases from Exercise 3a to structure your answer.

Test training

4 Work in pairs. Tell each other about your holidays. Talk about:
- where you usually go
- what you enjoy doing
- how you travel there
- and say what you enjoy most about travelling.

Task analysis

5 Work in pairs and discuss the questions.
1 Did you think about different things to say for each point?
2 Did you use language from Exercise 3a to structure your answer?

5a Module 5
The world around us

Writing (Task 1)

Organise information

1 Look at the graph below and answer the questions.
   1 What does it show?
   2 Which of these does it contain information about?
   - different regions of the world
   - different years
   - numbers of tourists
   - changes in income from tourism

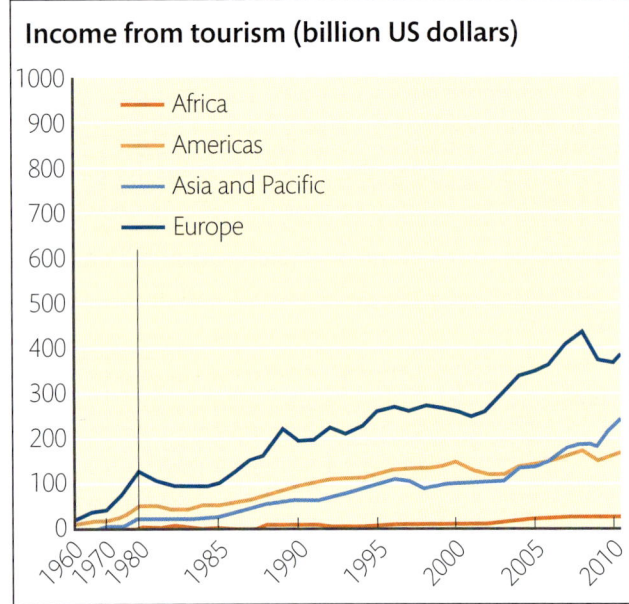

2a Read the writing task and underline the key words.

The graph shows the income from tourism in different regions over the period 1960–2010. Summarise the information by selecting and reporting the main features, and make comparisons where relevant.

b Look at some information from the graph that you could include in a summary. List three or four other pieces of information from the graph that you could include.
   - which region has the highest income from tourism
   - which years saw a peak in income from tourism

c Look at the plan for a summary. The four parts of the model answer below are in the wrong order. Read the plan and the model answer and number the parts of the model answer in the right order.

1 introduction explaining what the graph is about
2 overview of the general trend in the graph
3 paragraph outlining key differences between the areas shown, and some key data
4 paragraph outlining key similarities between the areas shown, and some key data

☐ The regions of the Americas, Asia and Pacific and Europe all show a similar pattern. After <u>reaching a peak</u> in 1980, income <u>remained fairly stable</u>. Since 2003 income <u>rose</u> more in Europe and the Asia and Pacific region than in other regions of the world, <u>peaking</u> at nearly 500 billion dollars in 2008.

☐ Although the graph shows some fluctuations from year to year, tourist income generally <u>increased</u> in all the areas shown.

☐ However, the different regions received very different amounts of tourist income. Europe earned between 50 and 200 billion dollars more each year than any other area, and Africa earned the least. Its income <u>stayed fairly constant</u>, at about 10 to 20 billion dollars. The Americas were in second place at the beginning of the period but by 2009, Asia and Pacific were in that position, receiving around 100 billion dollars more than the Americas. Although income everywhere <u>grew</u>, Europe had more fluctuation from year to year than other areas.

☐ The graph shows how much money different regions of the world received from tourism between 1960 and 2010. This income is given in billions of US dollars.

Describe changes and trends

3a Look at the verbs/verb phrases in the box for describing changes and trends. Write them in the correct place in the table.

decline decrease fall grow increase level off peak reach a peak remain stable remain unchanged rise stay constant

Going up	Going down	Staying the same

b Look at the underlined words in the model answer. What words from Exercise 3a could you use instead of the underlined words?

c Work in pairs. Look at the graph and complete the sentences with words from Exercise 3a. More than one answer may be possible.
   1 Tourist income in Europe reached _____ in 2008.
   2 Tourist income in Europe _____ in 1990.
   3 Tourist income in Africa _____ over the period 1997–2002.
   4 Tourist income in the Americas _____ during the 1990s.

4 Write two paragraphs reporting the main features of the graph. Use your ideas from Exercise 2b and words from Exercise 3a to describe changes and trends.

5b Our environment

Listening (Section 2: Table completion)

Before you listen

1 Do you have a favourite season? Which one? Why do you like it?

Test practice

> TEST STRATEGIES page 178

2 Work in pairs. Read the test task and answer the questions.
  1 You will hear a radio talk. What do you think it will be about?
  2 What main points will the speaker discuss? How do you know?
  3 Look at the words around each gap. What type of information is missing?

Questions 1–8
Complete the table below. Write **ONE** word for each answer.

Weather condition	Effects	Examples
Lack of sunlight	• symptoms of depression: difficulty sleeping, no 1 _____ • Seasonal Affective Disorder (SAD)	people living in areas with short days and little 2 _____ in winter
Season of birth	affects 3 _____ and temperament as an adult	• people born in winter: less bad-tempered • people born in autumn: less likely to suffer from 4 _____
Extreme weather	can cause 5 _____ and mental illness	• communities which rely on environment • people in high-risk areas
	makes people feel more 6 _____ to others	help from 7 _____ after New Orleans hurricane
High temperatures	possible link to increased 8 _____	study in Chicago: behaviour changes in late spring

> **HELP**

3 Listen for a phrase meaning 'as an adult'.
5 The answer is some sort of illness or medical condition.
6 Listen for an adjective to describe character.

3 🔊 5.4 Complete the test task.

Task analysis

4 Work in pairs and discuss the questions.
  1 How did the headings and the information in the left-hand column help you follow the talk?
  2 Did you correctly predict the type of information for each gap?
  3 Did you check:
    • that the words made sense with the words before and after each gap?
    • the number of words you wrote in each gap?
    • your spelling?

Discussion

5 Work in pairs. Are you affected by different seasons? In what way? Think about:
  • the light.
  • how warm or cold it is.
  • things like wind, rain and sun.
  • the kind of activities you do in different seasons.

5b Module 5
The world around us

Language development

Prepositions

▸ EXPERT GRAMMAR page 187

1 Underline the prepositions in the sentences. What does each one refer to? Write *T* for time, *P* for place or *M* for movement.
  1 The graph shows the temperatures in 2016.
  2 They were heading towards the river.
  3 The recycling centre is behind the post office.

Prepositions of place

2 Choose the correct prepositions to complete the sentences. There is one extra preposition for each sentence.
  1 We have a recycling centre _____ the main road, _____ the supermarket. (at, on, next to)
  2 There's a rubbish bin _____ the corner _____ the desk. (above, under, in)
  3 The storm caused damage to a building _____ the station and the post office _____ the end of the road. (at, below, between)
  4 You can't see the factory because it's _____ that wall, but you can see the smoke from it rising into the sky _____ the trees. (above, opposite, behind)
  5 People living _____ the airport don't like the noise from the aeroplanes flying _____ their houses. (near, below, above)
  6 The river runs _____ my house but there is a great deal of rubbish _____ it. (behind, in, over)

Prepositions of time

3a Which preposition do we use with each of the words/phrases in the box? Write them in the correct place in the table.

| 13 March 2015 7 o'clock autumn Diwali lunchtime Monday morning my birthday New Year night November Saturday evening the evening the past Wednesday |

on	at	in

b Work in pairs. Choose two different phrases from each category in Exercise 3a and use them to write questions for your partner. Then ask and answer your questions.

> What did you do on Saturday evening?

> I went to the cinema with a friend.

Prepositions of movement

4 Choose the correct options in *italics* to complete the sentences.
  1 We have to go *over / across* the street to leave our rubbish.
  2 They can't go *back / into* home because the flood damaged their houses.
  3 Driving slowly *through / over* a city is bad for air pollution.
  4 A lot of pollution comes from the road which goes right *across / round* the city.
  5 The water can't flow freely *under / back* the bridge because there is too much rubbish.
  6 The article had a photo of birds walking *down / over* a street, unable to fly because of air pollution.
  7 This is the first stage *across / towards* creating a cleaner city.
  8 We need to get *away / back* from the city because it's too polluted.

5 Choose the correct options in *italics* to complete the summary.

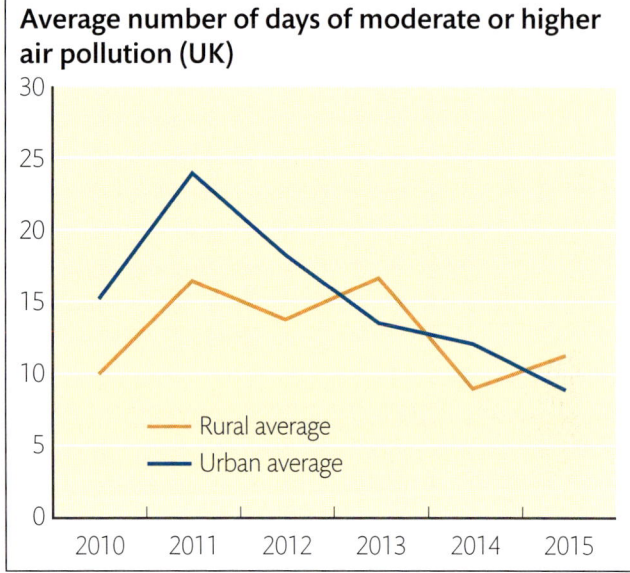

Average number of days of moderate or higher air pollution (UK)

The graph shows the number of days **1** *at / in / by* UK rural and urban areas when air pollution was medium or higher **2** *over / at / between* the years 2010 and 2015. It is clear that 2011 was a bad year for pollution as both figures went **3** *down / up / above* significantly, with the number of polluted days in rural areas rising **4** *to / up / by* five, and the number in urban areas increasing **5** *to / above / to* almost 25. However, in the following year, both figures went **6** *down / below / to*, with the urban average continuing to fall **7** *over / at / between* the next four years, until by 2015 it was down **8** *by / across / below* its 2010 figure. The rural average, on the other hand, went up and down in the same period and by 2015 was down to just **9** *in / over / for* ten, which is very similar to the figure **10** *at / on / in* the start of the period.

80 Student's Resource Book > Language development page 52 MyEnglishLab > 5b Language development

Vocabulary

Weather

1 Match the words in the box with the descriptions.

blizzard   drought   flood   fog   heat wave   hurricane   thunder and lightning

1 During the summer my country sometimes experiences strong violent winds that cause a lot of damage.
2 Last year we had a long period of dry weather with very little rain.
3 Last month some places had a lot of rain and many buildings and roads near rivers were damaged by the water.
4 At the moment we are having a long period of very high temperatures.
5 In the summer we often have electrical storms which are very noisy and light up the sky.
6 If we have a severe snow storm during the winter, it can be difficult to get to work or school.
7 Driving can be dangerous as it is very difficult to see through the thick cloud.

2a Choose the options in *italics* which <u>cannot</u> be used with the nouns.

1 *extreme / weak / severe* weather
2 *light / heavy / strong* rain
3 *tropical / violent / hot* storm
4 *solid / freezing / thick* fog
5 *mild / extreme / severe* climate
6 *hot / high / low* temperatures

b Complete the sentences with collocations from Exercise 2a.

1 _____ can be very dangerous and cause accidents on the road.
2 We have a(n) _____ , which means we have warm summers and cool winters.
3 Many people believe that _____ conditions like floods and droughts are caused by rising global temperatures.
4 Very _____ , often below 0°C, are very common here.
5 Last year we had very _____ for weeks, which caused floods.
6 The building was struck by lightning during a(n) _____ yesterday.

Climate change

3a Match words 1–5 with words A–E to make collocations.

1 global   A effect
2 polar   B fuels
3 forest   C warming
4 fossil   D ice cap
5 greenhouse   E fire

b Match the collocations in Exercise 3a with their meanings.

1 the frozen water that covers the top of the earth
2 coal, gas or oil you burn to produce heat or power
3 an increase in world temperatures
4 when pollution stops the sun's heat from escaping and the air gets warmer
5 when a large area of trees is burning

Environmental issues

4a Complete the sentences with the words in the box.

air quality   air pollution   noise pollution   recycling   rubbish   toxic waste

1 Airports should try to reduce _____ at night so that people living nearby can sleep.
2 There should be strict punishments for people who drop _____ in the streets.
3 Governments should do more to encourage _____ of waste products like newspapers and plastic.
4 It should be against the law for factories to put _____ in the sea or rivers.
5 Private cars should not be allowed in big cities, to reduce _____ .
6 The government needs to do something to improve the _____ in my city.

b Tick the sentences in Exercise 4a that you agree with. Discuss your ideas with a partner.

5 Choose the correct options in *italics* to complete the text.

Understanding noise pollution

Most of us are used to the sounds we hear in everyday life. Loud music, people talking on their phone and the traffic are part of our way of life. But we do not realise how much this can **1** *move / affect / effect* us. Pollution is not limited to nature and resources; noise that upsets the natural rhythm of life also **2** *supplies / delivers / produces* a form of pollution. By definition, noise pollution **3** *causes / brings / takes place* when there is a lot of noise which upsets us or is unhealthy. In our environment it has become difficult to escape noise. For example, many people have to live next to busy roads, which **4** *increases / spreads / grows* the amount of unwanted sounds they have to live with. Noise pollution is serious and can lead to disturbed sleep, so we do need to **5** *cope / deal / manage* with the problem. However, it is hard to think of ways to **6** *check / avoid / prevent* it increasing even more in the future.

5b Module 5
The world around us

Reading (Matching information)

Before you read

1a You are going to read a passage about visual pollution. Read this definition of the term. Do you have a similar term in your language?

> **visual pollution** (n) a term used to refer to structures or objects that make a view or environment unattractive

b Look at the list of things many of us see in our daily lives. How much do they annoy you? Number them 1–7 (1 = most annoying, 7 = least annoying). Can you think of other examples of visual pollution?

- billboards (advertising on the side of the road)
- bright lights in a city
- rubbish on the street
- graffiti on walls of buildings or public transport
- telephone towers
- power lines
- wind turbines

Test practice

> **TEST STRATEGIES** page 179

2a Read the test task and underline the key words. Label the underlined parts of each question A or B.

A type of information you are looking for
B detailed information you need

Questions 1-8

*The passage has seven paragraphs labelled **A-G**. Which paragraphs contain the following information? You may use any letter more than once.*

1 a reference to a problem that may no longer be possible to solve
2 examples of visual pollution having an impact on health
3 an example of a deliberate way of hiding something unattractive
4 definitions of different kinds of visual pollution
5 an example of a problem that may last for a long time
6 a reference to the fact that visual pollution can cause accidents
7 a reference to the impact of visual pollution on the economy
8 an example of different ways of viewing the same thing

b Complete the test task. Remember to:
- refer to the key words you underlined in Exercise 2a.
- only select a paragraph if it has the necessary information, not because it uses the same words as the question.
- underline the specific information in the passage.

> HELP

2 Paragraph C uses the word *health*, but does the information in the paragraph match the question? Does it give *examples* of health problems?
5 Many of the paragraphs refer to problems, but the right answer must also refer to how long people expect this problem to last.

Task analysis

3 Work in pairs and discuss the questions.
1 Which sentences in the passage gave you the detail you needed to match each statement?
2 Did the answer paragraphs use the same words as those in the question?
3 Did you use any letters more than once?
4 Did you use all the paragraphs?

Discussion

4 Work in pairs and discuss the questions.
1 Which do you think is the most serious problem in the place where you live – visual pollution, noise pollution or air pollution? Why?
2 What do you think we can do about visual pollution?

82 MyEnglishLab > 5b Reading

The problem of visual pollution

A Visual pollution means that people cannot enjoy what they see. There are two types of visual pollution in the modern world: one is when visibility is limited by haze*; another is visual untidiness, when buildings and signs spoil the view.

B Air pollution from cars and factories reduces visibility. It looks like a brown haze over cities, but it also affects the countryside. Scientists measured the visibility at a United States national park and found that on a clear day, it is possible to see for 320 kilometres. On a hazy day, that distance falls to 48 kilometres.

C Transport and industry are both major man-made causes of air pollution. But there are also natural sources of haze – smoke from forest fires, for instance. The pollution that creates haze can travel thousands of kilometres. In Southeast Asia, haze from enormous forest fires cost billions of dollars in health care. These fires have also stopped many tourists from visiting the area in the last decade. Fires in Sumatra and Borneo affected not only Indonesia, but also Malaysia, Singapore and Thailand. Developers started many of these fires – often illegally – because they wanted to use the land for building or farming. It is possible that some of the fires will continue to burn for years.

D Scientists can measure haze, but people have different opinions about other forms of visual pollution. Wind turbines, billboards, power lines, mobile phone towers, even modern buildings can all cause different feelings. To the businessman, a billboard in a good location may be beautiful. But to the traveller who would like to see the hills or the pretty village behind that billboard, it is visual pollution.

E When more people started to drive in the mid-20th century, businesses put large advertising hoardings next to busy roads. However, in the 1960s, many people began to complain about them, saying they were ugly and stopped drivers from focusing on the road. More modern examples of visual pollution are mobile phone towers and spray-painted graffiti. Some mobile phone towers have been made to look like trees or plants, which has reduced the visual impact, but attempts to ban the sale of spray paint to young people have not had much effect.

F But do these more subjective types of visual pollution really matter? The dangerous effects of air pollution are obvious, with more and more people suffering from breathing problems. However, research suggests that the other types of visual pollution can also have dangerous effects. One research study found that people who have an unpleasant view from their window are 40 percent more likely to feel sad or depressed. And there are several studies which show that physical environment affects stress levels. Being in beautiful surroundings – beside a lake or in a forest, for instance – tends to make people feel more relaxed.

G Moreover, another consequence of visual pollution is that it destroys the individual differences that make the world so special. In the past every town, city and suburb had its own unique character. Now they are starting to look the same all over the world. There are identical fast-food restaurants, billboards, motorways and petrol stations everywhere. Although this has a negative effect on the quality of life, it is probably already too late to change the situation.

*haze: air that contains something that makes it difficult to see through it, e.g. smoke or dust

5b Module 5
The world around us

Writing (Task 1)

Lead-in

1 Work in pairs and discuss the questions.
   1 Which do you think is the most serious of these problems: water shortages, air pollution, climate change or automobile emissions? Why?
   2 What do you think we can do about the problem of water shortages?

Understand the task

▶ EXPERT WRITING page 204

2a Read the writing task and underline the key words.

The graph below shows how serious people in four countries considered some environmental problems between 2000 and 2010. Summarise the information by selecting and reporting the main features, and make comparisons where relevant.

Seriousness of environmental issues
'Very serious,' average of 4 countries*, 2000–2010

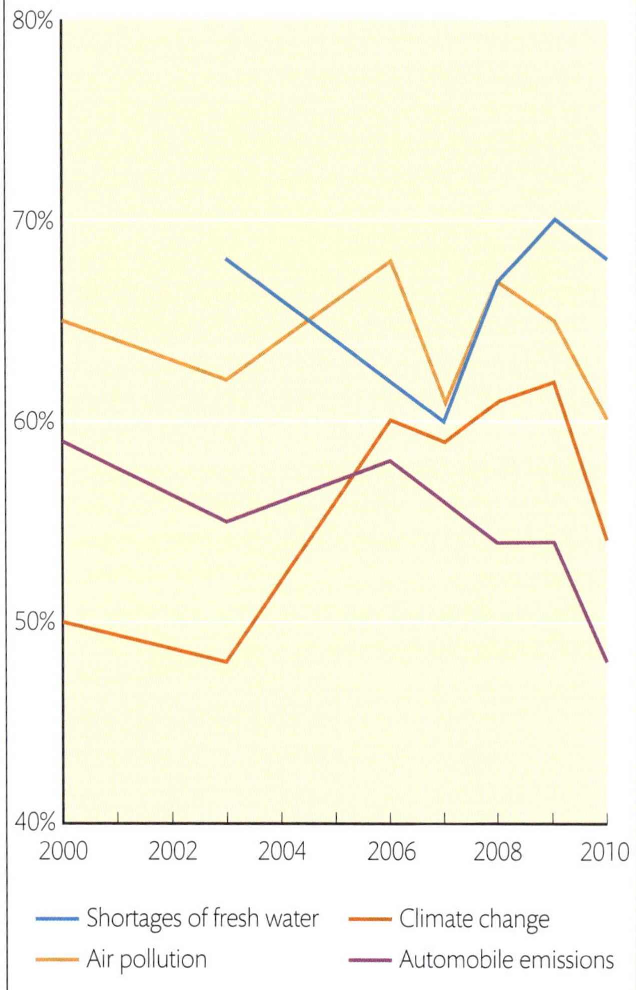

— Shortages of fresh water   — Climate change
— Air pollution   — Automobile emissions

*Average of China, India, Germany and USA

b Look at the words you underlined in Exercise 2a. What do you need to do in your answer?
   A explain why some issues are considered more serious than others
   B give reasons for fluctuations in people's attitudes
   C summarise the trends and main features in the graph

Language and content

3 Read the model answer below. Match the descriptions (1–4) with the parts (A–D).
   1 a description and comparison of the issues causing most concern
   2 an introduction to the graph
   3 a description and comparison of the issues causing least concern
   4 an overview summarising the main trends

A The graph shows how serious people in China, India, Germany and the USA thought four environmental issues were between 2000 and 2010.

B Overall, the graph shows that attitudes towards water shortages, air pollution, climate change and automobile emissions all fluctuated considerably over the period. ¹However, people were less worried about each of the issues in 2010 than in the previous years.

C In general, water shortages caused more anxiety in any one year than any other issue, with 70 percent of the population rating it as 'very serious' in 2009. ²In each year on the graph, either water shortages or air pollution was the problem which the highest proportion of people were very worried about. ³Concern about air pollution, for example, grew until 2006 before a sharp fall in 2007.

D In 2000 climate change was the issue fewest people (around 50 percent) expressed serious concern about. ⁴Between 2000 and 2003, there was a slow decline in anxiety about this. Although ⁵people were less worried about climate change than car emissions at the beginning of the period, the situation changed in 2006.

Module 5
The world around us — 5b

4a Look at the graph below and answer the questions.
1 Which line represents a sharp fall?
2 Which line represents a gradual fall?
3 Which line represents a slight rise?
4 Which line falls gradually?
5 Which line falls sharply?
6 Which line rises slightly?
7 Draw a line (D) on the graph to represent a slight decline.
8 Draw a line (E) that rises sharply.

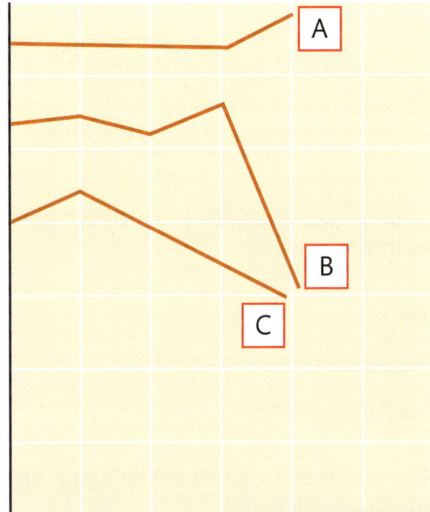

b Rewrite the sentences. Change the adjectives into adverbs and make any other necessary changes.
1 There was a steady rise in temperatures.
 Temperatures rose *steadily*.
2 There was a slight fall in numbers last month.
 Last month numbers fell _____ .
3 We saw a sharp decline in income.
 Income _____ .
4 In 2016 there was a sudden growth in student numbers.
5 We had a significant decrease in temperatures.
6 There was a gradual levelling off in income.
7 There was a dramatic increase in tourist numbers.

c Look at the underlined sentences (1–5) in the model answer. In which sentences does the student:
A describe a trend?   B make a comparison?

5 Work in pairs. Read the model answer again and answer the questions.
Has the student:
1 included an introduction and overview?
2 organised the information into clear sections?
3 used a range of nouns and verbs to describe trends? Can you find examples?
4 used a range of adjectives and adverbs to describe trends and make comparisons? Can you find examples?

Plan your summary

6a Look at the two final paragraphs of the model answer again. Which of these ways to organise the information has the student used?
A paragraph 1 on the first half of the decade and paragraph 2 on the second half of the decade
B paragraph 1 on the two issues causing most concern and paragraph 2 on the two issues causing least concern
C paragraph 1 on air pollution and automobile emissions and paragraph 2 on water shortages and climate change
D paragraph 1 on similarities between the trends for the four different issues and paragraph 2 on differences between trends for the four issues

b Now think about your own answer. Choose one of the ways in Exercise 6a to organise the information in the last two paragraphs. It does not have to be the same as the model answer.

c Organise the information you need for your paragraphs. Use your ideas from Exercise 6b and make notes in the table.

Paragraph	Main focus	Notes
1		
2		

d Look at your plan in Exercise 6c. Think about some useful language for describing changes and trends you can use for each point.

Write your summary

▶ TEST STRATEGIES page 181

7 Write your two paragraphs. Use your plan from Exercise 6c.

Assess and improve

8 Check your work. Did you do these things in your paragraphs?
1 I reported the main features and included some key data.
2 I made some comparisons.
3 I organised the information in each paragraph in a clear and logical way.
4 I used a range of language to describe changes and trends and make comparisons.

Student's Resource Book > Writing page 54

5b Module 5
The world around us

Speaking (Part 2)

Use time phrases

1a Which of these environmental problems does your local area suffer from?
- rubbish in the streets or countryside
- noise pollution
- poor air quality
- polluted sea or rivers
- something else?

b Do you think environmental problems in your local area are worse or better now than they were ten years ago?

2a Read the test task. Does it ask you to talk about the present, the past or both?

Describe a place you know that has an environmental problem.
You should say:
what the place is
what the environmental problem is
what caused the problem
and say whether the problem is better or worse now than in the past.

b 🔊 5.5 Listen to a candidate doing the task and answer the questions.
1 What place and environmental problem does he talk about?
2 Does he say the problem is better or worse now than in the past?

3 Look at audio script 5.5 on page 215. Find examples of time phrases the candidate uses and write them in the correct place in the table.

Time phrases used with present tenses	Time phrases used with past tenses

Use a range of grammar

4a Look at audio script 5.5 on page 215. Find one or more examples of:
1 a verb in the present simple.
2 a verb in the present continuous.
3 a verb in the past simple.
4 a modal verb (*can, should, must,* etc.).
5 an adverb of frequency.
6 a comparative.
7 a superlative.
8 an *-ing* form used as the subject of a sentence.

b Complete the sentences with the correct form of the word in brackets.
1 The streets in my town are much _____ (dirty) now than in the past.
2 When I was younger, I _____ (not care) about the environment.
3 The _____ (polluted) places in my country are the big cities.
4 I _____ (always/pick up) my litter.
5 The air quality in my capital city is so bad that it's difficult _____ (breathe).
6 People shouldn't _____ (leave) rubbish on the beach.
7 I think _____ (keep) the countryside clean and free from pollution is very important.
8 Pollution in my country is _____ (steady) increasing.

c Work in pairs. Do you agree or disagree with the sentences in Exercise 4b?

Test practice

▶ **TEST STRATEGIES** page 182
▶ **EXPERT SPEAKING** page 198

5a Look at the test task in Exercise 2a again and make notes for each point.

b Check your notes with a partner. Have you got enough information to talk for 1–2 minutes?

c Work in pairs. Follow the instructions and complete the test task. Then swap roles.
- Student A: Use your notes from Exercise 5a and talk about the topic. Try to:
  - speak for 1–2 minutes.
  - use words/phrases to structure your answer.
  - use a range of grammar.
- Student B: Listen and make notes in the table.

	Notes/Examples
Did your partner talk about all the points in the task?	
Did your partner structure his/her answer using appropriate words/phrases?	
Did your partner use a range of grammar?	
Did you hear any mistakes?	

Assess and improve

6 Work in the same pairs. How well did your partner do? Use your notes from Exercise 5c to give him/her feedback.

6 Buying and selling

6a Training
- **Reading:** Understand paraphrasing (Summary completion)
- **Language development:** *be going to*
- **Vocabulary:** Food and diet
- **Listening:** Follow a conversation (Section 1: Matching)
- **Speaking:** Say you are not sure (Part 3: Discussion)
- **Writing:** Structure a paragraph; Give examples (Task 2: Opinion essay)

6b Testing
- **Listening:** Section 1: Matching
- **Language development:** *will*; *will* and *be going to*
- **Vocabulary:** Shopping
- **Reading:** Summary completion
- **Writing:** Task 2: Opinion essay
- **Speaking:** Part 3: Discussion

Lead-in

Discuss the questions.
1. Do you enjoy shopping? Why/Why not?
2. Do you prefer shopping in big stores or small shops? Why?
3. What do you usually buy when you go shopping?
4. Which is the most popular place to shop in your town?

87

6a The food we eat

Reading (Summary completion)

Before you read

1 Work in pairs and discuss the questions.
   1 What is more important for you when you shop for food: price or quality? Why?
   2 What kind of information can you find on food labels? How often do you read the labels?

Understand paraphrasing

2a Read the passage quickly. What is its purpose?
   A to report on changes in farming
   B to suggest what kind of food we may have in the future
   C to describe a variety of new food types

b Read this summary of part of the passage. Which part of the passage does it summarise? Underline the parts of the summary and the passage that helped you to decide.

Some developments in high-tech food

Both companies and 1 _____ are putting money into developing **high-tech ways of producing artificial foods**. One such business says that its aim is to create meat in a 2 _____ without hurting animals. Another is already selling products that resemble meat but are actually made from 3 _____ from plants. You can find their range in the supermarket next to ordinary meat products. A third company produces food using artificial 4 _____ . This company's products are already selling to educational and health 5 _____ of different types in the USA. There is also a business which has put an unusual drink on the market. This, its developer says, will help consumers save time and also solve the problem of food 6 _____ .

c Which of these sentences is true about the summary in Exercise 2b?
   A It copies sentences from the passage, but only the important ones.
   B It expresses the same ideas as the passage, but in different words.

d Look at some paraphrases of different parts of the passage. Find the part of the passage each sentence is a paraphrase of.
   1 The number of people living on the planet will increase by over one quarter.
   2 Current farming methods will not be able to provide enough food for so many people.
   3 Even everyday food products are causing her concern.
   4 People do not realise what they are putting in their mouths.
   5 Her preference is to prepare meals from ingredients she buys from farms in her region.
   6 It is essential to make certain that new products not only taste good but are also healthy.

3 Work in pairs. Look at the first sentence of the summary and answer the questions.
   1 Which part of the passage does the sentence refer to? How do you know?
   2 What words in the passage express the same idea as the phrase in bold?
   3 What kind of information goes in the gap (a person, a place, a description, etc.)?
   4 Complete the gap using one word from the passage. Check the word you choose matches the grammar of the sentence.

Test training

4 Decide what kind of information goes in gaps 2–6 in the summary.

5 Read the passage again and complete the rest of the summary with words from the passage. Use only one word in each gap.

Task analysis

6 Work in pairs and discuss the questions.
   1 Did you identify paraphrases in the passage for each gapped sentence?
   2 Did you think about what kind of information went in each gap?
   3 Did you just write one word for each gap?
   4 Did you check that each word you wrote matched the grammar of the sentence?

Discussion

7 Work in groups. Would you like to try some of the high-tech food mentioned in the passage? Why/Why not?

The future of food?

Studies suggest that, over the next 25 years or so, the population of the world will grow by more than 25 percent. This means that there will be 9 billion people on earth by then. We must, therefore, change the systems we use to produce food or it will not be possible to feed a population of this size.

With this in mind, business people and governments are investing in a range of unusual new ways of producing food. Some companies, for example, are using technology to develop new artificial food products. One such business is Modern Meadow, which develops meat that does not involve killing animals. What that actually means is that scientists are working in the company's lab to find ways to create something that looks and tastes like meat. Another company called Beyond Meat already has such products in shops in the US. Its range includes 'burgers', 'chicken' strips and 'beef' for stews. Although they are actually made out of plant proteins, these products are almost impossible to distinguish from meat and shoppers find them on the same supermarket shelves as the genuine meat products. Another company, Hampton Creek, sells products that are made with man-made eggs. The main ingredient is a type of pea. Hampton Creek is already selling its foods to US hospitals, retirement homes, universities and other institutions.

A more extreme approach to dealing with the problem of getting enough food to feed the world involves drinking a special drink and not eating any food at all. Every day a businessman called Rob Rhinehart drinks three glasses of a thick, brownish liquid, which he says has all the nutrients the body needs. He has put his drink on sale and it is doing surprisingly well. Rhinehart says that this type of product will not only help to deal with food shortages but will also provide people with more time. 'There's no need to waste time cooking. I drink a litre of my liquid every day and don't even need to stop what I'm doing.'

However, the high-tech solutions that Rhinehart, Modern Meadows and others are suggesting worry many people. Food writer Joanna Blythman, for example, does not like the idea of eating things that we do not know enough about. She even worries about foods that are already familiar to us. Packets of salad leaves, for example, can be weeks old but still look fresh because of the chemicals on them. These chemicals are not always named on the label because they are not food. So consumers have no idea what they are eating. Blythman says, 'There are many examples of products we once thought were safe and then later discovered they weren't.' She prefers to cook her family meals using locally produced natural food that people have eaten for centuries. 'It's tried and tested, and we know it's healthy.'

It is easy to understand this point of view, but it is still very important to find some way to solve the problem of feeding the world. The answer must be to make sure we check very carefully the quality and safety of the high-tech solutions that scientists are developing.

6a Module 6
Buying and selling

Language development

be going to

▶ EXPERT GRAMMAR page 188

1 Match the sentences (1–6) with what they express (A–B).
   1 Look at the prices! This meal is going to be very expensive.
   2 I'm going to buy my vegetables at the market because the food is fresher there.
   3 Are you going to cook the meat in the oven or on the grill?
   4 I'm not going to buy any more fast food – it's too unhealthy.
   5 This cake smells amazing – it's going to taste delicious.
   6 You're going to get fat if you eat all that chocolate!

   A a planned future event
   B a prediction based on knowledge or evidence

2 Complete the sentences with the correct form of *be going to* and the verbs in brackets.
   1 This fish is not cooked, so I _____ (not eat) it.
   2 I need to go to the supermarket – I _____ (cook) a meal for my family tonight.
   3 There are too many things on this menu – it _____ (not be) easy to choose what to have.
   4 This table only seats four people, so we _____ (have to) find a bigger one.
   5 My friend has decided to stop eating meat, so I _____ (buy) her a vegetarian cook book.
   6 Drinking coffee gives him a headache, so he _____ (drink) tea instead.
   7 There's a new Korean restaurant opening soon and we _____ (try) it.
   8 I'd like to learn how to cook because I _____ (go) live on my own next year.
   9 That supermarket is quite expensive, so they _____ (not shop) there any longer.
   10 My doctor says I eat too many sweet things, so I _____ (stop) eating cakes and biscuits.

3a Write questions using be *going to*.
   1 where / you / have / lunch / tomorrow?
   2 who / cook / your evening meal / tonight?
   3 you / eat out / this weekend?
   4 you / cook / any meals / this week?
   5 it / be / easier or more difficult to eat healthily / in the future?
   6 you / have / a coffee / after class?
   7 we / have / more choice of food / in the future?
   8 food prices / go / up or down / this year?

 b Work in pairs and discuss the questions in Exercise 3a. Give reasons for your answers.

4 Write sentences for each of these situations. Use *be going to* and the prompts in brackets.
   1 You want to eat more healthy food. (chocolate and biscuits)
      I'm going to stop eating chocolate and biscuits.
   2 You want to spend less money on food. (grow vegetables)
   3 You want to become a vegetarian. (eat meat)
   4 You want to eat more healthily. (advice)
   5 You want to learn how to cook. (cookery course)
   6 You want to find out how to make a particular dish. (recipe)
   7 You want to find a good Japanese restaurant. (online)
   8 You want to try Thai food. (restaurant)

5 Work in pairs. Tell your partner about what you intend to do this year or next year. Think about:
   • your work or studies
   • your home and family life
   • your interests and hobbies.

   I'm going to apply for university next year.

   I'm going to join a tennis club later this year.

Module 6
Buying and selling — 6a

Vocabulary

Food groups

1 Write the words in the box in the correct place in the table. Some words can go in more than one group. Can you add more examples?

apples   bananas   bread   cheese   chicken   fish   milk   pasta

Protein	Carbohydrates	Dairy	Vitamins and minerals

Flavours

2 Choose the correct options in *italics* to complete the sentences.
   1 In general, I prefer *savoury / salty* food like meat and fish to *sweet / sour* desserts and puddings.
   2 Lemons and other fruit have a sharp acid taste and are too *sour / savoury* to eat without sugar.
   3 Crisps are not a healthy option because they are very *salty / spicy*.
   4 The sugar in soft drinks makes them bad for you and I find them far too *bitter / sweet*.
   5 Children don't like *bitter / salty* flavours like coffee.
   6 I like using chillies in my cooking, but some people find them too *sour / spicy*.

Types of food

3a Match the words in each pair with the descriptions.
   1 fattening / fast
      A food like burgers that is prepared quickly
      B food that will probably make you fat like cakes and chocolate
   2 junk / takeaway
      A food that is unhealthy because it contains a lot of sugar or fat
      B food you order from a restaurant to eat at home
   3 fresh / processed
      A food that is changed from its natural state to make it safer or easier to eat
      B food that you have just picked or prepared
   4 ready-made / home-cooked
      A food that is prepared and cooked in the home
      B food that is already prepared and ready to eat
   5 organic / nutritious
      A food that is produced without any chemicals
      B food that contains substances which help the body grow and stay healthy

b Work in pairs. Tell your partner how often you eat the types of food in Exercise 3a. Are there any you never eat? Are there any you would like to eat more or less of?

Diet

4 Cross out the adjective in italics that is not possible in each sentence.
   1 I am following a *strict / poor / special* diet where I can't eat anything but fruit and vegetables.
   2 Doctors say a(n) *low-fat / vegetarian / unhealthy* diet is good for your heart.
   3 If you want to have a *balanced / healthy / strict* diet, you should eat a variety of different foods.
   4 I have a number of food allergies, so I have to follow a *special / low-calorie / strict* diet.
   5 People with a(n) *poor / balanced / unhealthy* diet are more likely to have bad health.

5 Complete the text with the words in the box.

appetite   calories   dessert   dish   hunger   ingredients   main course   meal   snack   thirst

Dieting

There are different ways to lose weight. A popular one is to eat foods with fewer **1** _____ . However, some experts believe that this approach to dieting is confusing because foods with the same energy value can affect your **2** _____ in different ways, with some foods making you feel fuller for longer. So certain foods can produce a feeling of **3** _____ sooner because we digest them more quickly than others. This means that we are more likely to want a(n) **4** _____ rather than waiting for our next **5** _____ .

When you feel hungry, it is a good idea to have a drink of water before you eat, to see if that helps. Sometimes we think we are hungry when, in fact, we are experiencing **6** _____ .

Another thing you can do is to eat more slowly. It takes some time for the brain to register that we are full, so when you finish your **7** _____ , it's a good idea to wait a while before deciding if you want a(n) **8** _____ . After a few minutes you may realise that you're no longer hungry.

Finally, cooking your own food is generally better for you because you can choose healthier **9** _____ and you can see exactly what goes into each **10** _____ .

6a Complete the questions with the correct form of the verbs in the box.

go   have   lose   put on   spoil   watch

   1 Is eating less the best way to _____ weight?
   2 Is it a good idea for children to _____ on a diet?
   3 Why do some people _____ weight as they get older?
   4 Why is it important to _____ your weight if you want to be healthy?
   5 If you _____ a snack between meals, does that _____ your appetite?

b Work in pairs. Take turns to ask and answer the questions in Exercise 6a.

6a Module 6
Buying and selling

Listening (Section 1: Matching)

Before you listen

1 Work in pairs. Do you ever buy any of these things?
   - energy or sports drinks
   - protein or energy snack bars
   - vitamin and mineral supplements
   - ready-made diet meals
   - protein or diet drinks

Follow a conversation

2a 🔊 6.1 Listen and complete the conversations.
   1 A: The organic drink is €1.45 and the non-organic <u>one</u> is €1.15.
      B: _____ €1.45 for the organic one?
   2 A: I'm not sure which one to choose.
      B: _____ try these snack bars? <u>They</u>'re delicious and only have 55 calories.
   3 A: I think it would be better for you to buy these vitamins, which are on special offer.
      B: _____ . I'll go for the cheaper <u>ones</u>. How much are they?
   4 A: So, I'll order a couple of boxes of the energy drinks for you.
      B: Good – <u>that</u>'s the last thing on my list. _____ I'd like to ask you.
   5 A: We have a number of ready-made low-fat meals which I think you'd like.
      B: Hmm … _____ I want <u>one of those</u>, to be honest. I don't like them.

b Look at Exercise 2a again. What is the second speaker doing each time? Match the conversations (1–5) with the functions (A–E).
   A agreeing
   B disagreeing
   C checking information
   D making a suggestion
   E moving on to a new topic

c Look at the underlined words in Exercise 2a. What do they refer to?

Test training

3a Work in pairs. You will hear a conversation between a customer and a sales assistant. Read the test task. What type of shop do you think they are in?

*What comments do the speakers make about each product? Choose your answers from the box and write the correct letter **A–F** next to questions 1–5.*

Comments
A They are organic.
B They are the shop's best-selling product.
C They are suitable for people with allergies.
D They are suitable for vegetarians.
E They are for people on diets.
F They are on special offer.

Products
1 nutrition drinks   _____
2 snack bars   _____
3 energy drinks   _____
4 protein drinks   _____
5 vitamins and minerals _____

b 🔊 6.2 Complete the test task.

4 Look at the underlined words in audio script 6.2 on page 216. What do they refer to?

Task analysis

5 Work in pairs and discuss the questions.
   1 In what order did the speakers discuss the products?
   2 Did the list of products and comments help you to predict the information in the text? How?
   3 Look at the words you underlined in Exercise 4. How did they help you?

Discussion

6 Work in pairs. Do you think health products like the ones in the recording are effective or are they a waste of money? Why?

Module 6
6a Buying and selling

Speaking (Part 3)

Say you are not sure

1 Work in groups and discuss the questions.
   1 What food is your country famous for?
   2 How healthy do you think your country's diet is?

2a 🔊 6.3 Listen to two students talking about food. What country does the man come from? What food does he say his country is famous for?

b 🔊 6.3 Listen again and complete the phrases the speakers use to say they are not sure.
   1 I'm _____ I think it's from the north of the country originally.
   2 I _____ it's what we're best-known for.
   3 I _____ , but isn't that why people say you have one of the healthiest diets?
   4 It's _____ , but I know many people say that olive oil is very good for you.
   5 I _____ , but I think people in the cities are eating more fast food nowadays.

c Work in pairs. Take turns to respond to these points. Use phrases from Exercise 2b.
   1 Which are more popular in your country: fast food restaurants or traditional restaurants?
   2 Which countries do you think have the healthiest diets? Why?
   3 Do you think eating habits will change in the future? How?

Pronunciation: silent letters

3a 🔊 6.4 Listen to these words. What do you notice about the letters in bold?

ni**gh**t **t**wo recei**p**t lis**t**en is**l**and **k**now

b 🔊 6.5 Listen and circle the silent consonants in the words in bold.
   1 You **should** always be careful when using **knives** and **scissors**.
   2 **Who** is going to the **talk** next **Wednesday**?
   3 I hurt my **knee** when I went **climbing** last **autumn**.
   4 I don't **know** what to **write** because I wasn't **listening** to the lecture.
   5 To be **honest**, I think **half** of these **answers** are **wrong**.

c Work in pairs. Practise saying the sentences in Exercise 3b.

Test training

4 Work in pairs. Take turns to ask and answer the questions.
   1 What is the typical diet of people in your country?
   2 How are the eating habits now in your country different from eating habits in the past?
   3 What's the difference between restaurant food and home cooked food?
   4 Why do you think people eat junk food when they know it's bad for them?

Task analysis

5 Work in pairs and discuss the questions.
   1 Did you/your partner stay focused on the topic of each question?
   2 Did you/your partner give examples?
   3 Did you/your partner use any of the phrases from Exercise 2b to show you were not sure?

MyEnglishLab > 6a Speaking

6a Module 6
Buying and selling

Writing (Task 2)

Structure a paragraph

1a Read the writing task and underline the key words. Then choose the correct answer in the question below.

> People should only buy locally grown food; it is better for individuals and society.
>
> To what extent do you agree with this statement?

What do you need to do in your essay?
A describe a problem and present a solution
B present and explain your opinion
C discuss two sides of an argument

b Read the model answer. Does the student agree or disagree with the statement?

> Today supermarkets sell all sorts of natural and processed foods from all over the world. However, many people think that we should only eat meals we prepare ourselves from products that are grown locally. I totally agree with this statement.
>
> Firstly, we get many advantages from eating food that is grown in the part of the world where we live. Local foods, for instance, taste better because they are fresher. They also have all the natural vitamins and other nutrients that we need. Eating local food means that we cannot have, for example, strawberries at all times of the year, but I think this is a good thing. If you can only eat them when they are available locally, that makes them more special.
>
> ¹Secondly, buying food that has travelled a long way is not good for society. ²Flying produce to Europe or the USA from a place such as Australia or South Africa contributes to environmental problems like air pollution, one of the main reasons for climate change. ³When the food arrives at an airport on the other side of the world, it then usually goes by lorry to supermarkets across the continent. ⁴This leads to busy roads, which is bad for the environment and also makes driving more stressful for everyone.
>
> If we just buy food that has come from farms in our local area, our diet may be less varied, but this is not a serious problem. Both we and the planet will benefit.

2a Look at the second paragraph in the model answer and answer the questions.
1 What is the topic sentence in this paragraph?
2 Do the other sentences in the paragraph explain the idea in the topic sentence or do they introduce new ideas?
3 Do any of the other sentences give examples?

b Look at the third paragraph in the model answer. Which of the four sentences (1–4):
A is the topic sentence?
B describes the next stage in a process?
C gives a reason for the point made in the topic sentence?
D presents what happens as a result of the situation the writer described?

c Number the sentences in the best order (1–4) to make a paragraph.
A It also makes it more difficult for them to get all the vitamins and nutrients that their body needs.
B In this part of the country, for example, they can eat lots of potatoes, carrots and apples but they can't have rice, aubergines or bananas.
C People who only buy food that comes from their local area have a very limited diet.
D This means that meals are much less varied and interesting for them.

Give examples

3a Look at the words/phrases in the box for giving examples. Which ones does the student use in the model answer?

for example   for instance   one example (of …) is …
to give a(n) (simple/brief) example, …
take, for example, …   like   such as

b Write examples for each statement using phrases from Exercise 3a. You can write the examples in a new sentence or include them as part of each statement.
1 Many countries export food.
3 Exporting food is important for the economies of some countries.
2 Green vegetables are full of vitamins and other nutrients.
4 The farm sells dairy products.

4 Write the second and third paragraphs of an essay for the writing task in Exercise 1a. For each paragraph, remember to:
- begin with a topic sentence.
- explain/support the idea of the topic sentence in the rest of the paragraph.
- make clear links between the sentences in the paragraph.
- give examples using some of the words/phrases in Exercise 3a.

6b How we buy

Listening (Section 1: Matching)

Before you listen

1 Work in pairs and discuss the questions.
  1 How often do you buy these things?
    - books
    - magazines or newspapers
    - stationery (e.g. pens and paper)
    - DVDs
    - greetings cards (e.g. birthday cards)
  2 Where do you usually buy these things?
    - in a supermarket
    - in a department store
    - in a smaller shop
    - online

Test practice

▶ TEST STRATEGIES page 178

2 Work in pairs. Read the test task and answer the questions.
  1 Where do you think the conversation is taking place?
  2 In what order will the speakers discuss the products?
  3 Do you need to use all the options A–F?
  4 How can you use reference words (*this*, *that*, *it*, *they*, etc.) to help you follow the conversation?

Questions 1–5

What does the shop manager say about each product? Choose your answers from the box and write the correct letter **A–F** *next to questions 1–5.*

Comments
A They are in a temporary display.
B They are not in a busy department.
C They are on special offer.
D They are the most popular products.
E They make the most profit.
F They are at the front of the shop.

▶ **HELP**

B If a department is not busy, what is it?
C Listen for another way of saying 'on special offer'.
1 What other words might the speaker use instead of *stationery*?
3 Listen for an example of a greetings card.

Products
1 stationery   _____
2 newspapers and magazines _____
3 greetings cards   _____
4 books   _____
5 DVDs   _____

3 🔊 6.6 Complete the test task.

Task analysis

4 Work in pairs and discuss the questions.
  1 Look at audio script 6.6 on page 216. Can you find examples of reference words that helped you with the answers?
  2 Which option was not an answer? Why?

Discussion

5 Work in pairs. Do you agree that competition from online stores and streaming services affects sales of DVDs? Can you think of any other products affected in the same way?

6b Module 6
Buying and selling

Language development

will

▶ EXPERT GRAMMAR page 188

1 a Match the sentences (1–3) with what they express (A–C).
1 I think the price will go up next week.
2 OK. I'll buy it!
3 I'll drive you to the store as it's out of town.

A an offer
B a prediction
C a spontaneous decision

b Make sentences using *will* and *won't*.
1 there / probably / be / more people shopping online / in the future
2 I don't think / people / change / the way they shop
3 do you think / you / be able to / afford to go on holiday / this year?
4 I / lend / you some money if you like
5 I can't afford it, so I / buy / it / later
6 I / take / you to the supermarket / tomorrow
7 I'm tired, so I / go / home / now
8 we / probably / use / less cash / in the future

c Match the sentences in Exercise 1b (1–8) with the descriptions in Exercise 1a (A–C).

2 a Complete the sentences about the future of shopping. Use *will* or *won't* to give your opinion.
1 All companies _____ have an online store.
2 People _____ stop buying books in bookshops.
3 Large shopping centres _____ replace high street shops.
4 Musicians _____ only sell music online.
5 Companies _____ improve the way they deliver their products.
6 People _____ use cash to pay for things.

b Work in pairs. Choose two sentences from Exercise 2a and tell your partner the reasons for your prediction.

will and be going to

3 Choose the correct options in *italics* to complete the conversations.
1 A: Did you go to the new superstore yesterday?
  B: No, *we'll / we're we going to* drive over there this afternoon.
2 A: Look, your new watch is broken.
  B: Do you think the shop *will / is going to* exchange it?
3 A: I've got to go to the chemist's for my prescription.
  B: *I'll / I'm going to* go if you like – it's on my way.
4 A: We don't have that book in stock at the moment.
  B: OK, thanks. *I'll / I'm going to* try the online store.
5 A: Are you cutting your prices?
  B: Yes, I hope the sales *will / are going to* bring more customers into the store.
6 A: Everything in the new supermarket seems very expensive.
  B: Well, we *won't / aren't going to* shop there then!
7 A: Have you got all the ingredients you need?
  B: No, but Neil *will / is going to* get everything on his way home from work.

4 a Complete the sentences with the correct form of *will* or *be going to* and the verbs in brackets.
1 I don't think I _____ (have) more money than I do now in ten years time.
2 I'm hungry; I _____ (have) something to eat soon.
3 I'm sure I _____ (have to) go to the supermarket tomorrow.
4 I _____ (buy) some clothes this weekend.
5 I _____ (not have) much money left at the end of the month – my back account is empty.
6 I hope I _____ (be able to) afford to travel around the world one day.
7 I _____ (always / lend) money to my friends.
8 I've decided I _____ (not spend) any money on clothes this month.

b Work in pairs. Are any of the sentences in Exercise 4a true for you?

5 a Make notes about these things.
• something that you think you will do next year
• something that you're definitely going to do later in the year
• something that will probably happen to your country this year
• somewhere that you're going to visit soon
• somewhere that you hope you will go in the future
• something you are sure you'll do today

b Work in pairs. Use your notes from Exercise 5a to tell your partner about your plans, hopes and predictions.

> I hope I'll be able to get a good university degree.

> I'm going to buy a new coat next week.

Module 6
Buying and selling
6b

Vocabulary

Types of shops

1a Match the shops (1–8) with the products they sell (A–H).

1 chemist's
2 newsagent's
3 antique shop
4 florist's
5 bookshop
6 second-hand store
7 department store
8 sports shop

A maps, books, kindles, music
B many different types of things, including clothes and furniture
C sports clothes and equipment
D things people have used before
E flowers
F old and valuable furniture, paintings, jewellery
G sweets, newspapers and magazines
H medicines, soap, toothpaste, make up

b Work in pairs. When was the last time you went to the shops in Exercise 1a? What did you buy?

Shopping

2a Complete the sentences with the words in the box.

bill   customers   fitting room   order   receipt   sales assistant

1 A good _____ needs to be confident and friendly with the people they serve.
2 I never use the shop _____ when I'm buying clothes – I prefer to try them at home.
3 You should always get a(n) _____ in case you have to return the item to the shop.
4 In a restaurant I always check the _____ carefully before paying.
5 When you place a(n) _____ online, you often have to wait a long time to receive the product.
6 It is important for shops to provide good after-sales service for their _____ .

b Work in pairs. Do you agree or disagree with the sentences in Exercise 2a?

Verbs and verb phrases

3a Choose the correct options in *italics* to complete the sentences.

1 How much do you usually *spend / pay* on clothes every month?
2 Do you ever buy things that you can't really *afford / cost*?
3 For what reasons do people *exchange / serve* items they buy?
4 How much does it *buy / cost* to feed a family of four for a week?
5 Do you ever *offer / return* something to a shop because you find it at a better price somewhere else?
6 In a clothes shop, is it important that the people who *browse / serve* you are well-dressed?
7 Do you think companies should *advertise / serve* unhealthy food products?
8 Do you like *browsing / spending* in the shops without actually buying anything?

b Work in pairs. Take turns to ask and answer the questions in Exercise 3a.

Dependent prepositions

4 Complete the text with the prepositions in the box.

at   back   by   in (x2)   on (x5)

Online shopping

Although most people still shop regularly **1** _____ the high street, it is becoming more common for customers to shop online. The percentage of UK adults buying **2** _____ the internet is increasing rapidly, and websites can crash when a store puts a new or popular product **3** _____ sale. There are a number of reasons for this. Firstly, you can shop online using your phone or tablet anywhere and at any time, so it is far more convenient for busy customers. Secondly, online shopping gives us more choice of product and we can see which stores have the product we want **4** _____ stock. Finally, online shopping allows us to compare prices easily and find products that are **5** _____ special offer.

Of course, shopping online has disadvantages too. One of them is that you usually have to pay **6** _____ credit card as you can't pay **7** _____ cash. Buying clothes and shoes online is particularly popular but, of course, you are not able to try them **8** _____ before you buy them and it can be more difficult to take something **9** _____ if you're not happy with it. However, some shoppers overcome this problem by looking at and trying products in stores without buying, knowing that they can find the same product online **10** _____ a discount.

Student's Resource Book > Vocabulary page 63   MyEnglishLab > 6b Vocabulary

97

6b Module 6
Buying and selling

Reading (Summary completion)

Before you read

1 Work in pairs and discuss the questions.
   1 What kind of advertising makes you want to buy something?
      • advertisements in magazines
      • street advertising
      • online advertisements
      • TV commercials
   2 Do you often buy something because someone you know recommends it?

Test practice

➤ **TEST STRATEGIES** page 179

2a Read the first paragraph of the passage. What words or phrases from the paragraph do these paraphrases match?

   1 buyers   4 types
   2 convince   5 relatives
   3 companies   6 increase in popularity

b Read the test task. What do you have to do?
   A complete the summary with words from the passage
   B complete the summary with words from a list
   C complete the summary with words from both the passage and a list
   D complete the summary with your own words

Questions 1–8
Complete the summary using the list of words A–L below.

The characteristics of word-of mouth marketing

A big advantage of word-of-mouth marketing is the fact that no 1 _____ is involved. It is simply a matter of 2 _____ passing on information to people they know. This feature means that it has particular 3 _____ for smaller businesses. It is a very powerful type of marketing because people have more 4 _____ in friends than in advertisements. Although adverts reach a bigger audience, word-of-mouth marketing is often more likely to lead to 5 _____ . One of its disadvantages, however, is that businesses cannot control it. They have no 6 _____ when it comes to the comments people make about their products – consumers may also share their 7 _____ of something they have bought. Word of mouth may help a company's name to become known, but what people say about their business may in the end prove to be an actual 8 _____ for sales.

A problem   E sales   I buyers
B value   F dangers   J experience
C companies   G faith   K influence
D dislike   H manner   L money

3 Complete the test task. Remember to follow these steps.
   1 Find the part of the passage the summary relates to – underline matching words at the beginning of the summary and in the passage.
   2 Think about what kind of information you need for each gap.
   3 Read each sentence in the summary and match it with the right part of the passage. Remember that the summary uses paraphrases and not the same words as the passage.
   4 Find the word in the list which fits the gap. Check that it matches the meaning and grammar of the sentence.

➤ HELP

2 Who might share information? There are two words referring to people or organisations in the list, but only one matches the meaning in the passage.
7 There are different words in the list that are things that people can share. You need one with a negative meaning here.

Task analysis

4 Work in pairs and discuss the questions.
   1 Did you use the beginning of the summary to identify which part of the passage it was about?
   2 Did you think about what kind of information goes in each gap (e.g. a person, a place, a feeling)?
   3 Did you find the right word in the passage and think about paraphrases?

Discussion

5 Work in pairs and discuss the questions.
   1 What adverts have you seen that you remember? What do you think makes them memorable?
   2 To what extent do online reviews influence your decisions about whether to buy something or not?

98   MyEnglishLab > 6b Reading

WOMM: advantages and disadvantages

A business can make the best product in the world but if no one knows about it, they cannot sell it. To tell customers about their products and to persuade them to buy them, all businesses need marketing. One of the most powerful forms of marketing is WOMM: word-of-mouth marketing. This is when people tell their family and friends about a product – and the growth of social media means it has become even more effective.

Word-of-mouth marketing has both advantages and disadvantages for businesses. Firstly, a main advantage is that it costs the business nothing. If a customer likes a product or service, he or she just tells their friends and family about it without getting or expecting any payment. So, word-of-mouth marketing has always been especially useful for small and local businesses, which may have small advertising budgets.

There are other benefits to word-of-mouth marketing. People trust a friend's recommendation more than an advertisement. Magazine and television advertising is based on the idea of reaching a lot of customers and hoping that some of them will buy the product. In contrast, although one happy customer can only tell their friends about a positive experience with a business, a personal recommendation from a friend has more influence than a professional advertisement.

However, there are, of course, problems with word-of-mouth advertising and the main one is that companies cannot manage it. For example, they cannot increase it nor can they control what people say. Customers may say negative things about the products and this can discourage people from buying them.

Interactive and social media have made word-of-mouth marketing much more powerful. When someone tells a friend in a coffee shop about the wonderful new phone they've just bought, they are speaking to one person. When they write about it on their social network page, they are telling all their friends. If they mention it on a blog or on YouTube, they are telling anyone with web access. The impact of this can be enormous. After all, most people say that they check out online reviews before booking a holiday or buying a new electronic device.

The problem of control is still an issue for online word-of-mouth marketing, but less so than for basic face-to-face marketing. Businesses can have more influence on the internet. They can, for instance, monitor what people say about their products and add comments of their own. They can also identify bloggers and people who are popular online and who they feel may be able to influence others to use their products. They can do a great deal to encourage excitement about their product on social media.

Of course, the trust that people have in a friend's recommendation is stronger than their trust in a review that a stranger posts online. Everyone has heard stories about less honest businesses employing people to give their products five stars, or even to write negative reports of competitors' products or services. Even so, there is evidence to show that online reviews frequently determine the decision: to buy or not to buy. This means that word-of-mouth marketing is something today that no business, large or small, should ignore.

6b Module 6
Buying and selling

Writing (Task 2)

Lead-in

1 Work in pairs and discuss the questions.
   1 What have you bought recently? Why did you buy these things?
   2 Do you ever buy things you don't really need? If so, what made you buy them?

Understand the task

> EXPERT WRITING page 205

2 Read the writing task and underline the key words. Then choose the correct answer in the question below.

Write about the following topic.

Buying new things has too much importance in modern society.
To what extent do you agree with this statement?

Give reasons for your answer and include any relevant examples from your knowledge or experience. Write at least 250 words.

What do you need to write about?
A how often people today buy new things
B whether people today think too much about shopping
C how important buying new things is for you

Language and content

3 Read the model answer. Does the student agree or disagree with the statement in the task?

It is often said today that people spend too much time thinking about what they are going to buy next rather than more important aspects of life. I very much agree that modern society has become too commercial.

Firstly, I think this focus on buying things is bad for the individual person. If someone is always thinking about when they can upgrade their mobile phone or buy the latest fashion of clothes, then they are not taking the time to enjoy what they actually have. In addition, thinking about or shopping for new things all the time can be a waste of both money and time. There are certainly more constructive ways for people to spend their time, such as reading, doing sport or, more importantly, being with friends and family.

Secondly, getting new things also has negative consequences for society in general. For a start, many valuable resources are used to make things that no one really needs. Those resources will then not be available for people to use in the future. As well as this, wanting new things makes people throw away lots of items like last year's model of phone or handbag. Although these things may still be perfectly good, we no longer want them. As a result, there are mountains of rubbish near every town and city. All this is wasteful and has a very negative effect on the environment.

Therefore, even though I too sometimes enjoy buying new things, I agree with the statement that shopping has become too important in modern society. This approach to life has a negative impact on both the individual and the environment.

Module 6
6b Buying and selling

4a Work in pairs. Look at the underlined linking words/phrases in the model answer and write them in the correct place in the table.

Adding	Showing result	Showing contrast	Giving examples	Listing points

b Write the linking words/phrases in the box in the correct place in the table in Exercise 4a.

> but   finally   for instance   however   moreover
> on the one hand …   on the other hand
> one example (of …) is …   so

c Choose the correct options in *italics* to complete the sentences.
   A This is because such people choose, *such as / for instance / like*, to go to the shops rather than to visit an elderly neighbour or relative.
   B As a result *to / of / for* this, family and other relationships suffer.
   C If people are constantly thinking about what they want to buy next, *so / then / also* they do not have time to pay attention to more important aspects of life.
   D However, this is a serious mistake as most people get more pleasure not from things, *firstly / but / even though* from contact with others.
   E In *the one hand / the other hand / addition*, they seem to think it is more important to buy presents for others than to spend time with them.

d Number the sentences in Exercise 4c in the best order (1–5) to make a paragraph.

5 Work in pairs. Read the model answer again and answer the questions in the table.

	Notes/Examples
Is the essay organised into clear paragraphs?	
Does the student say how strongly they agree or disagree with the statement?	
Does the student explain their opinion?	
Does the student give examples to support their opinion?	
Does the student use words and phrases to link ideas?	

Plan your essay

6a Read the task in Exercise 2 again. To what extent do you agree with the statement? Mark with an *X* on the scale.

completely agree — neither agree nor disagree — completely disagree

b Work in pairs and follow these steps.
   1 Discuss reasons why you agree or disagree with the statement.
   2 Decide on examples you can use to support your points.
   3 Plan your essay. Make notes in the table.

Paragraph	Notes
Introduction	
Reason(s) to agree/disagree	
Reason(s) to agree/disagree	
Conclusion	

Write your essay

▶ **TEST STRATEGIES** page 181

7 Write your essay. Use your plan from Exercise 6b. Remember to:
   • make it clear how strongly you agree or disagree.
   • give examples to support your ideas.
   • use linking words and phrases to connect your ideas.

Assess and improve

8 Check your work. Answer the questions in Exercise 5 about your essay.

Student's Resource Book > Writing page 64

6b Module 6
Buying and selling

Speaking (Part 3)

1 Work in pairs. Which of these statements do you agree with? Give reasons and/or examples.
   1 There is definitely too much advertising these days.
   2 We possibly buy things we do not need because of advertising.
   3 We should probably control the amount of advertising we have.

Degrees of certainty

2a 🔊 6.7 Listen to a candidate doing Part 3 of the Speaking test and answer the questions.
   1 What is the main topic of the discussion?
   2 How certain is the student about each of her answers?

b Look at audio script 6.7 on page 216. The underlined words are words the speaker uses to express different degrees of certainty. Write them in the correct place in the table.

Certain	Not certain

c Work in pairs. Tell each other how certain you are on these points. Use words/phrases from Exercise 2b.
   1 We will eat more junk food in the future.
   2 Food from my culture will be more popular in other countries.
   3 More people will grow their own fruit and vegetables.
   4 People will have a healthier diet than they do now.

Use a range of vocabulary

3a Look at audio script 6.7 on page 216. Find two words/phrases the speaker uses to avoid repeating each of these words/phrases.
   1 everywhere   2 don't need   3 controls

b Match the words/phrases below with words/phrases from the box with a similar meaning.

be different   be hard   buy things   in my culture
in the coming years   in years to come   nations
not be easy   not be the same   parts of the world
spend money on   where I live

1 in my country   4 countries
2 in the future   5 change
3 be difficult   6 go shopping

c Work in pairs. Take turns to ask and answer the questions. Try to use different words/phrases to refer to the same thing more than once. Use Exercise 3b to help you.
   1 What types of things do people in your country like to go shopping for?
   2 Do you think shopping habits will change in the future?
   3 How do shops encourage customers to spend more money?

Test practice

▶ TEST STRATEGIES page 182

▶ EXPERT SPEAKING page 199

4a Read the test task. Think about what you can say for each question.

   1 Do you think there is too much advertising around us?
   2 Do you think we often buy things we don't need because of advertising?
   3 Do you think the amount of advertising we have should be controlled?

b Work in groups of three. Follow the instructions and complete the test task. Then swap roles.
   • Student A: Ask the questions.
   • Student B: Answer the questions. Remember to use words/phrases to show how certain you are. Avoid repeating the same words.
   • Student C: Listen and make notes in the table.

Did your partner:	Notes/Examples
stay focused on the topic of each question?	
use a range of words to talk about the same thing?	
use words/phrases to show different degrees of certainty?	

Assess and improve

5 Work in the same groups. How well did your partner do? Use your notes from Exercise 4b to give him/her feedback.

7 City life

7a Training
- **Reading:** Understand sequencing (Flow chart completion)
- **Language development:** Zero conditional
- **Vocabulary:** Communities; Crime
- **Listening:** Identify different types of information (Section 3: Short-answer questions)
- **Speaking:** Express opposing ideas (Part 3: Discussion)
- **Writing:** Write an introduction and overview; Describe numbers (Task 1: Tables)

7b Testing
- **Listening:** Section 3: Multiple choice; Short-answer questions
- **Language development:** First conditional
- **Vocabulary:** Public buildings; Public services
- **Reading:** Flow chart completion; Multiple choice
- **Writing:** Task 1: Tables
- **Speaking:** Part 3: Discussion

Lead-in

1. Look at the photos of different types of communities. What are the differences between the communities? Think about these points.
   - the amount of space each person has
   - how easy it is to get to areas of natural beauty
   - the type of services available

2. Which type of community would you prefer to be part of? Why?

7a Communities

Reading (Flow chart completion)

Before you read

1 Work in pairs. Talk about the town or city where you live. Talk about:
   - where exactly it is.
   - its history – why people started living there.
   - whether it has any factories and, if so, what they make.
   - what sports and other facilities it has.

Understand sequencing

2 Look at the flow chart. What does it show?
   A the steps in a process
   B some choices available
   C the order of events

The development of Bournville Village

| 1879: Cadburys moved their 1 _____ manufacturing business to outside the city |

| From 1890: Building of workers' houses, all with big 2 _____ |

| 1900: Trust set up, aiming to change Bourneville into a proper 3 _____ |

| 1906: Bournville tenants' association formed |

| 1920: Land bought in order to build a range of 4 _____ |

| 1950s and 1980: Bournville experienced considerable 5 _____ |

| 2000 onwards: large amount spent on a 6 _____ |

| Today: Bournville has 8,000 homes |

3a Read the passage and answer the questions.
   1 How did the Cadbury brothers treat their staff?
   2 How is Bournville today different from the beginning of the 20th century?

b Work in pairs. Underline all the words in paragraphs B–F that tell you when something happened (e.g. a year, a date, *then*).

c Look at the underlined words (1–8) in the passage. What do they refer to?

Test training

4 Look at question 1 in the flow chart, and the words before the gap. Follow these steps.
   1 Predict: what kind of information might be missing (a place, a person, etc.)?
   2 Find: which part of the passage contains the answer? How do you know?
   3 Look for similar meanings: which words in the passage have the same meaning as *moved* and *outside the city*?
   4 Complete the gap: what is the correct answer?

5 Read the passage again and complete questions 2–6 in the flow chart. Choose no more than two words from the passage for each answer. Follow the steps in Exercise 4 for each gap.

Task analysis

6 Work in pairs and discuss the questions.
   1 Did you use the flow chart to help you understand the order of events?
   2 What kind of words helped you with the order of events?
   3 Did you think about the type of information that was missing in each gap?

Discussion

7 Work in pairs and discuss the questions.
   1 Do you think life was better for Cadbury workers at the beginning of the 20th century than it is for most factory workers now? Why/Why not?
   2 What do you think companies should give their employees apart from a salary? Think about these points.
      - a pension
      - sports facilities or social clubs
      - holidays
      - transport

George Cadbury, 1839–1922

Bournville: an unusual community

A Villages, towns and cities usually grow slowly over a long period of time. However, in 19th-century Britain some places developed in a very different way. [1]This was thanks to some very unusual men.

B One of the most remarkable of [2]these was George Cadbury. He and his brother Richard had a chocolate factory in the industrial city of Birmingham. In 1879 they decided to find a new site for it and so left the city centre for a location about seven kilometres to the south. They took this decision because they thought the countryside was a healthier environment than a big city. They wanted their staff to work in a pleasant green place with fresh air. They chose a pretty location next to a little river called the Bourn.

C The Cadburys treated workers much better than most industrialists did at that time. [3]They paid them good salaries and provided pensions and a full medical service. However, they wanted to do more than just provide good working conditions. In 1890 George Cadbury bought a large area of land around the factory and starting creating, at his own expense, a whole village for the factory employees. He called the village Bournville. By 1900, the village already had 314 small houses. [4]These were traditional in design but with large gardens and modern rooms.

D In 1900 the Cadburys set up a *trust whose purpose was to transform the village from just a collection of houses to a community. They built shops, churches, parks, sports facilities and schools so that the people who lived in Bournville had everything [5]they could want. In order to make it look like a traditional English village, which typically has a green open space at [6]its centre, the Trust built the public buildings around a village green. In 1906 the Trust started a housing association called Bournville Tenants Limited. This was run by the people who lived in the village, which meant they could control their own affairs. This organisation planned new houses, chose tenants and dealt with repairs to the buildings.

E The brothers were very keen on health and fitness and in 1920 they bought a large area of land next to the village, where they constructed football and hockey pitches, a running track, an open-air swimming pool and a fishing lake. This area also contained a large pavilion which had both changing rooms and a large hall used for balls and formal dinners. All the sports facilities were free for Cadbury staff and their families.

F Since then Bournville has continued to expand, with strong periods of growth in the 1950s and then again in the 1980s. At the start of the 21st century Bournville went through a £25-million redevelopment programme. The Trust pulled down all the flats from the 1950s because [7]they wanted to build modern houses and apartments. In 2009 residents moved into the first of these modern homes, which have top-quality environmental standards and use much less energy than traditional houses.

G Bournville is, of course, very different today. Although the chocolate factory is still there, many of the 25,000 people who live [8]there now work elsewhere. The number of homes in the area has grown to almost 8,000 and these vary in size from one-bedroom flats to five-bedroom houses. Bournville is now very much part of the city of Birmingham rather than a country village, but it still has good facilities and plenty of green space. And it still considers itself a distinct community.

*trust: an organisation which controls money that will be used to help someone else

7a Module 7 — City life

Language development

Zero conditional

▶ EXPERT GRAMMAR page 188

1 Read this zero conditional sentence and answer the questions.

If people live in a small community, they generally feel safer.

1 How many parts are there in the sentence? What separates the two parts?
2 Which part of the sentence shows a condition? Which shows a result?
3 Can you change the order of the two parts of the sentence? What happens to the punctuation?
4 Can you think of another word you can use instead of *if*?

2a Match the sentence beginnings (1–6) with the endings (A–F).

1 If you live in a busy city,
2 You should check your doors and windows are locked
3 When you share a house with others,
4 If you have elderly neighbours,
5 Crime generally increases
6 Joining a social club is a good way to make friends

A when you go to bed.
B you need to be clean and tidy.
C you should try to help them.
D when you move to a new town.
E if there is high unemployment and poverty.
F you have more facilities than in a small town or village.

b Work in pairs. Choose two statements from Exercise 2a and discuss. Do you agree?

3 Complete the zero conditional sentences with the correct form of the verbs in brackets. Add commas where necessary.

1 When people *visit* (visit) villages, they usually *like* (like) the peace and quiet.
2 Cities _____ (work) well as communities if they _____ (offer) good public facilities.
3 If you _____ (live) in a big city you often _____ (have) very limited personal space.
4 When you _____ (buy) a house in the countryside it usually _____ (come) with a nice garden.
5 When a city _____ (have) a central square people _____ (use) it for all sorts of purposes.
6 If you _____ (want) to be part of a community it _____ (be) a good idea to join local clubs.
7 Travelling often _____ (take up) a lot of your time when you _____ (live) in a city.
8 There _____ (be) generally less crime when there _____ (be) a sense of community.

4 Complete the sentences with *if* or *unless*.

1 Crime rises _____ people lose their jobs.
2 Communities don't work well _____ they have a central point.
3 _____ people feel part of a community, they look after their property.
4 Young people often move away from an area _____ there are plenty of job opportunities.
5 A community is not successful _____ it has a group of leaders.
6 A town is very attractive _____ it has good schools and other facilities.

5a Make zero conditional sentences. Add commas where necessary.

1 I / not carry / much money on me / unless / I / really / have to
2 I / not feel / safe in the streets at night / if / I / be / on my own
3 when / I / see / my neighbours / I / always / stop / for a chat
4 I / always / lock / my doors / when / I / be / at home
5 children in my town / play / in the street / even when / it / get / dark
6 if / I / be / part of a community / it / make / me / feel safer

b Work in pairs. Are any of the sentences in Exercise 5a true for you?

6a Complete the questions with the correct form of the verbs in brackets.

1 What time _____ (you / wake up) if you _____ (not have to) work or study?
2 How _____ (you / entertain) yourself if you _____ (be) on a long journey?
3 What _____ (you / do) if you _____ (have) difficulty sleeping?
4 If you _____ (be) late, what _____ (your boss or teacher / do)?
5 When _____ (you / need) advice, who _____ (you / usually / talk) to?
6 If _____ (you / get) lost in a strange place, _____ (you / ask) someone for help?

b Work in pairs. Take turns to ask and answer the questions in Exercise 6a.

Vocabulary

Module 7
City life
7a

Communities

1 Complete the sentences with the correct form of the words in bold.
1. **citizen / resident**
   - A More than 60 percent of the local _____ are retired.
   - B Although I was born in France, I am now a Canadian _____ .
2. **service / facility**
   - A My town has some good sports _____ , including a swimming pool and a tennis court.
   - B There are going to be some job losses in public _____ , particularly in schools and hospitals.
3. **involvement / development**
   - A It is good to see young people's _____ in the community is increasing.
   - B There is a lot of _____ in my town, with new houses, shops and a new school built in the last year.
4. **council / society**
   - A The local _____ started a recycling scheme last year.
   - B The new law will benefit all members of _____ , particularly young people.
5. **cooperation / relationship**
   - A I have a very good _____ with all my neighbours.
   - B It would be good to have more _____ between local schools and businesses.

Adjectives

2 Choose the correct options in *italics* to complete the sentences.
1. People living in *urban / rural* communities usually have greater job opportunities.
2. My street is very *safe / noisy* as there is always a lot of traffic.
3. I live in Seoul, which is a very *crowded / urban* city, full of people and vehicles.
4. I am involved in a number of *near / local* community groups in my town.
5. Nowadays many families are moving from the cities to live a more *urban / rural* lifestyle.
6. It's very important that you feel *local / safe* in your own home.

Crime

3a Match the words (1–10) with their meanings (A–J).

1. judge
2. police officer
3. criminal
4. witness
5. burglar
6. mugger
7. thief
8. shoplifter
9. vandal
10. suspect

A someone who goes into buildings and steals things
B someone who does something illegal
C someone who steals things
D someone who destroys public property
E someone who takes things without paying in shops
F the person in a court who decides what punishment a criminal should get
G someone who sees an accident or crime
H someone the police think may be guilty of a crime
I someone who attacks people in public places and steals their money, phone, etc.
J someone whose job it is to catch criminals

b Complete the table.

Criminal	Crime
robber	robbery
burglar	
mugger	
thief	
vandal	
shoplifter	

c Complete the sentences with the correct form of words from Exercise 3b.
1. You shouldn't carry anything valuable on you as there have been a number of _____ recently.
2. They are putting more security cameras in the street to try and reduce car _____ in the area.
3. It's a shame that _____ are damaging parts of the city centre.
4. Most large stores have security guards to look out for _____ .
5. There was a serious _____ last night from the bank in the next street.

Verbs

4a Choose the correct options in *italics* to complete the sentences.
1. We should *send / arrest* everyone who *accuses / commits* a crime to prison.
2. Burglaries often *steal / take place* because people do not care about security in their homes.
3. *Stealing / Catching* things like paper and pens from your work is not a crime.
4. When you *accuse / arrest* someone of a crime, it's important to be sure that they are guilty.
5. If you see a crime, you should *report / send* it to the police immediately.
6. The police should *accuse / arrest* people even for very minor crimes like dropping litter.

b Work in pairs. Do you agree or disagree with the sentences in Exercise 4a?

7a Module 7
City life

Listening (Section 3: Short-answer questions)

Before you listen

1 Work in pairs and discuss the questions.
   1 In what ways is a university a type of community? Think about things that everyone has in common (e.g. study, living on campus, social life).
   2 What problems might you have with living as part of a community in a college or university?

Identify different types of information

2 Work in pairs. You will hear a conversation about crime on a university campus. Look at the questions and options below and follow steps i–iii.
   i Underline the key words in each question.
   ii Match the questions (1–6) with the type of information you need to listen for (A–F).
   iii Think about what words you expect to hear in answer to each question.

   1 What kind of crimes happen on campus?
   2 How many crimes are there every year?
   3 Who is committing the crimes?
   4 Where do the crimes usually happen?
   5 When do the crimes generally happen?
   6 What are we doing to make the campus safer?

   A a place on campus
   B a number
   C a time of day
   D an action that the university is taking
   E a category of person
   F a type of crime

3a 🔊 7.1 Listen to six extracts from the conversation and answer questions 1–6 in Exercise 2. Use no more than three words or a number for each answer.

  b Work in pairs and follow these steps.
   1 Compare your answers. Do they match the type of information you chose in Exercise 2?
   2 Check your partner's answers. Did he/she make any spelling mistakes?

Test training

4a Read the test task and underline the key words.

Answer the questions below. Write **NO MORE THAN TWO WORDS AND/OR A NUMBER** *for each answer.*

   1 What type of crime does the campus NOT experience?
   2 Which two crimes are increasing at the moment?
   3 Which crime is most common?
   4 What percentage of incidents were vandalism?
   5 What was stolen from the psychology department?
   6 Where do most thefts occur?
   7 What is the problem in the changing rooms?
   8 What does Claude suggest people need to be?

  b 🔊 7.2 Complete the test task.

Task analysis

5 Work in pairs and discuss the questions.
   1 Look at the key words you underlined. Did they help you to identify the key points in the conversation?
   2 Did you think about the type of information you needed for each answer?
   3 Did you check the number of words in your answers?
   4 Did you check your answers for spelling mistakes?

Discussion

6 Work in pairs. Suggest three ways you can reduce crime in a university community.

Module 7
City life
7a

Speaking (Part 3)

Express opposing ideas

1 Work in pairs. Think of two advantages and two disadvantages of:
   - living in a small community.
   - living in a large community.

2 Read the statements below expressing opinion. What does the speaker do in each one?

   A gives an example
   B gives a reason
   C expresses opposing ideas

   1 It can be difficult to have a private life in a small community because everyone knows everyone else.
   2 It's true that your neighbours know everything about you, but they can also help you in times of trouble.
   3 In my view, a small community can bring people together – for instance, when they are going through some difficult times.

3 Match the beginnings (1–6) and endings (A–F) of statements expressing opposing ideas.

   1 On the one hand, getting involved in a community can take up a lot of your free time.
   2 Some people think that there is a better sense of community in a small village
   3 Although in a large city you have lots of facilities and services available,
   4 It's wrong to say that living in a city can be lonely
   5 I don't enjoy living in a village because there are no facilities apart from one shop.
   6 There is always something happening in a busy city

   A but others say you can have the same community feel in a city.
   B On the contrary, I find it an excellent place to make friends.
   C but at the same time it can be a very lonely place to live.
   D On the other hand, it can give you a sense of belonging.
   E However, I do like the peace and quiet.
   F you also have more pollution, more noise and more stress.

4a 🔊 7.3 Listen to a candidate answering an examiner's questions about his community. Match the questions (1–4) with the candidate's answers (A–D).

   1 Do you think we are losing our sense of community nowadays?
   2 How much do you take part in your community?
   3 What kind of community do you live in?
   4 What do you think are the advantages of that?

b 🔊 7.3 Listen again and note down two opposing ideas for each answer the candidate gives.

5a Look at audio script 7.3 on page 217 and the words/phrases in the box for expressing opposing ideas. Which ones does the candidate use in his answers?

   … but at the same time …
   Although …
   However, …
   It's true that … but …
   On the contrary, …
   On the one hand, … On the other hand, …
   Some people think/feel/say/etc. … but …

b Complete the sentences with words/phrases from Exercise 5a.

   1 It's not easy to keep things private in a small village. _____ , everyone knows your personal business.
   2 _____ many people like getting involved in community activities, but not everyone does.
   3 _____ big cities offer many opportunities, there can be a lot of competition.
   4 _____ , I like having all the facilities nearby. _____ , I don't like the noise and pollution.
   5 I love living in a small village and am happy to stay here. _____ , my brother hates it and wants to move away.
   6 _____ think it's important to keep small traditional communities _____ others feel they are too old-fashioned.

c Work in pairs. Read these statements expressing opinion. Think of opposing ideas to add.

   1 Some people think we are losing our sense of community but others …
   2 It is true that living in a small community can be difficult but …
   3 Although living in the city can be very expensive, …
   4 It's good to know your neighbours well. However, …
   5 You are never far from a bus stop in the city but at the same time …
   6 On the one hand, small communities don't have many facilities but on the other hand, …

Test training

6 Work in pairs. Take turns to ask and answer the questions in Exercise 4a. Try to express opposing ideas in your answers.

Task analysis

7 Work in pairs and discuss the questions.

   1 Did you express opposing ideas for each question? Was it difficult to think of what to say?
   2 Did you use any of the words/phrases in Exercise 5a?
   3 Did you give reasons and/or examples?

MyEnglishLab > 7a Speaking

109

7a Module 7
City life

Writing (Task 1)

Write an introduction and overview

1 Read the writing task and underline the key words in the instructions.

The table below gives some information about thefts in the Helby region of the UK, compared to UK averages. Summarise the information by selecting and reporting the main features, and make comparisons where relevant.

Thefts in Helby region of UK, compared to UK averages

	Helby 2014	Helby 2015	UK average of types of theft 2014	UK average of types of theft 2015
Total number of thefts: Of which:	34,801	33,133		
Domestic burglary	31%	26%	40%	35%
Car theft	26%	33%	30%	31%
Bicycle theft	9%	7%	4%	9%
Shoplifting	34%	33%	26%	25%

2a The answer to the task in Exercise 1 has three parts. Match each part (1–3) with its description (A–C).

1 an introduction 3 key details from the data
2 an overview

A one or two paragraphs giving more detailed information about the data
B a sentence paraphrasing the title of the table
C one or two sentences summarising the main features shown in the table

b Read the model answer and match its parts with the descriptions (A–C) in Exercise 2a.

3a How has the student paraphrased or changed these words from the task instructions in their introductory sentence?

thefts   region   UK   compared to   UK averages

b Look at the overview in the model answer and answer the questions.
1 What does each sentence describe?
2 Do the sentences refer to all the information in the table?
3 Do they mention any specific figures?

The table provides data about different types of theft in the Helby area of the United Kingdom in 2014 and 2015, presenting national average figures for comparison.

Overall, there were fewer theft crimes in Helby in 2015 than in 2014. The majority of types of theft crime declined, but the number of car thefts increased.

In 2014 shoplifting represented just over a third of all thefts in Helby, and burglaries were just under one third. One in ten theft crimes was a bicycle theft and the remaining quarter involved the stealing of a car. Apart from shoplifting, the proportions were different in 2015, with burglaries falling to just over a quarter and car thefts rising to a third. Only six percent of thefts in Helby that year involved a bicycle.

Comparing the Helby percentages with national averages, it is clear that Helby patterns are not typical of the UK as a whole. Shoplifting, for example, makes up over one third of all theft crimes in Helby in both years while it is approximately one quarter across the UK.

Describe numbers

4a Match the words in the box with the percentages.

a fifth   a half   a quarter   a third   four fifths   one in ten   three quarters   two thirds

1 10%   3 25%   5 50%   7 75%
2 20%   4 33.3%   6 66.6%   8 80%

b Find examples of the words in Exercise 4a in the model answer.

5 Complete the test task below. Remember to divide your answer into three clear parts. Use Exercise 2a to help you.

The table below gives some information about types of crime in urban and rural areas of the Helby region of the UK. Summarise the information by selecting and reporting the main features, and make comparisons where relevant.

Traffic offences in Helby, 2015

	Urban areas	Rural areas
Driving without a licence	150 (35.4%)	100 (33.33%)
Speeding	1 (0.2%)	0
Dangerous driving	74 (17.4%)	50 (16.66%)
Illegal parking	200 (47%)	150 (50%)

7b Public services

Listening (Section 3: Multiple choice; Short-answer questions)

Before you listen

1 Which services or facilities in your community do you use most? Which ones are you happy with and which ones are you not so happy with?

Test practice

> TEST STRATEGIES page 178

2 You will hear a conversation. You must complete both of the tasks below while listening. Before you listen, follow these steps.
  1 Read the tasks. What do you think the conversation is about? Who is speaking?
  2 Read questions 1 and 2 and underline the key words. What do you need to listen for?
  3 Read questions 3–10. Underline the key words. Think about what type of information you need to listen for.

Questions 1 and 2
Choose TWO letters A–E.

Which TWO problems does the student say she had with her report?
A choosing suitable places to ask people
B analysing the results
C writing the questions for the survey
D finding enough people to ask
E finding different people to ask

Questions 3–10
Answer the questions below. Write no more than THREE WORDS AND/OR A NUMBER for each answer.

3 How many facilities did the student ask about?
4 Which facility did young people not use much?
5 Which facility do people use most?
6 Which age group were happier with the restaurants?
7 Which group of people all know about the community centre?
8 What classes are there for children at the community centre?
9 What are people not satisfied with at the community centre?
10 What are people unhappy with at the leisure centre?

3 🔊 7.4 Complete the test tasks.

> HELP

1–2 The student mentions all five options, so you need to listen carefully to see which were problems for her.
4 Listen for another way of saying 'young people'.
6 Listen for another way of saying 'restaurants'.
9–10 *Not satisfied* and *unhappy* mean the same thing, so listen out for both of these.

Task analysis

4 Work in pairs and discuss the questions.
  1 Were your predictions in Exercise 2 correct?
  2 Did the question words in questions 3–10 help you predict what kind of information to listen for?
  3 Could you identify where the first task ends and the second task begins?
  4 Did you use the correct number of words?
  5 Did you check your spelling?

Discussion

5 Work in pairs and discuss the questions.
  1 For what reasons do you think different age groups have different opinions about facilities?
  2 What recommendations would you make about facilities and services in your town?

Student's Resource Book > Listening page 71   MyEnglishLab > 7b Listening

111

7b Module 7
City life

Language development

First conditional

> EXPERT GRAMMAR page 188

1a Read these first conditional sentences and answer the questions.

If people are unhappy with a service, they will complain.
I won't go there again unless they improve security.

1 When do we use the first conditional?
   A to talk about past events that have happened
   B to talk about present events in progress
   C to talk about future events that are likely to happen
2 Which words can we use at the beginning of the *if* clause?
3 Which comes first, the condition or the result?
4 What do you need to remember about punctuation?

b Work in pairs. Match the beginnings of the sentences (1–3) with the endings (A–C). Then say which part is the condition and which part is the result in each sentence.

1 The museum will have to close
2 If people aren't satisfied with the service,
3 I'll join the sports centre

A we'll have to do something about it.
B if I can afford it.
C unless it gets more money from the government.

2 Complete the first conditional sentences with the correct form of the verbs in brackets. Add commas where necessary.

1 If we _____ (not get) enough money we _____ (never / be able to) open the new leisure centre.
2 The population in cities _____ (increase) if governments _____ (not control) it.
3 If they _____ (cut) the crime rate more people _____ (move) to the area.
4 Unless we _____ (reduce) the number of cars travelling _____ (take) longer.
5 If they _____ (open) a supermarket on campus I'm sure the students _____ (use) it.
6 The students _____ (not work) unless they _____ (be) well-paid.
7 Many people think we _____ (have to) spend more money if we _____ (want) to fight crime properly.
8 If the council _____ (not advertise) more then people _____ (not know) about their services.

3 Make first conditional sentences. Add commas where necessary.

1 they / open / the sports centre again / if they / can / repair the damage
2 if there / be / more job opportunities / more people / move / to the area
3 they / stay / in Helby / if they / find / a good school for their daughter
4 the local economy / not improve / if people / not support / local businesses
5 if they / get / the local council's permission / they / build / a new theatre here

4a Find and correct the mistakes in five of the questions.

1 Where do you go if you have free time this weekend?
2 If you will get home early tomorrow, what will you do?
3 What will happen if you get up late tomorrow?
4 If you go shopping next week, what do you buy?
5 What will you eat if you will feel hungry after class?
6 If you won't improve your English, what will happen?

b Work in pairs. Take turns to ask and answer the questions in Exercise 4a.

5 Rewrite the sentences using the words in brackets.

1 We won't keep the community centre open unless we have enough money. (if)
   We won't keep the community centre open if we don't have enough money.
2 Museums will close if they don't get more visitors. (unless)
3 The services will get worse if we don't support them. (unless)
4 If my neighbour doesn't stop making a noise, I'll complain. (unless)
5 Unless you live in this area, you won't have any problems with crime. (if)
6 I'm happy to do something for the community unless it takes up too much time. (if)

6 Complete the sentences so that they are true for you. Then share your answers with a partner.

1 If I have enough money, …
2 Unless I have time, …
3 If I have to move to another country, …
4 My English will improve if …
5 If I get bored this evening, …
6 Unless I save some more money, …

Vocabulary

Public buildings

1a Match words 1–8 with the words in the box to make compound nouns.

centre   hall   home   station

1 tourist information
2 retirement
3 town
4 fire
5 community
6 health
7 concert
8 leisure

b Match six buildings from Exercise 1a with their descriptions.
1 a building where doctors and other medical professionals see their patients
2 a building where old people live and where somebody looks after them
3 a place where people meet for social events and classes
4 a building containing government offices
5 a place where people do sports activities and exercise classes
6 a building where people go to hear music

c Write the compound nouns from Exercise 1a in the correct place in the table.

Accommodation	Attractions and entertainment	Public services

d Write the words in the box in the correct place in the table in Exercise 1c.

bed and breakfast   cinema   guesthouse   hospital
hostel   library   museum   prison   theatre

e Complete the sentences with buildings from the table in Exercise 1c.
1 I've got tickets to see my favourite band at our local _____ next month.
2 I don't often borrow books from the _____ but I sometimes study there.
3 I do voluntary work at a local _____ . I enjoy talking to the old people there.
4 When I go travelling, I usually stay in a youth _____ because it's so much cheaper than a hotel.
5 The local council have a meeting at the _____ every two weeks.
6 I prefer staying in a _____ or a _____ because you usually get better service than in a hotel.
7 My _____ is always really busy and it's sometimes difficult to see a doctor.
8 I'm going to start an art class at the _____ .

f Work in groups. Which of the buildings from the table in Exercise 1c are there in your town? How often do you use them? Which ones do you think are essential for every community?

Public services

2 Choose the correct definition of *public service*.
A a service which members of the public manage
B a service which a local company offers to the residents, which they pay for
C a service that the government or local council provides for its citizens

3a Complete the sentences with the words in the box.

education   environmental protection   health care
police and fire services   public housing   public spaces
public transport

1 Personally, I think spending money on children's _____ is more important than any other public service.
2 The _____ should be very well-paid because they do a very dangerous job.
3 Local councils should provide cheap _____ to stop people from using private cars.
4 I think all cities should have _____ where people can meet on important occasions.
5 It's a good idea to build _____ for people who cannot afford to buy or rent their own home.
6 It's impossible for governments to provide free _____ for its citizens because hospitals and medicines are very expensive.
7 Councils spend too much money on preventing pollution and other _____ services.

b Work in pairs. Do you agree or disagree with the sentences in Exercise 3a?

7b Module 7 — City life

Reading (Flow chart completion; Multiple choice)

Before you read

1 Work in pairs. What buildings can you think of that have a different use now from the one they had in the past?

2 Work in pairs. Read the extracts from articles below and answer the questions.
   1 Which event happened first in each extract? How do you know?
   2 What do the underlined words refer to?
   A A community group can have a very powerful influence on local government decisions. In our area one got together to organise a public protest. This stopped a plan to cut down some beautiful cherry trees along one of the city roads.
   B A key point for the decision to build a new library was the money that suddenly became available for it. Before this, it seemed very unlikely that the council would approve the plan.

Test practice

▶ TEST STRATEGIES page 179

3 Read the passage and the test tasks. Decide which section of the passage each task refers to.

Questions 1–7
Complete the flow chart below. Choose **NO MORE THAN TWO WORDS** from the passage for each answer.

The High Line in New York City

1840s:	• Trains started bringing 1 _____ into New York City • 'West side cowboys' were employed to reduce the number of 2 _____

1929:	West Side Improvement programme meant there were no more 3 _____

1934:	Trains moving on the High Line meant there were fewer 4 _____

1950s:	Less need for the railway because of less 5 _____ in New York

1980s:	Final thing transported before closure of High Line: 6 _____

2000s:	The work of a 7 _____ helped to get more support for saving the High Line space for the community

Questions 8–10
Choose **THREE** letters **A–G**.

Which **THREE** of these does the passage mention as features the community can enjoy in the High Line park?

A movie screenings
B special dog walking areas
C places for open air eating
D children's art clubs
E gardening activities
F spaces for informal work meetings
G organised fitness activities

4 Complete the test tasks.

▶ HELP

3 Look at the third paragraph. Find a paraphrase of the idea of having no more of something.
5 Look at the fourth paragraph. Find a verb that expresses the idea of something becoming less.

Task analysis

5 Work in pairs and discuss the questions.
   1 How easy was it to follow the sequence of events? What helped you?
   2 For questions 1–7, did you use the words before and after each gap to think about the kind of information you were looking for?
   3 Did you check the number of words in your answers?

Discussion

6 Work in pairs. Tell each other about a public green space in your town. Talk about:
   • who uses the space.
   • when they use it.
   • what they do there.
   • whether the space is looked after well.
   • what could be better there.

The New York City High Line

How an old railway line became an urban garden

The High Line is now one of New York's most attractive and popular city parks. However, its history is very unusual. It was once a railway line running above the city's busy streets.

Trains started making their way through the West Side of Manhattan in the 1840s, more than ten years before the start of the American Civil War. These trains were used mainly for goods rather than passengers, bringing food and other items to New York shops. They also carried raw materials to city factories and then took the products they made to markets outside New York. These early trains travelled through the city streets, crossing the path of pedestrians and horse-drawn vehicles. So many accidents happened that men were given jobs as 'west side cowboys'. Their role was to ride on horseback in front of the trains, waving a red flag in order to warn people that a train was coming.

In 1929 the railway company agreed to carry out a development programme, known as the West Side Improvement project. They built a railway above the level of the streets. This made the city much safer by getting rid of 105 level crossings. Trains began using the High Line in 1934. Factories and shops along the route had to make several changes so that items could come and go on an upper floor, without causing traffic problems at street level.

As manufacturing in the city declined during the 1950s, so did train traffic. The southern section of the High Line was demolished in the 1960s, and in 1980 three carriages of frozen turkeys were the last goods ever carried by the remaining section of the High Line railway. The track had now fallen completely out of use.

But then the problem was what to do with the two and a half kilometres of unused railway track. Many people thought the railway company that owned it should pull it down, but others saw some more interesting possibilities. They wanted to use the space in a way that would benefit the whole community. Discussions considered making it available for parking or for billboards, but the final decision was to transform the High Line into the city's most unusual park.

Interestingly, between 2000 and 2001 a photographer created public interest in the project when he took pictures of the disused railway line. These showed how beautiful wild flowers had started growing along the tracks and made people realise the line's potential. A Friends of the High Line group was formed to support the redevelopment of the space. There was some political and other opposition, but eventually plans were accepted, money was raised and work could begin.

Building of the first section of the park started in 2006. The first section was opened in 2009 and the second, from West 20th Street to West 30th Street, in 2011. The third section runs to the north, round the West Side Yards, which is still an active rail yard, and this was opened to the public in 2014. There are now eleven entrances to the park, five of which are accessible to people in wheelchairs.

So what is it like to walk along the High Line these days? The space has been developed in a very imaginative way, with lots of different things to see and do at different points. Many interesting plants grow along the walkway. Many New Yorkers give their time to plant and look after these, saying that it gives them the perfect opportunity after a busy day at work to enjoy spectacular views of New York and the Hudson River. There are playgrounds for children, as well as places to sit and relax or share a picnic. There are works of art to enjoy and it is often possible to watch performers. Dance parties and exercise classes are also held there. It is not surprising that the area has already been used in a number of films and TV programmes.

The High Line in New York is an extraordinary example of how a city was able to transform something ugly and unused into something of true beauty, enjoyed by the whole community.

7b Module 7
City life

Writing (Task 1)

Lead-in 1 Work in pairs. Talk about a health centre in your town. What do you think of the services and facilities? Think about these things.
- services for patients
- cost of services
- facilities for patients (think about different age groups: children, older people, etc.)
- facilities for visitors

Understand the task 2a Read the writing task and underline the key words.

> EXPERT WRITING page 206

The table below gives some information about how satisfied the population of Helby is with aspects of the facilities in its local health centre. Summarise the information by selecting and reporting the main features, and make comparisons where relevant.

Adult population satisfied with aspects of the facilities in the local health centre – Helby, UK

	Parking	Maps and signs	Automatic doors	Lifts	Waiting areas	Vending machines
Male	47%	66%	60%	58%	75%	89%
Female	45%	33%	66%	85%	74%	61%

b Work in pairs. Look at the table in the test task and decide which information is the most interesting or important. Which would you include in your summary?

Language and content 3a Read the model answer. Has the student included the information you chose in Exercise 2b?

The table presents information on how happy men and women are with various features of the health centre in Helby. It gives percentage figures for a number of areas.

It is clear from the table that men and women have similar levels of satisfaction with some features, such as the parking and waiting areas, but there is also considerable difference between how happy the two genders are with other aspects of the facilities, like lifts and maps and signs.

The feature of the health centre that men express most satisfaction with is the vending machines, with almost nine in ten men liking these, compared to only six in ten women. For women, the most satisfactory feature is the lifts, as over 85 percent said they were happy with these. The least popular feature is also different for the two genders. For men it is parking, whereas for women it is the maps and signs.

However, there are some areas where the figures for both genders are similar. Three quarters of both men and women said the waiting areas were good and just under half the population of each gender is satisfied with the parking facilities.

b Work in pairs and discuss the questions.
1 How many parts are there in the model answer?
2 Does the introduction repeat the words in the task?
3 What does the student do in the overview?
4 Does the student mention all the information from the table in their answer?

Module 7
7b City life

4a Look at some verbs/phrases for introducing and describing information. Which ones does the student use in the model answer?

Verbs to introduce information	Phrases to describe the type of information
describes gives illustrates presents represents shows	amount of level(s) of difference(s) between figure(s) for information on number of percentage of

Part	Notes
Introduction	
Overview	
Main features (2 paragraphs)	

b Complete the sentences with words from the second column of the table in Exercise 4a.
1. The table illustrates the _____ satisfaction that men and women express about different features of the health centre.
2. The table shows some significant _____ between the attitudes of men and women.
3. The _____ for both men and women are considerably different for some features.
4. The table gives _____ on the level of satisfaction of men and women with different aspects of the health centre.
5. The figures represent the _____ of men and women who are satisfied with each feature.

b Look at your plan in Exercise 5a. Think about some useful language you can use in each part. Think about:
A language to describe numbers.
B language to introduce and describe information.

Add your ideas in the spidergrams.

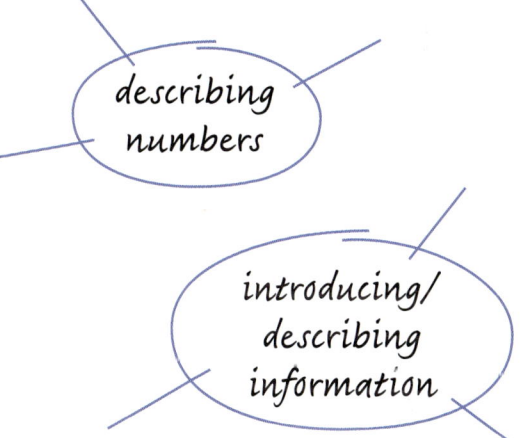

Plan your summary

5a Read the writing task and follow these steps.
1. Underline the key words.
2. Look at the table and think about what you need to include in your answer.
3. Select and organise the information you need. Make notes in the plan below.

The table below gives some information about how satisfied the population of Helby is with various aspects of their community. Summarise the information by selecting and reporting the main features, and make comparisons where relevant.

Adult population satisfied with aspects of the community – Helby, UK

	Male	Female
Work	55%	60%
Education	66%	67%
Sport	60%	80%
Transport	42%	38%
Entertainment	30%	35%
Shopping	55%	90%

Write your summary

▶ **TEST STRATEGIES** page 181

6 Write your summary. Use your plan from Exercise 5a and your ideas from Exercise 5b.

Assess and improve

7 Check your work. Did you do these things in your summary?
1. I organised my answer into three parts.
2. I wrote an introductory sentence paraphrasing the task.
3. I wrote an overview.
4. I selected and reported the key features.
5. I made comparisons where relevant.
6. I used a range of language to:
   - describe numbers.
   - introduce and describe information.

Student's Resource Book > Writing page 74

7b Module 7 — City life

Speaking (Part 3)

Give yourself time to think

1 a What public places do most towns and cities in your country have? What is the function of these public places?

  b 🔊 7.5 Listen to two candidates answering the questions in Exercise 1a. Which answer sounds better? Why?

2 a 🔊 7.6 Listen to the second candidate doing Part 3 of the test. Which of these things does she do in order to give herself time to think?

  A She comments on the question.
  B She pauses.
  C She repeats the question in a different way.
  D She says 'umm' and 'err' a lot.
  E She uses expressions to show she is thinking.

  b Look audio script 7.6 on page 218 and find examples of A, C and E in Exercise 2a.

  c Work in pairs. Take turns to ask and answer these questions. If you need time to think, use the ideas in Exercise 2a.

  1 What kind of buildings do you most enjoy visiting? Why?
  2 Do you prefer older or newer buildings? Why?
  3 Which public buildings are important to the community where you live?

Test practice

▶ TEST STRATEGIES page 182

3 a Read the test task. Think about what you can say for each question.

  1 What public places does your town or city have?
  2 How important are public places like these?
  3 Is there any difference between the appearance of public buildings today and those in the past?
  4 Are public buildings for everyone or just some people?

  b Work in groups of three. Follow the instructions and complete the test task. Then swap roles.

  - Student A: Ask the questions.
  - Student B: Answer the questions. Avoid too many pauses. If you need time to think, use the ideas in Exercise 2a.
  - Student C: Listen and make notes in the table.

Did your partner:	Notes/Examples
give an extended answer?	
discuss any opposing ideas? If so, did he/she use appropriate language to introduce them?	
use different ways to give him-/herself time to think?	
pause a lot?	

Assess and improve

4 Work in the same groups. How well did your partner do? Use your notes from Exercise 3b to give him/her feedback.

8 Activity

8a Training
- **Reading:** Understand the difference between detail and general information (Multiple choice)
- **Language development:** Present perfect
- **Vocabulary:** Sport
- **Listening:** Follow a talk (Section 4: Summary completion)
- **Speaking:** Balance information; Link ideas (Part 2: Long turn)
- **Writing:** Generate ideas and vocabulary; Introduce reasons and solutions (Task 2: Problem-solution essay)

8b Testing
- **Listening:** Section 4: Multiple choice; Summary completion
- **Language development:** Articles
- **Vocabulary:** Sports and business
- **Reading:** Notes completion; Multiple choice
- **Writing:** Task 2: Problem-solution essay
- **Speaking:** Part 2: Long turn

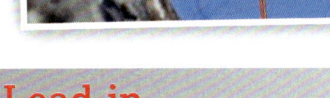

Lead-in

Discuss the questions.
1 Which sports are popular in your country?
2 Why do you think some sports are more popular than others?

8a Sport

Reading (Multiple choice)

Before you read

1 Work in pairs and discuss the questions.
   1 What stops a sportsperson from performing well?
   2 How important do you think it is for sportspeople to be prepared mentally as well as physically before a competition?

Understand the difference between detail and general information

2 Read the passage. According to the writer, how important is psychology for success in sport?

3 Read the passage again. Match paragraphs B–F with their topics 1–5.
   1 the importance of being positive
   2 the benefits of choosing what to concentrate on
   3 the importance of psychology in sports
   4 the effect of the way someone holds their body
   5 how the brain controls behaviour on and off the sports field

4 Work in pairs. Read the questions below about the passage. What is the focus of each question? Mark each question A or B.
   A This question asks about a detail.
   B This question asks about a general point.

   1 What is the writer's view on sport?
   2 According to the passage, how can football players deal with anger?
   3 According to the writer, what is one advantage of talking to yourself?
   4 What is the main point of the final paragraph?
   5 What was the writer's purpose in writing this passage?

5 Work in pairs. Look at question 1 in the test task on the right and underline the key words. Then follow steps 1–4 to answer it.
   1 Find the part of the passage the question refers to.
   2 Read this part of the passage and think about how you would answer the question without looking at options A–D.
   3 Consider whether you need to look for detail or for the general point of the paragraph.
   4 Decide which option is correct. Check by rereading the part of the passage that gives the answer.
   5 Find the parts of the passage that the other three options refer to. Why are they wrong?

Test training

6 Answer questions 2–7 in the test task. Follow the same steps you did for question 1.

1 What is the main point the writer wants to make about footballers in the first paragraph?
   A They respond best when people are watching them.
   B They are able to cope with a difficult situation.
   C They do something that is actually very simple.
   D People don't think they are very clever.

2 In the second paragraph, the writer mentions sports psychology as something which
   A is used by all football clubs.
   B needs to be taught to players.
   C can help build team spirit.
   D is more technical than people realise.

3 Busch mentions an area of the brain in order to
   A contrast it with other brain functions.
   B describe how things can go wrong.
   C give details about what he has studied.
   D show its significance for business and sport.

4 According to the writer, 'self-talk' can help players to
   A forget what people say.
   B respond to unhelpful comments.
   C perform to the same level as other players.
   D stop stress from affecting their behaviour.

5 The writer uses the example of a player thinking of 'ice' to show that
   A footballers have to be careful what they do on the pitch.
   B anyone can use this easy technique to help themselves.
   C it is best to think of something the brain can respond to quickly.
   D words are more powerful than actions.

6 Busch talks about a football striker to illustrate the point that
   A players need to take opportunities at the right time.
   B sport psychology is not as simple as it appears.
   C players should not concentrate on too many things.
   D self-control is important in sport.

7 What point is the writer trying to make in the passage?
   A how skills highlighted by sports psychology are relevant for everyone
   B how sportspeople pay too little attention to psychological knowledge
   C how many useful aspects of sports psychology there are
   D how difficult it is to overcome psychological limits in sport

Mind games

How footballers use sports psychology

A Footballers are not always famous for their intelligence off the pitch, but their mental skills in the middle of a competition are usually extraordinary. Most people find it hard to imagine successfully doing even something simple while 40,000 spectators watch. Yet every weekend, Premier League players perform brilliantly in packed stadiums under extreme pressure.

B For some players, the qualities of confidence and being calm are completely natural. But for the majority, mental skills involve ways of thinking and behaving which they have to learn and practise in the same way they learn physical or technical skills. That's why most Premier League clubs now work with sports psychologists, who teach the teams a range of mental techniques, including positive self-talk and anger management, as well as how to re-focus quickly as the game changes. The television cameras and fans cannot see these skills, but they do see the effect they have.

C Premier League footballers learn a number of special tricks, and those methods can help people in other professions too. Bradley Busch is a sports psychologist who has also worked with, for example, businessmen, teachers and students. 'Being confident, dealing with anger and being focused are just as important on football pitches as they are in the office or the classroom,' he says. 'And we now know that the key to a successful performance is the front area of the brain.' He explains that this area is very important for using information to think about what might happen next and for making decisions. If this part of the brain gets too much information or stress, then this affects the ability to decide quickly what to do next.

D Psychologists have shown that talking to oneself in a positive way can have a very powerful effect. Research proves that a person's internal conversations affect the chemistry in the brain. Negative comments cause stress which, in turn, reduces the ability of the brain to work at its best. In training, players practise taking a negative thought and changing it into a positive one. A difficult problem becomes an exciting challenge, for example. According to a study published by the *Journal of Sport* Behaviour in 2010, this self-talk really does make a difference. The study showed that introducing psychological techniques, such as the use of positive and motivating self-talk at half-time, improved the performance of some players in the second half. Many footballers also try to remember key words to control their behaviour. For example, a player who gets angry quickly might say 'Ice!' to remind them to stay in control. The brain finds it much easier to deal with one strong image than many complex processes. It only takes a second to get out of control, so speed is important.

E Sportspeople can even make good use of body language to help themselves get into a positive frame of mind and increase their confidence. 'We tell players to keep their eyes up, for example, because if they have their head and shoulders down, their brain chemistry changes for the worse. Holding their head up keeps their brain active,' says Busch. There is research evidence for this here, too. Studies by Harvard Business School showed that standing up straight can reduce levels of stress and increase confidence by a significant amount. This knowledge is something that many people who have to give major presentations at work can benefit from too.

F Psychological research suggests that when things go wrong, players should focus on three things only. They have to be things that they can control. A striker can't control goals but he can control his movement, his energy and the quality of his strikes. It is a matter of using the brain in the right way. Focusing on simple objectives can also help a player to identify and take more opportunities. 'There is so much information out there that the brain ignores what it does not need and focuses instead on what it understands to be important,' explains Busch.

G The knowledge that sports psychologists use so effectively with players is also useful for people who want to achieve more in their studies or their working lives. They, too, can benefit from what Busch recommends for his sports clients.

Task analysis

7 Work in pairs and discuss the questions.

   1 How easy was it to identify which part of the passage each question referred to?
   2 Did thinking about the main point in each paragraph help you to find the answers?
   3 Could you identify why the incorrect options were wrong for each question?

Discussion

8 Work in pairs and discuss the questions.

   1 What are the main pieces of advice the sports psychologist gives?
   2 How useful do you think each of these pieces of advice is for people when they are studying or working rather than playing sport?

8a Module 8 Activity

Language development

Present perfect

▶ EXPERT GRAMMAR page 189

1 Match the sentences (1–3) with what they express (A–C).
   1 He has been a professional football player for five years.
   2 Research has shown that sport can have a positive influence on behaviour.
   3 She has played in many international matches.

   A an experience or achievement
   B a state or situation that began in the past and continues in the present
   C an action that happened at an indefinite time in the past

2 Complete the table.

Infinitive	Past participle
be	
have	
go	
try	
win	
buy	
choose	
train	

3 Complete the sentences with the present perfect form of the verbs in brackets.
   1 I _____ (be) a member of the cricket club for quite a long time now.
   2 _____ (you / ever / see) a live rugby match?
   3 He _____ (choose) the team but not the captain.
   4 They lost the game because they _____ (not have) time to practise recently.
   5 _____ (you / buy) the tickets for the match on Saturday?
   6 She _____ (not be) to the gym at all this year.
   7 They _____ (win) most of their games this season.
   8 We _____ (never / swim) in a lake before.

4 Complete the sentences with *for* or *since*.
   1 Our national team has lost every match _____ March.
   2 We've only played two matches _____ the beginning of term.
   3 The football manager has been at the club _____ over five years.
   4 I have practised twice a week _____ the last three years.
   5 I think ice hockey has become more popular _____ we won the world championships.
   6 We haven't had a good Olympic team _____ a long time now.

5a Choose the correct options in *italics* to complete the sentences.
   1 I haven't been swimming *recently / ever*.
   2 I've *never / ever* played badminton before.
   3 I've *never / yet* been captain of a sports team.
   4 I haven't done any exercise today *yet / just*.
   5 I have *already / lately* been to the gym this week.
   6 I have *just / always* started a new sport.
   7 I don't think I've *ever / yet* been to a professional football match.
   8 I think I've been more active *before / lately*.

b Work in pairs. Are any of the sentences in Exercise 5a true for you?

6 Complete gaps 1–6 in the fact file with the present perfect form of the verbs in brackets. Then choose the correct options in *italics* in A–C.

Is Ultimate Frisbee the newest Olympic sport?

- The Olympic Committee **1** _____ (recently / recognise) Ultimate Frisbee, as well as a range of other flying disc sports.
- The game **2** _____ (not become) an official Olympic sport **A** *already / yet* but it may be at some point in the future.
- The Olympic Committee wants to attract younger audiences and that's why they **3** _____ (decide) to consider Ultimate Frisbee for future Olympic Games.
- It is unusual because the game relies on the players to keep to the rules without a referee.
- People in the USA **4** _____ (play) this game **B** *for / since* the 1960s. It **5** _____ (always / be) very popular there.
- **C** *Since / Already* the Olympic Committee accepted the sport in 2015, its popularity **6** _____ (grow) in many other countries.

7 Write six sentences about yourself and your activities using the present perfect and the time expressions in the box. Then discuss them with a partner.

   for over a year   for two weeks   recently
   since the beginning of the year   since Tuesday   yet

Module 8
Activity
8a

Vocabulary

Doing sports

1a Write the sports in the box in the correct category.

~~athletics~~ ~~baseball~~ basketball boxing football golf ice hockey ice skating rugby surfing table tennis taekwondo tennis

1 Team sports: *athletics,*
2 Played individually or in pairs: *baseball,*

b Can you add any more sports to the categories in Exercise 1a?

c Have you ever played any of the sports in Exercises 1a and 1b? Discuss in pairs.

2a Complete the sentences with *do, go* or *play*.

1 I _____ swimming once a week at my local leisure centre.
2 The number of people who _____ taekwondo and other martial arts has increased recently.
3 I'd like to learn how to _____ golf, so I'm going to join a club.
4 At my college we usually _____ rugby in winter and _____ athletics in summer.
5 People _____ football all around the world.
6 There is a beautiful lake near my home where people _____ sailing and fishing.

b Match the sports (1–7) with the venues where they are usually played (A–G).

1 golf   A pitch
2 football   B court
3 tennis   C rink
4 swimming   D course
5 running   E pool
6 boxing   F track
7 ice skating   G ring

Sporting equipment

3 Complete the sentences with the words in the box.

ball bat boots clubs helmet life jacket racquet skates surfboard

1 I'm going to take my _____ on holiday so I can play tennis.
2 I don't usually wear special _____ when I play football.
3 I like playing golf but the _____ can be expensive.
4 You don't have to buy _____ ; you can usually hire them from the rink.
5 When you are on a boat, you should always wear a _____ .
6 It can be very hard to stand up on a _____ .
7 When I go cycling, I always wear a _____ to protect my head.
8 You need a _____ and a _____ to play baseball.

People in sport

4 Choose the correct options in *italics* to complete the text.

Icelandic football heroes

When the Iceland football team took part in the European Football Championships in 2016, they didn't expect to become **1** *champions / spectators*. As the team from the smallest country to qualify for the tournament, nobody thought they would get very far. The team played their first two matches against Portugal and Hungary. In their third match against Austria, Iceland scored a goal in the final seconds before the **2** *coach / referee* blew his whistle for full time. They went forward to the next stage, where they beat England to reach the quarter-finals. This achievement was amazing when you consider that Iceland has a population of only about 330,000. This means it has far fewer people than other countries from which to choose its **3** *players / supporters*. Although most of the Icelandic team members, including the **4** *referee / captain*, play for professional football teams, some play football only part-time as they also have other jobs. This includes one of the team **5** *champions / coaches*, who as well as managing the team, also works as dentist. The team had excellent support from their **6** *players / fans*, with thousands travelling to France to watch them play. The **7** *supporters / coaches* delighted and entertained other **8** *spectators / captains* with their noisy and enthusiastic encouragement of their team.

Phrasal verbs

5a Complete the phrasal verbs in the questions with *out* or *up*.

1 Why do some people start a new sport or activity and then give it _____ after a few weeks?
2 What's the best way to warm _____ before you start exercising?
3 What sport or activity would you most like to take _____ in the future?
4 Do you like working _____ in the gym or do you prefer outdoor sports?
5 If you get injured, do you think you should drop _____ of the match?
6 Have you or anyone you know ever tried _____ for a professional team?

b In pairs, take turns to ask and answer the questions in Exercise 5a.

8a Module 8 Activity

Listening (Section 4: Summary completion)

Before you listen

1 Work in pairs. What qualities do you think you need to be successful at sport? Why? Use the ideas below to help you.
   - talent
   - support
   - a good coach
   - money
   - time
   - something else?

Follow a talk

2a 🔊 8.1 Listen to an extract from a talk by a sportswoman and answer the questions.
   1 What is the main purpose of the talk?
   2 What three main points does the speaker make?

b 🔊 8.1 Listen again. How does the speaker introduce each new point? How does she introduce her conclusion?

3 Read the summary of a lecture below and answer the questions.
   1 What do you think the lecture is going to be about?
   2 Underline six words/phrases in the summary which introduce a new point.
   3 What kind of information might be missing in each gap?

What can help make a successful sportsperson?

People think that you need a natural talent to be good at sport and even 1 _____ believe this. In fact, many students have given up sport by their 2 _____ . One important factor in sporting success is the time spent training. However, a study of 3 _____ found other key factors contributed to their success. The first of these is that they are 4 _____ to succeed and they set themselves clear goals. This enables them to succeed even when they have 5 _____ . Secondly, the way in which they deal with 6 _____ is also a good indicator of future success. In addition, successful sportspeople are mentally strong and have a lot of 7 _____ so that they can cope with losing and with difficult competition. Finally, they have a detailed knowledge of their sport, which includes studying the performance of other 8 _____ and competitors. In summary, although talent and hard work are important, it is not possible to succeed with these alone.

Test training

4a 🔊 8.2 Listen and complete the summary in Exercise 3. Use no more than two words for each answer.

b Look back at your answers. Check that they fit in the summary both in terms of content and grammar. Is your spelling correct?

Task analysis

5 Discuss the questions about the task in Exercise 3a.
   1 Did you find it easy to identify the main points of the talk?
   2 Look at audio script 8.2 on page 218 and find the words/phrases which introduce each new point. Did these words/phrases help you follow the talk?

Discussion

6 Work in pairs and discuss the questions.
   1 In which sports does your country have most success?
   2 Which are your country's most successful sportspeople?

Module 8 Activity 8a

Speaking (Part 2)

Balance information

1a Read the test task. What is the main topic? How many aspects of the topic do you need to talk about?

Describe a sport that is popular in your country.
You should say:
  what the sport is
  whether or not you play this sport
  where people play this sport
and explain why you think the sport is popular.

b Read the sentences from a candidate's response to the second point in the task. Number them in the correct order (1–4).

  A The reason I don't play now is because you have to be tall to be good, and I'm too short.
  B In fact, I did learn how to play at school, but I haven't played since then.
  C I have lots of friends who play and I know they really enjoy it although I don't actually play myself any more.
  D I gave it up because I didn't grow tall enough and I didn't think any team would want me!

c Match the sentences in Exercise 1b (A–D) with their functions (1–3).
  1 introducing the sub-topic
  2 giving more detail about the sub-topic
  3 closing the sub-topic

2 🔊 8.3 Listen to a candidate doing the task in Exercise 1a. Does he spend more time talking about some points? If so, which ones?

Link ideas

3a Look at audio script 8.3 on page 219. Find and underline the words/phrases in the box. Which of these words/phrases does the candidate use to:

although   as well   because   for instance   I think   so

  A give his opinion?
  B introduce a reason for something?
  C introduce the result of something?
  D link two different or opposing ideas together?
  E give an example?
  F add more information about something?

b Match the words/phrases in the box with the functions (A–F) in Exercise 3a.

also   as   as a result   due to   even though   however
I believe   in my view   like   such as   too

c Choose the correct options in *italics* to make the sentences true for you. Then complete the sentences with your own ideas.
  1 Basketball *is / isn't* very popular in my country because …
  2 *I'm / I'm not* very good at sports, so …
  3 I *like / don't really like* playing sports although …
  4 I watch *a lot of / a little* sport on TV. I also watch …
  5 Where I live there are *many / a few* sporting facilities. For instance, …

Pronunciation

4a 🔊 8.4 Listen to this sentence from the candidate's answer again. Notice how he uses very short pauses between groups of words (called thought groups). Work in pairs and practise saying the sentence, pausing where there is a /.

I have lots of friends who play / and I know they really enjoy it / although I don't actually play myself any more.

b 🔊 8.5 Mark a / where you think the speaker pauses in these sentences. Listen and check. Then work in pairs and practise saying the sentences.
  1 Most people follow a team and when there is an important match on, everyone watches it on TV.
  2 I think it's also a good sport to watch live and although I don't go to see games myself, I have friends who go and they say it's really exciting and there's a great atmosphere.

Test training

5 Work in pairs. Take turns to complete the test task in Exercise 1a. Make notes of your ideas before you start. Try to speak for 1–2 minutes.

Task analysis

6 Work in pairs and discuss the questions.
  1 Did you/your partner give more information on some points than on others? If so, which ones?
  2 Did you/your partner use linking words/phrases to connect your ideas?

MyEnglishLab > 8a Speaking

8a Module 8 Activity

Writing (Task 2)

Generate ideas and vocabulary

1 Read the writing task. How many paragraphs would you include in your essay? What would you include in each paragraph?

Write about the following topic.

> Children nowadays are playing less and less sport and this is having a bad effect on their health and their behaviour.
>
> Why do you think this is happening? What can we do to solve the problem?

Give reasons for your answer and include any relevant examples from your knowledge or experience. Write at least 250 words.

2a Work in pairs. Note down your ideas under each of these headings.
   1 Reasons why children play less sport
   2 Possible solutions

Introduce reasons and solutions

b Look at your notes from Exercise 2a. Think of phrases you can use to introduce:
   1 the reasons you thought of.
   2 the solutions you thought of.

3 Read the model answer on the right and answer the questions.
   1 Does it follow the structure you planned in Exercise 1?
   2 Does it mention any of the ideas you thought of in Exercise 2a?
   3 Does the student use any of the phrases you thought of in Exercise 2b?
   4 What other phrases does the student use to introduce reasons and solutions?

4 Match the sentence beginnings (1–6) with the endings (A–F). Then look at the words/phrases in bold for introducing reasons and solutions. Did you think of any of these words/phrases in Exercise 2b?
   1 The cost of joining a sports club **is one reason**
   2 Hoping to get fitter **is one of the main reasons**
   3 The opportunity to make friends **is another**
   4 A lot of children take up a sport
   5 We could solve the problem
   6 A further solution

   A **because** their friends like it.
   B **by** making sports club membership free for students.
   C **for** joining a walking club.
   D **reason for** becoming a member of a sports club.
   E **to the problem could be** to introduce compulsory sports lessons at school.
   F **why** some people don't do much sport.

5 Plan your answer to the task in Exercise 1. Think about these questions and use your ideas from Exercises 1 and 2.
   1 How will you introduce the topic in your own words?
   2 What reasons will you include?
   3 What examples will you give to support your reasons?
   4 What solutions will you include?
   5 How will you conclude your essay?

6 Write your essay.

Studies have shown that children today do not play as much sport as they did in the past. This is worrying because it means children are not as fit as they could be. Therefore, it is important, for several reasons, to try to get children back to the sports field.

Firstly, we need to understand why young people are less active nowadays. Probably the main reason is that there are too many other exciting things to do — there are so many attractive games to play on phones, tablets and laptops. Another reason is that there are so many amusing video clips and movies to watch — it is not surprising that children spend so much time looking at screens. Schoolwork is a further reason for this change in behaviour. Students today get much more homework than their parents did. This means that they have less time available for sport.

So what can we do about the situation? Firstly, I think schools could help by introducing students to a variety of sports. Not everyone enjoys football or tennis. But they may find that, for example, judo, canoeing or the trampoline becomes more exciting than a computer game. A further solution to the problem is for parents to do sports together with their children. If sport is a regular, fun, family activity, children learn to love sport from a young age.

If schools and parents do all they can to encourage children to play sport, then the situation will start to improve and young people will become fitter and better behaved as a result.

8b Work and play

Listening (Section 4: Multiple choice; Summary completion)

Before you listen

1 Work in pairs and discuss the questions.
   1 Which sports do you think make the most money?
   2 In what different ways can sportspeople, teams or organisations make money?

Test practice

▸ TEST STRATEGIES page 178

2 You will hear part of a lecture to a group of business students. You must complete both of the tasks below while listening. Before you listen, answer these questions.
   1 Read the tasks. What do you think the talk is about?
   2 Underline the key words in questions 1 and 2.
   3 Underline any words or phrases in the summary which introduce a new point.
   4 What kind of information might be missing in each gap in the summary?

Questions 1 and 2
Choose the correct letter, A, B or C.

1 How did football clubs make most of their money 30 years ago?
   A from selling food and drink at matches
   B from advertising and sponsorship
   C from selling match tickets
2 The main reason for the creation of the English Premier League was
   A so that matches could be shown live on TV.
   B to raise ticket prices for football matches.
   C to encourage more ticket sales for matches.

Questions 3–10
Complete the summary below. Write NO MORE THAN THREE WORDS for each answer.

How top teams make their money

Important new sources of income have appeared for football clubs during the last 30 years. The first of these was a major contract between Premier League clubs and 3 _____ , which is currently worth £81 million for each club per season. This deal also attracts major 4 _____ , who put their name on players' shirts and use 5 _____ in the football grounds. In some cases, sponsorship involves a change of 6 _____ for the stadium. An additional source of income is from the sale of 7 _____ and other products, which has increased recently due to a rise in the number of fans and the global 8 _____ . The final source of income, which gets the most 9 _____ , is from transfer deals, when a football club sells one of their players to another club. In some cases, this can result in a large 10 _____ for the original club.

3 🔊 8.6 Complete the test tasks.

▸ HELP

4 Listen for the adjective from the verb *attract*.
6 Listen for another word for *stadium*.
8 Listen for a phrase that has the same meaning as *global* in the summary.

Task analysis

4 Work in pairs and discuss the questions.
   1 Did underlining the key words in questions 1 and 2 help you? How?
   2 Did the words you underlined in the summary help you? How?
   3 Did you read the completed summary? Did you check:
      • that your answers fitted grammatically and in terms of content?
      • the number of words in each gap?
      • your spelling?

Discussion

5 Work in groups. Do you agree with the amount of money paid to sports stars? Are some paid too much? Are some paid too little?

Module 8
Activity

Language development

Articles

➤ EXPERT GRAMMAR page 189

1 Look at the words in bold and match the sentences (1–4) with the explanations (A–D).
   1 **Dr Marks** lectures us on sports psychology.
   2 He broke **the 100-metre world record**.
   3 **Athletes** usually eat very healthily.
   4 **A shuttlecock** is something you use to play badminton.

   A Don't use an article with plural or uncountable nouns when talking about something in general.
   B Use *the* to talk about something unique.
   C Use *a/an* with countable nouns, to talk about something in general.
   D Don't use an article with most names/proper nouns.

Definite or indefinite article?

2a Complete the sentences with *a/an* or *the*.
   1 _____ Olympic Games are _____ most important sporting event in _____ world.
   2 I generally prefer watching _____ football match on TV than seeing it live.
   3 _____ equipment you need for sports like skiing makes it too expensive for many people.
   4 Being _____ football manager is a very difficult job.
   5 Sportswomen should receive _____ same prize money as sportsmen.
   6 To be successful at any sport, you need to have _____ professional coach.
   7 Running is _____ easy sport – anyone can take it up.
   8 Sport should be _____ compulsory subject at all schools until the age of 16.

   b Work in pairs. Do you agree or disagree with the sentences in Exercise 2a? Give reasons for your answers.

Definite or zero article?

3a Choose the correct options in *italics* to complete the questions.
   1 Do you like - / *the* winter sports like - / *the* ice-skating and - / *the* snowboarding?
   2 What is - / *the* national sport in your country?
   3 Which sports did you learn at - / *the* school?
   4 Do you follow - / *the* football World Cup?
   5 How can we encourage - / *the* people to be more active?
   6 Do countries with - / *the* big populations like - / *the* United States and - / *the* China have an advantage in - / *the* international competitions?
   7 Do you think - / *the* women and - / *the* men can do - / *the* same sports?
   8 What do you think is - / *the* most dangerous sport?

   b Work in pairs. Take turns to ask and answer the questions in Exercise 3a.

4a Find and correct mistakes with articles in six of the sentences.
   1 When I was the child, I dreamed of becoming professional athlete.
   2 I've never been to the live sporting event.
   3 I don't like doing sporting activities when I'm on holiday.
   4 I would love to visit the famous football stadium like Old Trafford in the Manchester or Maracana in the Rio de Janeiro.
   5 I have no interest in a sport and hate talking about it.
   6 I always support my country in international sporting events like Olympic Games.
   7 I don't like the violent sports like the boxing.

   b Work in pairs. Are any of the sentences in Exercise 4a true for you?

5 Complete the text with *a/an*, *the* or – (no article).

Keeping fit at work

It is a well-known fact that sitting at **1** _____ desk all day is not good for you. So some workplaces are starting to think of ways to help their employees take part in sporting activities while at **2** _____ work. Some firms provide **3** _____ exercise classes before and after **4** _____ work. Other companies have also installed **5** _____ treadmill desks for some of their workers. **6** _____ desks allow people to walk at a steady pace as they work.

Some scientists have suggested that standing up more while working could be **7** _____ substitute for active sporting activity. Dr Mike Loosemore, **8** _____ doctor specialising in sports medicine, says that standing for three hours every day has the same health benefits as running ten marathons **9** _____ year! Dr Loosemore, who is **10** _____ head of exercise medicine at **11** _____ University College London, says that very low-level exercise is enough to keep someone fit and healthy.

Module 8
Activity 8b

Vocabulary

Sporting events

1 Match the words (1–6) with their meanings (A–F).
   1 championship   3 race   5 semi-final
   2 marathon   4 match   6 final

   A a competition where people run very long distances
   B one of the two games in a competition, whose winners compete in the last part
   C a competition to find which player, team, etc. is the best at a sport
   D the last and most important game in a competition
   E a game between two teams or people
   F a competition where people try to run, drive, etc. fastest and finish first

Sports and business

2a Replace the verbs in bold with the verbs in the box in the correct form.

   compete host sign sponsor support train

   1 Only rich countries can **organise** a major sporting event like the Olympic Games.
   2 It's more interesting when a less well-known team **takes part** in an important sporting final.
   3 It is better to **prepare and practise** on your own than with other people.
   4 **Following** your national team gives you a feeling of pride.
   5 It's wrong that fast food companies **provide money for** big sporting events by advertising their products.
   6 Big football clubs often **hire** players for far too much money.

 b Work in pairs. Do you agree or disagree with the sentences in Exercise 2a? Give reasons.

Compound nouns

3 Complete the sentences with the compound nouns in the box.

   life lesson   peer pressure   personal best   self-discipline
   self-belief   team work

   1 It takes a lot of _____ to get up at 5 a.m. every morning in winter to train.
   2 Some teenagers stop doing sport because of _____ from their friends and classmates.
   3 To be successful at sport, you need to have _____ and be confident in your own abilities.
   4 Training with the other players has taught me a lot about _____ .
   5 One _____ sport has taught me is 'always learn from your mistakes'.
   6 Even if I don't win, I always aim to achieve my _____ .

Collocations

4a Write the words in the box in the correct place in the table. One word can go in two columns.

   a championship   a competition   a game   a goal
   a match   a penalty   a point   a race   a stronger team
   a tournament   an opponent   Real Madrid

to win/lose	to beat	to score/miss

 b Complete the sentences with verbs from Exercise 4a in the correct form.

   1 We played France in the final and _____ them 1–0.
   2 It was an exciting match but unfortunately, Sri Lanka _____ in the end.
   3 I _____ the winning goal in the match on Saturday.
   4 He played well but he couldn't _____ his opponent.
   5 I didn't expect to _____ a medal, so I was delighted to come third.
   6 I had to take a penalty but unfortunately, I _____ !
   7 My team has a good chance of being champions – they haven't _____ a game so far this season.
   8 Although we didn't _____ the match, I was pleased with the way we played against a strong team.

5a Complete the sentences with the correct form of the verbs in the box.

   do set play make break (x2)

   1 Professional sportspeople are more interested in winning than in _____ records.
   2 If you don't _____ yourself goals, you will never achieve your dreams.
   3 People who _____ the rules in sport should be banned from competing again.
   4 It doesn't matter if you don't win; it's more important to _____ an effort and _____ your best.
   5 To be successful, you need to _____ by the rules.

 b Work in pairs. Do you agree or disagree with the sentences in Exercise 5a? Give reasons.

Student's Resource Book > Vocabulary page 83   MyEnglishLab > 8b Vocabulary

8b Module 8
Activity

Reading (Notes completion; Multiple choice)

Before you read

1 Work in pairs and discuss the questions.
   1 What types of work are available for people who want to work in the fitness industry?
   2 Why do you think people enjoy working in the fitness industry?

Test practice

▶ TEST STRATEGIES page 179

2 Read the test tasks and answer the questions.
   1 Look at questions 1–6. Do you need to look for specific details or a general point in the passage?
   2 Look at questions 7–10. Which questions are about a general point? Which are about specific details?

3 Complete the test tasks.

▶ HELP

9 The question asks about key advice, so think about the main point Nick Wood makes.
10 This asks what the writer's conclusion is, so be careful to read the whole paragraph and think about the main point.

Task analysis

4 Work in pairs and discuss the questions.
   1 Did thinking about whether a question is asking about detail or a general point help you to find the right answer?
   2 Were both tasks about the same parts of the passage or different ones?
   3 Which task did you find harder? Why?

Discussion

5 Work in pairs. Would you like to work as a personal trainer? Why/Why not?

Questions 1–6
*Complete the notes below. Choose **NO MORE THAN TWO WORDS** from the passage for each answer.*

Personal training in the UK today
- 1 _____ in UK valued at just under £4 billion
- Growth in the role of personal trainers predicted by a 2 _____
- People like using a trainer because:
  - training is personalised
  - they prefer the environment of their 3 _____
  - they like the 4 _____ a trainer provides
- To set up a personal training business, people need:
  - qualifications
  - 5 _____
  - transport
  - 6 _____ they can use

Questions 7–10
*Choose the appropriate letters, **A**, **B**, **C** or **D**.*

7 The writer says that a career in fitness training
   A is rewarding despite a need to work long hours.
   B suits people already working in the fitness industry.
   C offers flexibility and a variety of work opportunities.
   D provides a good income and interesting work.

8 Which aspect of his work does Nick Wood enjoy most?
   A helping clients recover from an injury
   B encouraging people to do their best
   C finding new ways to motivate people
   D watching his customers achieve their aims

9 The key advice Nick Wood gives people who want to start a training business is
   A to become known by teaching groups well.
   B to make sure they keep fit themselves.
   C to advertise in local gyms and sports clubs.
   D to make good use of social media.

10 What is the writer's conclusion about personal training?
   A It is likely to grow in popularity for a long time.
   B It helps both trainer and clients to keep fit.
   C It may be good for both the trainer and society.
   D It will prevent many health problems in the future.

Personal training in the UK

Studies have shown that average weights for British men, women and children have increased considerably over the last 20 years. Recent research predicts that half the UK population will be seriously overweight by the year 2050.

Reports of this type often lead to a sudden rush of people deciding to join a gym or buy an exercise bike to use at home. The fitness industry has become very big business and is now worth approximately £3.92 billion. One aspect of this that is growing particularly fast at the moment is the personal training business. More and more people are choosing to pay a coach to give them regular individual fitness advice. And more and more people are choosing to become personal trainers.

Once only the rich – successful film stars and professional footballers, for example – used personal trainers but now they provide their services for bank clerks, teachers and builders as well. A number of recent television programmes have raised people's awareness of personal training and made them realise that it is no longer something that only the wealthy can afford. One major leisure company has identified personal training – either for individuals or for small groups of friends – as a key area of future growth. The company understands that people prefer a more tailored and personal programme over a one-size-fits-all approach.

The main reason for this preference is the clients' belief that personalised training will be matched to their individual fitness needs and so will help them achieve the great results they want. But there is another reason as well. Many people feel uncomfortable working out in a gym where everyone else seems so much more athletic. People like this feel much happier exercising in privacy at home. Of course, they could do this without a personal trainer but most people find it motivating to have someone else give them encouragement.

For all these reasons, then, it is a good time to set up a personal training business and there are only a few requirements for anyone wishing to do so. Firstly, they must get a general qualification in personal training. This can cost them from £300 to several thousand, depending on their previous knowledge and on the specific focus of the course. They must also take out insurance and they will need transport and access to fitness equipment. They should also identify a specialism to offer their clients. This could mean focusing on helping people to lose weight or to improve their muscle tone, or it could mean specialising in helping women during pregnancy or athletes.

Fitness training offers a flexible career as trainers can work on a full-time or a part-time basis. It is possible to fit in training around an existing job so that trainers can see if the business is going to be right for them before they give up a regular salary. Most fitness trainers work on a *freelance basis, advertising for their own clients. This is popular because trainers can choose their own hours and can set their own charges. However, others are associated with gyms or sports clubs where they provide fitness classes as well as offering private sessions to individual customers. Despite the fact that there are many more personal trainers in the country than there were ten years ago, there are still plenty of clients to keep them busy and this allows them to make a good living.

It can be a satisfying career choice. Nick Wood, a freelance personal trainer in London, says, 'For me, nothing is better than helping someone towards their dream. They might want to lose weight, gain muscle or get better after an injury – I just love seeing them reach their goal. This is a big motivator for me and the reason why I became a personal trainer.'

Wood says anyone setting up as a trainer should start by teaching keep-fit classes locally. 'I put a lot of energy into every single one I do and, trust me, if people think you are a good motivator in a studio, then it is only a matter of time before they want your advice to achieve their own personal goals. Posters, social media and other types of ad have also helped me get clients, but you have to get out there and get noticed.'

So, the personal training industry in the UK may not only be an interesting career choice, but also an important way of stopping those predictions of serious weight problems by 2050 from coming true.

---

*freelance: someone who does freelance work is not employed by one company but sells their services to several different companies

8b Module 8 Activity

Writing (Task 2)

Lead-in

1 Work in pairs and discuss the questions.
   1 Why can it be good to try different sports?
   2 Which sports have you tried once or twice but not continued with? Why did you stop doing them?

Understand the task

> EXPERT WRITING page 207

2a Read the writing task and underline the key words.

Write about the following topic.

People often stop doing a new sport soon after taking it up. This is a pity as it means that they are missing an opportunity to do something healthy and enjoyable.
What do you think are the reasons for this? What solutions can you suggest to deal with this situation?

Give reasons for your answer and include any relevant examples from your knowledge or experience. Write at least 250 words.

b Which of these things do you need to do in your essay?
   A explain why you think this situation exists
   B say whether you agree or disagree with the statement in the task
   C present ideas for solving the problem

Language and content

3a Read the model answer below and answer the questions.
   1 How many paragraphs are there? What is each paragraph about?
   2 Has the student given reasons? Where?
   3 Has the student supported the reasons with examples or explanations?
   4 Has the student suggested solutions? Where?
   5 Has the student given examples or explanations about how the suggested solutions could work?

There are lots of different sports for everyone to try today. There are more traditional ones like football, tennis and golf, of course, but there are also newer ones like wind-surfing, jet-skiing and scuba diving. Unfortunately, many people have a go at a sport once or twice and then never try it again.

There are a number of reasons for this, in my opinion. A main reason is that doing a sport can be very expensive. Take golf, for instance. As with any sport, a good coach charges a lot for a lesson. Moreover, if you want to play it seriously, you need to have your own golf clubs. So many people decide that it is all going to cost too much for them. A further reason is that it is often necessary to travel a long way to be able to do the sport. There may not be a golf course near your home, for example.

So what can we do about this? One solution is for people to share the cost of doing the sport. Having lessons with a group of friends will be much cheaper than individual lessons and perhaps you can share your equipment as well. Also, I think another solution would be for the government to do more to help people get and stay involved in sport. They should build more sports facilities so that doing a sport is easier for people. This may be expensive for the government but it will be good for the nation's health and happiness.

It is a pity that people do not keep up with all the sports that interest them. I think individuals and governments too should do all they can to solve this problem.

Module 8
Activity 8b

b Work in pairs. Look at a student's notes for this task. Decide if each point refers to a reason or a solution.

1 takes a long time to learn
2 organise open days in sports clubs to let people try out lots of different things
3 no one wants to play with a beginner
4 give people questionnaires to make them think about what they really want
5 not as much fun as it looks
6 have more TV programmes teaching people about sports

c Match the sentences (A–F) with the points in Exercise 3b (1–6). Then compare and discuss your answers with a partner.

A This solution would help people analyse their own aims.
B This solution would help teach people some simple things they can quickly enjoy doing.
C The solution to this problem is to make sure the coaches are good at motivating people.
D This solution would mean people have more information before they try the sports themselves.
E You could solve this problem by organising groups of people who are also new to the sport.
F This would help solve the problem by helping people to quickly find out what they like and what they don't like.

4a Look at the words/phrases in the box for adding information. Which ones has the student used in the model answer?

also   as well (as this)   furthermore   in addition
moreover   too

b Underline the words and phrases for adding information in the sentences. Then complete them using your own ideas.

1 Swimming is an excellent sport. It is very enjoyable. In addition, …
2 Greater investment in sport will help to make the population of the country healthier. Furthermore, it will …
3 Joining one of the college's sports clubs is a good way to make friends. Moreover, …
4 The university has an excellent fitness centre, with a well-equipped gym and also …

Plan your essay

5a Work in pairs. Think of reasons and solutions you could include in your essay.

b Plan your essay. Make notes in the table. Use your ideas from Exercise 5a.

Paragraph	Notes
Introduction	
Reasons	
Solutions	
Conclusion	

Write your essay

▶ **TEST STRATEGIES** page 181

6 Write your essay. Use your plan from Exercise 5b. Remember to:
- introduce the topic in your own words.
- use topic sentences in your paragraphs.
- support your reasons and solutions with explanations and/or examples.
- use appropriate phrases to introduce your reasons and solutions and to add information.

Assess and improve

7 Check your work. Did you do these things in your essay?

1 I used my own words in the introduction and did not copy the statement in the task.
2 I included reasons and supported them with explanations and/or examples.
3 I suggested solutions and explained why they would work.
4 I used appropriate phrases to introduce reasons and solutions and to add information.

Student's Resource Book > Writing page 84

133

8b Module 8 Activity

Speaking (Part 2)

Develop a topic

1 Work in pairs. Think about sports you have learned. Which one was the easiest to learn? Which was the most difficult? Think about:
   - the skill involved.
   - the instructor/coach.
   - any equipment needed.
   - the cost.
   - how much you enjoyed it.

2a 🔊 8.7 Read the test task. Listen to a candidate doing the task and make a note of <u>one</u> thing she says about each point.

Describe your experience with a sport you have tried to learn.

You should say:

    why you decided to learn this sport

    what you did to learn it

    what kind of equipment you needed

and explain how successful you have been.

b Compare your notes from Exercise 2a with a partner. Did you note down the same points?

c Look at some ways to expand your answer in Part 2 of the Speaking test. Then look at audio script 8.7 on page 219. Which of these does the candidate do in her answer? Can you find examples?
  1 Give examples.
  2 Give reasons.
  3 Talk about the advantages and/or disadvantages of a situation.
  4 Talk about someone you know.
  5 Clarify: explain what you have just said; be more specific.

Make yourself clear

3a 🔊 8.7 Listen again and complete the phrases the candidate uses to make herself clear.
  1 What I _____ I wanted to make new friends.
  2 In _____ , it was my friend who got me into playing tennis.
  3 What I'm _____ is I always followed tennis tournaments on TV.
  4 To put it _____ , I suppose it was quite easy for me because I already knew the rules.
  5 What I _____ is you don't need much equipment.
  6 What I _____ is I'm good enough to play in club matches.

b Work in pairs. Look at the questions in Exercise 1 again. Choose one sport to talk about. This time, try to talk about each of the points listed for as long as you can. Use some of the techniques in Exercise 2c and phrases from Exercise 3a.

Test practice

▶ TEST STRATEGIES page 182

4a Look at the task in Exercise 2a again and make notes for each point.

b Check your notes with a partner. Have you got enough information to talk for 1–2 minutes?

c Work in pairs. Follow the instructions and complete the test task. Then swap roles.
  - Student A: Use your notes from Exercise 4a. Try to speak for 1–2 minutes and think carefully about giving enough information for each point.
  - Student B: Listen and make notes in the table.

Did your partner:	Notes/Examples
talk about all the points in the task?	
develop each point, giving enough information?	
use phrases to make him-/herself clear?	
use linking words to connect his/her ideas?	

Assess and improve

5 Work in the same pairs. How well did your partner do? Use your notes from Exercise 4c to give him/her feedback.

9 Media

9A Training
- **Reading:** Understand connections (Matching features)
- **Language development:** Present perfect and past simple
- **Vocabulary:** Media and social media
- **Listening:** Locate information (Section 1: Form completion)
- **Speaking:** Express attitude (Part 3: Discussion)
- **Writing:** Compare and contrast data (Task 1: Pie charts)

9B Testing
- **Listening:** Section 1: Matching; Form completion
- **Language development:** Possessives, pronouns, quantifiers
- **Vocabulary:** Technology
- **Reading:** Matching features; Sentence completion
- **Writing:** Task 1: Bar charts and line graphs
- **Speaking:** Part 3: Discussion

Lead-in

Look at the photos of different ways we get news and discuss the questions below. Think about:
- the number of people who read, watch or use each one.
- the types of information available.
- the speed with which each one can give information.
- who is writing the information.

1 Which do you think is the most/least important?
2 Which is the most/least reliable?
3 Which is the most/least interesting?

135

9a The news

Reading (Matching features)

Before you read
1 Work in pairs and discuss the questions.
   1 Do you think it's important to follow the news? Why/Why not?
   2 How do you like to get your news? Why?

Understand connections
2a Read the passage quickly. What was the subject of the Pew Center research study?

b Read the test task and look at the groups of people A–D. Which section of the passage focuses on each group?

Look at the following features (questions 1–8) and the list of groups below. Match each feature with the group the writer associates it with. Choose the correct letter, A–D. You may use any letter more than once.

Features of groups
1 well-informed about political affairs
2 a smaller proportion of women in this group
3 have technology but do not use it fully
4 one particular section of this group is growing
5 earn a lot of money
6 prefer a visual presentation of information
7 have typically spent the least time in education
8 fewer people in this group than the other groups

Groups of people	
A Traditionalists	C Integrators
B Net-newsers	D Disengaged

c Now look at features 1–8 in the test task. Underline the key words.

3a Work in pairs. Try to think of another way to express each of the features in the test task.
   1 knowing a lot about politics

b Find words in paragraphs 1 and 2 of the passage that match these synonyms.
   1 currently
   2 prefer
   3 on the internet
   4 carried out
   5 across the whole country
   6 discover
   7 dividing

4 Look at the underlined words in the passage (1–8). What do they refer to?

5 Read the section of the passage relating to group A and follow these steps.
   1 Read the features carefully and decide which one/ones match/matches group A.
   2 Underline the part of the passage that matches each feature.
   3 Check the feature and the underlined text to make sure they are saying the same thing.

Test training
6 Complete the test task in Exercise 2a. Follow the same steps as in Exercise 5 for the remaining paragraphs.

Task analysis
7 Work in pairs and discuss the questions.
   1 Did underlining key words in the features help you? How?
   2 Did thinking about how the same thing can be said in different ways help you find the answers? How?
   3 Do you think looking at each of the relevant paragraphs in turn was a good way for you to approach the task?

Discussion
8 Work in pairs and discuss the questions.
   1 Which of the four groups do you belong to?
   2 What kinds of news stories interest you the most?

Changing habits in accessing the news

1 There are many different ways to get the news nowadays. Some people buy a daily newspaper, others watch television or listen to the radio and still others choose to get their news online. ¹Many, of course, make regular use of more than one source.

2 The Pew Research Center in the US recently conducted a survey with 3,612 adults nationwide. Researchers wanted to find out how ²they currently learn about the news. They ended up classifying the people they interviewed into four groups: Traditionalists, Net-newsers, Integrators and the Disengaged.

3 The researchers called the largest group Traditionalists. As the name suggests, ³they prefer to access the news in a traditional way, typically by watching television. They do ⁴this a great deal – in the morning, in the afternoon and in the evening. They explain that they understand the news better when they see pictures rather than just reading or listening to a news story. Their level of education is relatively low, with over 60 percent of this group having no more than a high school education. This group tends to be middle-aged or older, and is less well-paid than people who access the news in other ways. They say they like to get information about the weather but do not find stories about science or technology interesting. Most people in this group have a computer at home but they almost never use it to find out about the news. Although they are still a large group – 46 percent of the population – their numbers have been going down for ten years now.

4 Net-newsers, on the other hand, choose to get the majority of their news from the internet. Sometimes they read online news articles or blogs and sometimes they watch video clips of news stories. Their online access to the news is highest during the day. They use technology in other aspects of their lives too and like to follow stories relating to science. The smallest of the four groups, they are also the youngest, with a typical age of 35. They are better educated than other groups; eight in ten of them have at least attended college. Nearly 60 percent of the group are men and they also tend to be relatively well-off. Although the internet is by far the main source of news for Net-newsers, they do occasionally use other sources too. They are, for example, at least as likely as Integrators and Traditionalists to read serious news magazines.

5 The third group are the Integrators. These are people who regularly use both television and the internet as their source of news. They usually watch the news on television in the evenings and log on to the internet from work in order to keep up with the news during the day. Almost half of them also get some of their news from the radio. Integrators are people with a particularly strong interest in the news and spend more time following ⁵it than any of the other groups. They keep up-to-date with national and international politics and they also follow sports news. They currently represent 23 percent of the population but this proportion is growing steadily. They typically have higher education and a high salary. Most of them are middle-aged.

6 The researchers reported that 14 percent of the US population fall into the fourth and final group, which ⁶they called the Disengaged. This group has little or no interest in the news. Almost half of the group do not watch the television news even once a day and one-fifth do not know which party is in power in Washington. In general, they have even fewer academic qualifications than the Traditionalists. There are signs that the proportion of young people in the Disengaged category is rising. Slightly over one-third of the under-25 age group reported that on a typical day, ⁷they read or see no news, up from one quarter in 1998.

7 The Pew Center's research study highlights interesting trends in the ways people access news today. One of ⁸these is the fact that there are increasing extremes of behaviour in the US population. While there are many people who are accessing news stories much more frequently and in a variety of different ways, the number of people who pay no attention at all to the news is also on the increase.

9a Module 9 Media

Language development

Present perfect and past simple

▶ EXPERT GRAMMAR page 190

1 Read the sentences and look at the verb forms in bold. Match the sentences (1–4) with the descriptions (A–D).
1 I've read three newspapers this week.
2 I've seen that film – it's good.
3 I read the news online yesterday.
4 I've been on Facebook since 2010.

A something that happened in the past and is now finished but we don't know the time
B something that started in the past and continues in the present
C something that started and finished at a specific point in the past
D something that happened in a time period that has not yet finished (*this year*, *today*, etc.)

2 Complete the sentences with the time words/phrases in the box. There are two extra words/phrases you do not need to use.

ago   already   ever   for   just   last year   lately   never   since   still   when   yesterday   yet

1 I've _____ bought a newspaper but I sometimes read my friend's.
2 My father has read the same newspaper _____ he was 18.
3 Did you see the news _____ ? There was a serious accident on the motorway and they _____ haven't opened the road.
4 The election was two days _____ but they haven't announced the result _____ .
5 I don't want to watch the news now because I've _____ seen it once today.
6 The figures for newspapers sales fell a lot _____ but have increased a little _____ .
7 I started using a news app _____ I got my tablet.
8 The country has suffered from economic difficulties _____ a number of years.

3 Complete the sentences with the present perfect or past simple form of the verbs in brackets.
1 I _____ (not use) social media for months.
2 _____ (you / hear) the news about the new university?
3 My brother _____ (decide) to close his Twitter account last Monday.
4 They _____ (not make) enough money this year, so the paper is going to close.
5 I _____ (not see) the news this evening but I _____ (see) it at lunchtime.
6 I _____ (stop) buying that paper when the price _____ (go up).

4a Complete the questions with the present perfect or past simple form of the verbs in brackets.

News and the media
1 How _____ (people / get) their news 50 or 60 years ago?
2 How _____ (technology / change) the way we get news?
3 Do you think the media _____ (be) more or less powerful in the past than it is now?
4 _____ (people / become) less sensitive to bad news stories in recent years? Why/Why not?
5 _____ (there / be) more or less media choice in the past?
6 _____ (social media / make) people more or less involved in the news?

b Work in pairs. Take turns to ask and answer the questions in Exercise 4a.

5 Complete the text with the words in the box.

ago   been   did   has (x2)   have   in   last   since   was (x2)   were

Breaking news

There is no doubt that the way we get our news **1** _____ experienced a major change in the **2** _____ two decades. One of the most remarkable changes has **3** _____ the way in which a news story breaks. 20 or 30 years **4** _____ , reporters and journalists **5** _____ the first people to announce breaking news. For many years, our only source of news **6** _____ the traditional media of newspapers, radio and TV but this is no longer the case. **7** _____ 2011, when Japan suffered a serious earthquake, reporters and journalists **8** _____ not break the news. Instead, it **9** _____ social media users who first told the world what was happening. **10** _____ the introduction of social media, it has become common for members of the public to post photos and videos of news events. It **11** _____ also become far easier in recent years to comment on and share news stories instantly. This means that many people **12** _____ become more engaged with the news than ever before.

6 Write questions to ask a partner about their activities using the words/phrases in the box. Then work in pairs and take turns to ask and answer your questions.

last week   last year   on Saturday   recently   since Tuesday   yet

138   Student's Resource Book > Language development page 88   MyEnglishLab > 9a Language development

Vocabulary

Module 9
Media
9a

Media

1a Match the words (1–8) with their meanings (A–H).
1 headline
2 journalism
3 mass media
4 news story
5 paparazzi
6 the press
7 privacy
8 tabloid

A the photographers who chase celebrities to get photos of them
B when other people don't know what you are doing
C the job of writing reports for newspapers, TV and radio
D newspapers and magazines
E the title of a newspaper report
F all the news media together
G a newspaper with small pages, short reports and not very much serious news
H an article in a newspaper about new events

b Complete the sentences with words from Exercise 1a in the correct form.
1 _____ can sell photographs of celebrities for a lot of money.
2 I'd like to write for newspapers, so I'm thinking of doing a course in _____ .
3 I think everyone, even famous people, have a right to _____ in their personal lives.
4 Although I don't often buy a newspaper, I sometimes look at the _____ to see what the main _____ are.
5 The report about the fire was in the local _____ but it didn't appear in national newspapers.
6 You shouldn't use _____ newspapers for academic research because they do not contain much important news.

Adjectives

2 Complete the sentences with the words in the box.

believable boring depressing effective entertaining informative

1 Newspaper articles are more detailed and _____ than TV news, so you can learn a lot from them.
2 I never watch the TV news because I find it too _____ ; it is full of wars and disasters.
3 The news is not supposed to be _____ or funny.
4 I find that many news stories about celebrities are not very _____ ; I think a lot of them are invented.
5 TV news can be very _____ in raising people's awareness about world events, particularly disasters in other countries.
6 I find the news is _____ because it seems to be the same every day.

Social media

3a Complete the questions with the words in the box.

instant messaging likes emoticons chat rooms podcasts blogs

1 In what ways can students listen to _____ for educational purposes?
2 Is _____ the most convenient means of communicating nowadays?
3 For what reason do people keep _____ ? How are they different from writing a diary?
4 Do you think student discussions in _____ can replace discussions in class?
5 Do you often use _____ in your messages?
6 Do people worry too much about how many _____ they get on social media?

b Work in pairs. Take turns to ask and answer the questions in Exercise 3a.

4a Complete the questions with the words in the box.

comment follow go post reply subscribe tag update

1 Do you _____ to any websites or blogs?
2 Do friends often _____ you in their photos?
3 Do you often _____ photos on social media?
4 Do you _____ famous people on social media?
5 Do you ever use social media to _____ on serious news stories?
6 Do you ever _____ to a stranger's comments on social media?
7 How often do you _____ your status?
8 What type of topics _____ viral on social media?

b Work in pairs. Take turns to ask and answer the questions in Exercise 4a.

Phrasal verbs

5 Choose the correct options in *italics* to complete the phrasal verbs in the sentences.
1 Privacy in the media was one of the subjects they brought *up / on* at the meeting.
2 In my house we all have to be quiet when the news comes *in / on* because my dad likes to watch it.
3 Some people buy the latest smartphone as soon as it comes *out / off*.
4 I sometimes flick *through / over* a magazine to see if there are any interesting articles to read.
5 I prefer reading articles in serious newspapers because they go *onto / into* more detail.
6 When looking *up / out* information on the internet, make sure the website is reliable.
7 You shouldn't believe the news stories you read in the tabloids; they often make them *off / up*.

9a Module 9
Media

Listening (Section 1: Form completion)

Before you listen

1 Work in pairs and discuss the questions.
   1 What qualities do you need to work in journalism?
   2 Have you ever been involved with writing or publishing a newspaper, newsletter or similar?

Locate information

2a 🔊 9.1 Listen to the first part of a conversation between a student and the editor of a newspaper. What are they discussing?

b 🔊 9.2 Listen to the next part of the conversation and choose the correct answers below to complete the notes.

Education: Degree course in 1 _____ at 2 _____

1 journalism / media and communications
2 Midlands University / Central College

c 🔊 9.2 Listen again. The speakers mention both options for each gap in Exercise 2b. Why are the incorrect options wrong?

d Look at audio script 9.2 on page 220. Underline the questions which signal when an answer is coming for each of the gaps in Exercise 2b.

Test training

3a Work in pairs. Read the test task below and answer the questions.
   1 What kind of information goes in each gap?
   2 Can you think of possible questions you might hear that will signal when an answer is coming for each gap?

Complete the form below. Write **NO MORE THAN THREE WORDS AND/OR A NUMBER** for each answer.

Wynmouth Weekly News – Work experience
Particular interest: 1 _____ media
Experience: deputy editor of 2 _____
Availability: available 3 _____
Own transport?   can use 4 _____
Name: James 5 _____
Nationality: 6 _____
Email: 7 _____ @bmail.com
Notes: away last two weeks of 8 _____

b 🔊 9.3 Complete the test task.

Task analysis

4 Work in pairs. Look at audio script 9.3 on page 220 and discuss the questions.
   1 Did you correctly predict the type of information for each gap?
   2 Which questions/phrases showed you when an answer was coming for each gap? Did you hear them all?
   3 Did you get any answers wrong? If so, why were they wrong (e.g. wrong spelling, wrong word, too many words)?

Discussion

5 Do you think traditional newspapers have a future in the age of the internet?

Module 9
Media
9a

Speaking (Part 3)

Express attitude

1 Choose the correct definition of *attitude*.
   A a way of doing something or dealing with a problem
   B what you think or feel about someone or something
   C how polite you are when you speak to somebody

2 🔊 9.4 Listen to five people talking about news stories and look at the words/phrases in bold. Which ones introduce the speaker's opinion (O)? Which ones show their attitude (A)?
   1 **Thankfully**, everyone escaped safe and well from the floods.
   2 **I believe that** privacy laws should change as soon as possible.
   3 House prices are **obviously** going to rise.
   4 **My view is that** the politicians involved should apologise.
   5 **Sadly**, two people died in the accident and many more were injured.

3 Match the attitude adverbs (1–6) with their uses (A–F).
   1 worryingly   4 apparently
   2 hopefully   5 obviously
   3 naturally   6 definitely

   The adverb shows that the speaker:
   A expects the listener to know or agree with something.
   B feels there is no doubt about something.
   C hopes that something is true or will happen.
   D is concerned about something.
   E has heard or read that something is true, although they are not certain.
   F thinks that something is normal and not surprising.

4 Change each word so that it can be used to express attitude.
   1 surprise   _____
   2 important   _____
   3 basic   _____
   4 serious   _____
   5 clear   _____
   6 fortunate   _____

5 Rewrite the sentences replacing the phrases in bold with attitude adverbs.
   1 **It is clear that** the situation is getting worse every day.
      Clearly, the situation is getting worse every day.
   2 **It is sad that** tabloids report news inaccurately.
   3 **I am hopeful that** prices will fall next year.
   4 **I am concerned that** these reports on social media might be true.
   5 **It was a surprise that** the president resigned.
   6 **I am thankful that** nobody was hurt.

6a 🔊 9.5 Listen to a candidate doing Part 3 of the Speaking test. What subjects are they talking about?

 b Look at audio script 9.5 on page 220 and underline the attitude adverbs.

7 Work in pairs. Talk about some recent news stories using ideas from the box. Try to use adverbs from Exercises 2–5 to express your attitude on the news stories.

   news about disasters   news from other countries
   news about famous people   sports news   weather news

> Apparently, it's going to be extremely hot in Europe this summer.

> Sadly, the football team I support didn't win last week.

Test training

8 Work in pairs. Take turns to ask and answer the questions.
   1 How much do you think the way we get news has changed in the last few years?
   2 Why do you think some people are so interested in news about celebrities?
   3 How far do you think we can control the stories that newspapers and TV programmes publish?

Task analysis

9 Work in pairs and discuss the questions.
   1 Did you give reasons for your point of view?
   2 Did you give any examples?
   3 Did you use attitude adverbs in your answers?

MyEnglishLab > 9a Speaking

9a Module 9 Media

Writing (Task 1)

Compare and contrast data

1 Read the test task. What information do you need to include in your answer? Do you need to give your personal point of view?

The charts below show how people of different age groups access the news. Summarise the information by selecting and reporting the main features, and make comparisons where relevant. Write at least 150 words.

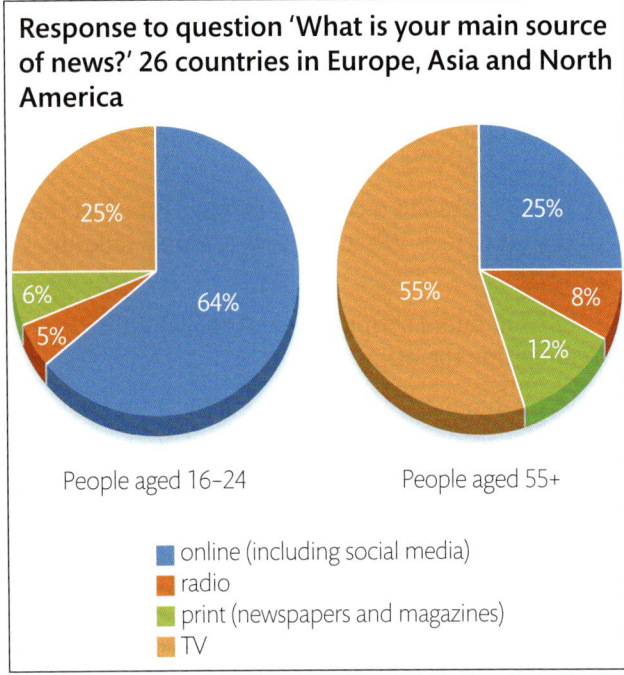

Response to question 'What is your main source of news?' 26 countries in Europe, Asia and North America

People aged 16–24: online 64%, TV 25%, print 6%, radio 5%
People aged 55+: TV 55%, online 25%, print 12%, radio 8%

- online (including social media)
- radio
- print (newspapers and magazines)
- TV

2a Read the model answer. How many parts are there? What does the student do in each part?

The charts illustrate the principal source of news for young adults (aged 16–24) and for people over 55. They summarise information gathered from 26 European, Asian and North American countries.

The charts show that the two age groups access news in rather different ways. A majority of the younger people get their news online, while the older generation, in contrast, choose television as their main source.

Although use of TV and the internet differ for these two age groups, the radio is the least important source of information for both groups. A similarly small proportion of each group – 5 percent and 8 percent – name the radio as their main source of news.

Printed newspapers and magazines, the most traditional way of accessing news, still has some importance for both the age groups illustrated in the charts. However, they are more popular with older people: 12 percent of the over-55s name this as their main source of information, in comparison with only 6 percent of 16- to 24-year-olds.

b Read the model answer again and underline the parts where the student compares/contrasts data.

3a Look at the words/phrases in the box for comparing and contrasting data. Which ones has the student used in the model answer?

although   but   comparing   however   in comparison
in contrast   on the other hand   while

b Look at some more sentences comparing and contrasting data. Rewrite them using the words in brackets.

1 Many people still watch television in the traditional way. However, more and more young people are choosing to watch TV programmes online. (while)
While many people still watch television in the traditional way, more and more young people are choosing to watch TV programmes online.

2 Nowadays more people own tablets than laptops. However, laptops are still popular, particularly with businesspeople and students. (although)

3 Women watch the news on television more than men do, while men make more use of online news sources. (on the other hand)

4 If we look at data from Europe and the US, we can see some interesting differences. (comparing)

5 Adults say they discuss the news at least once a day. Teenagers, on the other hand, do so less than once a week. (in contrast)

4a Plan your answer to the writing task in Exercise 1. Make notes in the table. Think about:
- your introduction and how you can describe the main topic of the charts in your own words.
- your overview.
- what main features to report and how to organise them.
- how to compare/contrast data using some of the words/phrases in Exercise 3a.

Paragraph	Notes
Introduction	
Overview	
Main body paragraph 1	
Main body paragraph 2	

b Write your answer. Use your plan from Exercise 4a.

9b Technology

Listening (Section 1: Matching; Form completion)

Before you listen

1 Work in pairs. Talk about what technology skills you are good/bad at.
   - communications
   - creating presentations
   - web surfing
   - making and uploading videos
   - creating websites
   - other?

Test practice

> TEST STRATEGIES page 178

2a You will hear a conversation between a woman and a college advisor. You must complete both of the tasks below while listening. Before you listen, answer these questions.
   1 Read the first task. Can you use options A–C more than once?
   2 Read the second task. What kind of information might go in each gap?
   3 Can you think of possible questions you might hear that will signal when an answer is coming for each gap?

Questions 1–4

Which description matches each course? Choose your answers from the box and write the correct letter **A–C** next to questions 1–4. You may choose any letter more than once.

| A is a full-time course |
| B is not suitable for beginners |
| C is on a different campus |

1 Introduction to Email and the Internet _____
2 Computing Level 1 _____
3 Introduction to Website Design _____
4 Desktop Publishing _____

Questions 5–10

Complete the form below. Write **NO MORE THAN TWO WORDS AND/OR A NUMBER** for each answer.

Central College – Student enrolment

Name: Maria 5 _____
Nationality: Russian
First language: 6 _____
Telephone: 7 _____
Education: university
Highest qualification: 8 _____ in jewellery design
Special needs: 9 _____
Amount paid: 10 _____

b  9.6 Complete the test tasks.

> HELP

B Listen for another way of saying that someone is not a beginner.
5 The speaker spells her name. Make sure you get it right the first time because it is not repeated.
9 Listen for another word for 'not any'.

Task analysis

3 Work in pairs and discuss the questions.
   1 Which of the two tasks did you find more difficult? Why?
   2 Did you listen out for signal words or questions?
   3 Were you confused by any of the words that could fit in the gaps but were wrong? Look at audio script 9.6 on page 220. Can you see why they are wrong?

Discussion

4 Discuss the questions.
   1 Have you ever taken any courses to help you with computer skills? If so, what were they?
   2 Is there a computer skill that you would like to improve by doing a course?
   3 Do you think it is possible to succeed in business without computer skills?

Module 9
Media

Language development

Possessives, pronouns, quantifiers

▶ EXPERT GRAMMAR page 190

1 Complete the sentences with possessive adjectives (*my, your, his, her*, etc.) or possessive pronouns (*mine, yours, his, hers*, etc.).
   1 Some students in my department have won a prize for _____ research.
   2 My laptop isn't working. Can I use _____ , please?
   3 Can I have a look at _____ newspaper, please?
   4 My sister and I both have Facebook accounts but she doesn't use _____ very much.
   5 That DVD is _____ . Can I have it back, please?
   6 This newspaper is well-known for _____ excellent articles on the environment.
   7 My uncle is a journalist and I've just read _____ latest article.
   8 My brother and I have known Callum for a long time; he's a good friend of _____ .

2a Choose the correct options in *italics* to complete the sentences.
   1 *Both / Either* cost and design are equally important when you buy an electronic device.
   2 *Neither / Either* texting or instant messaging are appropriate ways to give someone bad news.
   3 Even *most / no* older people these days know how to use the internet.
   4 *Every / All* website I use has too many pop-ups.
   5 *None / Neither* of the electronic devices we use nowadays last a long time.
   6 There's *no / none* excuse for not owning a smartphone nowadays.
   7 *Several / Each* people I know have their own websites or blogs.
   8 *Each / Either* person in my house owns at least two electronic devices.

   b Work in pairs. Which of the sentences in Exercise 2a do you agree with? Which are true for you?

3 Complete the sentences with the correct form of the missing word.
   1 Neither of these laptops _____ working. (is / are)
   2 Neither _____ has the features I want. (phone / phones)
   3 In my house each person _____ their own tablet. (has / have)
   4 Every _____ on the page mentioned the same problem. (comment / comments)
   5 Either of these two apps _____ you to create music. (helps / help)
   6 None of us _____ how to fix the device. (knows / know)
   7 Both the laptop and the tablet _____ too expensive. (was / were)

4 Complete the sentences with the words in the box.

amount couple deal number plenty

   1 The new software took a great _____ of time and effort to create.
   2 Technology affects education in many ways but, in my view, only a(n) _____ of them are positive.
   3 Parents often complain about the _____ of time their children spend online.
   4 The article made a(n) _____ of points in favour of going digital and I agreed with all of them.
   5 Fortunately, we can afford the new computer system as we have _____ of money at the moment.

5a Complete the table.

	some-	*any-*	*no-*	*every-*
People	someone		no one	
		anybody		everybody
Things		anything		everything

b Choose the correct options in *italics* to complete the exchanges.
   1 A: Do you think there is *anything / everything* we can do to stop people making nasty comments on social media?
      B: Well, the problem is *no one / anyone* takes responsibility for this.
   2 A: Do you think the internet should be available to *everybody / somebody*?
      B: Yes, but the problem is not everybody *want / wants* to use it.
   3 A: Is there *anything / everything* we can do to make the internet safer?
      B: I think we should do *everything / nothing* possible but unfortunately, nobody *seems / doesn't seem* to know the best thing to do.
   4 A: Do you think *anybody / somebody* can learn how to use a computer?
      B: Of course *he / they* can. I believe *somebody / everyone* can learn *anything / nothing*.

6 Choose the correct options in *italics* to complete the text.

Emoji diversity

Almost 1 *everyone / all* who communicates by text or instant messaging uses emoji. For 2 *anyone / someone* who doesn't know, emoji are the little pictures you can add to your message to express an emotion. There are 3 *every / all* kinds of emoji to choose from. In fact, there is probably an emoji to express almost 4 *something / everything* you want, including pictures of animals, jobs, sports and weather. However, until recently, nearly 5 *most / every* emoji in the jobs category featured a man, with only a few represented by women. Therefore, a new set of jobs emoji with 6 *either / both* male and female versions will soon appear so users can choose 7 *their / your* favourite. This comes after a 8 *number / plenty* of different skin tones were introduced to the range of emoji characters, to make them more diverse.

Vocabulary

Technology

1 Choose the correct options in *italics* to complete the sentences.
   1 I usually use an app like WhatsApp to *access / message* my friends.
   2 When you *google / attach* something, you often get too many websites to choose from.
   3 This is a good site for research but you have to pay to *go / access* some parts of it.
   4 I spend a lot of time *downloading / browsing* news and current affairs websites.
   5 If a file is very big, it can take a long time to *download / upgrade*.
   6 My computer always seems to *attach / crash* at important times.
   7 I usually *upgrade / browse* my mobile every year because I like to have the latest features.
   8 My computer is very old, so it takes ages to *attach / browse* large files.

2a Complete the questions with the words/phrases in the box.

apps   connection   devices   digital age   e-books
equipment   gadget   software

   1 What advantages does living in the _____ give us?
   2 Do you ever read _____ ? Why/Why not?
   3 How many electronic _____ do you own?
   4 How fast is your internet _____ ?
   5 How many _____ do you have on your phone? Do you use all of them?
   6 Do you always upgrade your computer _____ every time you need to?
   7 What electronic _____ do you use for work or study?
   8 Do you always buy the latest _____ or do you prefer to wait?

b Work in pairs. Take turns to ask and answer the questions in Exercise 2a.

Word formation

3a Complete the table.

Verb	Noun
develop	
	progress
advance	
	impact
influence	
change	
	effect

b Complete the sentences with words from Exercise 3a in the correct form. More than one answer may be possible.
   1 Reports say that they are making good _____ towards a peace agreement.
   2 Parents have enormous _____ on what and how much TV their children watch.
   3 World leaders are meeting to consider the environmental _____ of global warming.
   4 It can be difficult to keep up with the speed of recent technological _____ , which have changed our lives enormously.
   5 One way that technology has _____ news reporting is that we can get news updates instantly.
   6 When Twitter first appeared in 2006, no one could imagine how quickly it would _____ .

Phrasal verbs

4a Complete the questions with *up, into* or *out*. Then underline the phrasal verb in each question.
   1 Are you worried about someone hacking _____ your bank account?
   2 Do you find it easy or difficult to set _____ software on your computer?
   3 Do you remember to back _____ your files regularly?
   4 How often do you run _____ of space in your computer or phone?
   5 Do you find adverts that pop _____ on your screen annoying?
   6 Do you use _____ all your data quickly on your mobile?
   7 Do you read on screen or do you prefer to print things _____ ?
   8 Do you like to sign _____ for special offers?

b Work in pairs. Take turns to and answer the questions in Exercise 4a.

9b Module 9 Media

Reading (Matching features; Sentence completion)

Before you read

1a Work in pairs. Read the extracts below from three articles about technology. Find paraphrases of these words/phrases.

1 research study
2 the majority
3 cannot
4 on the internet
5 resembles
6 finding the answers in
7 say
8 change
9 based on
10 developments

A A survey published earlier this year found that four out of five 18- to 30-year-olds are unable to find their way without help from a satnav device. So if <u>they</u> lose their smartphone, they are quite literally lost.

B Searching and browsing online exercises the brain in a way that is similar to solving a crossword puzzle. So <u>it</u> may not be such a waste of time as some people argue.

C We can identify anyone we point a phone at; when we shop online, the shop may adjust prices according to what we can pay. <u>These</u> are advances in technology that many people regret.

b Look at the underlined words in the extracts. What do they refer to?

Test practice

▶ TEST STRATEGIES page 179

2 Complete the test tasks.

Questions 1–5
Look at the following features (questions 1–5) and the types of technology below. Match each feature with the type of technology that has that feature.

Features
1 can accompany other activities
2 means that distance is no longer a problem
3 helps record achievements
4 helps make everyday decisions
5 informs when something is too much or too little

Types of technology
A technology related to exercise
B technology related to music
C technology related to diet
D technology related to social networking
E technology related to mental challenge

Questions 6–10
Complete the sentences below. Choose **ONE WORD ONLY** from the passage for each answer.

6 Elderly people with several good _____ are happier than those without any.
7 Being on a different _____ is not a problem for communication these days.
8 People with similar _____ can get to know each other on the web.
9 Being mentally active can increase the number of _____ that brain neurons create.
10 Taking advantage of online options for _____ can help challenge the mind.

▶ HELP

1 Look for a paragraph that gives examples of different activities and the key words *while* and *during*.
9 To find the part of the passage this question relates to, look for the key word *neurons* in the passage.

Task analysis

3 Work in pairs and discuss the questions.
1 Did you identify which parts of the passage each task referred to? How easy did you find this?
2 Did you use underlining to help you find information? What did you underline?
3 Did looking for paraphrases help you to find answers to the questions?
4 Did you have any difficulties understanding reference words like *it*, *their*, *that*, etc.?

Discussion

4 Work in pairs. What do you think are the best ways for teachers to make use of technology? Think about the examples in the passage and how technology can help improve brain function.

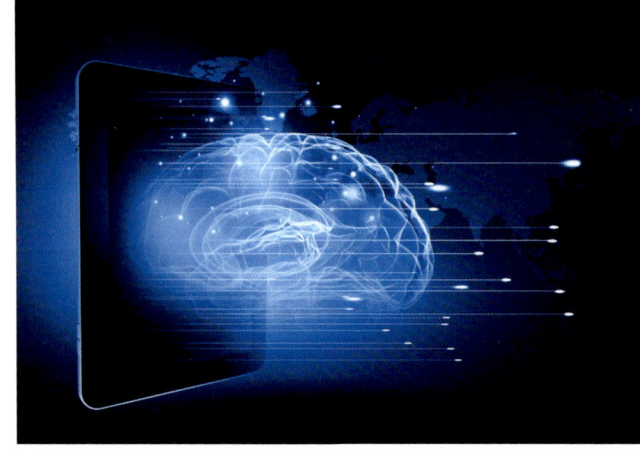

Brain health and technology

We live in the digital age but some people say that too much use of technology will have a negative effect on our psychology and mental abilities. According to them, if school children use, for example, calculators instead of working out a sum in their head, they will not be able to understand basic arithmetic. Similarly, adults will become too lazy to check their spelling if they can rely on a spell-check program. In other words, if computers do the work for people, they may not learn to think for themselves. However, a number of research studies have shown that technology does not necessarily limit mental abilities. It seems that it can, in fact, actually have a positive impact on them.

The brain is extremely important when it comes to being healthy and living well. Exercise makes more blood flow to the brain, so it is one of the simplest ways to get the brain working better. It also improves the chemicals which protect *nerves from damage. However, exercise must be energetic enough to be effective. People can use technology like heart monitors to check that they are exercising at the right level. Another way to use technology to make exercise more effective is to use devices with a GPS (Global Positioning System). This allows people to know, for example, how great a distance they have run and to plan future runs in their area.

Music is known to have a positive impact on feelings of happiness and well-being. In addition, there is a theory, called the Mozart Effect, that listening to classical music makes a person cleverer. Experiments have indeed shown that listening to music has improved language ability in patients with certain illnesses. Electronic devices now make it possible to listen to music on public transport, at work, while exercising or at any other time during the day. So this is another way in which digital devices may be making people's mental abilities stronger.

Changes in diet can also help to improve brain function. Omega-3 fats, for instance, are good for the brain and provide important support to the *nervous system. Similarly, research shows that having coconut oil in the diet is especially helpful for the brain and can help improve memory. Vitamin D is also good as it improves nerve growth in the brain. Technology provides a quick and easy way for people to check what nutrients there are in specific foods. Having this information easily available on a smartphone app is very convenient when shoppers are selecting food. They can choose products based on accurate information rather than just guessing what a particular food contains.

Many people use their electronic devices to help them stay in contact with others. And having a network of social relationships is also important in keeping the brain working well. Research shows this to be a key factor in keeping older people happy. Social media sites, texting and video calls all make staying in touch with one another so much easier than it used to be, even if they live on different continents. Moreover, the internet means it is possible for people who share the same interests to make contact with each other.

Another way for people to improve their brain function is by exercising it with challenging mental tasks. Psychologists have shown that learning new things actually changes the size and structure of brain *neurons and develops more connections between them. Smartphones, tablets and computers make it very easy for people to have access to information and tasks that are both fun and stimulating. For instance, the internet offers all sorts of amazing opportunities for study. Research has shown that surfing the web increases activity in the parts of the brain used for decision-making.

To sum up, despite frequent criticisms of the impact of technology on people today, electronic devices can have a very positive impact on brain health and mental powers. They can help people exercise, listen to music, diet, stay in contact with friends and find mental challenges. All these activities play a very valuable role in improving not only health and happiness but also mental ability.

* nerves: parts inside the body which carry messages between the brain and other parts of the body
* nervous system: all the nerves in the body that make moving, feeling pain, feeling heat, etc. possible
* neuron: a cell (= the smallest living part of a plant or animal) that sends and receives messages to and from the brain

9b Module 9 Media

Writing (Task 1)

Lead-in

1 Work in pairs and discuss the questions.
  1 Which of these devices do you own? When did you first get them?
    - mobile phone
    - e-reader
    - laptop
    - tablet
    - games console
  2 Do you think ownership of these devices has grown or declined over the last five years? Why?

Understand the task

> EXPERT WRITING page 208

2 Read the writing task and underline the key words. What do you need to do in your answer?
  A explain why ownership of different devices has changed between 2010 and 2015
  B compare ownership of devices in your country to those in the US
  C describe the key information in the charts in your own words

The charts below show changes in the percentages of US adults owning different types of electronic device. Summarise the information by selecting and reporting the main features, and make comparisons where relevant. Write at least 150 words.

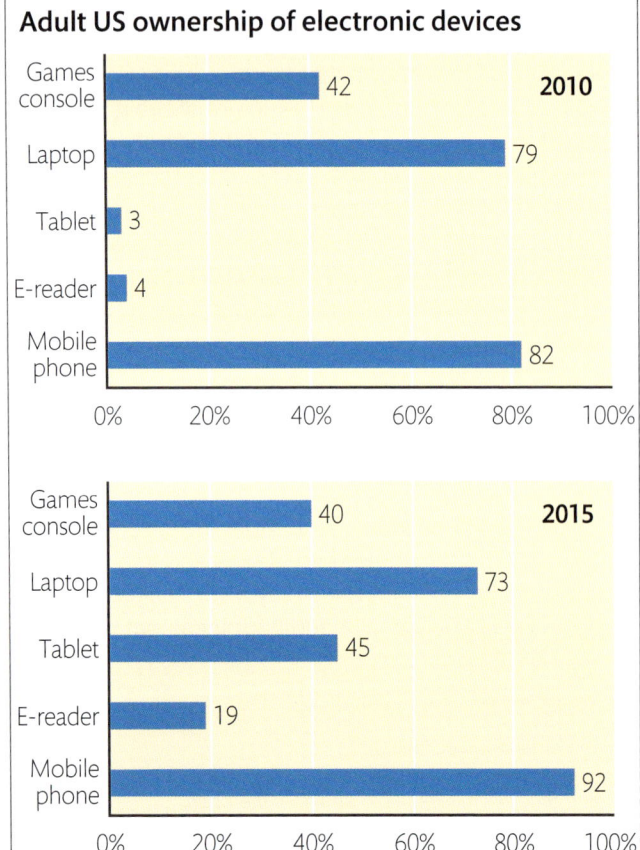

Language and content

3a Work in pairs. Look at the charts and discuss the questions.
  1 What are the main features?
  2 What differences are there between the charts?
  3 What similarities can you see?

b Read the model answer. Does the student:
  1 report the features you selected in Exercise 3a?
  2 make the same comparisons?

> The charts illustrate the proportions of adults in the USA who owned five different types of digital equipment in the years 2010 and 2015.
>
> The charts show that in 2015 a higher percentage of people owned mobile phones, e-readers and tablets than in 2010. However, ownership of laptops and games consoles declined over the period.
>
> The device that the largest number of people owned in both years was the mobile phone. Ownership rose from just over 80 percent to 92 percent. The increase in ownership was greatest for tablets. Only 3 percent had one in 2010, in comparison with 45 percent in 2015. The third device whose popularity increased in a similar way was the e-reader. Although ownership of this rose, it was the least frequently owned of all five devices in 2015.
>
> In contrast, ownership of both laptops and games consoles fell over the period. Ownership of laptops declined slightly and the fall in games console ownership was similarly small.

4a Read the model answer again and underline the words/phrases the student uses to compare and contrast data.

b Look at the words/phrases in the box for describing similarities. Which ones has the student used in the model answer?

both x and y …   in the same/a similar way   like x, y …   similarly

c Look at some more sentences describing similarities. Complete them using the words/phrases in Exercise 4b.
  1 The charts show that ownership of _____ laptops _____ games consoles fell between 2010 and 2015.
  2 Ownership of e-readers increased in 2015 _____ that ownership of mobile phones did.
  3 It is clear that ownership of games consoles is decreasing. _____ , ownership of laptops is falling.
  4 _____ e-readers, tablets became much more popular between 2010 and 2015.

148

Module 9
Media
9b

Plan your summary

5 Read the writing task below and follow these steps to plan your answer. Make notes in the table.
1 Underline the key words in the task and look carefully at the graphs.
2 Select the main features to report.
3 Think about what comparisons you can make: what differences and similarities are there?
4 Think about your introduction.
5 Think about your overview.
6 Decide how you will organise the points you want to make.

Paragraph	Notes
Introduction	
Overview	
Main body paragraph 1	
Main body paragraph 2	

The graphs below give information about ownership of some electronic devices in the USA. Summarise the information by selecting and reporting the main features, and make comparisons where relevant. Write at least 150 words.

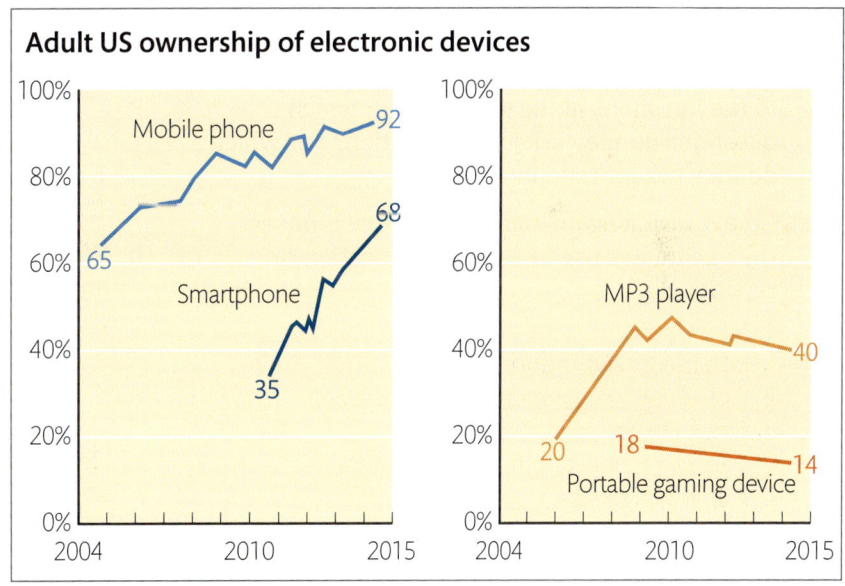

Write your summary
▶ TEST STRATEGIES page 181

6 Write your summary. Use your plan from Exercise 5.

Assess and improve

7 Check your work. Did you do these things in your answer?
1 I used my own words in the introduction.
2 I wrote an overview.
3 I selected and reported key details.
4 I made some comparisons.
5 I used some words and phrases for comparing/contrasting data and for describing similarities.

Module 9
Media

Speaking (Part 3)

Ask for clarification/repetition

1a Work in pairs. Read the test task below and discuss these questions.
   A Do you find any of the questions difficult to understand?
   B Are there any words or phrases in the questions that you are not sure about?
   C What can you do if you don't understand part or all of a question?

   1 Do you think we rely too much on technology nowadays?
   2 Do you think technology has improved education?
   3 Why do people always want to have the latest gadget?
   4 Do you think the recent rate of technological development will continue in the future?
   5 What are the differences in attitude between older and younger people towards technology?
   6 What are some of the benefits of technology in the workplace?

b 🔊 9.7 Listen to two candidates responding to the questions in the test task. For which questions do they ask for clarification? For which do they ask for repetition?

c 🔊 9.7 Listen again and complete the phrases the candidates use to ask for clarification or repetition.
   1 When you _____ 'technology', do you _____ computers and mobile phones?
   2 Could you _____ the _____ , please?
   3 Sorry, I'm not _____ what 'gadget' _____ . Could you _____ it in another _____ , please?
   4 Could you please _____ what 'rate' _____ ?
   5 Sorry, I don't _____ the _____ . Could you _____ ?
   6 Sorry, _____ you _____ repeating the question?

2 Work in pairs. Take turns to ask and answer the questions. Start your response by asking for clarification or repetition.
   1 Do you think it's true that children nowadays use too much technology?
   2 What can parents do to control the amount of technology their children use?
   3 What are the negative effects of technology in the workplace?
   4 Do you think men and women use technology for communication in different ways?

Speak fluently

3a 🔊 9.8 Listen to the male candidate's complete answers to three of the questions in Exercise 1a. Which of the following does he do to help him speak fluently?
   1 He gives opinions.
   2 He repeats himself.
   3 He gives examples.
   4 He gives different or opposing points of view.
   5 He pauses a lot.
   6 He uses discourse markers (e.g. linking words, adverbs of attitude).

b Look at audio script 9.8 on page 221 and find examples of:
   1 phrases to introduce examples.
   2 attitude adverbs.
   3 phrases to express an opinion.
   4 phrases to express different or opposing views.

Test practice

▶ TEST STRATEGIES page 182

4a Read the test task. Think about what you can say for each question.

   1 Do you think that technology has improved education?
   2 Do you think that the recent rate of technological development will continue in the future?
   3 What are some of the benefits of technology in the workplace?

b Work in groups of three. Follow the instructions and complete the test task. Then swap roles.
   • Student A: Ask the questions.
   • Student B: Answer the questions.
   • Student C: Listen and make notes in the table.

Did your partner:	Notes/Examples
have to ask for clarification or repetition? If so, did he/she use appropriate phrases?	
use adverbs to express his/her attitude?	
give reasons/examples?	
repeat him-/herself?	
pause a lot?	

Assess and improve

5 Work in the same groups. How well did your partner do? Use your notes from Exercise 4b to give him/her feedback.

10 Communicating

10a Training
- **Reading:** Identify ideas and opinions (*Yes/No/Not given*)
- **Language development:** Relative clauses
- **Vocabulary:** Communicating; Spoken communication; Non-verbal communication
- **Listening:** Connect information to a visual (Section 4: Label a diagram)
- **Speaking:** Emphasise a point (Part 2: Long turn)
- **Writing:** Write a conclusion; Concluding phrases (Task 2: Opinion essay)

10b Testing
- **Listening:** Section 4: Label a diagram; Notes completion
- **Language development:** *may/might* for possibility and permission; *could* for ability, possibility and requests
- **Vocabulary:** Intercultural communication
- **Reading:** Short-answer questions; *Yes/No/Not given*
- **Writing:** Task 2: Opinion essay
- **Speaking:** Part 2: Long turn

Lead-in

1 Think about the people you communicate with and answer the questions below. Think about:
- colleagues.
- friends.
- family.
- people you don't know but want to know.

　1 What are the different ways you usually keep in touch with these people?
　2 How often do you communicate with them?
　3 What is your favourite form of communication? Why?

2 Do you think it's easy to communicate with people from other countries? Why/Why not?

10a Being understood

Reading (Yes/No/Not given)

Before you read

1. Work in groups. How far do you think technology affects the way we communicate?

Identify ideas and opinions

2. Read the passage about technology and communication. Does it focus on the benefits or problems of using technology for communication?

3a. Work in pairs. Read the question from a test task and answer the questions below.

Do the following statements agree with views of the writer in the reading passage?

   1. Do you need to look for facts, details or opinions?
   2. Will the statements in the task follow the order of the passage?
   3. If the opinion is one that you believe to be true but is not in the passage, is the answer *Yes* or *No*?

b. Work in pairs. Read this statement and follow the steps below.

It is surprising that people today rely on new digital devices as much as they do.

   1. Underline the key words in the statement.
   2. Which part of the passage does the statement refer to? Underline it.
   3. Find words in the part of the passage you underlined which have a similar meaning to words in the statement.
   4. Read the part of the passage you underlined again. Does the statement agree or disagree with what the writer says? Which word makes this clear?
   5. Write *Yes* or *No* next to the statement.

c. Read the question in Exercise 3a again. Match the answers (1–2) with the explanations (A–B).

   1. No   2. Not given

   A. It is impossible to say what the writer thinks about this.
   B. The statement contradicts the writer's view.

d. Work in pairs. Read these statements about the second paragraph of the passage and answer the questions below.

   1. People love the experience of communicating using modern devices.
   2. Geoffrey Tumlin is a well-known writer on the topic of modern communication.

   A. The answer for statement 1 is *No*. It contradicts the information in the passage. Which words in the second paragraph tell you this?
   B. The answer for statement 2 is *Not given*. Some words from this statement are mentioned or paraphrased in the paragraph. What are they?
   C. What information from statement 2 is not mentioned in the passage?

Test training

4. Complete the test task. Remember to follow the same steps as you did in Exercises 3b and 3d.

Do the following statements agree with the views of the writer in the reading passage? Write:

YES   if the statement agrees with the views of the writer.
NO   if the statement contradicts the views of the writer.
NOT GIVEN   if it is impossible to say what the writer thinks about this.

   1. The process of email communication is complete only when the receiver has finished reading it.
   2. Only certain people are able to communicate effectively.
   3. Electronic communication is having a negative impact on face-to-face communication.
   4. Better communicators can communicate well without having to think about it.
   5. Younger people are more likely than older ones to send the same message to a lot of people.
   6. Sending a message to 20 people should require the same amount of thought as sending one to 10 people.
   7. It is important to consider the impact a message will have on people in different situations.

Task analysis

5. Work in pairs and discuss the questions.
   1. What helped you to find the correct part of the passage for each statement?
   2. Did you make sure all your *Yes/No* answers were in the passage and not your own point of view?

Discussion

6. How far do you agree with the points in the passage?

THIS WEEK

Considering modern communication

Advertisements for the latest smartphones, tablets, laptops and other gadgets say that they will make communication faster and more efficient. Naturally enough, because new technology can do so many things so easily, people have come to depend on it. But this has some unfortunate consequences.

Geoffrey Tumlin is the author of a book on the theme of communications in our contemporary world. His basic argument – that people today give too much importance to gadgets rather than each other – will surprise many people but it is strong and clear. He says the result of such dependency is that people feel dissatisfied with their experience of using these gadgets to communicate.

Electronic devices have certainly made the sending and receiving of messages much simpler than it was in the past, but there is more to communication than just hitting the 'Send' button or clicking to open a message. Real communication does not happen until the other person understands the message, and people forget about this important stage in far too many cases. Tumlin says that adding an extra step – considering whether or not the message is understood – can make a person a much more effective communicator. His argument is that most people are focusing only on efficiency when they approach the majority of their exchanges. They want to clear their inboxes and respond to new text or voice messages as soon as they come in. Similarly, they are in the habit of getting face-to-face conversations over as quickly as possible so they can move on to the next thing. They feel that they have so many communication tasks to deal with every day that they spend as little time on each one as they can and are satisfied just by crossing one more job off their to-do list.

However, meaningful and effective communication is possible only when the speaker or writer think about their goals. 'In contrast with average communicators, great communicators think carefully about what they would like to achieve rather than about what they would like to say,' Tumlin says. He makes the point that it can be very difficult for people to stop themselves from saying something, especially when they are feeling angry or upset. By making it so easy for everyone to share their thoughts and feelings, technology has encouraged them to do so. But these same emotional messages, unfortunately, are also the ones that stop them from achieving their communication goals.

One of the greatest problems with the digital age is that sending a message to lots of people is just as easy as sending a message to one person. But having a conversation with someone much older or younger than you may be different from speaking to someone your age. Similarly, a conversation with one friend is different from a discussion with 100 friends. But because all people have to do is click to send an email to all of their contacts or to post a social media message for the world to see, they think, incorrectly, that adding people to a message does not require any extra thought. Tumlin argues that communication gets much more difficult as the number of people receiving a message is increased. Including more people means there are more points of view to take into account. When people do not remember these additional viewpoints, it may mean that the other person ignores what was said or, more seriously perhaps, is upset by a thoughtless message. So before someone sends a message to a group, he or she should ask questions like, 'What's my uncle going to think about this post?' or 'I wonder how this email is going to come across to the other departments in my workplace.' Adding people complicates communication and when that is forgotten, misunderstandings will follow.

People now just use their devices without pausing to think. But these can never automatically copy all the features that traditional communication includes. Eventually, people will realise that these devices have a remarkable *potential only when used with thoughtful human *input. If people are in less of a hurry to press 'Send', they will be able to take full advantage of all the amazing opportunities for meaningful communication that the digital age can offer.

*potential: the possibility to develop or succeed in the future
*input: ideas, effort, time, money, etc. that you put into something

10a Module 10: Communicating

Language development

Relative clauses

➤ EXPERT GRAMMAR page 191

1 Read sentences A–D below and look at the parts in bold. Which one identifies or gives more information about:
   1 a person/people?
   2 a place?
   3 a thing?
   4 possession?

   A Email is the main form of communication **which is used in business settings**.
   B Having a conversation with someone **who is much older than you** is different from speaking to someone your age.
   C I prefer to work in places **where I can get access to the internet**.
   D Students **whose phones ring during class** will be asked to leave.

2a Complete the sentences with *who*, *which*, *where* or *whose*.
   1 I have a new messaging app _____ I can use without an internet connection or phone signal.
   2 I think people _____ don't use smartphones to communicate are behind the times.
   3 There are a number of places near here _____ we can sit quietly and talk.
   4 My father is the only person I know _____ still writes letters regularly.
   5 I'm receiving messages from someone _____ email address is very similar to mine.
   6 I'd like to spend some time living in a country _____ I can learn another language.
   7 This is the only mobile telephone network _____ signal is strong in my area.
   8 I've spent all morning reading the emails _____ I received while I was away.

b Tick the sentences in Exercise 2a where the relative pronoun can be replaced with *that*.

3 Join the sentences using relative clauses.
   1 Members receive important updates. They join our mailing list.
      Members who join our mailing list receive important updates.
   2 My inbox is full of emails. I've never read them.
   3 I think there should be more public places. You can get free wi-fi there.
   4 People use their phones at the dinner table. I don't like them.
   5 There are one or two authors. I always read their books.
   6 Letter writing is an important skill. People no longer develop it.
   7 There's a psychology professor at my university. His lectures are really interesting.

4a Read the text and underline the relative clauses. Circle the relative pronouns that can be omitted.

Public speaking

Making a speech is something (which) politicians do all the time and the ability to deliver a successful speech can make all the difference to a politician's career. However, it is a skill which is difficult to teach and there are many people who find public speaking a terrifying experience. But making a speech or giving a presentation is something which most of us will have to perform at some point in our lives. And although there are very few people who are natural public speakers, there are a few things which the nervous speech-maker can do to make the experience easier.

Probably the most important thing to remember is that the speech should have a clear message or aim. This could be as simple as congratulating the couple who have just got married or persuading clients to buy the product which you are trying to sell. Everything you say should aim to get the main message across. The next point to remember is to practise the speech, preferably in front of a small audience whose feedback can help improve the performance. Another useful method is the use of body language which will make the speaker look confident, for example by standing straight and making direct contact with the audience. Finally, if the speaker feels anxious on the day, there are a number of relaxation techniques which can help reduce the anxiety. To read about some of them, click **here**.

b Look at the underlined relative clauses in Exercise 4a. In which clauses can the relative pronoun be replaced with *that*?

5 Circle one extra word in each sentence.
   1 I have a couple of friends who they are doing a degree in languages and communication.
   2 He has an accent I find difficult to understand it.
   3 I've sent you the information you asked for it.
   4 There are a number of phone companies whose their sales have increased recently.
   5 There's a woman in my street who she speaks five different languages.
   6 One of the students who I live with her spends hours on her phone every evening.

6 Finish the sentences to make them true for you. Use relative clauses. Then discuss your ideas with a partner.
   1 I usually socialise *with people who have similar interests to mine.*
   2 I prefer to study in a place …
   3 I think the most difficult languages to learn are those …
   4 I am the kind of person …
   5 I usually read books …
   6 In the future we will use communication methods …

Module 10
Communicating
10a

Vocabulary

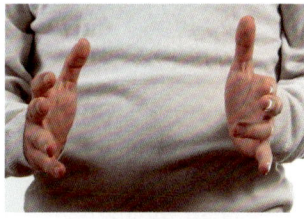
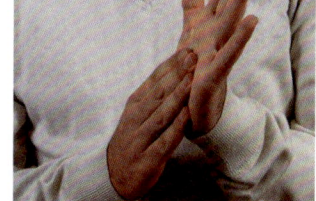
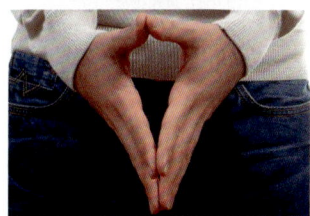
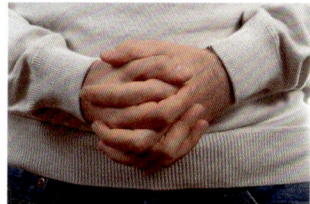

Communicating

1a Choose the correct options in *italics* to complete the sentences.

1 It's difficult to live with people who are always *arguing / promising*.
2 You shouldn't use social media to *announce / inform* important news like an engagement or birth.
3 You don't have to *confirm / reply to* every email you receive.
4 When you receive an invitation to a social event, it is polite to *announce / confirm* if you can go or not.
5 In an argument, it is much easier to *convince / repeat* someone if you have all the facts.
6 In the workplace, email is the best way to *inform / convince* everybody about what's going on.
7 If you *convince / promise* to do something, you should always do it.
8 Some people think that if they keep *repeating / announcing* the same point, you will believe them.

b Work in pairs. Do you agree or disagree with the sentences in Exercise 1a?

2 Complete the sentences with the words in the box.

effective   face to face   formal   informal   instant   verbal

1 It is common in many cultures to use _____ language with people you don't know very well.
2 A lot of my business is done by email, so I rarely meet my clients _____ .
3 You can help children develop their _____ communication skills by talking to them and encouraging them to speak more.
4 Some of these expressions are too _____ to use in a letter to your boss.
5 Communicating with people by text is not very _____ when you want to say something serious.
6 In the past, when people didn't have _____ communication like email and texting, they had to wait for days for letters to arrive.

Spoken communication

3a Choose the correct options in *italics* to complete the questions.

1 How often do you telephone you best friend to *hold / have* a chat?
2 When a large group of people are talking, do you find it easy to *make / join in* the conversation?
3 Should we encourage children to *take / have* part in family discussions?
4 Have you ever *made / done* a speech?
5 Did your school *hold / give* debates for students to discuss controversial topics?
6 How do you feel about *giving / making* an academic presentation?

b Work in pairs. Take turns to ask and answer the questions in Exercise 3a.

Non-verbal communication

4 Match the words in the box with the descriptions.

body language   eye contact   facial expression   gesture   posture   tone

1 You can communicate what you are thinking or feeling by the way you move and place your body.
2 People trust you more if you look at them directly when you're talking to them.
3 Moving your hands or head in certain ways can mean different things in different cultures.
4 The look on your face and whether you are smiling or not can tell someone a great deal about your mood.
5 You can change the sound of your voice to show people how you feel about something.
6 The position you hold your body when you're standing or sitting can indicate your attitude.

5a Complete the sentences with the verbs in the box.

give   look   lower   nod   point   raise   shake   shrug

1 It's rude to _____ your shoulders instead of saying, 'I don't know.'
2 In my country it's common for friends to _____ each other a hug when they meet.
3 You can't trust a person who doesn't _____ you in the eye when they're talking to you.
4 It is a good idea to _____ your head when someone is talking – it shows you are listening.
5 If you _____ your head, it can be a sign of sadness as well as meaning 'no'.
6 I only _____ my voice when I'm very angry.
7 If you want to talk in the library, you should always _____ your voice.
8 It's very rude to _____ your finger at someone.

b Work in pairs. Do you agree or disagree with the sentences in Exercise 5a?

Student's Resource Book > Vocabulary page 99   MyEnglishLab > 10a Vocabulary

10a Module 10
Communicating

Listening (Section 4: Label a diagram)

Before you listen 1 How much of our communication do you think depends on words?

Connect information to a visual 2a Look at the diagram below showing information from a lecture and answer the questions.
1 What do you think the lecture is going to be about?
2 What do the three different sections of the pie chart show?

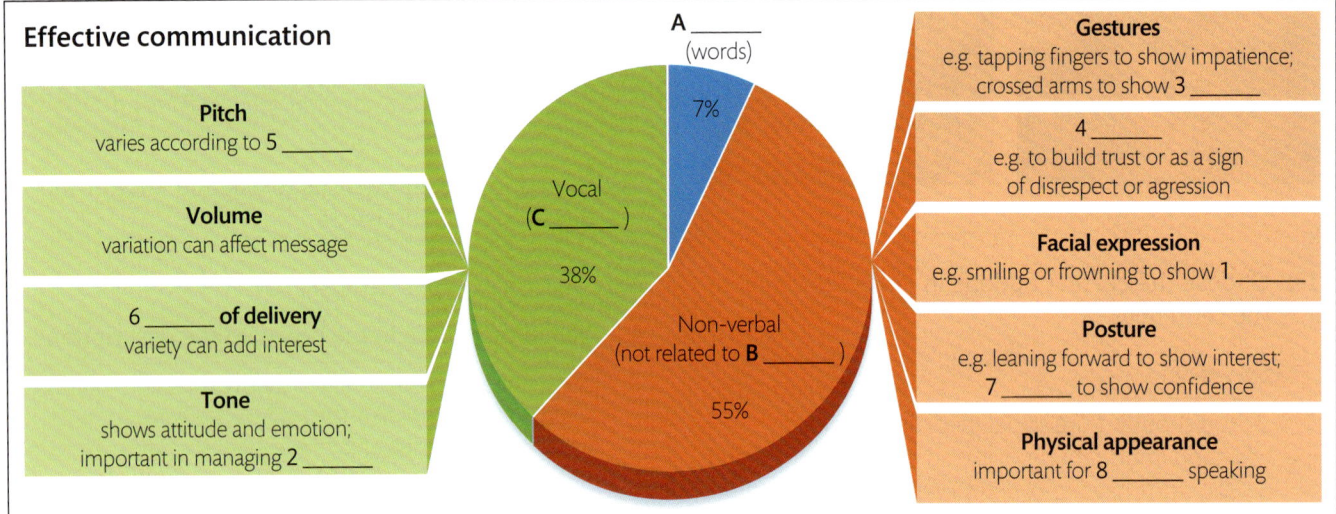

b 🔊 10.1 Listen to an extract from the lecture. What information does this extract give you?
A the details of what is in each section on the diagram
B a description of the main parts of the diagram
C an opinion on why the diagram is important

c Work in pairs. Look at gaps A–C in the diagram and answer the questions.
1 What different words might the speaker use to refer to each section of the pie chart (e.g. the smallest, the largest)?
2 What type of information goes in each gap?

d 🔊 10.1 Listen again and compete gaps A–C in the diagram. Use only one word in each gap.

Test training 3a Work in pairs. Look at gaps 1–8 in the diagram and answer the questions.
1 What does the numbering tell you about the order in which you will hear the information?
2 What type of information goes in each gap?

b 🔊 10.2 Listen to the rest of the lecture and complete gaps 1–8 in the diagram. Write no more than three words for each answer.

Task analysis 4 Work in pairs and discuss the questions.
1 Did you use the introductory part of the lecture to help you understand the diagram?
2 Did the numbering help you to follow the structure of the talk?
3 Did you hear the speaker use cues to help you know which part of the diagram she was discussing? Look at audio script 10.2 on page 221. Can you find these cues?

Discussion 5 Work in pairs. Which of the communication features on the diagram do you use most? Why?

Module 10
Communicating
10a

Speaking (Part 2)

Emphasise a point

1. Work in pairs. Look at the reasons people give for learning a language. Which do you think are the most important? Which are not so important?
   - to travel
   - to increase job opportunities
   - because it's compulsory at school
   - to help with studies
   - to discover new cultures
   - to improve your brain and memory
   - to meet new people and make new friends
   - because it's necessary in your current job

2. 🔊 10.3 Listen to a candidate doing the test task below. Which of the points in Exercise 1 does he mention?

   Describe a language you would like to learn.
   You should say:
   what the language is
   where it is spoken
   how easy or difficult you think it would be
   and explain why you want to learn this language.

3. a Work in pairs. Look at the phrases in the box for emphasising a point. Then look at audio script 10.3 on page 222. Which phrases does the candidate use?

   Don't forget that …
   I want to stress that …
   It's important to remember that …
   One of the points I'd like to highlight is that …
   The essential point is …
   The important thing (about …) is …

   b 🔊 10.4 Read this question and the answers from three different candidates below. Complete the phrases they use to emphasise a point. Then listen and check.

   What are the main differences between spoken and written communication?

   1 I suppose _____ is that written communication is much more permanent than spoken communication.
   2 One of the differences _____ is that when we speak, we are usually quite informal compared to some of the things we write.
   3 There are quite a few differences but _____ is that when we write something, we take time to think about it.

   c Work in pairs. Take turns to answer this question. Use a phrase from Exercise 3a to emphasise the most important point.

   Do you think there are differences in the way older and younger people communicate?

Pronunciation: intonation

4. a 🔊 10.5 Listen to three different people saying the same sentence. Match the speakers (1–3) with how they feel (A–C). How do you know how each person feels?

   'You speak Spanish.'
   A The speaker finds the fact surprising.
   B The speaker is not sure about the fact.
   C The speaker does not show any particular emotion.

   b Work in pairs. Practise saying the sentence in Exercise 4a expressing the different feelings A–C.

   c 🔊 10.6 Work in pairs. Practise saying this sentence. Use intonation to show the different feelings A–C. Then listen and check. Did your intonation match the speakers'?

   'You've got a new phone.'
   A surprise   B neutral statement   C unsure

Test training

5. a Look at the test task in Exercise 2 again and make notes for each point.

   b Work in pairs. Take turns to complete the test task in Exercise 2. Use your notes to help you. Try to speak for 1–2 minutes.

Task analysis

6. Work in pairs and discuss the questions.
   1 Did you talk about all the points?
   2 Did you use phrases to emphasise points?
   3 Did you use intonation to show how you felt about some points?
   4 Did you speak for 1–2 minutes?

10a

Module 10
Communicating

Writing (Task 2)

Write a conclusion

1 Work in pairs. Read the test task and discuss the questions below.

Write about the following topic.

> Face-to-face communication is better than other ways of communicating, such as email, phone calls or social networking.
> To what extent do you agree or disagree?

Give reasons for your answer and include any relevant examples from your knowledge or experience. Write at least 250 words.

1 How many paragraphs do you need?
2 Which of these two possible options (A or B) would you choose for your two main body paragraphs?
  A i reason 1 for agreeing/disagreeing
      ii reason 2 for agreeing/disagreeing
  B i reasons for agreeing
      ii reasons for disagreeing
3 Do you need to give your personal point of view?

2 Read the model answer. Which option from Exercise 1 has the student used for the main body paragraphs?

Nowadays it is no longer necessary to meet face to face in order to have a conversation. We can email, telephone, text message or share our news on a social network. However, many people argue that none of these modern means of communication is as good as talking to someone directly.

In my opinion, modern ways of communication have many advantages. Firstly, the ability to text friends and family probably means that we communicate with them more often than in the past and this has to be a positive thing. Technology like Skype means we can have close and satisfying contact with relatives in other countries. Secondly, using social media means we can make connections with new people in other cultures and this must be good for improving international understanding.

However, it is true that face-to-face communication has many advantages too. There is nothing better than spending a long evening with a friend chatting and laughing, as well as talking about more serious things. You can tell a lot about how someone is feeling through their body language and their tone of voice, and you don't get these from texts or social network posts. Moreover, you can't hug your mum or share a cup of tea with a friend when you're on the phone or the laptop.

In conclusion, I think that the different ways of communication we enjoy today are wonderful and have enriched people's lives a great deal. However, talking to someone face to face remains the best form of contact that we can have with another person.

3a Work in pairs. Read the conclusion in the model answer again and answer the questions.
  1 How many sentences are there?
  2 Does the paragraph refer back to the question?
  3 What does the student do in this paragraph?
      A lists all the points mentioned in the essay
      B summarises his/her point of view

b Work in pairs. Which of these sentences about concluding paragraphs are true?
  1 They usually give specific reasons and examples.
  2 They often refer back to the introductory paragraph.
  3 They are often longer than either of the main body paragraphs.
  4 They often use different words to summarise points made in the main body.

Concluding phrases

4 Look at the words/phrases in the box and answer the questions.

Firstly, …   In conclusion, …   In summary, …   Moreover, …
To conclude, …   To sum up, …

---

1 Which words/phrases can be used to introduce a conclusion in an essay? Underline them.
2 Which one has the student used in the model answer?
3 Can the words/phrases you underlined be used in the same way? Can they replace the one the student has used in the model answer?

5a Plan your answer to the writing task in Exercise 1. Make notes in the table.

Introduction	
Main body paragraph 1	
Main body paragraph 2	
Conclusion	

b Write your essay. Think about the questions in Exercise 3a and the sentences in Exercise 3b to help you write a good conclusion.

10b Understanding others

Listening (Section 4: Label a diagram; Notes completion)

Before you listen

1 Work in pairs. Which of these are the most important features of a country's culture?
   - the language
   - the customs and traditions
   - the food
   - the history
   - the art and literature
   - the beliefs and values
   - something else?

2 Work in pairs. You will hear part of a lecture. Read the test tasks and answer the questions.
   1 What do you think the lecture is going to be about?
   2 How does the numbering in the diagram help you understand the structure of the lecture?
   3 For questions 1–6, do you have to use all the words in the box?
   4 For questions 7–10, how many words can you use in each gap?
   5 What type of information goes in the gaps in questions 7–10?

Questions 1–6

Label the diagram below. Choose FIVE answers from the box and write the correct letters A–H next to questions 1–6.

The cultural iceberg

External or surface culture
- Visible 1 _____ and traditions
- Food, 2 _____, dress, music, literature, etc.

Internal or deep culture
- Types of 4 _____
- 5 _____ of behaviour
- Attitudes to important life issues
- Ideas about 6 _____ in society
- Hidden 3 _____ and beliefs

A rules	D roles	G communication
B values	E behaviour	H customs
C language	F culture	

Questions 7–10

Complete the notes below. Write NO MORE THAN TWO WORDS for each answer.

Understanding core values of culture
- Factors influencing core values:
  - family
  - 7 _____
  - history, religion and economics
  - the media
- These factors allow core values to continue to the 8 _____ without changing
- To learn about a culture – not enough to 9 _____ in it; have to be part of it
- Living in another culture: like a 10 _____, the deeper you go, the more you understand

Test practice

▶ TEST STRATEGIES page 178

3a 🔊 10.7 Complete the test tasks.

▶ HELP

1 The explanation comes after the answer. Listen carefully because if you miss the answer, this explanation can help you identify the correct word.
3 Listen for a word meaning 'hidden'.
4–6 Listen for cues which show you when the speaker moves from point to point.

Task analysis

4 Work in pairs and discuss the questions.
   1 Did the numbering in the diagram help you to follow the structure of the lecture?
   2 Did you hear the speaker using cues to say which part of the diagram he was talking about? Can you find them in audio script 10.7 on page 222?
   3 Did you correctly predict the type of missing words in questions 7–10?

Discussion

5 Work in pairs. Look at the diagram in the test task and discuss the questions.
   1 What are the most significant external features of your culture?
   2 How do you think the internal features of your culture are different from other cultures?

Module 10
Communicating

Language development

may/might for possibility and permission

> EXPERT GRAMMAR page 191

1 Match the sentences (1–3) with what they express (A–C).
  1 Students may not use the library computers for Skype calls.
  2 May I borrow your phone, please?
  3 We may/might all have to learn several languages in the future.

  A asking for permission
  B saying that something is possible
  C giving or refusing permission

2 Rewrite the sentences using *may* or *might*.
  1 It's possible that people will think you are rude if you don't smile.
     People may think you are rude if you don't smile.
  2 You are allowed to leave now.
  3 There's a possibility that people will all communicate online in the future.
  4 Maybe some people don't like using email.
  5 Is it OK if I use my mobile phone in here?
  6 It's possible that intercultural communication is the most important skill of all.
  7 There's a chance that everyone will need training in intercultural skills.
  8 Maybe the whole world will have to speak one language.
  9 Is it alright for me to print out a copy of this report?
  10 Students are not allowed to share notes during an exam.

could for ability, possibility and requests

3 Match the sentences (1–6) with what they express (A–C).
  1 Could you help me with this video call, please?
  2 He couldn't speak English when I first met him.
  3 Technology could change the way we communicate.
  4 Could you translate this report for me?
  5 I could hear them arguing in the meeting room.
  6 That could be the right answer.

  A saying that something is possible
  B making a polite request
  C talking about ability in the past

4a Rewrite the sentences using *could* or *couldn't*.
  1 Did you know how to use a laptop when you were five?
  2 It's possible we will be able to speak on Sunday.
  3 I was not able to speak to her face to face.
  4 Maybe we will meet up for a chat this evening.
  5 Is it possible for me to join your Skype meeting?
  6 In those days, the only way people were able to communicate over long distances was by mail.
  7 There is a possibility that technology will allow more new forms of communication.
  8 Would it be possible for us to attend the lecture later?

b What do the sentences in Exercise 4a express? Mark them *P* (possibility), *A* (ability) or *R* (request).

5 Complete the text with *may/may not* or *could/couldn't*. More than one answer may be possible.

Culture shock

Many people dream about moving to a different country to work or study, or even to retire. However, the reality of living in a different culture **1** _____ be as bright as they imagined – there are a number of difficulties which **2** _____ contribute to a feeling of culture shock. Of course, one of the main reasons for this is a problem with communication which **3** _____ make you feel weak and helpless in some situations. This **4** _____ even make you wish you were back in your home country, where you **5** _____ communicate without difficulty. Even if you are familiar with the language, you **6** _____ find that the language you learned at school is very different to that which you hear in the street. Another difficulty is the difference in culture, whether that be in the workplace, in shops or in social situations. You **7** _____ find yourself feeling very unsure about what to do in normal everyday situations. Another thing that may surprise you is differences in laws between your home country and your new one, so it's a good idea to check these before you arrive. You **8** _____ find that there are things you can do in your new country which you **9** _____ do when you were back home or things that you **10** _____ do back home that you **11** _____ do in your new country because it is against the law.

Vocabulary

Intercultural communication

1 Complete the pairs of sentences with the correct word in bold.
   1 values / beliefs
      A It can be difficult for people to get on if they have very different political _____ .
      B I think there has been a fall in the moral _____ of many young people.
   2 way of life / tradition
      A Things that are unusual in one country are just a normal _____ in another.
      B If you have a family _____ , you should try to pass it on to the next generation.
   3 cultures /customs
      A It's important to find out about local _____ before visiting another country.
      B Learning about different countries and _____ should be compulsory in all schools.
   4 manners / behaviour
      A People who use a mobile at the dinner table have no _____ .
      B Parents should reward their children for good _____ .

2 Complete the sentences with the verbs in the box.

   build   get (x2)   make   show   stay

   1 I can never _____ sense of other languages.
   2 I think it's great to _____ to know people from other countries.
   3 It's hard to _____ used to a new way of life.
   4 It's important to _____ respect for other cultures.
   5 If people can _____ relationships with people in other countries, it's good for business.
   6 Nowadays it's very easy to _____ in touch with people all round the world.

Attitudes

3a Choose the correct options in *italics* to complete the sentences.
    1 People who are *flexible / polite* find it easier to manage change in their lives.
    2 People should be *tolerant / honest* about other ways of doing things.
    3 They are very *open-minded / loyal* people, always willing to accept new ideas.
    4 Some things can take a long time, so it's necessary to be *loyal / patient*.
    5 I think it's very important to be *polite / honest* when you are travelling in other countries.
    6 It's usually better to be *honest / friendly* and say if you don't understand something.
    7 People who are *sensitive / tolerant* usually think about how the other person is feeling.

b Work in pairs. Choose four words from Exercise 3a and for each word, tell each other an example of when you behaved in this way.

c Complete the first two columns of the table.

Noun	Positive adjective	Negative adjective
flexibility	flexible	inflexible
	tolerant	
patience		
	polite	
honesty		
	friendly	
sensitivity		
	loyal	

d Complete the third column of the table in Exercise 3c with negative adjectives. Use *in-*, *im-*, *dis-* or *un-*.

4 Choose the correct options in *italics* to complete the text.

Multi-cultural understanding

In the 21st century we live in a world of fast and easy communication, which means it is becoming more common to live, work or study with people from different **1** *customs / cultures*. This experience can be beneficial because it can make us less **2** *tolerant / intolerant* and allow us to develop more **3** *sensitivity / honesty* towards people whose beliefs and **4** *values / manners* may be very different to ours. However, it would be **5** *honest / dishonest* to say that these differences are not sometimes challenging. Even if your neighbours or colleagues are very **6** *loyal / polite* and friendly, communicating every day with people who do not speak your language can test your **7** *patient / patience*. So when someone moves to a different country, it is important to adapt to the customs and **8** *traditions / cultures* of the new home. Although this may make them feel **9** *disloyal / dishonest* to their home country, being **10** *flexible / inflexible* will help them settle in more quickly. In a similar way, it is important to remember that it can take new arrivals some time to **11** *stay / get* used to their new environment. Living and working in a multi-cultural environment can really help **12** *build / make* relationships and understanding between different cultures.

Module 10
Communicating

Reading (Short-answer questions; *Yes/No/Not given*)

Before you read

1   Discuss the question in pairs.
   1   What do you think it is like working in a company which employs people from lots of different cultures?
   2   What difficulties might there be? What could the company do to deal with those difficulties?

Test practice

➤ TEST STRATEGIES page 179

2   Read the test tasks and underline the key words.

Questions 1–5

Answer the questions below. Choose **NO MORE THAN TWO WORDS** *from the passage for each answer.*

   1   What do Germans prefer more of than Americans?
   2   What do some Asian cultures think a person is failing to show if they look directly at you most of the time?
   3   What involves physical contact in some cultures but just a word in others?
   4   Who developed the idea of high- and low-context cultures?
   5   Which aspect of communication do people in low-context cultures find most effective?

Questions 6–10

Do the following statements agree with the claims of the writer in the reading passage? Write:

YES   *if the statement agrees with the claims of the writer.*
NO   *if the statement contradicts the claims of the writer.*
NOT GIVEN *if it is impossible to say what the writer thinks about this.*

   6   If employees are unhappy with communication at their workplace, they may want to stop working there.
   7   People are not always honest about how much they have understood.
   8   Low-context cultures tend to be more successful in business than high-context cultures.
   9   Many men feel uncomfortable about having a boss who is a woman.
   10 A language programme is the most important way for a company to deal with cultural diversity among its employees.

3   Work in pairs. Read the passage quickly and answer the questions.
   1   Which paragraphs do questions 1–5 relate to?
   2   Which paragraph does each of questions 6–10 relate to?
   3   What helped you to find the right part of the text?

4   Complete the test tasks.

➤ HELP

3   Look for two examples of physical contact and one specific word people use.
9   The writer mentions 'many men'. But can you find anything about this in the passage?

Task analysis

5   Work in pairs and discuss the questions.
   1   Which test task focused on facts? Which focused on opinions?
   2   Which test task did you find harder? Why?
   3   How much did the order of the statements in the second test task help you?

Discussion

6   Work in pairs. Which of the differences between cultures mentioned in the passage did you already know about? Can you think of any other examples?

162

Cultural diversity in business today

A Many businesses today employ people from a range of different cultures. This means that communication issues may sometimes cause problems. Therefore, companies need to do all they can to make sure that managers and employees are communicating effectively. Business success depends on good communications between a company and its staff.

B Poor communication practices within a company can lead to personal conflicts and unsatisfactory work, as well as an incorrect understanding of the business's goals. All of these factors can make staff unhappy and may even make them decide to leave their job. On the other hand, effective communication means there is trust between members of staff, which helps the company produce more and perform at its best.

C When considering cultural *diversity, one of the most obvious areas of difficulty is language. It is important for a business to think about how to deal with this. If it fails to do so, misunderstandings will occur. An employee may say they understand an instruction when they do not, especially if they are embarrassed or frustrated with the language problem, and this can have a very serious effect on the quality of a company's work.

D However, there are other less obvious cultural differences that affect communication. There is the issue of personal space, for example. An American is used to being about 1.5 metres away from the other person when talking to them. Germans and the Japanese may find that distance uncomfortably close while Arabs and Latin Americans may feel that that is too far apart to be friendly. The amount of eye contact that people make with one another is also different in different cultures. Europeans and North Americans feel that eye contact is necessary and shows attention and honesty, while in some Asian and Latin cultures too much eye contact can suggest a lack of respect. Greeting people can also vary a great deal between cultures. Some cultures typically shake hands when they meet, others give each other a kiss and others simply say *hello*.

E Sociologists divide cultures into two types, which they call 'high-context' and 'low-context'. High-context cultures are those that give a lot of importance to non-verbal communication, actions and contexts. In other words, body language, behaviour and relationships communicate almost as powerfully as words. Japan, India and the Middle East are examples of high-context cultures. Low-context cultures, on the other hand, emphasise the importance of language for communication and do not pay as much attention to other information. Examples of low-context cultures are the US, the UK and Germany. Neither type, of course, is better than the other; the important thing is simply to be aware of the difference in values.

F It is also important to remember that cultural differences relating to roles and status can also have an impact on communication in the workplace. For instance, different attitudes to the roles and status of men and women can affect how a male employee feels about having a female manager or how comfortable a female employee feels when a male colleague talks to her. Moreover, some cultures accept quite informal relationships between people with a different status in an organisation or between people of different ages, while others feel that younger people or those in a lower position should treat their managers or their elders in a formal, respectful way.

G It is very important for businesses with employees from a number of different countries to do all they can to make sure that communication works as well as possible. The best way for companies to do this is to provide training in cultural awareness for all members of staff. This should explain some of the differences between cultures and encourage staff to respect and be interested in all the cultures of their fellow workers. The company should, however, remember to avoid *stereotyping. A culture may have certain typical characteristics but that does not mean that such things are true of each individual. A simple way to indicate the company's respect for all its staff is for it to know when a culture has its main festivals and to allow people from those cultures time off to celebrate them. A language programme can also be very useful. This should show managers how to avoid using very difficult language when they are talking to staff with a different first language. It should teach them how to explain information simply and clearly, using pictures and diagrams whenever that is possible, to support what they are saying.

H If a business values the cultural diversity of its staff and encourages them all to understand and respect one another, the company will gain many advantages. It will not only be more productive but it will also be a happier place for all the people who work there.

*diversity: the fact of including many different types of people or things
*stereotype: when you have a fixed idea about what a particular type of person is like

Module 10
Communicating

Writing (Task 2)

Lead-in

1 Work in pairs. To what extent do you think that global communication is making people all over the world more similar? Think about these points.
- food
- clothing
- entertainment
- business

Understand the task

➤ EXPERT WRITING page 209

2 Read the writing task and underline the key words. Then choose the correct answer in the question below.

Write about the following topic.

It is almost impossible to keep our traditions in a global community.
To what extent do you agree or disagree?

Give reasons for your answer and include any relevant examples from your knowledge or experience. Write at least 250 words.

What does 'to what extent do you agree or disagree' ask you?
A if you agree or not with the statement
B how strongly you agree or disagree
C the reasons other people agree or disagree

Language and content

3 Read the model answer. Match the paragraphs (A–D) with their content (1–4).
1 reasons for agreeing
2 summing up of theme and of writer's point of view
3 reasons for disagreeing
4 brief explanation of the theme of the essay

A It is undoubtedly true that nowadays more and more people are travelling round the world. They do this not just for holidays, but also to live and work abroad. Some people are afraid that this means we will all lose our unique cultures and traditions.

B I strongly disagree with this point of view. First of all, we need to think about where we learn these traditions. We usually learn them in our family, so we get in the habit of doing what our family does every year. If we go to live in a different place, there is no doubt that it will feel strange at first. As a result, family traditions can feel even more important to us than they were when we were living in our home country.

C Another point is that people in the countries which you go to are often very interested in other countries' traditions. If we look at the example of some big cities, we can see they celebrate everyone's special days, not just those of their own country. London, for example, has big Chinese and West Indian festivals as well as English ones. In other words, people are clearly happy to take on new traditions rather than losing or forgetting their old ones.

D To conclude, it is certainly true that many people these days are moving away from their original communities and there is much more contact between people of different cultures than ever before. However, I believe that this may actually be making many traditions stronger rather than weaker.

4a Look at the words/phrases in the box for expressing certainty. Which ones has the student used in the model answer?

certainly   clearly   definitely   obviously   there is no doubt that   undoubtedly

Module 10 10b
Communicating

b Rewrite the sentences using the words in brackets.
1 It is obvious that most people want their country to keep its unique traditions. (obviously)
2 People are undoubtedly travelling more than ever before. (doubt)
3 It is certain that global communications will continue to increase. (certainly)
4 There is a definite feeling that globalisation can cause problems. (definitely)
5 It is clear that many people are worried by the thought of losing their traditions. (clearly)

Plan your essay

5 Plan your answer to the test task in Exercise 2a. Make notes in the table.

Introduction	
Main body paragraph 1	
Main body paragraph 2	
Conclusion	

Write your essay
▶ TEST STRATEGIES page 181

6 Write your essay. Use your plan from Exercise 5.

Assess and improve

7 Use the table below to check your essay.

Answering the question	
Is my answer at least 250 words long?	
Have I answered the question in the task?	
Is my opinion clear?	
Is each paragraph clearly connected to the topic?	
Have I given reasons and/or examples to support my opinion?	
Organisation	
Are there four paragraphs (an introduction, two main body paragraphs and a conclusion)?	
Have I stated the topic in my own words in the introduction?	
Do the main body paragraphs start with a topic sentence?	
Have I included supporting points after the topic sentence?	
Are the paragraphs clearly linked to each other?	
Are the sentences in each paragraph linked to each other?	
Does the conclusion summarise my opinion?	
Language	
Have I used a range of grammatical structures (e.g. tenses, modal verbs, conditionals)?	
Have I avoided using the same words lots of times?	
Have I used a range of linking words/phrases to connect ideas?	
Is my spelling correct?	
Is my punctuation correct?	
Have I checked for grammar mistakes?	

Student's Resource Book > Writing page 104

Module 10
Communicating

Speaking (Part 2)

1 Work in pairs and discuss the questions.
  1 What is the best way to learn about a different culture?
  2 Do you think you can learn about another culture without visiting the country?

2a Read the test task. Do you have to describe visiting a country or could you talk about somewhere in your country?

Describe a place where you enjoyed learning about another culture.

You should say:

  what the place is

  why you went there

  what you learned there

and explain why you enjoyed learning about this culture.

b 🔊 10.8 Listen to a candidate doing the test task in Exercise 2a. What culture did he find out about and how?

Explain manner, means and purpose

3a 🔊 10.8 Listen again and complete the phrases the candidate uses to explain manner, means and purpose.
  1 We went to Chinatown _____ get a Chinese meal.
  2 We decided to return the next day _____ explore the area more _____ .
  3 We decided _____ to find out about the history was _____ the museum there.
  4 The museum has lots of pictures and videos and it's done _____ that you really get a good idea of what it was like to be a Chinese immigrant.
  5 We asked the people in the museum for a recommendation _____ miss the best food.
  6 We only found the place _____ because it was in a little back street.
  7 You can often find out more about a culture just _____ to someone.
  8 It has really made me interested in Chinese culture _____ now I'd like to visit China.

b Complete the sentences with your own ideas. Then compare with a partner.
  1 People like to learn a language **to** …
  2 You can find out about another culture **by** …
  3 You should travel to another country **in order to** …
  4 One way to experience a different culture's food is **by** …
  5 You should do some background research on a country **so as (not) to** …
  6 It's a good idea to find out about local customs and behaviour **so that** …

Use correct stress and intonation

4a 🔊 10.9 Listen to an extract from the candidate's answer said in two different ways. Which one sounds more interesting? Why? What is different?
  A the speed
  B the way the speaker pronounces the words
  C the intonation
  D the way the speaker stresses some words

b 🔊 10.10 Look at audio script 10.9–10.10 on page 223. Listen again and underline the words the candidate stresses. Take turns to repeat, using the correct stress and intonation.

Test practice

▶ **TEST STRATEGIES** page 182

5a Look at the test task in Exercise 2a again and make notes for each point.

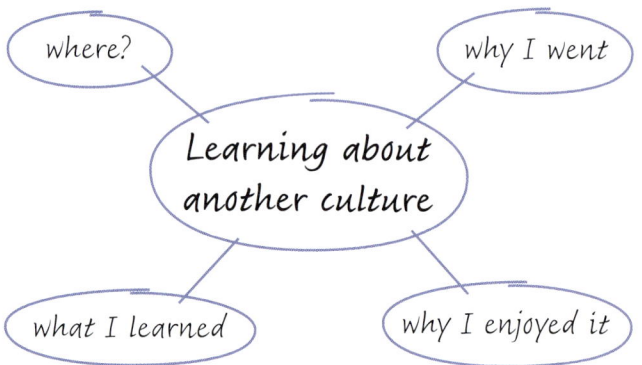

b Check your notes with a partner. Have you got enough information to talk for 1–2 minutes?

c Work in pairs. Follow the instructions and complete the test task. Then swap roles.
  • Student A: Use your notes from Exercise 5a and talk about the topic. Try to speak for 1–2 minutes. Think carefully about giving enough information to answer each point.
  • Student B: Listen and make notes in the table.

Did your partner:	Notes/Examples
talk about all the points in the task?	
use language to express manner, means and purpose?	
use phrases to emphasise any points?	
use stress and intonation to sound interesting?	

Assess and improve

6 Work in the same pairs. How well did your partner do? Use your notes from Exercise 5c to give him/her feedback.

Expert reference

	page
Module reviews 1–10	**168**
Test strategies	**178**
Expert grammar	**183**
Expert speaking: useful language	**193**
Expert speaking	**194**
Expert writing	**200**
Audio scripts	**210**

Review 1

1 Read the descriptions and complete the words/phrases. The first letter of each word is given.
   1 one section of a university where people study the same subject: d_____
   2 the most important university teacher in a department: p_____
   3 a place where you can borrow books and study: l_____
   4 a university teacher: l_____
   5 all the buildings and land of a university: c_____
   6 a room where scientists do experiments: l_____
   7 a teacher at a university that teaches one student or a small group of students: t_____
   8 a group of departments in a university, specialising in a particular subject: f_____

2 Make the positive statements negative and the negative statements positive.
   1 My university has got very good sports facilities.
   2 The library is open today.
   3 My family doesn't live near the university.
   4 I usually work at the weekends.
   5 My best friend studies the same subject as me.
   6 I don't usually go to the library in the afternoon.
   7 My tutor speaks Chinese.
   8 The buildings on campus are very modern.

3 Rewrite the sentences putting the adverbs in the correct place.
   1 I study in the library because my house is quiet. (normally, rarely)
   I normally study in the library because my house is rarely quiet.
   2 I don't get the bus but I take it when it rains. (usually, occasionally)
   3 I am the first to finish my assignments. (often)
   4 My friend is late to lectures because she gets up late. (always, always)
   5 I use the sports facilities before lectures; they are too busy later in the day. (sometimes, always)

4 Complete the text with the present simple form of the verbs in brackets.

If you are the sort of person who 1 _____ (worry) about exams, you 2 _____ (not be) alone. A recent survey shows that more than 90 percent of students 3 _____ (feel) anxious about exams and worry about what will happen if they 4 _____ (not get) the results they need. This means that many students 5 _____ (spend) so much time studying that they 6 _____ (not eat) properly and they 7 _____ (rarely / sleep). However, you 8 _____ (not have to) work 24 hours a day to pass your exams and it 9 _____ (not matter) if you give yourself a day off occasionally. In fact, rest and relaxation 10 _____ (be) very important in helping you deal with the stress of exams.

5a Rewrite the sentences using *can* or *can't*.
   1 I'm fluent in Arabic and French.
   I can speak Arabic and French.
   2 I'm good at understanding other people's problems.
   3 She's not a good cook.
   4 I'm not very good at telling people what to do.
   5 I'm finding it very difficult to write this report.
   6 I'm able to help my friends with their computer problems.

b Match sentences 1–6 in Exercise 3a with the skills in the box.

IT skills   language skills   management skills   people skills   practical skills   writing skills

6 Choose the correct options in *italics* to complete the student's responses.

What do you like most and least about your studies?

I really like 1 *producing / carrying out* research for my assignments and I quite like 2 *making / writing* essays. I find it quite difficult to 3 *do / take* notes in lectures and I don't like 4 *doing / making* exams.

Do you enjoy working with other students?

Yes, I do. I like working with my classmates to 5 *complete / make* a project or to 6 *give / have* a presentation and I find it useful to work together to 7 *produce / prepare* for a test.

What do you hope to do when you finish your course?

If I 8 *get / make* good grades in my exams, I hope to continue my studies and 9 *do / make* a post-graduate course. But I'm a bit worried in case I 10 *miss / fail* an exam.

Review 2

1 Complete the sentences with the words in the box and choose the correct options in *italics*.

after (x2)   in (x2)   out   up   with (x2)

1 It's easy to lose touch _____ your old *classmates / colleagues* after you leave school.
2 I often look _____ my sister's son; his name is Jamie and he's my favourite *nephew / cousin*.
3 It can be difficult if you don't get on well _____ your *neighbours / acquaintances* as you see them every day.
4 If you fall _____ with your *housemates / co-workers*, it can make it very difficult to continue living together.
5 My father had to bring me _____ on his own until he married my *mother-in-law / stepmother*.
6 I take _____ my *father-in-law / grandfather* – we have the same character and we look the same too!
7 I want to keep _____ touch with some of my *roommates / co-workers* when I leave my job.
8 I don't have much _____ common with my *neighbours / colleagues*, apart from working together.

2 Complete the sentences with the words in the box. There are two extra words you do not need to use.

better   fewer   greater   less   more   most   much   worse

1 My brother is the _____ confident member of the family; the rest of us are very shy.
2 I'd like to spend _____ time with my grandparents. I only see them twice a year.
3 My sister's exam results are _____ than mine because she works harder than I do.
4 There are _____ families living in our road now; all the children have grown up and moved away.
5 A _____ number of people live alone now than 20 years ago.
6 Rajesh is a much _____ driver than I am; he seems to have an accident every week!

3 Rewrite the sentences using the words in brackets. Do not change the words in brackets.

1 Marcos is shorter than his sister. (tall)
Marco _____ his sister.
2 Girls aren't as noisy as boys. (than)
Boys _____ girls.
3 Big families are not as popular these days. (popular)
Big families are _____ these days.
4 My old tutor was not as friendly as my new one. (than)
My new tutor _____ my new one.
5 No one in my family is as intelligent as my sister. (the)
My sister _____ person in my family.
6 Our new house is smaller than our old one. (not)
Our new house is _____ our old one.

4 Complete the time words/phrases in the sentences. The first letter of each word is given.

1 I see my grandparents three t_____ a w_____ – on Tuesday, Friday and Sunday.
2 I go on holiday t_____ a y_____ – once in June and once in December.
3 My family all get together o_____ a month – we have a big family celebration every three or four weeks.
4 My mother rings me several t_____ a d_____ – once in the morning and two or three times in the evening!
5 I rarely see my cousins – we live in different countries, so we h_____ ever get together.
6 I meet my old classmates from time to time; we're all very busy, so we can only see each other o_____ in a w_____ .
7 I visit my parents e_____ w_____ for a meal – every Friday night, in fact.
8 My best friend and I see each other d_____ – we usually have a coffee together every morning before work.

5 Complete the sentences with the correct form of the adjectives in brackets.

1 We can travel to other countries very _____ (easy) nowadays.
2 The world population is increasing _____ (rapid).
3 This year prices are rising _____ (steady).
4 Sadly, some people don't get on _____ (good) with their family.
5 It's difficult to complete this exercise _____ (correct).
6 I don't feel very _____ (strong) about this subject.

6 Complete the student's response with the words in the box.

celebrate   culture   days off   decorate   dress up
fireworks   gifts   invite   public holiday   takes place

Can you tell me about an important celebration in your country?

A popular celebration in my country is Diwali – it's an important part of my **1** _____ and many Indian people **2** _____ it all around the world. It **3** _____ in October or November and because it's a **4** _____ here, many places close and we have several **5** _____ work or school. One of the things we do is clean the house and **6** _____ it with lots of lights. We **7** _____ in our best clothes and **8** _____ all our family to be with us. Everyone gives each other special **9** _____ and sweets. My favourite part is when we go outside in the evening and watch the **10** _____ in the sky.

Review 3

1 Complete the paragraph from a student's essay with the words in the box. There are three extra words you do not need to use.

career   conditions   employment   living   opportunities
promotion   repetitive   rewarding   salary   satisfaction
voluntary

You can only enjoy your job if you earn a lot of money. Do you agree or disagree?

There are many jobs that give you job **1** _____ but which are not very well-paid. For example, a **2** _____ which involves looking after people like nursing is probably very **3** _____ but does not have a high **4** _____ compared to other jobs. People who do **5** _____ work do not get paid at all but usually enjoy what they do. In my opinion, people who make their **6** _____ doing challenging jobs probably enjoy these more than people who do boring and **7** _____ work. People are also more likely to enjoy their jobs if they have **8** _____ to do further training, learn new skills and improve themselves.

2 Match the sentence beginnings (1–6) with the endings (A–F). Then choose the correct modal verbs in *italics* to complete the sentences.

1. I wear what I like to work
2. When I finish my apprenticeship, I start full-time work
3. I always have my lunch in the cafeteria
4. You have all the necessary qualifications for that job
5. His job involves a lot of paperwork
6. It's easy to make mistakes in an email
7. I'm working nights at the moment
8. I do a lot of business with international customers

A. so I often *have to / must* travel overseas.
B. because we *mustn't / don't have to* wear a uniform.
C. so I *need to / should* sleep during the day.
D. so you *should / have to* always check it carefully before you click 'Send'.
E. because we *mustn't / don't have to* eat at our desks.
F. so you *should / don't have to* think about applying for it.
G. so I *mustn't / don't need to* worry about looking for a job.
H. and he *has to / should* write a long report every week.

3 Complete the sentences with the present simple or present continuous form of the verbs in brackets.

1. I _____ (not like) my job because I _____ (have to) work at weekends.
2. I _____ (live) with my parents at the moment because I _____ (look for) my first job.
3. My brother _____ (have) good qualifications but he _____ (find) it difficult to get a good job at the moment.
4. I _____ (work) near my home, so I _____ (walk) to work every day.
5. She _____ (work) in a different office this week, so she _____ (stay) with her cousin in London.
6. I _____ (know) he's not in his office at the moment because he _____ (meet) a customer.
7. I _____ (study) medicine because I _____ (want) a job that is rewarding and well-paid.
8. My job _____ (become) harder because we _____ (get) a lot more customers.

4 Replace the underlined words/phrases in the student's responses with the words/phrases in the box. There are two extra words you do not need to use.

applicant   application   bonus   employee   employer
experience   interviewer   overtime   pay rise   promotion
shift work   working conditions

How can you prepare for a job interview?

It's important that you prepare well for an interview as you won't be the only **1** candidate for the job. You should find out everything you can about the **2** company before you go. You should also look at the **3** form you completed carefully because the **4** person asking the questions will probably ask you about this. You can also practise talking about your skills and **5** practical knowledge and why you want the job.

What are some of the important things a candidate should find out before accepting a job?

First of all, you need to find out about the hours of work – if the job is full- or part-time or if you have to do **6** days and nights. You can also ask if you can do **7** extra hours. It's important to find out about the **8** environment in which you will work and also what opportunities there are for training and **9** moving to a more important position. Finally, you can ask about money and whether there is a pension or **10** extra money scheme.

Review 4

1a Read the symptoms and complete the illnesses and injuries. The first and last letters of each word are given.
1. being sick, stomachache: f_____d p_____g
2. a painful purple mark on your skin: b_____e
3. pain in the chest, difficulty breathing: h_____t a_____k
4. difficulty breathing, a cough: a_____a
5. a runny nose, sore eyes, itchy skin: a_____y
6. feeling tired and worried: s_____s
7. an itchy red spot on your skin: mosquito b_____e
8. a high temperature, aching legs: f_____u

b Choose the correct options in *italics* to complete the possible treatments (A–D). Then match them with four of the illnesses and injuries (1–8) in Exercise 1a.

A First I had to **1** *have / take* surgery. Now I make sure I **2** *stay in / keep on* shape by doing sport to **3** *treat / prevent* it happening again. I also try to **4** *make / have* a balanced diet.

B I have to **5** *go / get* for regular medical check-ups and the doctors **6** *make / give* me a prescription to help with my symptoms. I hope that one day they'll **7** *treat / find* a cure for my condition.

C The best way to **8** *treat / have* this infection is to stop eating, rest and drink plenty of water. If it's very serious, you have to **9** *take / make* antibiotics.

D I didn't see a doctor but I talked to my friend about my problems, which made me **10** *keep / feel* a little better. She also advised me to **11** *get / take* plenty of sleep and to **12** *do / have* regular exercise.

2 Find and correct the mistakes in six of the sentences.
1. I'd like to get a few more information about the national parks near here.
2. You should only eat a little sugars a day because it's bad for your teeth.
3. There are too many endangered animal, and people are not doing enough to protect them.
4. Some beautiful natural places are ruined because too much people visit them.
5. I'm not sure how many money the government should spend on protecting the natural world.
6. I don't think we have not enough time to go to the beach.
7. Do you know how many tigers there are left in the wild?
8. Many people have health problems because they don't do enough exercise.

3 Complete the student's response with the past simple or past continuous form of the verbs in brackets.

Describe a health problem you had. You should say:
  what it was
  how you got this health problem
  what you did to get better
and explain how you felt about this health problem.

I'm usually very healthy but last year I **1** _____ (suffer) a serious injury to my arm while I **2** _____ (play) tennis. Fortunately, I **3** _____ (not break) it and at first I **4** _____ (not think) it was too bad although it was very painful. I **5** _____ (not go) to the doctor and I just **6** _____ (take) some medicine to help with the pain. However, after a few weeks my arm **7** _____ (not get) better. It was still very painful and I **8** _____ (find) it difficult to use it to do anything. I went to the doctor, who decided I **9** _____ (need to) have surgery. It **10** _____ (be) difficult after the surgery because I couldn't move my arm while I **11** _____ (recover), so my family **12** _____ (have to) help me do everything.

4 Complete the paragraph from a student's essay with the words in the box.

endangered farm fish fur habitat hunt ocean protect rainforest species

What are the effects of human activity on wildlife?

Sadly, humans are destroying the natural **1** _____ of many animals. For example, humans cut down trees in the **2** _____ so that they can use the land to **3** _____ and produce more crops. This means that some **4** _____ of animals, birds and insects that live there are **5** _____ because they have nowhere to live. In addition, some people **6** _____ wild animals for their meat or **7** _____, or even just for sport. Humans also produce a lot of rubbish, which often ends up in the **8** _____ and can affect the sea life, and pollution in rivers can kill all the **9** _____ . It is important that governments introduce policies to **10** _____ the natural world and the wildlife that lives there.

Review 5

1 Read the descriptions and complete the words. The first letter of each word is given.
   1 a journey or holiday by ship, visiting different places: c_____
   2 cheap accommodation, often for young people or students: h_____
   3 a type of holiday where the travel company organises everything: p_____ holiday
   4 you stay in this when you go camping: t_____
   5 visiting interesting places as a tourist: s_____

2 Complete the student's responses with the prepositions in the box.

   around (x3) by off on (x2) out to with

   Do you often travel abroad?

   Not very often because I don't like flying – especially when the plane takes 1 _____ . I sometimes travel to Thailand because I can get 2 _____ Bangkok 3 _____ train. Last year I had to go there 4 _____ business but I also had time to look 5 _____ the city.

   What would you recommend a visitor to your country should do?

   My country gets lots of visitors from all 6 _____ the world. It's well-known for its food and so I would recommend that they eat 7 _____ as much as they can and try the local food. The main cities are very busy and public transport is always crowded 8 _____ people, so the best way to get 9 _____ is probably 10 _____ foot.

3 Complete the paragraph from a student's essay on environmental problems with the words in the box.

   air extreme floods fuels global heavy polar pollution temperatures toxic

   The number of 1 _____ weather events in many countries is increasing every year. For example, some regions are experiencing far more 2 _____ rain than in the past, leading to 3 _____ in many areas. Average 4 _____ are also changing, with warmer winters and hotter summers. This 5 _____ warming is causing the 6 _____ ice caps to melt, which is having a harmful effect on people and wildlife in some regions. Many cities have very poor 7 _____ quality caused by the burning of fossil 8 _____ from the increasing number of cars on the roads and industrial air 9 _____ . Factories also produce a great deal of poisonous chemicals and other 10 _____ waste which can seriously affect health.

4 Complete the student's response with the correct form of the verbs in brackets.

   Describe the weather in your country. You should say
     what the weather is like at different times of year
     what your favourite season is
   and explain how the weather affects your mood.

   In my country we generally have very hot summers, but you can usually expect 1 _____ (have) quite a bit of rain during the summer too. It can 2 _____ (be) quite cold in winter but it doesn't get cold enough 3 _____ (snow), except in the mountains. Actually, instead of 4 _____ (get) snow, we usually have very heavy rain at this time of year. That's why I don't like winter – it makes me 5 _____ (feel) depressed, especially when it gets dark so early too. I prefer 6 _____ (stay) inside when it's like that. I always look forward to summer 7 _____ (come). When it gets hotter, I enjoy 8 _____ (go) to the beach near my home. I love the summer – 9 _____ (spend) time outdoors is my favourite thing and when it's hot and the sun is shining, it's easy 10 _____ (forget) the winter!

5 Choose the correct options in *italics* to complete the sentences.
   1 As we drove *through / between* the city, we noticed that there was a lot of rubbish *in / on* every street corner.
   2 They usually collect our rubbish *in / on* Monday morning but this week they did it *in / on* the afternoon.
   3 You can tell how polluted the city is from the clouds of black smoke rising *above / under* the trees and all the rubbish *in / on* the river.
   4 *At / In* the past people were less concerned about environmental issues but *in / on* recent years they are taking more notice.
   5 In the desert, temperatures are very high *at / in* midday but they fall very quickly *at / in* the evening.
   6 We get a lot of noise from the train station which is *at / on* the end of the road and the bus station which is *next to / between* it.
   7 We rarely go on holiday *in / on* autumn, but last year we went on a six-day cruise *on / at* my birthday, which is *in / on* October.

Review 6

1 Complete the text with the words in the box. There are two extra words you do not need to use.

bitter calories carbohydrate dairy fattening fresh
ingredients minerals nutritious processed
ready-made weight

Studies show that there is a clear link between a country's diet and the health of its population. In many western countries, people eat a lot of fast or **1** _____ food for convenience. However, such food is not very **2** _____ and does not have enough of the necessary vitamins and **3** _____ we need to stay healthy. On the contrary, junk food is often full of salt and sugar, and contains far too many **4** _____ , which can lead to people putting on **5** _____ and suffering health problems. In contrast, people are generally healthier and live longer in countries like Greece and Spain, where there is a diet high in **6** _____ fruit and vegetables and where they usually have home-cooked food rather than buying **7** _____ meals from the supermarket. Although many people think that food like rice and pasta is **8** _____ , the Japanese, who live longer than any other country, eat this type of **9** _____ every day. And although some people find Indian food too spicy, chillies and ginger and some of the other **10** _____ in Indian dishes can protect against certain diseases.

2 Match the sentence beginnings (1–6) with the endings (A–F). Then complete the sentences with the correct form of *be going to* and the verbs in brackets.

1 The reviews of the new Chinese restaurant are not very good,
2 I'm eating too much junk food at the moment,
3 They don't eat meat,
4 Jenna's trying to lose weight,
5 They're worried about their health,
6 I'm not a very good cook,

A so I _____ (make) a vegetarian dish for them.
B so my flatmate _____ (help) me prepare the meal.
C so we _____ (not eat) there.
D so they _____ (go) on a diet.
E so I _____ (put on) weight.
F so she _____ (not have) dessert.

3 Read the descriptions and complete the words. The first letter of each word is given.

1 you need this to return an item to a shop: r_____
2 this person serves you in a shop: s_____ a_____
3 a large shop where you can buy almost anything: d_____ s_____
4 where you go to buy flowers and plants: f_____
5 you can buy newspapers and magazines here: n_____
6 where you try on clothes in a shop: f_____ r_____
7 you ask for this at the end of a meal in a restaurant: b_____
8 where you go to buy medicines: c_____

4 Choose the correct options in *italics* to complete the student's response.

Describe a shop you often go to. You should say
  what it sells
  how often you go there
and explain what you like about it.

A shop I often go to in my town is the bookshop. I don't often shop **1** *on / at* the high street as I do most of my shopping online but I really like this shop, so I go there a lot – probably every month. They have a good range of books and if something is not **2** *on / in* stock, they can order it for you. It's not very cheap and I can't always **3** *afford / pay* to buy anything, so sometimes I just **4** *browse / serve* and see what new books there are. You can't really buy anything **5** *at / on* a discount like you can online, but occasionally they have new books **6** *on / in* special offer and they have a large section of cheap **7** *antique / second-hand* books. One of the things I like about this shop is that they give very good service to all their **8** *assistants / customers* and you can always take something **9** *back / up* if you change your mind, which is more difficult to do if you **10** *order / offer* online.

5 Complete the responses with the correct form of *will* or *be going to* and the verbs in brackets.

What are your plans for tonight?

A I **1** _____ (finish) my essay first and then my flatmate **2** _____ (cook) my favourite meal for me.
B My brother **3** _____ (take) me to the cinema and afterwards we **4** _____ (probably / go) for something to eat.
C I'm feeling very tired, so I **5** _____ (have) something to eat and then I **6** _____ (go) to bed.

What are your plans for the future?

A I'm not sure at the moment. I **7** _____ (take) my exams in December and then I think I **8** _____ (take) a holiday before I decide what to do next.
B I **9** _____ (start) looking for a job. There aren't many jobs in my field, so it **10** _____ (not be) easy.
C I **11** _____ (visit) my sister in France; she invited me to stay for the summer. I hope I **12** _____ (be able to) travel around a bit and see some of the country.

Review 7

1a Complete the sentences with the past simple form of a suitable verb. The first letter of each verb is given.
1. They stopped him leaving the store and a_____ him of taking £500 worth of goods.
2. The judge s_____ him to prison for stealing from a number of houses in the local area.
3. A number of attacks on local residents t_____ place in the streets this year, with the criminals taking money and mobile phones.
4. Yesterday the police c_____ the man who stole my car.
5. The men c_____ a number of crimes in the area, including stealing money from banks and post offices.

b What crimes do the sentences in Exercise 1a describe?

2 Complete the student's responses with the words in the box.

community concert health leisure public (x2)
retirement town

What facilities does your town have?

We have the usual **1** _____ buildings like schools and hospitals. In the main square we have the **2** _____ hall – it's where they have government offices and you can get married there too. Next to it is a beautiful **3** _____ hall – but I don't often get to go inside because tickets are so expensive. We also have a big modern **4** _____ centre, which opened last year - my mum's a doctor and she works there.

Is your town a good place for young people?

Actually, there are probably more old people living in my town – we have lots of **5** _____ homes. But I suppose it is quite good for young people. We have a lot of **6** _____ spaces like parks where young people can meet, and there is also a new **7** _____ centre which is great if you like sport. I think there are also youth groups and clubs that meet at the **8** _____ centre but I have never used them.

3 Complete the text with the words in the box. There are two extra words you do not need to use.

care council crowded involvement leisure lifestyle
public residents rural urban

People who live in a town or city probably have access to more facilities than those who live in a(n) **1** _____ community. These include not only shops, but also public buildings like schools and health **2** _____ facilities. Many people living in **3** _____ communities find it difficult to imagine what it is like to live in a small village with limited facilities. Even if there is a shop in the village, it probably only sells essential items, so **4** _____ have to travel to do most of their shopping. Unless they have their own car, they have to rely on **5** _____ transport and they may also have to travel some distance to see a doctor. However, a rural **6** _____ does have some advantages; a village is less **7** _____ and noisy and generally safer than a city. In addition, there is often a greater sense of **8** _____ in the local community.

4 Match the sentence beginnings (1–6) with the endings (A–F). Then complete the conditional sentences with the correct form of the verbs in brackets.
1. Transport services won't improve
2. You are more likely to know your neighbours
3. When my grandmother is ill,
4. Unless more people use it,
5. If you witness a crime,
6. If a town doesn't have good facilities,
7. A community needs good health care facilities

A the community centre _____ (close).
B if you _____ (live) in a small rural community.
C when there _____ (be) many older people living there.
D young people _____ (not want) to stay there.
E she _____ (travel) 15 km to the nearest doctor.
F unless the council _____ (spend) more money on them.
G it _____ (be) important to report it to the police.

5 Find and correct one mistake in each sentence.
1. I will feel safe in my town even when I'm at home alone.
2. I don't stay here unless I can find a good job.
3. If the council closes the community centre, I am very angry.
4. Our community works best unless all the residents work together.
5. My neighbours always help me if I will need them.
6. Crime will increase unless there is more facilities for young people.
7. When you live in a city, you usually will have access to good public facilities.
8. If I'll manage to get a better job, I'll rent a bigger flat in the centre.

Review 8

1 Complete the student's response with the verbs in the box.

> beat do give go lose make play score support work

Describe your favourite sport. You should say
  what the sport is
  how often you play or watch it
  who you play or watch it with
and explain why it is your favourite sport.

I love sport and I spend a lot of time playing or watching it. I 1 _____ swimming regularly, I 2 _____ out in the gym twice a week and I also 3 _____ a martial art called aikido. But I think my favourite sport is football, although I don't actually 4 _____ it any more. I was in the football team at school but I had to 5 _____ it up because I injured my back quite badly. However, I watch it all the time, either on TV or I go to matches. I 6 _____ my local team and I try to watch them play whenever I can. Of course, it's much easier to do that when they are playing at home but sometimes I 7 _____ the effort to travel to an away match too. I usually go to matches with my cousin who is a big fan too. We both get very upset when the team 8 _____ , but at the moment they are doing really well – last week they 9 _____ a much stronger team when they managed to 10 _____ three goals in the last ten minutes. It was very exciting – that's why I love football.

2a Complete the paragraph from a student's summary with the present perfect form of the verbs in brackets.

According to the table, the number of people taking regular exercise 1 _____ (increase) significantly in the last ten years, although numbers for some individual sports 2 _____ (fall). For example, team sports like football and hockey 3 _____ (see) a decrease in numbers and the number of people going to the gym regularly 4 _____ (also / go down) slightly. This could be because gym membership 5 _____ (become) more expensive in recent years. However, sports which do not require expensive fees or equipment, like running, 6 _____ (rise) in popularity. One sport that is becoming increasingly popular is cycling; more than 200,000 people 7 _____ (take up) this activity during the last decade, particularly in urban areas, where cycle use 8 _____ (grow) by 48 percent.

b Cross out the option in *italics* that is not possible in each sentence.

1 I've *recently / just / before* taken up rugby.
2 I haven't been to the gym *never / recently / since last year*.
3 Has the game finished *yet / just / already*?
4 We've *never / before / just* beaten a stronger team.
5 I've played baseball *ever / for ages / before*.
6 Have you *so far / ever / recently* played table tennis?
7 We've *already / just / yet* scored 20 points.
8 I haven't won a match *ever / before / lately*.

3 Read the descriptions and complete the words. The first letter of each word is given.

1 this protects your head when you're cycling: h_____
2 you use this to hit the ball in tennis: r_____
3 athletes run around this: t_____
4 the people who watch a sporting event: s_____
5 this is where a football match takes place: p_____
6 this person trains an athlete or a team: c_____
7 you need this to play golf: c_____
8 you wear this on a boat so that you are safe if you fall into the water: l_____ j_____
9 this is where you play tennis: c_____
10 this person makes sure football players follow the rules: r_____

4a Complete the sentences with *a*, *the* or – (no article).

1 Playing football has taught me many things, including _____ importance of following the rules.
2 When I was _____ teenager, I almost let my classmates make me give up sport.
3 I can't make myself train every day like _____ professional sportspeople do.
4 To be successful at sport, you need to have _____ confidence in your ability.
5 Taking part in _____ sport like football shows employers that you can work with others.
6 Even if you can't be _____ champion, you should always aim to beat your own time in every race.

b Complete the compound nouns that the sentences in Exercise 4a describe.

1 _____ lessons
2 peer _____
3 _____ discipline
4 self _____
5 team _____
6 personal _____

Review 9

1 Replace the underlined verbs/phrases in the student's responses with the correct form of the phrasal verbs in the box.

back up   come on   come out   flick through   go into
look up   pop up   print out   set up

Where do you usually get the news from?

I get most news from social media because you can see a story as soon as it **1** <u>appears</u>. I sometimes listen to the radio news if it **2** <u>starts</u> when I'm in the car. I don't usually read newspapers although sometimes I **3** <u>quickly read</u> them at the weekend. I suppose newspaper articles do **4** <u>describe</u> more detail but I don't have time to read them.

Have you ever taken a course to improve your computer skills?

No, but I often ask my sister to help me with something because she's a computer expert. For example, I got a new laptop recently and she showed me how to **5** <u>make</u> it <u>ready to use</u>; she also did something to stop those annoying adverts from **6** <u>appearing</u> on my screen all the time. She's always telling me to **7** <u>make copies of</u> my files but I always forget!

What device do you use for browsing the internet?

I use my smartphone for most things – it's useful if I want to **8** <u>search for</u> something quickly when I'm out. When I'm at home, I usually use my laptop but if I want to read an article on the internet, I usually **9** <u>make a copy of</u> it <u>on paper</u> because I find it difficult to read on a screen.

2 Read the definitions and complete the words. The first letter of each word is given.

1 a webpage where a person writes regularly about topics that interest them or recent events: b_____
2 the title of a newspaper article, printed in large letters at the top: h_____
3 newspapers and magazines: p_____
4 a small device or tool that does something useful: g_____
5 the sets of programs that tell a computer how to do a particular job: s_____
6 a special sign that is used to show an emotion, especially in text messages and on the internet: e_____
7 a newspaper with small pages, a lot of photographs and not much serious news: t_____

3 Choose the correct options in *italics* to complete the paragraph from a student's summary.

Over the last ten years, the number of people using social media to access news **1** *increased / has increased* steadily, with significantly more people using this method now compared to a decade **2** *yet / ago*. However, **3** *for / since* 2006 the two different age groups have shown slight differences. In 2012 there **4** *was / has been* a small fall in the number of people under 40 using social media to access their news. **5** *For / Since* the last four years, numbers in this age group have remained steady. In comparison, the number of over 40s who use social media to access news **6** *rose / has risen* considerably each year until 2014. **7** *For / Since* then, although figures in this age group **8** *continued / have continued* to grow, it **9** *was / has been* at a much slower pace; the older age group has not **10** *yet / already* reached the level of the younger one.

4 Complete the paragraph from a student's essay with the words in the box.

app   comment   digital age   effective   follow
informative   journalism   media   press   update

Compare the advantages and disadvantages of traditional media and social media for communicating news.

Although we live in the **1** _____ , I believe all forms of mass **2** _____ have their advantages and disadvantages. One obvious advantage of social media is that it can **3** _____ the news continuously and this means people can use a(n) **4** _____ on their phone or tablet to **5** _____ a news story as it happens; they can't do this with traditional media. I also think social media is more **6** _____ at involving people in the news because it allows them to **7** _____ on news stories and give their opinion. On the other hand, the traditional **8** _____ is usually more detailed and **9** _____ than social media, and you are more likely to find serious **10** _____ in a newspaper article.

5 Find and correct the mistakes in eight of the sentences.

1 Not everybody are able to use a computer confidently.
2 Neither printer are working today.
3 I read lots of articles about this subject but only a number of them were useful.
4 Is there everything I can do to stop these pop-up adverts?
5 Both Sandra and I buy a newspaper but she rarely reads her.
6 Each of these two apps has the same function.
7 Unfortunately, I have none paper, so I can't print this out.
8 That tabloid is famous for it's unbelievable stories.
9 Every friend of mine have a smartphone.
10 Both of my parents are journalists and work for the local newspaper.

Review 10

1 Match the sentence beginnings (1–7) with the endings (A–G) and join them with *who, which, where* or *whose*. Then choose the correct options in *italics* to complete the sentences.

1 I have a very shy friend who D
2 That's a really nice café
3 I have some good advice for anyone
4 There's a lecturer at my college
5 Leaning forward and nodding are gestures
6 There is one part of the library
7 There are many students in my class

A gets nervous when they have to *make / do* a speech.
B like *giving / holding* debates about various issues.
C you are not allowed to *raise / rise* your voice at all.
D finds it difficult to *see / look* other people in the eye.
E body language when he *gives / makes* a lecture is very funny.
F you can use when *taking / having* part in a discussion.
G I often go to *do / have* a chat with my friends.

2 Complete the student's responses with one word in each gap. The first and last letters of each word are given.

What form of communication do you use most?

Nowadays I suppose the form of communication I use most is probably **1** i_____t messaging and texting. This is definitely the quickest way but one thing I don't like is that people expect you to **2** r_____y to a message immediately. I definitely don't like using this type of communication to **3** a_____e important news – I think if you want to **4** i_____m people of an important event, you should telephone them or even send them a more **5** f_____l letter.

3a Choose the correct options in *italics* to complete the sentences.

1 I *couldn't / mightn't* attend the meeting because I was ill.
2 You *may / might* not ask questions until the presentation is finished.
3 *Might / Could* you explain what this expression means, please?
4 If you speak too quickly, they *may / could* not understand you.
5 He was very upset but he *couldn't / mightn't* tell us what the problem was.
6 If you are very traditional, you *might / might not* find it difficult to get used to a modern lifestyle.

b What do the sentences in Exercise 3a express? Write *A* for *ability*, *PO* for *possibility*, *PE* for *permission* or *R* for *a request*.

4 Rewrite the sentences using the correct form of *may, might* or *could*.

1 It is possible that this translation is incorrect.
2 I wasn't able to understand what he was talking about.
3 Perhaps that gesture means something different in Europe.
4 You are not allowed to use a dictionary in the exam.
5 Is it possible for me to join in the discussion?
6 Perhaps they don't want to talk to us.
7 There's a chance that our beliefs are going to change in the future.
8 Did you know how to write like that at the start of the course?

5 Complete the student's response with the words/ phrases in the box.

custom   friendliness   get to know   get used
keep in touch   manners   polite   show respect
traditions   way

Describe a foreign culture that you like. You should say
what culture it is and how you know about it
what differences there are between that culture and your own
and explain why you like that foreign culture.

I'm interested in Japanese culture and I know a little about it because last year I spent a month in Japan. I stayed with the family of a friend who I've tried to **1** _____ with since I met her a few years ago. It was good to **2** _____ her family and find out about their **3** _____ of life. One of the differences I noticed is that Japanese people bow to each other all the time. Another thing they do is use the word 'san' after a name – I think it's to **4** _____ to someone and, in fact, they always seem to be very **5** _____ . Of course, they use chopsticks when they eat, which was difficult for me, but I soon managed to **6** _____ to it. Another difference is that you shouldn't eat or drink while walking in the street – they consider it bad **7** _____ . Another Japanese **8** _____ is that you have to take off your shoes when you enter the house. The thing I like most about Japanese culture is their **9** _____ to guests and I also love some of their **10** _____ – particularly their famous tea ceremony.

Test strategies

Listening Paper

The **Listening Paper** tests your ability to understand spoken English. The test is approximately 30 minutes, with 10 minutes at the end to transfer your answers from the question paper to the answer sheet. There are four different recordings with ten questions each. There will be more than one task type for each recording. You will hear each recording only once. You must write in pencil.

General advice

> **DO** use the time given to read any headings and the next set of questions.
>
> **DO** use the questions to help you predict what the recording will be about and what the answers might be. This will help you focus on the recording when you listen.
>
> **DO** listen very carefully to the introduction because it gives you more information about what you will hear.
>
> **DON'T** panic if you miss an answer. Forget that question and move on to the next one so you do not miss that.
>
> **DO** listen carefully for signposting language (*the first factor*, *the second reason*, etc.) so you know when the speaker is moving on to next question.
>
> **DON'T** worry if you don't understand some words. You may not need to know them to answer the question.
>
> **DON'T** spend time checking answers you have already written down. You can do this when transferring your answers to the answer sheet.
>
> **DO** make sure you transfer your answers to the answer sheet carefully so you do not lose points by writing an incorrect number, letter or word.
>
> **DO** spell words correctly or your answers will be marked wrong. You can write in small letters or capital letters.

Gap-fill tasks (sentence/summary/form/notes completion) and short-answer questions

In these listening tasks, there will be sentences, a summary, a form or notes with gaps. You need to complete each gap with a word/words or a number from the recording. With short-answer questions, there are questions and you need to write down words from the recording to answer them.

Before you listen

- Read the instructions to find out how many words or numbers you can write in each gap (e.g. *NO MORE THAN TWO WORDS*).
- Read the sentence, summary, form, notes or question and think about what type of information goes in each gap. Decide what part of speech it is (noun, verb, etc.). Think about key words you need to listen for.
- If there is a box of options given to you, look at those options and think about which words could fit which gap.

While you listen

- Follow the information you have in the sentence, summary, form, notes or questions. Listen for key words or other ways of expressing these. Remember to write the exact word/words that you hear on the recording in each gap on the question paper as you listen.
- Write your answer quickly and then move on to the next gap. Don't worry about spelling at this stage. Remember that the word should be exactly as it is on the recording and must not be changed.
- If you choose your answers from a box of options, remember that these words may appear in the recording but not all will be the correct answers.

After you listen

- Read the sentences, summary, table and notes in full to check that the meaning and grammar of the words fit correctly. For short-answer questions, check that the words answer the questions correctly.
- When the recording of the whole test has finished, write your answers on the answer sheet.
- Check your spelling because if you spell a word incorrectly, it will be marked as wrong. You can write numbers as a number (*2*) or a word (*two*).

Multiple choice

There are three types of multiple-choice listening tasks. In the first, you read a question or sentence prompt and choose one correct answer or ending from three options A–C. In the second, you have a question and choose one correct image such as a diagram or chart. In the third, you have a question and choose more than one answer from a set of options.

Before you listen

- Read the instructions so you know how many options you need to choose.
- Read the questions or sentence prompts and options and underline the key words. This will give you an idea of what the recording will be about and what to listen for.

While you listen

- Listen for a signal word from the question/stem that will signal the answer is coming. Listen for other ways of expressing the key words you underlined.
- All of the information in the options will be mentioned in the recording – these are distractors. Do not choose an option just because you heard it. Listen carefully to the whole recording.
- Circle the option on the question paper that best fits the information you heard.

After you listen

- When the recording of the whole test has finished, write your answers on the answer sheet.
- Check you have written the correct letter next to each number.

Matching (information/features/sentence endings)

In this listening task type you may have to match objects, places, etc. to their features, or speakers to their opinions. You may also need to match the first half of a sentence to a second. You will be given options to choose from.

Before you listen
Underline the objects, places, speakers, etc., and key words in the options. Think about how each option differs. Use these ideas to predict the content of the recording.

While you listen
- Listen for mention of the objects, places, speakers, etc. Listen for key words or other ways of expressing these.
- Do not stop listening simply because you hear an option mentioned in connection with one of the objects, etc., as it might be a distractor. Keep listening to be sure it is the correct answer.
- The numbered items will be in the same order as the recording. The lettered items will not.
- Write the correct letter next to each number on the question paper.

After you listen
- When the recording of the whole test has finished, write your answers on the answer sheet.
- Check you have written the correct letter next to each number.

Plan/Map/Diagram labelling, Flow chart completion

In this listening task type you will have a map, plan, diagram or flow chart to label or complete.

Before you listen
- Read the instructions so you know how many words or numbers you can write in each gap (e.g. *NO MORE THAN THREE WORDS*).
- Look at what information is in the map, plan, diagram or flow chart. Read the prompts and predict the missing word or part of speech. If there are options, read them and try to guess which could fit each gap.
- Underline key words to listen for in the recording or think about location/direction words you might hear (e.g. *opposite, below, above*). Look at the numbers as the information in the recording will follow these in order.

While you listen
- With a diagram or flow chart, listen for key words and other ways of expressing the information in the diagram/flow chart that you have.
- With a map or plan, make sure you listen carefully at the beginning to find out where you are currently on the map/plan. Listen for language of direction (e.g. *north, west, on the right*) so you know where different items are on the map/plan.
- Note down the missing words on the question paper as you hear them. Remember that if there are options, all of them will appear on the recording but only some will be correct answers, so listen carefully at all times.

After you listen
- When the recording of the whole test has finished, write your answers on the answer sheet.
- Check that your spelling is correct and that you have used a capital letter at the beginning of a word where necessary.

Reading Paper

The **Academic Reading Paper** tests your ability to understand written English in an academic environment. The total time for the test is 60 minutes and there are 40 questions to answer. In total, the passages are 2,000–2,750 words long and this is spread over three different passages. There are a variety of question types and you will have up to four question types for each text.

In the Reading test, you must write your answers on the answer sheet during the 60-minute time limit. Write your answers next to the correct number.

General advice

> **DO** think about the time you need for each question – you have 40 questions and only 60 minutes. Spend about 20 minutes on each passage.
>
> **DO** start with Part 1 and work through the passages in order, as they become increasingly difficult.
>
> **DO** move on if you can't find an answer in 2 minutes.
>
> **DO** start by reading the questions. These are often written in easier language and you can get a feel for the main ideas in the passage from the questions.
>
> **DON'T** go back and change answers unless you are sure. Studies show that test-takers more often change correct answers to the wrong answers.
>
> **DON'T** read everything. Even native speakers cannot read all 2,750 words carefully and complete the tasks. Scan to find information, then read carefully for the answer.

Gap-fill tasks (sentence/summary/table/notes completion and short-answer questions)

In this reading task type you will have sentences, a summary, a table, or notes with a gap that you need to complete, or a question that needs a short answer. They usually test more factual information and detail. The answers usually appear in the same order as in the passage.

Test strategies

Before you read
- Read the instructions so that you know how many words or numbers you can use in each gap.
- Predict what kind of word might be missing. Even if you predict incorrectly, it will help you to focus your attention on the right piece of information.

While you read
- Underline the key words and then scan the passage to see where the answer might be.
- Copy the word or words directly from the passage. You will not need to make any changes.
- Watch the time. If a question is taking more than 2 minutes, it might be too difficult for you.

After you read
- If you have a whole sentence, check that it makes sense and you have respected the word limit.
- Check your spelling and check that you have used a capital letter at the beginning of a word where necessary.

Multiple-choice questions and short-answer questions

In short-answer questions, there will be questions for you to answer. In multiple-choice questions, there will be either a question or the first half of a sentence and four possible answers or ways of continuing that sentence. These questions usually test opinions and ideas and may be related to a specific part of the passage or test global understanding. The questions usually appear in the same order as the information in the passage.

Before you read
Read the question or sentence beginning and the options quickly. Try to decide quickly what the question is asking for (e.g. a main idea, detailed information, an opinion).

While you read
- Underline key words that might help you to find the correct answer in the passage.
- Remember that answers to this type of question usually appear in the same order as they appear in the passage.
- Read the relevant part of the passage carefully. Try to understand the main point and supporting points.
- Try to guess the meaning of the words you do not know by looking at the other words in the sentence – but only do this for words that are important to answer the question.

After you read
- Quickly work through the options one by one. Try to decide if each is correct or incorrect.
- When you think you have found the correct answer, read the passage again quickly to be sure you are correct.
- Match up sentences in the passage that paraphrase the idea in the option you think is correct.
- Watch the time. Multiple-choice questions can require more reading, but are still only worth 1 mark each.

True/False/Not given, Yes/No/Not given

In this reading task type you will have statements and you have to decide if the passage says the same thing, says the opposite or if that information is not in the passage. *True/False* statements are usually opinions and *Yes/No* statements are usually factual. The answers usually appear in the same order as in the passage.

Before you read
Underline key words in the options that might help you to find the correct answer in the passage.

While you read
- Read the passage quickly to find where the answers are.
- Answers to *True/False/Not given* questions appear in the same order in the questions and passage.
- Find the easiest answers first and then look before or after for more difficult answers.
- Try to guess the meaning of the words you do not know by looking at the other words in the sentence – but only do this for words that are important to answer the question.

After you read
- Remember that *False* means that the opposite idea is paraphrased and stated in the passage. *Not given* is for anything that is not in the passage.
- Watch your time. Do not spend too long looking for *Not given* answers.

Matching (information/features/sentence endings)

In this reading task type you may have to match objects, ideas, historical periods, etc. to their features. You may also need to match the first half of a sentence to a second. You will be given options to choose from in the questions.

Before you read
- Underline the key words in the questions.
- Think about how each option is different.

While you read
- Read the passage quickly to find the relevant parts.
- Read to see if there are any key ideas from the options that are paraphrased there.
- Look at words that show how ideas relate to each other (examples, causes, effects, contrasts, etc.). Sometimes this is tested.

After you read
- When you think you have found the correct answer, read the passage again quickly to be sure you are correct.
- If you are matching sentence beginnings and endings, re-read the sentence to make sure it makes sense grammatically.

Matching headings

In this reading task type you will be given a list of headings and you will have to match them with paragraphs or sections of the passage.

Before you read
- Read the headings quickly.
- Identify the topic and the focus of each heading. For example, in a passage on shopping, there might be several headings on the topic of healthy food, but one will focus on the cost of healthy food, another on the availability of healthy food, a third on displaying healthy food, etc.
- Read the instructions carefully. Sometimes you either have to match a summary with sections or find the section where an idea is mentioned.
- Look at the example. Sometimes you can get a feel for how the test-writer summarises ideas.

While you read
- There are two possible ways of answering this task type: (1) Quickly read each section in the passage, summarise it in your own words, then find a heading that matches your summary. (2) Underline key words in the headings and then quickly read each section in the passage to find paraphrases of the key words. Experiment with both and see which suits you.
- As you match sections, make a mark next to the options you have used already.

After you read
- Guess any that you have not matched.
- Watch your time. Don't try to read the whole passage in detail.

Writing Paper

The **Academic Writing Paper** tests your ability to write academic texts. You have to interpret and describe visual information in Task 1 and write an essay in Task 2. The paper is one hour long, with 20 minutes recommended for Task 1 and 40 minutes recommended for Task 2. You can write in either pen or pencil.

General advice

DO read the questions carefully and make sure you understand them.
DO plan each task to make sure you answer all parts of the question and organise your ideas well when you write.
DON'T spend too much time planning. No more than 5 minutes for Task 1 and no more than 10 minutes for Task 2.
DON'T write a first draft in full and then write a second. You will not have time for this.
DO write in paragraphs.
DO use a variety of language and connecting words/phrases to join ideas together (e.g. *as a result*, *however*).
DO leave time to review your writing. Read it once to check it makes sense. Then read it again and check for any incorrect language, punctuation and spelling.

Task 1: Factual description

Task 1 is a factual description. The question might ask you to describe a chart, diagram or map. You might have more than one chart or image on a connected theme. You should write at least 150 words.

Before you write
- Study the image and the title to understand what information you have.
- Pay attention to any information in the image. You need to include all the main points.
- Organise information into groups. Try to see connections or relationships between information.
- Identify an overview (the main information given by the image).

While you write
- Start with an introduction sentence and one or two overview sentences.
- Continue with one or two paragraphs that give more detail.
- Include facts and numbers to illustrate your main points.
- Highlight the main points.
- Don't add your opinion or try to explain why things happen. Just describe what you see.
- Write clearly so the examiner can read your handwriting.
- Write at least 150 words or you will lose marks.

After you write
- Read your description and check that it makes sense and that the ideas are organised logically.
- Correct any incorrect language, punctuation and spelling.
- Cross out any changes neatly and write the correction neatly above or below them.

Task 2: Essay

Task 2 is an academic essay. The question might ask you to discuss an opinion, provide solutions to a problem or explain the causes and/or effects of something. There are usually two parts to the question and you must make sure you address both parts in the essay. You should write at least 250 words.

Before you write
- Read the question carefully and underline the key words.
- Identify the type of essay required.
- Generate ideas on how to answer the question and note down key words.
- Write down useful words or phrases you could use.
- Organise the ideas and words/phrases into a paragraph plan.
- Aim to write four paragraphs (an introduction, two main body paragraphs and a conclusion).

Test strategies

While you write
- Follow your paragraph plan. Start with an introduction which introduces the topic, gives some background information and makes a statement which the essay will discuss. Paraphrase the essay question.
- Start each main body paragraph with a topic sentence and then give supporting points. Expand your ideas where possible by giving explanations, examples or reasons.
- End with a conclusion which summarises the key points. Paraphrase rather than repeat the points you made earlier.
- Write clearly so the examiner can read your handwriting.
- Write at least 250 words or you will lose marks.

After you write
- Read your essay and check that it makes sense and that the ideas are organised logically.
- Correct any incorrect language, punctuation and spelling.
- Cross out any changes neatly and write the correction neatly above or below them.

Speaking Paper

The **Speaking Paper** tests your ability to communicate on a variety of topics and speak at length on a topic. The test lasts 11–14 minutes and has three parts.

General advice

> **DO** speak as much as you can. You have 11–14 minutes to show the examiner all your skills, so use the best language you can. Expand your answers by giving examples or reasons.
> **DO** try to look confident even if you do not feel it. Smile, sit up in your chair and take deep breaths.
> **DO** speak clearly and try to sound interested.
> **DO** try to speak fluently, without pausing too much.
> **DO** give yourself time to think with phrases like *Let me see* or by rephrasing the question.
> **DO** speak as clearly as possible.
> **DO** use intonation to sound more interested.
> **DO** use a wide variety of language.
> **DO** try to be as accurate as possible, but do not worry too much about making mistakes.
> **DO** use connecting words/phrases to join ideas together (e.g. *so, because, but, although*).

Part 1: Introduction and general questions

Part 1 focuses on general questions about your life. It lasts 4–5 minutes. The examiner will start by asking you to introduce yourself and will then ask further general questions.

Before you speak
Listen carefully to the questions. If you do not hear the question, ask the examiner to repeat it.

While you speak
- Give yourself time to think with phrases like *Let me see* or *That's an interesting question*.
- Answer the question and then give extra information to expand the topic. This could be two reasons why you enjoy something or a reason and an example.

Part 2: Individual long turn

In **Part 2** the examiner will give you a task card which has a topic and four points to talk about. Three of these points usually focus on describing something and the final point asks for reasons for something. You have one minute to prepare and then should talk for 1–2 minutes. The examiner might then ask you one or two more questions on this topic.

Before you speak
- Read the task card carefully and think about what you can talk about.
- Write down key words if it helps you.
- Make sure you use all the one-minute preparation time to plan what you want to say.

While you speak
- Start by saying what you are going to talk about (e.g. *I'd like to talk about a famous historical building in my city.*).
- Follow the prompts on the task card to make sure you talk about all the points.
- Use a range of language.
- Speak for at least one minute. You can expand your answer for the final point by giving several reasons and/or examples to help you keep talking.
- Listen carefully to any follow-up questions that the examiner might ask before moving on to Part 3. Give yourself time to think with phrases like *I'm not sure about that* or *That's a good question*.

Part 3: Two-way discussion

In **Part 3** the examiner will ask you questions on the topic from Part 2 and you will have a conversation on that topic. This part lasts 4–5 minutes.

Before you speak
Listen carefully to the questions. If you don't understand, ask the examiner to repeat the question, speak more slowly or explain a word.

While you speak
- Give yourself time to think with phrases like *Let me see* or *That's an interesting question*.
- Answer the question and expand your answer as much as possible. Give reasons, explanations or examples to support your ideas. Be prepared for the examiner to ask you to explain or justify your ideas.
- Do not feel you have to speak for 4–5 minutes on just one question. The examiner will ask you follow-up questions to help you keep talking.

Expert grammar

Module 1

Present simple (page 10)

A Use

We use the present simple to talk about:

1 regular repeated actions, routines and habits.

   We **study** in the library most of the time.
   Doctor Meyer **gives** lectures every Monday and Friday.

2 permanent situations.

   We **live** in Madrid.
   My brother **goes** to college in York.

3 general truths and facts that are always true.

   The sun **rises** in the east.
   People **exercise** for good health.
   The course **lasts** three years.

B Form

To form the present simple, we use the base form of the verb. He/She/It forms are different.

Positive

I/You/We/They **speak** German.
He/She/It **speaks** German.

Negative

We use don't/doesn't to form negative sentences.

I/You/We/They **don't speak** German.
He/She/It **doesn't speak** German.

Questions

We use do/does to form questions.

Do I/you/we/they speak German?
Yes, I/you/we/they **do**.   No, I/you/we/they **don't**.
Does he/she/it speak German?
Yes, he/she/it **does**.   No, he/she/it **doesn't**.

Present simple with adverbs of frequency (page 16)

We often use adverbs of frequency with the present simple, to say how often something happens. Some common adverbs of frequency are: *always, frequently, generally, never, normally, occasionally, often, rarely, sometimes, usually*.

Adverbs of frequency come:

1 before main verbs.

   We **usually study** together.
   I don't **normally have** lectures on Fridays.
   Do you **often give** presentations?

2 after the verb *be*.

   I **am always** tired after work.
   My tutor **isn't usually** late.
   Are you **often** busy at weekends?

Note: We also use other time phrases with the present simple to say how often something happens (e.g. *every day/week/month, once/twice/three times a week/month/year, on Mondays/Fridays*). These phrases can come at the beginning or end of the sentence.

On Thursday afternoons we have a tutorial.
I have lunch on campus **every day**.

can for ability, possibility and permission (page 16)

Can is a modal verb. Remember that:

1 after modal verbs, we use the infinitive without *to*.

   I **can speak** French and Italian.

2 modal verbs don't add -s after *he/she/it*.

   Professor Murray **can** help you with your assignment.

3 in negative sentences and questions, the auxiliary *do* is not necessary.

   I **can't** read these notes.
   Can you read my essay?

We use *can/can't*:

1 to talk about ability in the present.

   He **can** play the guitar and the piano.
   I **can't** swim very well.

2 to say that something is or isn't possible.

   You **can** meet your tutor tomorrow.
   I **can't** go out tonight – I'm too busy.

3 to ask for, give or refuse permission.

   Can we use this classroom?
   You **can** come in now.
   You **can't** eat in here.

Module 2

Comparatives and superlatives (page 26)

A Comparative and superlative forms of adjectives

1 One-syllable adjectives

   We add *-er* and *-est* to form the comparative and superlative forms of one-syllable adjectives.

   My sister is only a year **older** than me.
   I am the **youngest** person in my family.

   With adjectives that end in one vowel + consonant, we double the consonant before adding *-er* or *-est*.

   bi**g** – bi**gg**er – bi**gg**est   sa**d** – sa**dd**er – sa**dd**est

   With adjectives that end in -e, we add -r and -st.

   saf**e** – saf**er** – saf**est**

183

Expert grammar

2 Two-syllable adjectives

With use *more* and *the most* with most two-syllable adjectives.

*It is **more common** to have a small family these days.*
*I think history is the **most boring** subject.*

With two-syllable adjectives that end in *-y*, we replace the *-y* with *-i* and add *-er* and *-est*.

*hea**vy** – hea**vier** – hea**viest***

3 Long adjectives

With adjectives that have three or more syllables, we use *more* and *the most*.

*I'm much **more confident** than my brother.*
*My cousin is **the most intelligent** person I know.*

Note: We also use *less* and *the least* with two-syllable and longer adjectives.

*Martin is **less friendly** than his sister.*
*He's **the least interesting** teacher we have.*

4 Irregular comparative and superlative adjectives

These are the most common irregular forms:

good – better – best
bad – worse – worst
far – further – furthest

B (not) as … as …

We use *(just) as* + adjective + *as* to show that two people, things, places, etc. are similar, the same or equal.

*This computer is **just as expensive as** that one.*

We use *not as* + adjective + *as* to mean 'less … than'.

*I'm **not as confident as** I want to be.*

C Making comparisons with nouns

1 We can use *more*, *the most*, *less*, *the least*, *fewer* and *the fewest* with nouns to compare quantities.

*People have **less free time** these days than 50 years ago.*
*Our group has **the fewest students**.*

2 We use *more* and *the most* + uncountable/plural countable noun.

*There were **more people** at the lecture today than on Friday.*
*Of all the people in our group, Jamie does **the most work**.*

3 We use *less* and *the least* + uncountable noun.

*Students have **less money** than people who work.*
*My brother does **the least work** out all of us.*

4 We use *fewer* and *the fewest* + plural countable noun.

***Fewer people** live with their grandparents now.*
*My town gets **the fewest visitors** in January.*

Adverbs and adverbial phrases (page 32)

A Adverbs of manner

1 Adverbs of manner tell us how we do something. To form them, we add *-ly* to adjectives.

*I learn languages quite **easily**.*
*She speaks very **slowly** and **clearly**.*

2 Some adverbs of manner are the same as the adjective:
fast – fast   hard – hard.

*I can't run very **fast**.*
*My mother always works very **hard**.*

3 Some adverbs are irregular: *good – well*.

*I usually do **well** in exams.*

B Adverbs and adverbial phrases of frequency

To say how often something happens, we can use:

1 adverbs of frequency (e.g. *always, sometimes, usually, rarely, never*).

*I **rarely** visit my aunt and uncle.*
*He is **always** polite and friendly.*

2 time phrases (e.g. *once/twice a week, every day/month/year, in the morning/afternoon/evening*).

*I speak to my mum on the phone **every day**.*
***Once a week** I have dinner at my grandparents' house.*

C Adverbial phrases of place and time

1 We use adverbials of place to show location, direction or distance (e.g. *here, there, abroad, past the bookshop, down the road*).

*My cousins live **down the road** from us.*
*I can't study **here** – it's too noisy.*

2 We use adverbials of time to say when something happens, or for how long (e.g. *today, later, at the moment, during the day, after the summer, from May to July*).

*My family always goes on holiday **in June**.*
*I have a part-time job **at the weekend**.*

Module 3

Present continuous (page 42)

A Use

We use the present continuous to talk about:

1 actions happening now.

*I'm **trying** to finish this report.*
*You're **not listening** to me.*

2 temporary situations.

*I'm **working** in a different office this week.*
*My computer **isn't working** at the moment.*

B Form

To form the present continuous, we use *be* + *-ing* form.

Positive

I'm/You're/He's/She's/It's/We're/They're waiting.

Negative

I'm not/You aren't/He isn't/She isn't/It isn't/We aren't/They aren't waiting.

Questions

Am I waiting?
Is he/she/it waiting?
Are you/we/they waiting?

C Spelling rules for verbs + *-ing*

1 most verbs: add *-ing*

   start – starting   work – working

2 verbs ending in *-e*: drop the *-e* and add *-ing*

   live – living   take – taking

3 verbs ending in *-ee*: add *-ing*

   agree – agreeing   see – seeing

4 verbs ending in *-ie*: change *-ie* to *-y* and add *-ing*

   lie – lying   die – dying

5 verbs ending in one vowel + consonant: double the final consonant and add *-ing*

   sit – sitting   stop – stopping

D Stative verbs

Stative verbs describe states, not actions, and we don't normally use them in continuous forms. Some common stative verbs are:

1 mental/thinking verbs: *agree, believe, know, remember, think, understand.*
2 attitude verbs: *hate, like, love, need, prefer, want, wish.*
3 sense verbs: *hear, see, smell, taste.*
4 verbs that describe appearance or qualities: *appear, look (= seem), seem, sound.*
5 verbs that describe owning things: *belong, have, own.*
6 other verbs: *be, cost, mean.*

*I **need** some help.   I **don't know** what you **mean**.*

have to and must (page 48)

1 We use *have to* and *must* to talk about something that is necessary. *Have to* shows that the action is necessary because someone else says so or because there is a rule or law. *Must* shows that we think the action is necessary or important.

   *I **have to** start work at 8.30 every morning.*
   *I **must** remember to book the tickets tonight.*

2 We use *mustn't* to show that it is necessary **not** to do something or that something is not allowed.

   *You **mustn't** eat a lot before exercising.* (It is important that you don't – it isn't good for you.)
   *We **mustn't** use our phones in here.* (It's not allowed.)

3 We use *don't have to* to show that something is not necessary.

   *I **don't have to** wear a uniform at work.* (It's not necessary – I wear what I like.)
   *My brother **doesn't have to** get up early because he starts work at 4 p.m.*

need to (page 48)

Need to is similar to *have to*. We use *need to* to show that something is necessary, and *don't need to* to show that something is not necessary.

*I **need to** make some important phone calls this morning.*
*He **doesn't need to** complete the report now – he can do it tomorrow.*

should (page 48)

We use *should* and *shouldn't* to give advice, to say that something is or isn't a good idea.

*You **should** check your spelling before you print a document.*
*You **shouldn't** speak to your boss like that.*

Module 4

Past simple (page 58)

A Use

We use the past simple to talk about actions, states or situations that started and finished in the past. We often use it with time expressions like *yesterday, two days/months/years ago, last week/month/year, in 2016*.

*I **joined** the course two weeks ago.*
*Last year I **was** very ill with food poisoning.*

B Form

1 To form the past simple of regular verbs, we add *-ed* to the verb.

   *We **finished** work early yesterday.*

2 Some verbs do not form the past simple with *-ed*. They are irregular. (See p. 192 for a list of common irregular verbs.)

   *He **wrote** his first book when he **was** a student in Madrid.*

3 In negative sentences we use *didn't* + the base form of the verb.

   *I **didn't walk** to work today.*
   *In the past people **didn't understand** that smoking was unhealthy.*

4 In questions we use *did* + subject + the base form of the verb.

   ***Did** you **do** any exercise last week?*
   *When **did** your brother **finish** his studies?*

Expert grammar

C Spelling rules for verbs + -ed

1 most verbs: add -ed
   start – start**ed**   work – work**ed**
2 verbs ending in -e or -ee: add -d
   live – live**d**   agree – agree**d**
3 verbs ending in consonant + -y: change -y to -i and add -ed
   stu**dy** – stu**died**   car**ry** – car**ried**
4 verbs ending in one vowel + consonant: double the final consonant and add -ed
   s**top** – s**topped**   pl**an** – pl**anned**

Past continuous (page 58)

A Use

We use the past continuous:

1 to talk about an action that was in progress at a particular time the past.
   We **were working** at 10 o'clock this morning.
2 to talk about two actions that were in progress at the same time in the past, often with *while*.
   I **was studying** while my friends **were enjoying** themselves.
3 to describe a background scene in a story.
   It **was raining** and it **was getting** colder and colder.

B Form

To form the past continuous, we use *was/were* + *-ing* form.

Positive
I/He/She/It **was** work**ing**.
You/We/They **were** work**ing**.

Negative
I/He/She/It **wasn't** work**ing**.
You/We/They **weren't** work**ing**.

Questions
Was I/he/she/it work**ing**?
Were you/we/they work**ing**?

Past simple and past continuous (page 58)

1 We often use the past continuous with the past simple together, to talk about an action that happened while another action was in progress. We use the past continuous for the longer action that was in progress. We use the past simple for the shorter action.
   I **was waiting** for the bus when it **began** to rain.
   You **weren't listening** when I **told** you what to do.
2 We often use *when* before the action in the past simple and *while* before the action in the past continuous.
   I **was running** in the park **when** I **met** Ana.
   While I **was swimming**, somebody stole my purse.

Note: When one action happens after another, we use the past simple for both actions.
I **fell** over and **hurt** my leg.
We use the past simple, not the past continuous, with stative verbs.
I **didn't understand** what he was saying.

Countable and uncountable nouns; Quantifiers (page 64)

A Countable or uncountable?

1 Countable nouns refer to things we can count. They have a singular and a plural form (e.g. *country – countries, animal – animals*). A singular countable noun is followed by a singular verb. A plural countable noun is followed by a plural verb.
   This **plant is** very common in my region.
   There **are** a number of **animals** in my country which **are** endangered.
2 Uncountable nouns refer to things we cannot count. They don't have a plural form (e.g. *information, advice, traffic, money*). An uncountable noun is always followed by a singular verb.
   The doctor's **advice was** very helpful.

B Quantifiers

Singular countable nouns	a/an
Plural countable nouns	some, any, a lot of, (how) many, a few, too many, (not) enough
Uncountable nouns	some, any, a lot of, (how) much, a little, too much, (not) enough

1 We use *a/an* with singular countable nouns.
   There's **a** beautiful **beach** near here.
2 We can use *some, any* and *a lot of* with both countable and uncountable nouns. We use *some* in positive sentences and *any* in negative sentences and questions.
   You can see **a lot of** interesting **birds** in the park.
   It's very dry at the moment – we need **some** more **rain**.
   We haven't got **any** high **mountains** in my country.
   I don't need to do **any** more **research** on the subject.
   Are there **any rivers** in your city?
   Have you got **any information** about the wildlife on the island?
3 We use *(how) many* with plural countable nouns and *(how) much* with uncountable nouns. We use *how much/many* in questions. We usually use *much/many* in negative sentences.
   How **much money** do we need to take?
   How **many** different **animals** are there in the zoo?
   We haven't got **much time** to finish this.
   There aren't **many tigers** left in the wild.

Expert grammar

4 We use *a few* with plural countable nouns and *a little* with uncountable nouns, to mean 'a small number/amount'.

There are **a few** good **beaches** near here.
I've only got **a little time** to see the country.

5 We use *too many* with plural countable nouns and *too much* with uncountable nouns, to mean 'more than we need'.

There are **too many animals** in that zoo.
I take **too much luggage** when I travel.

6 We use *enough* with plural countable nouns and uncountable nouns, to mean 'as much/many as we need'.

I think we have **enough information** about the area.
There are**n't enough parks** in my city.

Module 5

-ing forms and infinitives (page 74)

A -ing forms

We use *-ing* forms:

1 as the subject of a sentence, like a noun.

   Travelling by plane is very expensive.
   I think **visiting** the country is a good way to help learn a language.

2 after certain verbs, e.g. *avoid, begin, (can't) stand, consider, continue, enjoy, finish, hate, imagine, keep, like, love, miss, prefer, start, stop, suggest.*

   I really don't **like flying**.
   I **avoid going** there in the summer when it's too hot.

3 after prepositions.

   We took some photographs **before going** home.
   After seeing the main attractions, we went back to the hotel.

B Infinitives

We use an infinitive with *to*:

1 to express purpose.

   I went to London **to go** shopping.
   I'd like to go to Russia **to visit** my uncle.

2 after certain verbs, e.g. *advise, agree, allow, arrange, ask, can't afford, can't wait, decide, expect, forget, help, hope, learn, offer, plan, promise, refuse, want, would like.*

   They **advised** us **to travel** by coach.
   I **can't afford to go** on holiday this year.

3 after certain adjectives that describe feelings or opinions, e.g. *amazed, disappointed, pleased, sorry, surprised, careless, difficult, nice, wrong*. We usually use these structures: subject + *be* + adjective + *to*-infinitive or *it* + *be* + adjective + *to*-infinitive.

   I was very **surprised to find** the city was so modern.
   It is **difficult to find** cheap accommodation.

We use an infinitive without *to*:

1 after modal verbs, e.g. *can, could, may, might, must, should.*

   You **should** definitely **go** to the mountains.
   You **can't get** there by train.

2 after the verbs *make* and *let*.

   You can't **make** him **apologise** if he doesn't want to.
   My parents didn't **let** me **travel** alone when I was younger.

Prepositions (page 80)

A Prepositions of place

Some common prepositions of place are: *above, among, at, below, beside, between, in, near, next to, on, under.*

There is a lot of rubbish **under** the bridge.
I live right **next to** the train station.
The bus stop is very **near** the college.

B Prepositions of time

The main prepositions of time are *at, in* and *on*.

1 We use *at* with clock times, periods of time, meals, festivals and to refer to someone's age.

   at 12 o'clock   at midnight   at night   at the weekend
   at breakfast   at Diwali   at the age of 25

2 We use *in* with parts of the day, months, seasons, years and centuries.

   in the morning   in March   in winter   in 2015
   in the 19th century

3 We use *on* with days and dates.

   on Monday   on my birthday   on New Year's Day
   on weekdays   on 13 April

Some other common prepositions of time are: *before, after, by, since, for, during, until.*

I can't afford to go on holiday **until** I start work.
I went skiing **during** the winter holidays.

C Prepositions of movement

Some common prepositions of movement are: *across, along, down, into, off, onto, out of, over, through, to, towards, up*. We use them to show movement in the direction of or away from a place.

I like walking **through** the old part of the city.
We ran **up** the hill.

Expert grammar

Module 6

be going to (page 90)

A Use

We use *be going to*:

1 to talk about intentions.
   We're going to join a gym next week.
2 to make a prediction, say what we expect to happen in the future, based on something we know or can see now.
   *This meal **is going to be** amazing – I hear the restaurant is very good.*

B Form

Positive
I'm going to stay.
*He/She/It **is going to stay**.*
*You/We/They **are going to stay**.*

Negative
I'm not going to stay.
*He/She/It **isn't going to stay**.*
*You/We/They **aren't going to stay**.*

Questions
*Am I **going to stay**?*
*Is he/she/it **going to stay**?*
*Are you/we/they **going to stay**?*

will and *be going to* (page 96)

A *will*

We use *will*:

1 to make predictions about the future, often with phrases like *I think*, *I'm sure*, *probably*, *definitely*.
   *I think this recipe **will be** quite difficult.*
2 for decisions we make at the moment of speaking.
   *I'm not hungry, so I'll just **have** a coffee, please.*
3 for offers.
   *I'll **help** you make dinner.*

B *will* and *be going to*

Be careful:

1 We use both *will* and *be going to* for predictions. But with *be going to*, our predictions are based on evidence.
   *I think it'**ll be** better to shop online.*
   *I don't think those biscuits **are going to** taste very good – they look burnt.*
2 We use both *will* and *be going to* for future actions. With *will*, we are talking about something we have **just** decided to do. With *be going to*, we are talking about something we have **already** decided and planned to do.
   *I'm not sure what to have – I think I'**ll have** pizza.*
   *We'**re going to meet** next weekend and go for a meal.*

Module 7

Zero conditional (page 106)

1 We use the zero conditional to talk about things that are always or generally true or that always happen as a result of an action or situation. To form zero conditional sentences, we use: *if/when* + present simple (*if* clause), present simple (main clause).
   *If/When you **live** in the city centre, you probably **live** in a flat or apartment.*
   *I always **stop** and talk to my neighbours **if/when** I **see** them.*
2 The *if* clause can come at the beginning of the sentence or after the main clause. When it comes at the beginning, we use a comma between the two clauses.
   If I'm home alone, I always lock all the doors and windows.
   I always lock all the doors and windows if I'm home alone.
3 We can use *unless* in the *if* clause, to mean 'if not'.
   *A town isn't very attractive to young people **unless it has** good facilities.*
   *A town isn't very attractive to young people **if it doesn't have** good facilities.*

First conditional (page 112)

1 We use the first conditional to talk about something that may happen in the future as a result of an action or situation. To form first conditional sentences, we use: *if* + present simple (*if* clause), *will* + infinitive (main clause).
   *If they **open** a community centre, it'**ll be** very popular.*
   *If they **build** a new shopping centre, it **will be** good for the local community.*
2 The *if* clause can come at the beginning of the sentence or after the main clause. When it comes at the beginning, we use a comma between the two clauses.
   If crime continues to rise, people won't want to go out at night.
   People won't want to go out at night if crime continues to rise.
3 We can use *unless* in the *if* clause, to mean 'if not'.
   *The sports centre will have to close **unless they raise** prices.*
   *The sports centre will have to close **if they don't raise** prices.*

Module 8

Present perfect (page 122)

A Use

We use the present perfect to talk about:

1 an action that started and finished in the past. We don't say when it happened because the time is not known or not important. When we use the present perfect in this way, there is often a present result to the action.

   I've been ice skating a few times but I didn't like it.
   My sister *has hurt* her arm playing tennis.

2 an action or state that started in the past and continues in the present, often with *for* or *since*. *For* shows how long something has continued (e.g. *for a year, for two months*). *Since* shows when something began (e.g. *since 2013, since Monday*).

   I *haven't played* football *for* six months.
   I've been team captain *since* last year.

3 experiences in someone's life up to now. We often use *ever* and *never* when we talk about experiences.

   He's *taken part* in a number of national competitions.
   I've *never watched* a rugby match.
   Have you *ever played* hockey?

4 to refer to a period of time that is still continuing (e.g. *today, this morning, this week, this year*).

   I've *run* ten kilometres this morning. (It's still morning.)

B Form

To form the present perfect, we use *have/has* + past participle.

Positive

I/you/we/they **have eaten**
he/she/it **has eaten**

Negative

I/you/we/they **haven't eaten**
he/she/it **hasn't eaten**

Questions

Have I/you/we/they *eaten*?
Has he/she/it *eaten*?

Note: To form the past participle of regular verbs, we add -*ed* to the verb. Irregular verbs do not form the past participle with -*ed*. (See p. 192 for a list of common irregular verbs.)

work – worked   study – studied   finish – finished
drive – driven   taught – taught   see – seen

C Time phrases

We often use these time phrases with the present perfect:

1 *just* (= a very short time ago)

   My team **has just scored** a goal.

2 *already*

   I've **already bought** tickets for the match.

3 *yet* (in negative sentences and questions)

   I **haven't decided** whether to go **yet**.
   Have you **heard** the football results **yet**?

4 other phrases like *ever, never for, since, before, recently, lately, so far*

   I **haven't had** time to do any exercise **lately**.
   We've **won** six matches **so far** this season.

Articles (page 128)

A Indefinite article (*a/an*)

We use *a/an* with singular countable nouns:

1 when we talk about something for the first time.

   There's **a good swimming pool** near my house.

2 to refer to something or someone in general, meaning 'all'.

   A leisure centre often has facilities for different sporting events.

3 when we talk about a thing or person but we do not say exactly which thing or person we mean.

   You need **a lifejacket** to do many water sports.

4 to describe something with the verb *to be*, or to talk about a person's job.

   It's **an enormous stadium** on the other side of the city.
   My cousin is **a professional football player**.

B Definite article (*the*)

We use *the*:

1 to refer to something specific.

   The sports centre in my town is excellent.

2 to refer to something that we have mentioned before.

   My team has **a new coach** and **a new training ground**.
   The coach is very experienced and **the training ground** is much better than our old one.

3 when there is only one of something.

   People play football all around **the world**.

4 with the names of oceans, seas, rivers, deserts, groups of islands, mountain ranges and the names of some countries.

   the Atlantic Ocean   the Mediterranean   the Nile
   the Gobi Desert   the Pacific Islands   the Andes
   the Netherlands   the USA

5 with the names of buildings, monuments, hotels, theatres, museums and cinemas.

   the Tower of London   the Vietnam Memorial
   the Hilton   the National Theatre
   the Natural History Museum   the Odeon

Expert grammar

C Zero article

We don't use an article:

1 before plural countable nouns or uncountable nouns, when we refer to people and things in general.
   Football fans follow their teams all over the world.
   Sports equipment is very expensive.
   To be successful at *sport*, you need *strength* and *determination*.

2 with the names of people.
   Usain Bolt has won a number of Olympic medals.

3 with the names of lakes, mountains, continents, most countries, cities, towns, villages and streets
   Lake Superior   Everest   Europe   Italy   Madrid   California   Oxford Street

4 with games, sports, subjects and languages.
   chess   hockey   economics   Italian

5 with meals.
   What time do you usually have *breakfast*?

6 with institutions like *school, college, university, hospital, prison, church*.
   I did a lot of sport at *school* but I don't do any at *college*.
   You should go to *hospital* with that injury.

   However, when we talk about these as physical buildings, not as institutions, we use an article. Compare:
   I spent two days in *hospital* when I broke my leg.
   I went to *the hospital* yesterday to visit my team mate, who has broken his leg.

Module 9

Present perfect and past simple (page 138)

We use the present perfect, not the past simple:
1 for actions that happened at an indefinite time in the past.
2 for actions that started in the past and are continuing in the present.
3 to refer to a period of time that is still continuing.

We use the past simple, not the present perfect:
1 for past actions, when we say or know when they happened.
2 for actions that started and finished in the past.
3 to refer to a period of time that has finished.

Compare:
1 *I've been* to Spain. (We are not interested in when.)
   I was in Spain last weekend. (We say when.)
2 My brother *has worked* here since 2015. (He still works here.)
   My brother *worked* here for five years. (He no longer works here.)

3 *I've been* to the library four times this week. (The week has not finished yet.)
   I went to the library four times last week. (The week has finished.)

Possessives, pronouns, quantifiers (page 144)

A Possessives

1 Possessive adjectives (*my, your, his, her, its, our, their*) are followed by a noun.
   My mother rarely uses *her* mobile.

2 Possessive pronouns (*mine, yours, his, hers, its, ours, theirs*) are used instead of a noun/noun phrase.
   You'll have to use Keith's printer – *mine* isn't working.

B Quantifiers

1 *each* and *every*
   We use *each* and *every* + singular noun + singular verb to talk about the people or things in a group. We prefer *each* when we are thinking about each person/thing separately. We prefer *every* when we are thinking about all of the people/things together.
   I read *each article* in the magazine very carefully.
   Every TV programme seems to be the same.

2 *all, most, some*
   We can use *all (of)/most (of)/some (of)* + plural noun + plural verb to refer to people or things in a specific group. We can also use them with uncountable nouns + singular verb.
   All the electronic *devices* I own *are* very old.
   Most news these days *is* very depressing.
   I think *some of* the *information* on this website *is* wrong.

3 *no, none of*
   We use *no* + plural/uncountable noun to mean 'not one' or 'not any'. *No* has a negative meaning, so we use it with an affirmative verb.
   There *are no* messaging apps on my phone.
   There *is no* ink in the printer.

   We use *none of* + plural or uncountable noun. It has a negative meaning, so we use it with an affirmative verb. When we use *none of* with an uncountable noun, the verb is singular. When we use *none of* with a plural noun, we can use either a singular or a plural verb.
   None of the *information was* very helpful.
   None of these news *articles is/are* very interesting.

4 *several*
   We use *several* + plural noun + plural verb, to mean 'more than a few but not a lot'.
   Several friends of mine *are studying* journalism.

5 *plenty of*
   We use *plenty of* + plural or uncountable noun, to mean 'a large number or amount'.
   There are *plenty of books* to help you with your research.
   You need *plenty of money* to set up a business.

Expert grammar

6 *both, either, neither*

We use *both (of)* + plural noun + plural verb and *either/neither (of)* + singular noun + singular verb to refer to two people or things. *Both* means 'one and the other'. *Either* means 'one or the other'. *Neither* means 'not one or the other'.

Both of these **articles are** useful for your assignment.
Either of these **laptops is** suitable for you.
Unfortunately, **neither of** these **tablets has** the right software.

7 We can also use these phrases to refer to quantities: *a great deal of* + uncountable noun; *a small/large/considerable/*etc. *amount of* + uncountable noun; *a large/great/small/limited/*etc. *number of* + plural noun; *a couple of* + plural noun.

I don't have **a great deal of money** to spend on electronic devices.
I only spend **a small amount of time** on my computer.
There are **a large number of** useful **travel apps** for smartphones.
There are **a couple of** good **TV programmes** on tonight.

C Indefinite pronouns

	People	Things
some-	someone/somebody	something
any-	anyone/anybody	anything
no-	no one/nobody	nothing
every-	everyone/everybody	everything

1 We use *someone/somebody* and *something* in positive sentences.

I know **someone** who works in film production.
We need to find **something** good to watch.

2 We use *anyone/anybody* and *anything* in negative sentences and questions. We can also use them in positive sentences, to mean 'any person or thing' when it is not important to say exactly which.

I don't know **anyone** who works in journalism.
Is there **anything** interesting in the newspaper?
Anyone can take good photographs with a smartphone.
It seems that you can do **anything** with technology these days.

3 *No one/Nobody* and *nothing* have a negative meaning, so we use them with affirmative verbs.

Nobody seems to know the answer.
I've worked all day but I've produced **nothing**.

4 *Everyone/Everybody* and *everything* contain the meaning of 'all', but we use them with singular verbs.

Everyone in my family **uses** instant messaging.
Everything I know about politics **comes** from the media.

Note: We use all indefinite pronouns with singular verbs. But when we refer back to *somebody, everybody,* etc., we use *they, them, their* or *themselves*.

Everyone should carry a mobile so **they** can use it in an emergency.

Module 10

Relative clauses (page 154)

1 We use defining relative clauses to give more information about a person, thing or place and make it clear exactly which one we are talking about.

2 We use these relative pronouns:
who or *that* for people.
There are very few people **who/that** write letters these days.
which or *that* for things.
I'd like to get a phone **which/that** has a good camera.
whose to show possession.
I think I know **whose** telephone number this is.
where for a place.
There's a café next door **where** you can get free wi-fi.

3 A relative pronoun can be the subject or object of a relative clause.

There are a number of messaging apps **which** are free.
There's a new messaging app **which** I want to get.
When the relative pronoun is the object of a relative clause, we can leave it out.
There's a new messaging app I want to get.

Note: The relative pronoun *that* can replace *who* or *which* but not *whose* or *where*.

may/might for possibility and permission
(page 160)

1 We can use *may* or *might* to show possibility, when we think that something is possible now or in the future.

My dictionary isn't on my desk – it **may/might** be in my bag.
People **may/might not** have to learn English in the future.

2 We use *may* (but not *might*) to ask for, give or refuse permission.

May I borrow your dictionary?
You **may** use my notes.
You **may not** take any of the books from the library.

could for ability, possibility and requests
(page 160)

We can use *could*:

1 to express ability in the past.

I **could** speak very good French by the time I was nine or ten.
He **couldn't** communicate with his grandmother until he learned German.

2 like *may/might*, to express possibility. In negative sentences, we use *may not* or *might not* but not *couldn't*.

Intercultural communication **could** become even more important in the future.
You ~~couldn't~~ **may not** be able to understand her accent.

3 to make polite requests.

Could you translate this for me, please?

Expert grammar

Irregular verbs

Infinitive	Past simple	Past participle
be	was/were	been
beat	beat	beat
become	became	become
begin	began	begun
bend	bent	bent
bite	bit	bitten
blow	blew	blown
break	broke	broken
bring	brought	brought
broadcast	broadcast	broadcast
build	built	built
burn	burned/burnt	burned/burnt
buy	bought	bought
catch	caught	caught
choose	chose	chosen
come	came	come
cost	cost	cost
cut	cut	cut
do	did	done
draw	drew	drawn
dream	dreamed/dreamt	dreamed/dreamt
drink	drank	drunk
drive	drove	driven
eat	ate	eaten
fall	fell	fallen
feed	fed	fed
feel	felt	felt
fight	fought	fought
find	found	found
fly	flew	flown
forget	forgot	forgotten
forgive	forgave	forgiven
freeze	froze	frozen
get	got	got
give	gave	given
go	went	gone
grow	grew	grown
hang	hung	hung
have	had	had
hear	heard	heard
hide	hid	hidden
hit	hit	hit
hold	held	held
hurt	hurt	hurt
keep	kept	kept
know	knew	known
lay	laid	laid
lead	led	led
learn	learned/learnt	learned/learnt

Infinitive	Past simple	Past participle
leave	left	left
lend	lent	lent
let	let	let
lie	lay	lain
light	lit	lit
lose	lost	lost
make	made	made
mean	meant	meant
meet	met	met
pay	paid	paid
put	put	put
read	read	read
ride	rode	ridden
ring	rang	rung
rise	rose	risen
run	ran	run
say	said	said
see	saw	seen
sell	sold	sold
send	sent	sent
set	set	set
shake	shook	shaken
shoot	shot	shot
show	showed	shown
shut	shut	shut
sing	sang	sung
sit	sat	sat
sleep	slept	slept
smell	smelled/smelt	smelled/smelt
speak	spoke	spoken
spell	spelled/spelt	spelled/spelt
spend	spent	spent
spread	spread	spread
stand	stood	stood
steal	stole	stolen
strike	struck	struck
swear	swore	sworn
swim	swam	swum
take	took	taken
teach	taught	taught
tell	told	told
think	thought	thought
throw	threw	thrown
understand	understood	understood
wake	woke	woken
wear	wore	worn
win	won	won
write	wrote	written

Expert speaking: useful language

Give opinions
- I think/I don't think …
- I believe …
- In my opinion, …
- In my view, …

Give reasons
- because
- as
- so
- due to
- that's why

Give examples
- like
- such as
- for example
- for instance

Add another idea
- also
- as well
- too
- Another thing (I like) is …
- Another (important) point is …

Make generalisations
- Generally, …
- On the whole, …
- Overall, …

Sequence ideas
- To start with, …
- First of all, …
- Lastly, …

Agree and disagree

Agree
- I totally agree (with that).
- I agree (with that).
- I couldn't agree more.
- (Yes,) I see your point.
- That's true.
- You're absolutely right.

Partially agree
- I agree up to a point.
- I agree to some extent.
- I suppose you might be right.

Disagree
- I'm not so sure about that.
- I'm not sure I agree (with that).
- I totally disagree (with that).

Express opposing ideas
- Although …
- However, …
- It's true that … , but …
- On the one hand, … On the other hand, …
- Some people think/feel/say/believe … but …
- … but at the same time …
- On the contrary, …

Make yourself clear
- What I mean is …
- In other words, …
- What I'm trying to say is …
- To put it another way, …
- What I mean by that is …
- What I want to say is …

Say you are not sure
- I'm not sure, but …
- I could be wrong, but …
- It's difficult to say, but …
- I can't say for sure, but …
- I suppose …

Express different degrees of certainty

When you are certain
- certainly
- absolutely
- definitely
- clearly
- of course

When you are not certain
- maybe
- probably
- possibly
- perhaps

Express attitude
- Obviously, …
- Naturally, …
- Interestingly, …
- Hopefully, …
- Surprisingly, …
- Apparently, …
- Worryingly, …

Give yourself time to think
- To be honest, I haven't thought about that before.
- That's an interesting question.
- Well, I suppose …
- How can I explain?
- I guess …
- Let me see …

Ask for clarification/repetition
- When you say 'technology', do you mean …?
- Sorry, I'm not sure what 'gadget' means. Could you explain it in another way, please?
- Could you please explain what 'gadget' means?
- Sorry, I don't understand the question. Could you explain?
- Could you repeat the question, please?
- Sorry, would you mind repeating the question?

Emphasise a point
- Don't forget that …
- I want to stress that …
- It's important to remember that …
- One of the points I'd like to highlight is …
- The essential point is …
- The important thing (about …) is …

Expert speaking Test 1

Test 1 (Part 1)

Before you watch

1 Work in pairs and answer the questions about the IELTS Speaking test.
   1 How many parts are there?
      A two   B three
   2 In which part of the test do you have to:
      A answer questions about important issues in the world?
      B answer questions about yourself and your life?
      C describe a person, place, event or object.
   3 How long does the test last?
      A 11–14 minutes   B 15–20 minutes

2a You are going to watch an examiner answering the questions below. Work in pairs and try to predict what the examiner will say.

> **IELTS Speaking – FAQs**
> 1 What will the examiner ask me about?
> 2 What if I don't understand a question?
> 3 What if I have no ideas on the topic?
> 4 What if I make a mistake?

b 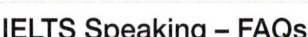 1.1 Watch the examiner and check your ideas from Exercise 2a.

3 You are going to watch a candidate, Nouf, doing Part 1 of the Speaking test. Read the questions. What topic words do you think she might use? Make two lists: one for *family* and one for *television*.

Part 1

Tell me about your family.
1 Who are you most like in your family?
2 In what ways are you similar?
3 Who do you get on best with in your family? Why?
4 How important is family to you?

Let's talk about television.
5 How often do you watch television? Why?
6 What type of programmes DON'T you like? Why not?

While you watch

4a ▶ 1.2 Watch and tick the words on your lists from Exercise 3 that Nouf uses.

b ▶ 1.2 Look at the responses below and watch Nouf again. What answers does Nouf give? How would you complete the sentences for yourself? Use the questions in brackets to give you ideas to improve your fluency.
   1 I'm similar to my _____ . (*What do you share? How are you different?*)
   2 I get on best with my _____ . (*What do you enjoy doing together? What do you like about this person?*)
   3 Family is important because _____ . (*How can family help you? Who else is also important?*)
   4 I watch television _____ a week. (*What do you watch? Why do you watch it?*)

5 ▶ 1.3 Watch the examiner talking about Nouf's interview. What does the examiner say about these things?
   1 Does Nouf speak fluently?
   2 Does she use connectors?

After you watch

6 Look at sentences 1–5. Make them better responses by joining them with extra information A–E. Then underline the connectors or introduction phrases.
   1 I'm not sure, but I think I am very similar to my brother;
   2 I get on well with my mum, of course,
   3 Well, family is really important to everyone,
   4 In general, I watch TV most evenings,
   5 To be honest, I really hate sport,

   A if you have a family that love you, things are easier.
   B especially when there's a good American programme on.
   C for example, we both have dark hair and very similar faces.
   D so I never watch that, unless it's an important game like the World Cup.
   E because she's very relaxed and also because we like the same things.

7 Work in pairs. Take turns to ask and answer the questions in Exercise 3. Remember to give extra information and use connectors.

Test 1 (Part 2)

Before you watch

1 What do you have to do in Part 2 of the Speaking test? Put the activities (A–D) in the order they happen (1–4).
   A You speak for 1–2 minutes.
   B You have a card with some instructions.
   C The examiner sometimes asks extra questions.
   D You have a minute to make notes.

2a You are going to watch an examiner answering the questions below. Work in pairs and try to predict what the examiner will say.

IELTS Speaking Part 2 – FAQs
1 Do I need to make notes?
2 What if I don't know the words in English?
3 What if I can't speak for two minutes?
4 How do I know when to stop?

b 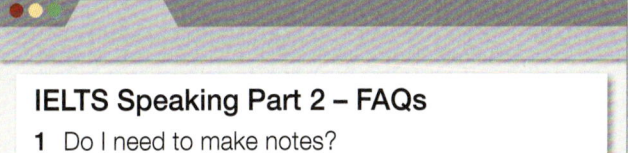 1.4 Watch the examiner and check your ideas from Exercise 2a.

3a Read the test task and make notes. Write a few key words in each section below. You have one minute.

Part 2

Describe a country you would like to visit.
You should say:
   which country this is
   what you would like to do there
   whether you would travel alone or with others
and explain why you would like to visit this country.

Which country?	What to do there?
Alone?	Why visit?

b Look at your notes from Exercise 3a again. Use these questions to improve them.
   1 Have you written something in each section?
   2 Can you add any more details (e.g. what? where? when? who? how? why?)?
   3 Have you included any verbs?
   4 Have you decided which tenses to use?

While you watch

4a ▶ 1.5 Watch Nouf doing the Part 2 task from Exercise 3a. Which country does she want to visit? Why?

b ▶ 1.5 Watch again and complete the sentences Nouf uses.
   1 I _____ (like) to visit France.
   2 I _____ (be) at school.
   3 But now I _____ (be) free.
   4 I _____ (want) to plan for this trip.

5 ▶ 1.6 Watch the examiner talking about Nouf's performance. What does the examiner say about these things?
   1 the variety of tenses
   2 how the connectors help the grammar

After you watch

6 Complete the sentences from a candidate's response with the correct form of the verbs in brackets.
   1 I _would like_ (like) to go to Spain.
   2 I know that the people there _____ (be) very friendly.
   3 My friend _____ (go) there two years ago.
   4 She _____ (tell) me there are some great clothes shops in Spain.
   5 I _____ (like) to go with my best friend, Christina.
   6 She always _____ (make) a day out feel special.
   7 I _____ (read) about this country in class last year.
   8 My brother _____ (go) there next year and I want to get there before him.

7 Work in pairs. Take turns to complete the Part 2 task in Exercise 3a. If possible, record your answer so that you can listen back to it.

8 How can you improve in Part 2 of the test? Make a list of three goals and share them with a partner.

Expert speaking Test 1

Test 1 (Part 3)

Before you watch

1 Choose the correct option in *italics* to complete the sentence about Part 3 of the Speaking test.

The examiner will ask you questions about *you and your experiences / things in the news or world issues*.

2 Look at two students' comments. Which student do you think has a better understanding of Part 3 of the Speaking test?

1 You need to answer questions about yourself again, but this time you need to ask the examiner for his or her opinion because it's a discussion.
2 You have to give opinions on more difficult topics and be able to give reasons for those opinions. You might also need to show you understand the opposite opinion.

While you watch

3 ▶ 1.7 Watch the examiner answering some frequently asked questions on Part 3 and check your answer to Exercise 2. Why is the other student wrong?

4a ▶ 1.8 The examiner asks Nouf about international travel and tourism. Write ten words/phrases you think she might use. Then watch Nouf doing Part 3 and check your ideas.

b ▶ 1.8 Watch again and complete the examiner's questions.

Part 3

1 _____ do people learn from travelling?
2 _____ do you think some people prefer to travel in their own country, not in new countries?
3 _____ that tourism and travel has changed a lot in the last 100 years?
4 _____ it's a good thing that we go on holiday a lot these days?
5 _____ has [your country] changed because of tourism?
6 _____ better with the tourists?

After you watch

5 How can Nouf check she has understood the questions? Write a question she could ask to:

1 ask the examiner to repeat.
2 ask the examiner to explain a difficult word.
3 tell the examiner what she understood and check that's correct.

6 Look at the words/phrases in the box that Nouf used in the test. Match them with words/phrases 1–6 with a similar meaning.

accommodation   respect the rules   rude
there are four seasons in one day   this depends
unfortunately

1 not do bad things
2 not polite
3 a place to stay
4 sadly
5 the weather changes a lot
6 there are good things and bad things

7a Look at these sentences from a candidate's answers. Think of a different word to replace the words in brackets. The first letter of each word is given.

1 I think that people would like (want) to stay at home.
2 I'm not sure everyone wants to go a_____ (to new countries).
3 At home, you don't need to worry about problems with c_____ (speaking to people) in a different language.
4 Also, some people don't like f_____ (travelling by plane).
5 Tourism has changed completely in the last c_____ (100 years).
6 We didn't really have f_____ (journeys by plane) 100 years ago.
7 Everyone b_____ (reserves) their holiday online these days.
8 Travelling is great but planes aren't good for the e_____ (air and planet).

b Work in pairs. Practise reading the sentences in Exercise 7a aloud.

8 ▶ 1.9 Watch the examiner talking about Nouf's performance. Does Nouf use a good range of vocabulary?

9 Work in pairs. Follow the instructions and answer the Part 3 questions in Exercise 4b. Then swap roles.

1 Student A: Ask the questions.
2 Student B: Answer the questions.
3 Student A: Try and keep Student B talking. Ask him/her for more details, examples, reasons or about the opposite opinion.

10 What three tips would you give another student doing Part 3 of the Speaking test?

Expert speaking Test 2

Test 2 (Part 1)

Before you watch

1 You are going to watch a candidate, Yuka, complete an IELTS Speaking test. Which of these things will the examiner mark her on?
   1 fluency
   2 pronunciation
   3 quality of ideas
   4 vocabulary
   5 grammar

2 In Part 1, the examiner is going to ask Yuka questions about her studies or work. Work in pairs and write three questions you think the examiner could ask.

While you watch

3a ▶ 2.1 Watch the first half of Part 1 of the test and check your ideas from Exercise 2.

  b ▶ 2.1 Watch again and complete the examiner's questions.
   1 Are you a _____ or do you _____ ?
   2 Why did you choose that _____ ?
   3 What are the _____ and _____ things about your course?

  c ▶ 2.2 Watch the second half of Part 1 of the test. What is the topic?

  d ▶ 2.2 Watch again and complete the examiner's questions.
   1 Do you have a _____ ?
   2 What do you think are the _____ of having a hobby?
   3 Which hobbies do you think are most _____ with your friends? Why?

4a Answer the questions about Yuka's fluency in Part 1.
   1 Does Yuka generally pause to prepare her answers?
   2 Do you think Yuka speaks slowly?
   3 Does Yuka use connectors (e.g. *and, but, also, because, so*)?
   4 Does Yuka answer all the questions?

  b ▶ 2.3 Watch the examiner talking about Yuka's interview and check your answers to Exercise 4a.

After you watch

5a Look at another candidate's answer to one of the questions. Complete it with the connectors in the box.

   also   because   but   so   unfortunately   when

   > Well, I don't have a lot of time **1** _____ I study, **2** _____ I like going to concerts. My friends are in a band and **3** _____ they play, I go to see them. **4** _____ , I don't play an instrument and I can't sing, **5** _____ I can only watch them. I **6** _____ enjoy writing in my free time, and I hope to write about music for a newspaper or magazine one day.

  b Work in pairs. Take turns to ask and answer the questions in Exercises 3b and 3d. Use at least three connectors from Exercise 5a in your answers.

6a Think about your answers to these Part 1 questions. Think of extra information to add for each answer. What connectors can you use?

   Part 1

   Let's talk about the internet.
   1 How important is the internet for you?
   2 What websites do you usually visit?
   3 Is there anything you dislike about using the internet?
   4 Do you think you will use the internet more in the future?

  b Work in pairs. Take turns to ask and answer the questions in Exercise 6a. Remember to give extra information and use connectors. If possible, record your answers so that you can listen and check your fluency.

Expert speaking Test 2

Test 2 (Part 2)

Before you watch

1a Read the test task and make notes. Write a few key words in each section below. You have one minute.

Part 2

Describe an important decision you have made.
You should say:
- what the decision was
- how you made your decision
- whether your decision involved other people

and explain why it was important to you or others.

What?	How?
Other people?	Why important?

b Think about the grammar that you need to use in your response. What tense(s) could you use to talk about:

1 how you made the decision?
2 how the decision affects you now?
3 who you spoke to?
4 your hopes for the future after making that decision?

2 You are going to watch Yuka doing Part 2 of the test. Which of these things do you think the examiner will listen for when she marks Yuka's grammar?

1 using a range of tenses
2 mistakes with grammar
3 using complete sentences rather than just words
4 using longer, more complex sentences
5 expressing a lot of different ideas

While you watch

3a ▶ 2.4 Watch Yuka doing Part 2 of the test. What was her important decision? Is she happy she made that decision?

b ▶ 2.4 Watch again and complete the sentences Yuka uses.

1 My important decision _____ (be) to come here.
2 My dad _____ (recommend) it.
3 Studying abroad _____ (be) one of my dreams.
4 I _____ (meet) a lot of people from a lot of countries.

4 ▶ 2.5 Watch the examiner talking about Yuka's performance in grammar. What does the examiner say about:

1 how Yuka uses the past simple?
2 the mistakes Yuka makes?
3 connectors like *whenever* and *also*?
4 the extra question the examiner asks Yuka?

After you watch

5 Look at these sentences from another candidate's response. Find and correct the mistakes with grammar. The number of mistakes in each sentence is given in brackets.

1 A important decision I made was to buy a new mobile phone. (1)
2 It was difficult decision because you need to use a mobile phone for a long time and I didn't wanted to make a mistake. (2)
3 Before I bought the phone, I speak with my friends who have a new mobile and I was reading a lot about different kinds of mobiles. (2)
4 It was one of the biggest decision I made in the last year. (1)

6 Work in pairs. Take turns to complete the Part 2 task in Exercise 1a. If possible, record your answer so that you can listen and check your performance in grammar. Try to listen for 1–4 in Exercise 2.

Test 2 (Part 3)

Before you watch

1. In Part 2, Yuka talked about an important decision. Look at these phrases on the topic of decisions and cross out the option in *italics* that is not possible in each phrase.

   1. *do / make / take / think about* a decision
   2. *choose / apply for / make / qualify for* a job
   3. *take / study for / make / do* a course
   4. *learn / take / choose / need* a new skill
   5. *leave / move into a new / buy a / make* home
   6. *set / achieve / make / reach* goals
   7. *start / do / make / build* a career
   8. *solve / have / deal with / answer* problems

2. Work in pairs. Think of three questions the examiner might ask in Part 3 about the topic of decisions.

While you watch

3a ▶ 2.6 Watch Yuka doing Part 3 of the test. Does the examiner ask any of your questions from Exercise 2?

b ▶ 2.6 Watch again. Match words 1–6 with words A–F to make collocations Yuka uses in her answers.

   1. strongly   A decision
   2. right   B deep things
   3. bring up   C job
   4. specific   D related
   5. improve your   E children
   6. think about   F skills

4a Work in pairs. Do you think Yuka has enough vocabulary to answer the questions? Does she use a range of vocabulary in her answers?

b ▶ 2.7 Now watch the examiner talking about Yuka's performance. What does she say about Yuka's vocabulary? Her pronunciation?

After you watch

5a Work in pairs. Read the Part 3 questions and look at the useful words/phrases in the box below. Could you use any of these in your answers? Can you think of any other useful words/phrases?

Part 3

1. Do you think parents' decisions affect their children's lives? (Why? How?)
2. What other things affect children's education? (Why? When?)
3. Do you think school prepares young people for working life well? (Why/Why not?)
4. Do you think students are responsible for their own learning? (How? Why?)
5. How has education changed in your country in recent years? (Give examples.)

---

bring up children   complete work on time
friends and classmates   hobbies and interests
more pressure   more technology   punctual
stay in school longer   the media   work in a team
work skills

---

b Work in pairs. Follow the instructions and answer the Part 3 questions in Exercise 5a. Then swap roles.

   1. Student A: Ask the questions.
   2. Student B: Answer the questions.
   3. Student A: Try and keep Student B talking. Ask him/her to give more information for each answer.

6. What three tips would you give another student doing Part 3 of the Speaking test?

Expert writing

Module 1

Task 2: Advantages-disadvantages essay

Task

Write about the following topic.

Many students choose to study in a different country from their own. What are the advantages and disadvantages of studying abroad?

Give reasons for your answer and include any relevant examples from your knowledge or experience. Write at least 250 words.

- Remember to write about both advantages and disadvantages.
- Don't forget to include reasons and examples.

Model answer

Nowadays a lot of students decide to go to college or university abroad. There are many reasons why this is a sensible decision, but being a student in a foreign country can also sometimes be difficult.

The main advantage of studying abroad is that the student not only gets a degree in, say, engineering or medicine, but also becomes fluent in a foreign language. Knowing another language is always useful but it can be a particular plus when the student starts looking for a job. A second advantage is that a student who does a course in a foreign country gains an understanding of a completely different culture from his or her own. This is valuable in many different ways. It usually makes the student more tolerant of other ways of looking at the world and it also introduces them to new singers and writers.

But studying abroad is not always easy. My cousin who did a degree in the USA felt very lonely for his first term or two. He missed his family and friends and, to begin with, he did not like the food or the way of life there. Gradually, however, he got used to being in Texas and by the end of the course he was sorry to leave.

To sum up, doing a degree or some other course in a foreign country can be hard but, for most students, it offers more advantages than disadvantages and so is a very positive thing to consider if you have the opportunity to do so.

- Plan your essay before you start writing. Note down ideas and make a paragraph plan.
- Make the first sentence of each body paragraph a topic sentence.
- Paraphrase the statement from the writing task in your introduction.
- Write in clear paragraphs.
- Remember to re-read and check your essay carefully.

Module 2

Task 1: Describe a chart

Task

The chart below gives information about the number of social networking sites people used in the US in 2013 and 2014. Summarise the information by selecting and reporting the main features, and make comparisons where relevant. Write at least 150 words.

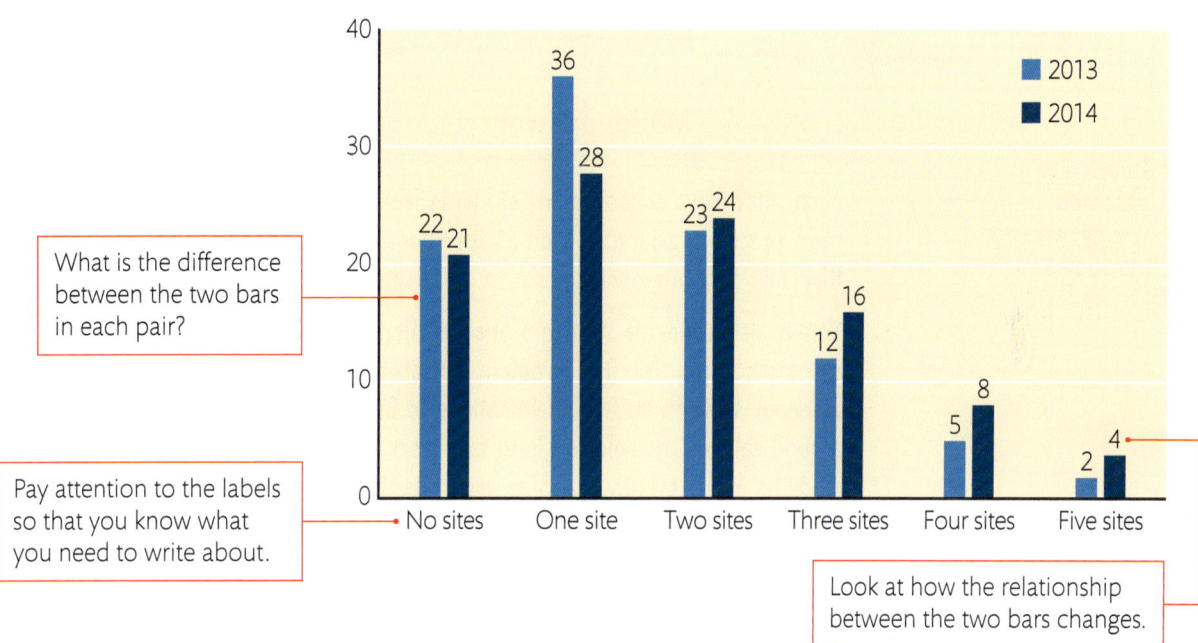

What is the difference between the two bars in each pair?

Pay attention to the labels so that you know what you need to write about.

Look at how the relationship between the two bars changes.

Model answer

Introduce the topic of the graph. Try to paraphrase the original sentence.

The bar chart shows the number of social networking sites visited by internet users in the USA in 2013 and in 2014. We can see from the data that, in general, there was a growing tendency to use more than one site.

Include an overview, describing the main trend.

Write about the main features. Mention some of the most significant figures shown in the chart.

Although just over one fifth of internet users did not use any social networking sites in either of the years, the proportion in this category decreased from 22 percent in 2013 to 21 percent in 2014. In both years the highest proportion of users in any group fell into the 'One site' category. However, this group declined sharply from 36 percent in 2013 to 28 percent in 2014.

Linking words and phrases like *in contrast* help to show the connection between the sentences or paragraphs.

In contrast, the numbers who reported using two sites, three sites, four sites and five sites all grew over the period analysed. In both years the proportion of internet users fell as the number of social networking sites increased, with only 2 percent using five sites in 2013 compared to 4 percent in 2014.

Use a variety of verbs like *grow*, *fall*, *increase* and *decrease* to describe trends.

Module 3

Task 2: Problem-solution essay

Task

Write about the following topic.

- *Some young people decide to get a job straight after leaving school instead of going to university.* — The problem.
- *What problems might this decision cause them? What can they do to solve these problems?* — What you have to write about. / Write about at least two problems. / Suggest at least one solution for each of the problems you mention.

Give reasons for your answer and include any relevant examples from your knowledge or experience. Write at least 250 words.

Model answer

When they leave school, many students feel that they need to earn a salary as soon as they possibly can. They therefore take the decision not to go to university.

[*Paraphrase the statement from the writing task in your introduction.*]

This decision may be the right one for them but it can cause problems. The first problem is that it is hard for a school-leaver with few qualifications to find a job with a good salary. One solution is to take work but continue studying in the evenings and at weekends. In that way, it is possible to gain qualifications and earn money at the same time. Once the person has got more qualifications, he or she can start looking for a better job. Another solution is to find work where it is possible to learn useful skills on the job. That is the best way to become, for example, a mechanic or an electrician.

[*Give reasons to explain why your solutions are appropriate.*]

Another problem in going straight to work after leaving school is that it can be hard to get down to a serious job starting work at nine and finishing at five, five days a week, when friends are living a more relaxed and independent life at university. I know my brother found that very difficult when he got his first job when he was eighteen. He solved the problem by making sure he had a good social life. He formed a band and they had a lot of fun playing together every weekend.

[*Give examples to explain your ideas.*]

In conclusion, although there are problems going to work straight after leaving school, it is not too difficult to find solutions to these problems.

[*Summarise your point of view in your conclusion.*]

Module 4

Task 2: Opinion essay

Task

Write about the following topic.
Some people believe it is wrong to keep animals in zoos.
Do you think the advantages of keeping animals in zoos outweigh the disadvantages?
Give reasons for your answer and include any relevant examples from your knowledge or experience. Write at least 250 words.

You need to decide which side is stronger – the advantages or the disadvantages – and explain your opinion.

Model answer

> Introduce the topic by explaining it in your own words.

Some people argue that it is cruel and unnecessary to keep animals in captivity. In my opinion, although zoos have both good and bad points, the advantages are greater than the disadvantages.

> Summarise your own view.

> Use phrases like *The main advantage …* , *A further advantage …* .

The main advantage of zoos is that they help to protect some animals that are in danger of becoming extinct. They give them the chance to produce young and to survive in a safe environment. This means that future generations will be able to enjoy looking at and learning about more of the wonderful animals that live on our planet. A further advantage is that zoos make it possible to see animals that come from very different places. Children in Europe, for example, can see elephants and giraffes and children in Brazil can enjoy watching kangaroos and emus. I believe this is a very special and important experience for young people.

> Explain the main point in more detail and give examples where possible. Make sure all the information is relevant.

> Give examples to support the points you make.

> Write more about the side that you think is stronger.

However, there are disadvantages to zoos. The main one is that the animals that live there are not free. They are not living in a totally natural way, able to go where they want when they want. Many people believe that it is not right to keep animals in this kind of prison. But you can also argue that the natural world is a cruel place for wild animals. It is hard for them to find food and they are likely to be attacked by other animals. They may well live longer in a zoo than in their natural environment.

> *In conclusion* can be a useful phrase to introduce your final paragraph.

In conclusion, I am in favour of zoos. I believe the benefits they bring us are more important that any disadvantages.

> Give your opinion in the conclusion, summarising the reasons.

Module 5

Task 1: Describe a graph

Task

The graph below gives information about petrol and diesel prices in the UK. Summarise the information by selecting and reporting the main features, and make comparisons where relevant. Write at least 150 words.

Look at the graph carefully. What do the numbers on the x and y axes represent?

What does each line show?

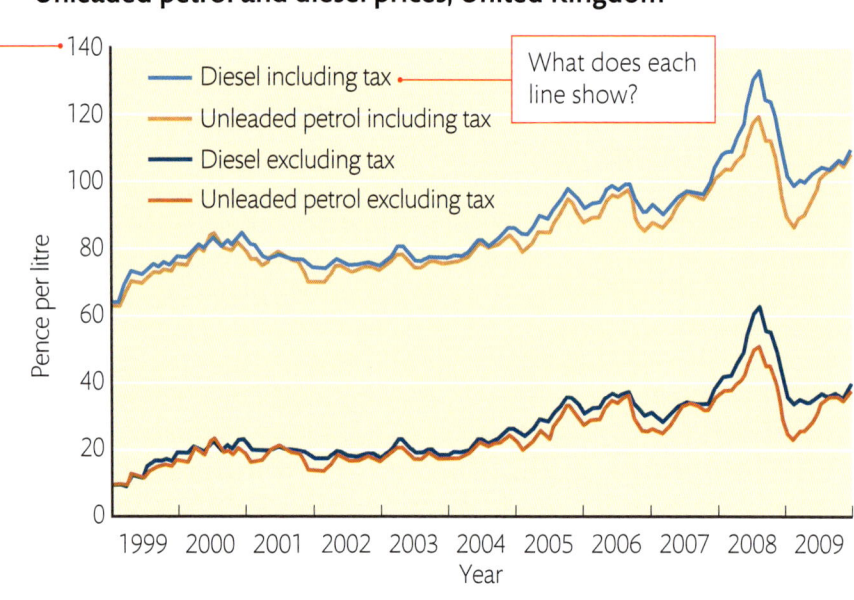

Model answer

Start by introducing the topic of the graph but paraphrase the sentence in the writing task.

The graph shows changes in the cost of fuel in the United Kingdom over the decade 1999-2009. It shows the cost in pence of a litre of unleaded petrol compared to a litre of diesel. It also indicates how much of the price is tax. We can see from the data that prices fluctuated considerably over the period but generally showed an upward trend.

Give an overview of the graph. What is the main thing you learn?

There was a peak in 2008, when unleaded petrol cost a high of 120 pence per litre and diesel cost approximately 135 pence per litre. The lowest price was at the beginning of the period, in 1999, when both types of fuel cost around 65 pence a litre.

Give more detailed information in the following paragraphs.

Identify some general trends in the graph.

Two things are consistent over the period. One is that unleaded petrol is always either slightly cheaper than or costs the same as diesel. The other is that tax on a litre of fuel accounts for at least half of the price. For example, without tax, the 65-pence a litre fuel in 1999 would only have cost 10 pence.

Give specific examples, using figures, to illustrate the trends you describe.

Check your work carefully. Make sure the information from the graph is correct.

Module 6

Task 2: Opinion essay

Task

You must say if you agree or disagree with the statement and give reasons.

You can invent some examples if you cannot think of any from your own experience.

Write about the following topic.

People these days give too much importance to following fashions, for example wearing fashionable clothes and having the latest model of phone.

To what extent do you agree with this statement?

Give reasons for your answer and include any relevant examples from your knowledge or experience. Write at least 250 words.

If you have no strong feelings about the topic, remember you do not have to tell the truth. Choose a possible point of view and argue it as well as you can.

Model answer

A lot of people these days spend a great deal of money keeping up with fashion. They always want to have the newest electronic gadget and the latest style of shoes.

I believe this to be the case because I often see it with my own eyes. The people I know love to keep up with the latest fashions. My best friend, for example, always wants to upgrade his phone as soon as a new model is released. My sister hates wearing clothes that were fashionable several years ago because she says they look out of date now.

It is not just people that I know. I often read articles in a newspaper or magazine describing how someone is in serious debt because they bought some expensive new clothes or the latest design of television or oven on their credit card. The media criticise people who get into money problems but the press is itself partly to blame. People only want fashionable things as a result of reading about them in the press.

Of course, everyone likes having nice possessions but I think being fashionable has too much importance these days. It would be better to think more about relationships with other people and less about material goods. In the end we get more pleasure from our friends and our family than we do from having the latest fridge or handbag. If our clothes are comfortable, what does it really matter if they are a few years old?

Try to put the topic in your own words in the introduction.

Make sure each paragraph deals with a distinct aspect of the topic.

Use linking words like *because*, *as* and *as a result* to explain and give reasons for the points you make.

Explain and support the points you made in previous paragraphs.

A question can be an effective way to begin or end an essay.

Expert writing

Module 7

Task 1: Describe a table

Task

Read the task carefully as it summarises what the table shows.

Remember: you have to write about the main points, not every detail.

The table below gives information about UK independent films. Summarise the information by selecting and reporting the main features, and make comparisons where relevant. Write at least 150 words.

Independent films released in the UK and Republic of Ireland by genre, 2012			
Genre	Number of releases	% of all releases	% of income from ticket sales
Comedy	26	17.6	45.4
Horror	14	9.5	20.2
Biopic	1	0.7	9.1
Drama	35	23.6	8.3
Crime	7	4.7	4.7
Action	4	2.7	4.1
Documentary	35	23.6	2.9
Thriller	13	8.8	1.3
Romance	5	3.4	0.8
Other	8	5.4	3.2
Total	148	100.0	100.0

Model answer

Spend time planning your answer before you start writing.

The table provides information about different types of independent films released in the UK and the Republic of Ireland in 2012. It indicates how many films of different genres were made and also shows what proportion of total ticket sales was made by each kind of film.

Avoid repeating words where possible; say *type, kind* or *sort of film* instead of always *genre* as in the table.

Linking words and phrases like *for example* and *however* help the reader understand your line of thinking.

The table makes it very clear that there is no correlation between the number of films made in any category and the proportion of ticket sales earned by that sort of film. For example, the largest numbers of films were made in the Drama and Documentary categories – 35 of each of these were released. However, they earned only 8.3 and 2.9 percent of total ticket sales respectively.

Write about the information in the table that you find the most interesting.

Comedy films were the most financially successful: 26 films, out of a total of 148, earned 45.4 percent of all the income from ticket sales. Another very successful type of film in 2012 was the biopic. Although only one of these was released, it accounted for 9.1 percent of ticket sales.

Make sure you use correct punctuation.

Module 8

Task 2: Problem-solution essay

Task

[This is the problem you need to consider.]

[There are two parts to the question: reasons for the problem and solutions to the problem.]

Write about the following topic.
Many adults nowadays do no physical activity in their free time.
Why do you think this is happening? What can we do to solve the problem?
Give reasons for your answer and include any relevant examples from your knowledge or experience. Write at least 250 words.

Model answer

[Introduce the problem in your own words.]

It is a sad fact that many people today do no sport or other physical exercise in their spare time.

[Begin your main body paragraphs with a topic sentence.]

One reason for this is that there are so many other tempting things for people to do. At home there are hundreds of different TV channels to watch, there are lots of exciting computer games to play or you can easily spend hours on social networking sites. If you are out, there are cafés, cinemas and shops to keep you away from the gym.

[Write two or three main body paragraphs.]

A further reason is that people have to work very long hours these days. The journey to work is also longer and more stressful than it was for most people in the past. As a result, people do not have enough energy to go for a run or a game of tennis when they eventually get home from work.

[Use linking words and phrases.]

[Use appropriate phrases to refer to solutions, e.g. *find a solution, provide a solution, one solution might be, another possible solution*.]

It will not be easy to find a solution to this problem. I think schools have a key role to play. Young children need to learn how important and how enjoyable physical activity is. In addition, teachers should help each student find a sport they can enjoy. Not everyone likes football or tennis, for example; some will find swimming or athletics more fun. Funding can also help provide a solution. The government should fund sports centres to make it possible for everyone to participate in sport even if they do not have much money.

[Explain how your solutions might help.]

Lack of activity is a serious problem for the health of many people, but the solutions suggested above could do a great deal to help solve it.

[Re-read your essay. Check that your ideas are organised well. Then check your use of language and your spelling.]

Module 9

Task 1: Describe a chart

Task

Read the task carefully. It will help you to understand the data.

The graphs below give information about how many hours people spent every day using different media and how many hours they spent using the media in different parts of the world from 2012 to 2015. Summarise the information by selecting and reporting the main features, and make comparisons where relevant. Write at least 150 words.

Study the graphs carefully before you start writing. Look for differences and connections between the two graphs.

The world's media consumption

Hours spent using media per day, average, by source

Hours spent using media per day, average, by region

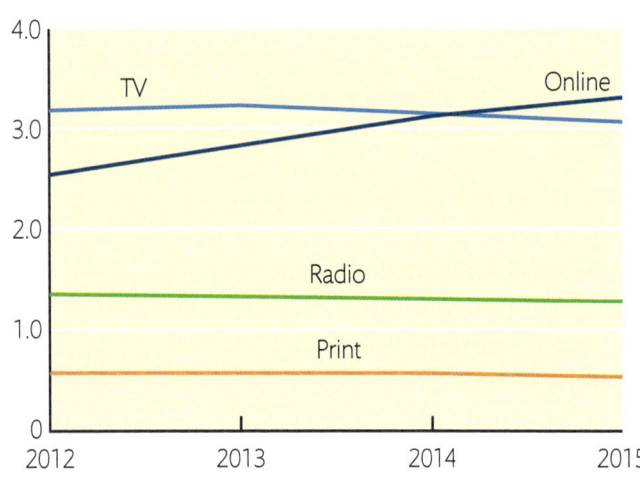
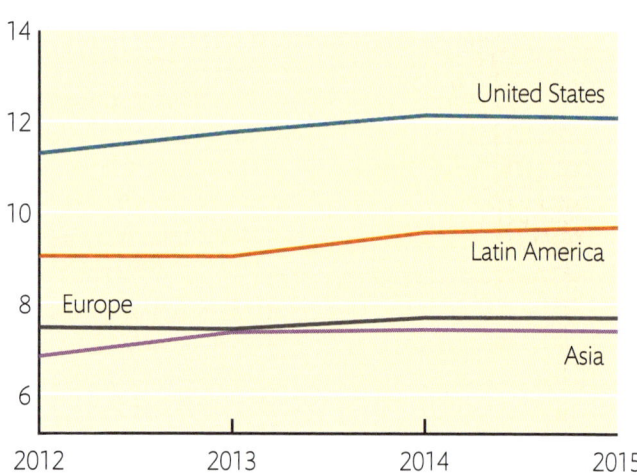

Model answer

Start by saying what the graphs show, but paraphrase the writing task.

The charts provide data about the use of different media in different areas of the world over the period 2012–2015. They compare online use with use of TV, radio and print media over the period. They also show the average hours spent per day on media use in the USA, Latin America, Europe and Asia.

Use *approximately* or *about* when you are not sure of exact figures.

We can see from the data that online consumption increased over the period from approximately 2.5 hours per day to about 3.3 hours per day. This meant that in 2014, going online overtook TV as the type of media people gave most time to. TV, radio and print all showed a very slight decline between 2012 and 2015 in terms of hours spent per day on them.

Use words like *this* and *that* to refer back to ideas.

You can write a separate paragraph about each of the graphs.

Use comparative and superlative forms.

Use figures from the graphs to illustrate the points you make.

Of the four geographical areas illustrated in the charts, people in the USA spent the most hours per day using media, rising from 11 to 12 hours per day over the period. People in Asia spent the least time on media, averaging over four hours per day less than US citizens.

Module 10

Task 2: Opinion essay

> There are two parts to this statement that you need to think about: English becoming more widely spoken and other languages dying out.

> You must say if you agree or disagree with the statement and give reasons.

Task

Write about the following topic.

Soon almost everyone in the world will speak English and most other languages will die out.

To what extent do you agree with this point of view?

Give reasons for your answer and include any relevant examples from your knowledge or experience. Write at least 250 words.

Model answer

Some people say that it will not be long before English is spoken everywhere in the world. They believe that the majority of other languages will become extinct.

> You can start your first body paragraph by stating your opinion.

I partly agree with their opinion. It is clearly true that English is becoming widely spoken all over the world. Everywhere you go now you see English. Even in countries where English is not the native language, you often find that menus, tourist brochures and street signs are in English. Many international businesses use English in their offices even when those offices are in Switzerland, Delhi or Hong Kong. When a Chinese person meets a Brazilian, they will probably talk to each other in English rather than Chinese or Portuguese. That is the situation now and I think English will become even more important in the next few years.

> Give examples to help make your ideas clear.

> Start a new paragraph to discuss the second part of the statement.

However, I do not think that most other languages will disappear. In my opinion, people will still speak their native languages when they are at home. Most people are proud of their own language. They want to pass it on to the next generation. A language is not just words – it is also stories and songs and poetry. Parents will always want to share these aspects of their language culture with their children and they will want schools to teach their children their own language as well as English.

> Use the language of opinion.

> State your opinion in the conclusion.

In conclusion, I agree that English will become more and more important as the international language of business and travel. But I do not believe that this will lead to the death of other languages.

> Allow time to check your work carefully.

Audio scripts

Module 1

1.1

T = Tutor   S = Student

T: So Rashad, we've talked about your presentation and we've also looked at your last essay. Are you happy with the feedback for that?
S: Yes, thanks – it's quite clear.
T: Good. So is there anything else I can help you with?
S: Well, yes, there is, actually. It's about my exams. I'm really not sure how best to prepare for them and I'd like some advice, please.
T: Did you go to Dr Green's talk last month – the one about assessment and exams?
S: Um, no, I wasn't able to go.
T: Well, these talks are well worth going to and Dr Green gives some really good advice about exam revision.
S: Oh dear, I wish I'd gone but I was too busy writing my essay!
T: Well, I believe she's giving the talk again next week. Um, let's see … yes, on Tuesday. Why don't you go along to that?
S: Do you know what time it is?
T: Let's see … you have a seminar at two o'clock, right? Well, it's straight after that, at 3.15, in room C52.
S: Oh that's great. Yes, I'll do that, thanks. Is there anything else I can do?
T: Have you ever used Student Services?
S: No, I haven't.
T: Well, they offer very good advice about this sort of thing. Why don't you go there and see if you can talk to one of the advisors? You'll probably need to make an appointment.
S: OK, I'll do that too. Thanks, Dr Milton, that's been really helpful.
T: No problem. So your next tutorial is in three weeks' time, on the seventeenth of April. Can you make 10.30 again?
S: The seventeenth … let's see … yes, that's fine. Thanks again, Dr Milton. Bye.

1.2

N = Narrator   A = Advisor   S = Student

N: You will hear a student talking to a student advisor about problems he is having preparing for his exams.
A: Come in and sit down, Rashad. My name's Lin Wood. I understand you wanted to talk to me about your exams?
S: Yes, I'm getting a bit stressed. My exams are coming up soon, but I'm finding it difficult to prepare. There seems to be so much to do – I don't really know where to start.
A: Well, you still have plenty of time before your exams start, which is good. So the first thing you need to do is to organise your time effectively: decide which areas or subjects you need to spend more time on.
S: Should I make a revision timetable?
A: Yes. They can be very helpful and give structure to your study time. One thing you definitely need to do is exam practice: try to look at as many past exam papers as you can and practise doing them under exam conditions.
S: Yes, I've done a few of those, but I don't know … I'm not sure how useful it was – I really wanted to discuss them with someone.
A: Well, why don't you then? You could set up a study group with some other students. Discussing exam questions and sharing ideas will really help you.
S: That sounds like a great idea. I'll ask some of the others later today.
A: Good. So, how much time do you spend revising?
S: Well, I seem to spend all my free time studying at the moment. I usually stay up late every night.
A: Well, it sounds to me as if you might be working too hard. You need to make sure you take plenty of study breaks. They say you should stop for ten minutes every hour, so fifty minutes of study time followed by a break; get up and walk around, have a drink or a snack, but don't sit at your computer or desk for long periods.
S: Yes, I do spend too long sitting at my desk sometimes.
A: And you also need to make time for other things. Make sure you have some relaxation time and get out and do things, even if it's just going for a walk or meeting a friend for a coffee.
S: I suppose I haven't been out much recently and I stopped playing football last term because I didn't have much time.
A: Well, I suggest you start playing again.
S: Yeah, maybe I will. Thank you, Lin, that's really useful.
A: I'm glad to help. Now remember: if you want to see me again, I'm here every weekday morning and Wednesday afternoons. You don't always need an appointment to see me – you can just pop in. Now have you got my contact details?
S: I've got your email address, I think. Do you think you could give me your phone number too?
A: Of course. You can leave me a message any time and I'll try to get back to you. And I'll be interested to hear how you get on with that study group. Ready? It's 0776 8123656.
S: Got that. Thanks again, Lin. Bye.
A: Bye, Rashad.

1.3

A: Hello, I'm Janine. Are you on the business studies course too?
B: Yes. Nice to meet you, Janine. I'm Martin. So do you like the course so far?
A: Yes, the work's quite hard but I'm enjoying it – the lectures are really interesting. I don't like all the reading we have to do though.
B: No, neither do I. Some of it's so boring! Do you live on campus?
A: Yes, my accommodation's only five minutes from here, so it's not difficult to get to lectures in the morning! My room's very small but it's really comfortable and living on campus is great – it's so easy to meet people. What about you? Where do you live?
B: I'm sharing a flat in the city centre. It's convenient to be in the centre of things but the rent is quite expensive. And I have a thirty-minute journey to get here every day.
A: How do you travel to classes?
B: I usually come by bike, but sometimes I get the bus if I'm feeling lazy.
A: So, who do you live with?
B: My cousin and his friend – they're in the second year, doing biology. It's quite difficult to meet people if you're not on campus, but I sometimes go out with my cousin and I play tennis with him too.
A: Oh. Do you do a lot of sport?
B: Not much apart from the tennis. I sometimes go to the gym but I get bored! What about you?
A: Well, I like watching football and rugby on TV but I'm not very good at sports, really. I prefer going to the theatre and cinema and things like that.
B: What type of films do you like?
A: Anything, really, but I especially like action adventure films.
B: They're my favourite too. We'll have to go to the cinema some time.
A: That would be great. Look, give me your number and I'll text you at the weekend and we can arrange something.
B: OK, it's 0795 …

1.5

N = Narrator   A = Advisor   S = Student

N: You will hear a student asking a course advisor about what to study.
A: Matt, nice to see you. How are you?
S: Fine. Busy, but fine!
A: Good … How can I help you?
S: Well, I've got to choose my course for next year and I'm getting very confused. Maybe you can help me?
A: Sure. What's the problem?
S: Well, I want to do engineering, but I think you need top marks to get on the course, don't you?
A: Hmm … Yes, they ask for a Grade A in maths. And I know they are very strict about that. Is there anything else you like?
S: Well, I quite like economics – or business studies maybe?
A: Yes, they're not as strict as engineering, but I know they both ask for good English language skills. You've got those already, so that's OK.
S: Yes. Business studies may be better for me anyway.
A: Well, the good thing about this course is you spend three days in lectures learning about the subject, and then the other two days you spend working in a company.
S: Yeah, that sounds great, but how do I find the work experience?

A: Well, that's another good thing about this course – the organiser can put you in touch with employers in the local area to help you find your position. I think most students who do the course are very happy with it. Why don't you go and see Professor Lyatt and talk to him about it and see what he says?
S: Sorry, can you spell that?
A: Yes, it's L-Y-A-T-T. He's one of the course organisers.
S: OK, thanks. Do you know where I can find him?
A: Let's see … His office is in the business school – do you know where that is?
S: I think so, yes.
A: Yes, here we are: Room 251, on the second floor.
S: Thanks.
A: One other thing you might be interested in: next week the business school is having a week of special events, including a number of talks. They're open to anyone and they have some guest speakers coming in. Why don't you go along? It might help you make your decision.
S: That sounds interesting. Do I have to book?
A: Well, the talks will probably be very popular, so I would ring them to reserve a place. Let's see … The number is 7682 9331.
S: Right, got that.
A: By the way, you do know you haven't got long to decide, don't you? It's already March, so you need to be quick.
S: Oh, Um, yes – when do you need to know?
A: You need to decide by the end of April.
S: OK, thanks. I'll get back to you soon.

1.6

E = Examiner   C = Candidate

E: Can you tell me about your studies?
C: Yes. I'm doing engineering. It's my first year.
E: Do you like it?
C: Yes, I do – I think the course is quite exciting because the subject is new for me. One of the reasons why I like it is that the other students on the course are really great and we enjoy studying together.
E: Is there anything you don't like about the course?
C: Well, in my opinion, it's quite hard work and sometimes it's difficult as there are so many students on the course. I don't think you can ask as many questions as you'd like to because there isn't enough time for everyone.
E: Why did you choose that course?
C: Mainly because I believe I can get a good job when I finish. To be honest, it's quite easy to get jobs in engineering. But I also think the work will be very interesting.

Module 2

2.1

N = Narrator   I = Interviewer   M = Melissa

N: You will hear part of a radio programme about relationships.
I: Now I'd like to welcome to our show psychologist Melissa Duck, who's going to tell us about what makes us choose our friends.
M: Thanks, Dave. Yes, I'm going to talk about friendships and why we find some people more attractive as friends than others. It's a topic that almost everyone finds interesting and we all think we are experts on the subject. But we might not necessarily know everything or be correct.

2.2

N = Narrator   I = Interviewer   M = Melissa

N: You will hear part of a radio programme about relationships.
I: Now I'd like to welcome to our show psychologist Melissa Duck, who's going to tell us about what makes us choose our friends.
M: Thanks, Dave. Yes, I'm going to talk about friendships and why we find some people more attractive as friends than others. It's a topic that almost everyone finds interesting and we all think we are experts on the subject. But we might not necessarily know everything or be correct. For example, lots of us believe that we find people with opposite characters attractive but this is not correct. Recent research has shown that people like those who have similar opinions and ideas to their own. The study found that people with similar beliefs are attractive to us but we usually keep away from those who don't agree with our ideas. So what does this mean for you and me? Well, it shows that if we want to make friends with someone, we should concentrate on things we have in common instead of things that make us different.
To find out how important being similar is when forming friendships, researchers asked pairs of people, including couples, friends and acquaintances, to answer questions about their personality, beliefs and opinions. They then compared this information to see how similar or different each pair was, and if people in close or long relationships had more in common than people in shorter or more distant ones. The results showed that all the pairs had similar beliefs – even if they didn't know each other well.
In a second experiment, the researchers studied pairs on two different occasions: once when they did not know each other well, and then again some time later, when they knew each other better. There was almost no difference in their opinions during this time, which suggests that it's not easy to change someone's opinions. So if friends go into a relationship hoping to do this, they probably won't be successful.
I: So we don't have any control over our friends' beliefs?
M: Well, it's possible that we have some control, but it's a mistake for friends to enter a relationship thinking that they can change the other person. That's why it's better to pick a friend who has similar beliefs and goals to ours from the beginning.
I: Do you have any other advice for our listeners?
M: Well, the researchers warn that if we always look for friends who are very similar to us, we will not come into contact with different ideas and beliefs. So although we usually make friends with people who are similar to us, it is useful to also get to know people who are different from us.
So my advice is, you should try to get to know people who can show you new ideas and ways of thinking.
I: Thanks, Melissa!

2.3

A: Hi, Ken. I'm doing some research into family relationships for my sociology course and I'd like to ask you a few questions if that's OK.
B: Sure, what would you like to know?
A: Well, one of the things I'm looking at is the relationships between people in big and small families, so the first question is: do you have a large or small family?
B: Well, it's not that big, but I've got one brother and one sister. They're both older than me.
A: And how well do you get on with them?
B: I guess I get on better with my brother because we're closer in age – he's only two years older than me. And we also have similar interests, like surfboarding and chess.
A: OK, thanks. What about your sister?
B: Well, I'm eight years younger than her, so we're not as close and we don't have that much in common, really.
A: What about your parents? Do you have a good relationship with them, do you think?
B: Um, well, I think I'm quite close to my mum. I take after her in many ways; we're both confident but I'm not as sociable as she is.
A: And your dad?
B: Well, I don't always get on with him so well. I really look up to him but I think we have very different personalities and that's why we sometimes disagree.
A: And does anyone else live with you?
B: Yes, my grandmother.
A: What's your relationship with her like?
B: We're very close. In fact, she's probably my favourite person as although she's in poor health, she's the most cheerful person I know.
A: Well, thanks very much for answering my questions. That was very helpful.

2.6

N = Narrator   W = Woman

N: You will hear a woman talking at a careers conference about her job as an events organiser.

211

Audio scripts

W: I'm here today to talk to you about my job as an events organiser. Now, many people are interested in this type of work and it looks like fun, but I should warn you it is very hard work!

I'm sure you all know we need to do many different things in order to make a successful event, but when you are working for someone else, you really need to do things in the right order. The very first thing you need to do is choose the date and also decide on the budget – that is the amount of money you are going to spend. I say this because it's easy for the customer to forget about the cost as they are so excited about the event itself. So it's very important that you discuss the costs in detail right at the start, before you have to make choices about what you can and can't have.

OK, so after that, the next thing to do is find and book somewhere to hold the event. Some places are very popular, so don't forget you have to reserve them before you do anything else. Decide if it's indoor or outdoor and before you book, make sure your client can afford it: discuss and agree on a good price for them. Then order the invitations as they will take a while to print and you need to tell guests in good time – the earlier the better! And do remember to look at the invitations carefully before you send them, to check they have all the necessary details.

The next thing to do is start thinking about the food. You will need to make quite a few decisions with your client. For example, is it going to be a sit-down dinner or a buffet? And apart from the food itself, there are smaller things to decide, like table decorations and flowers. Then you can start organising things like the entertainment – you may have to book a musician or band. If it's a big event, you will have to decide how many staff you will need to help on the day. As you plan the event, it's not a problem if you have to go back to your customer and change a few small things. This is normal and all part of the job of keeping your client happy and making sure they get what they want.

One of the most difficult parts of being an events planner is remembering all the things you have to do, so perhaps my most important advice is to make a list of everything you need to do. You can add things to this and you can tick things as you complete them. In this way you won't forget. And finally, my last piece of advice is: always stay in touch with your client.

2.7

A Yes, yes I do. I like meeting up with my family and friends for a special event, like a birthday or wedding. We all get on really well, so when it's someone's birthday, we usually get together at someone's house or at a restaurant to celebrate and have a special meal. I like having a meal out in a restaurant but to be honest, I prefer having a celebration at home because my mum is a very good cook.

B Oh lots! In my family we celebrate lots of things together, such as birthdays, passing exams, a new baby in the family, getting a new job … In fact, we celebrate everything! We usually do the same thing for each celebration – we have a big meal at home and we invite all our family and friends. They're a very special family time and everyone is happy, and that's why I like them.

C Well, we have quite a few big national festivals. For instance, New Year is probably the most important as everyone celebrates this and lots of people travel long distances to be with their families. I like New Year but sometimes it's very busy, especially on trains and buses, and this makes it difficult if you want to travel. I prefer the smaller celebrations we have in my town because I don't have to travel far!

Module 3

3.1

A = Advisor   S = Student

A: So, Louis, tell me, what sort of job are you looking for?
S: Well, my degree is in biological sciences, so there are various options open to me. My parents are both science teachers but although I did consider it, I don't think that's for me. I'm quite interested in food manufacture – you know, developing and testing new products for some of the big food companies. In fact, that appeals to me much more than the drugs industry – that's what many of my friends are interested in.
A: What about working for a drugs company – in the sales department? I think that's quite popular too.
S: Yes, I know. But I don't think I'm a good salesman. I'm not sure I would enjoy meeting customers. I prefer spending time in the laboratory. So possibly some sort of research – maybe in a university or hospital.

3.2

N = Narrator   A = Advisor   S = Student

N: You will hear a university careers advisor talking to a student about the best way to find a job.
A: So, Louis, how are you getting on with your job search?
S: Hm, not too well, really. I'm studying really hard for my exams at the moment, so I don't have much time, but I'm trying my best to look for suitable jobs.
A: What are you doing at the moment then?
S: Well, I'm sending out my CV to some large companies, but that hasn't been very successful. I've only had one reply and that wasn't very positive.
A: Lots of the university departments have got a jobs notice board – have you looked?
S: They don't put up job adverts in my department. They did have a few large employers come to speak to students, but it was on a day when I couldn't go. My tutor also suggested I look for job adverts in science journals, but I don't think people advertise much in those these days, do they?
A: Not as much, maybe. What about online?
S: Well, there are a few good websites where they advertise jobs in science-related fields, so I'm checking those quite a lot. I've seen a couple of really interesting jobs.
A: OK. Well, that's a good start but there are quite a few other things you could start doing. And don't stop looking online; it's probably one of the best places to look these days – much easier than looking in newspapers. In fact, I suggest you get yourself more of an online profile. Maybe you should start using LinkedIn or sites like that – that's where many firms seem to advertise jobs these days. And you can follow the employers you're interested in.
S: That's a good idea. Some of my friends are already doing that, so I'll ask them to help me.
A: Now, I don't think there's any point in you going to a job agency – not for the type of job you're looking for. But I do suggest you think about a specialist job fair. Let's see … City University are holding one in two weeks – there'll be many employers there looking for graduates in your line of study. I really think you should go.
S: Yes, I think I will. Thanks, that's really good advice.
A: Good – I'm glad to help. Is there anything else you would like to know? Don't forget you can't continue to use our careers service when you leave the university and that's very soon, isn't it?
S: Yes, next month. No, I think I've got everything I need for now. Thank you very much for your help.

3.3

A: So I'm delighted to welcome Richard Adams here today. He's going to tell us a little about working in engineering and answer all your questions. So before that, Richard, could you just give us a very short description of your job?
B: Yes, of course. So I'll start by telling you a bit about my employer. I work for a large international engineering company. We have offices all over the world and employ all sorts of people – not just engineers – so I meet lots of different people, which is brilliant. I'm an engineer, but I also have a management position, so I manage a team of engineers. At the moment we're working on an exciting new project quite near here – it's a new road system on the other side of the city. So this is a local job. But I often have to travel too because some of our projects are a long way from here, even overseas, which can be fascinating. Some of my office work and paperwork is rather routine but that's true for many jobs, so I don't mind. What I like best is working with other people, travelling to new countries and working on different projects. I find solving problems is very rewarding and I also enjoy seeing my ideas come to life. I think I enjoy everything about my job, and actually prefer the more difficult and demanding parts of the job to the easier ones – these can become boring. So if you're good at maths and science, have a creative mind and like solving problems, engineering might be a good career for you.

A: Thanks. That's great. Before you answer questions, could you just explain a little bit about your qualifications and training – I'm sure everyone here …

3.6

N = Narrator   S1 = Student 1   S2 = Student 2

N: You will hear a discussion between two students about a presentation on a business project they are studying.
S1: OK, so have you got any ideas for our presentation?
S2: Well, there's an interesting article in this magazine about people who are very successful selling on online marketplaces. Some of them have made millions and what they have in common is they started by selling things on eBay.
S1: That does sound interesting. So how shall we organise the presentation?
S2: Well, I think we need to talk about the challenges of setting up this type of business and then we can discuss the benefits.
S1: Alright, so what can you tell me about the difficulties? I would imagine it's quite difficult to set up any kind of business without any money to finance it.
S2: But that's the whole point of these success stories. Many of them start with very little and then they grow very quickly. In fact, one of the main difficulties for many of these companies is just that: they find they are increasing in size so quickly that it is difficult for them to keep up with all the orders and they don't have enough things to sell to all the customers.
S1: Yes, I can see how that would be a problem. And what about all the paperwork you have to do if you run your own business – the tax and things like that? Don't you need a lot of experience to do that?
S2: Not really. You have to be organised, of course, but I think anyone can do it. Now, another problem some of the sellers have is finding enough room to store their products. You need to have lots of products to sell, but if you're working from home, that can soon start to be a problem – you need to find somewhere to put everything.
S1: Right. And what are the benefits of running this type of business? I don't expect it's the most rewarding job, is it?
S2: Well, maybe not, but it's one of the easiest types of business to set up – all you need is a camera to photograph the products, a computer and some packaging to post the products – it's as simple as that.
S1: But you have to get the products from somewhere?
S2: Yes, but the key thing is to start small, perhaps by selling things you already have in your home. Then you can start looking for new and different products.
S1: I suppose it's important to offer products the customer wants?
S2: Exactly. And the main advantage of online selling like this is that it's possible to have millions of buyers all around the world – much more than you have with just a normal High Street shop.
S1: But it must get difficult trying to keep all of them happy.
S2: Yes, I suppose giving good customer service might be difficult sometimes, so that is possibly a disadvantage.
S1: OK, so we've got some ideas. Let's do some more research and see if we can find some actual case studies. Why don't we …

3.7

E = Examiner   C = Candidate

E: Can you start speaking now, please?
C: Well, the job I'm going to talk about is a teacher. Of course, the job involves teaching, but there are many different kinds of teachers. For example, some teachers work in schools and others work in colleges or universities. Some teachers specialise in one or two subjects but most primary school teachers have to teach many different subjects. I think it's a demanding and stressful job because apart from teaching, they have to work very hard. For example, they have to spend a lot of time preparing for their classes and marking homework and assignments. They also have to attend meetings and they probably have to do a lot of paperwork.
I think most teachers have a degree and probably other teaching qualifications too, so they probably spend quite a few years training. And I think most teachers continue to do some training throughout their careers.
Of course, teaching is a very important job – we need good teachers in schools so that children learn well and get good qualifications. Teachers can also teach their students about other things apart from academic studies. They can teach them life skills and about how to behave well – that sort of thing. And teachers are important role models for their students. I think teaching can be a difficult and stressful job, but it can also be a fantastic job – and very rewarding.

Module 4

4.1

So now I'm going to talk a little about some of the most significant medical breakthroughs and discoveries of the last two or three hundred years. In the modern age, it's sometimes difficult to believe that some of the treatments and procedures we now take for granted were not available until relatively recently. For example, until the late nineteenth century, people had surgery without anaesthetic. And it wasn't until the 1900s that scientists realised there were different blood groups, which meant it was safer to give people blood during or after an operation. Many people consider the nineteenth century to be one of the most important periods for scientific discovery and it is true that this was a time of huge progress in the medical field, particularly regarding the cause and prevention of infectious diseases. A key development of this time was French scientist Louis Pasteur's discovery that the main cause of infectious diseases were tiny living things, or germs, that are so small we can only see them under a microscope. He also realised that these grew in food, making it go bad, and that we can kill them by heating them to a certain temperature – what we now call pasteurisation. And he was also responsible for developing vaccinations, which people now take to stop themselves getting certain diseases. His work with vaccinations continued the work of British scientist Edward Jenner, who successfully created the first vaccination to stop people getting the disease smallpox earlier, at the end of the previous century.
Pasteur's theories about bacteria influenced other scientists, including Joseph Lister, who realised that hospitals and medical equipment needed to be free of dirt and germs to prevent infection. Until his discovery in the 1860s, many people died after surgery because they developed infections from dirty hospitals and instruments. Lister's discovery changed people's ideas about cleanliness and saved many lives.

4.2

N = Narrator   L = Lecturer

N: You will hear part of a lecture about medical discoveries and breakthroughs.
L: So I've already discussed Louis Pasteur and Joseph Lister, but of course, these were just two of many doctors and scientists at this time who were making important medical breakthroughs. Another one was a Scottish doctor called Henry Gray, who in 1858 published the first edition of his work on the human body. It had hundreds of beautiful illustrations. It was used in schools and homes and, most importantly, in the teaching of medical students. Although it is over a hundred and fifty years old, people still use it today and doctors consider it one of the most important medical publications.

Another scientist working at this time who had a special interest in the human body was Czech-born Jan Purkinje. He studied cells and made important discoveries about the eye, the brain and the heart. He also made an important contribution to the study of medicine by establishing the first university department specialising in how the body works. He later set up the world's first specialist laboratory where scientists could examine human cells in detail.

As knowledge about the human body increased, so did knowledge about diseases, with many scientists continuing Pasteur's work. You remember that Pasteur discovered that germs could cause disease. Well, a German doctor named Robert Koch took this one step further and discovered how to grow germs or bacteria in the laboratory. Towards the end of the nineteenth century he identified the germs which cause tuberculosis and cholera, two major killers at that time. Koch's work in this area was an important breakthrough for which he received the Nobel prize for medicine in 1905.

Audio scripts

Another area of medical science that was developing at this time concerned how lifestyle can affect health. Many scientists in the nineteenth century were investigating the food people ate. Although they realised that particular foods could protect you from certain diseases, nobody knew why. In the early part of the twentieth century, a Polish scientist called Casimir Funk was investigating the health benefits of certain foods, when he found four substances in foods that could prevent or cure certain diseases. Funk suggested that we needed to eat food containing these substances in order to keep us healthy. He called the substances vitamins, and in later years other scientists identified more of these substances. We now know there are thirteen in total. Another scientist who made a significant discovery at this time was …

4.3

W = Woman   M = Man

W: Look at this, Marco – there's an article in this magazine with a list of factors which can keep you healthy. Hmm … I'm not so sure about some of these.
M: Why, what does it say?
W: Well, some of them are obvious – not smoking, for example; everyone knows it's not good for you.
M: Uh huh.
W: And doing regular exercise – I totally agree with that.
M: Doing regular exercise? Well, I agree up to a point – my grandfather never did any exercise and lived to the age of ninety-two. What other factors does it mention?
W: Well, a good diet – yes, I agree with that. But having a job you enjoy? I'm not sure I agree with that one.
M: I agree to some extent – after all, if you're unhappy in your job, it can affect your health negatively.
W: Hmm … What about this one then? Having friends and family around you?
M: I couldn't agree more with that. I think it's really important in keeping us happy and therefore healthy.
W: Yes, I see your point. What about this one – sleeping well? I totally disagree with that one. I never get a good night's sleep but I'm healthy. What do you think?
M: I don't agree with you. I think poor sleep can lead to problems later in life.
W: I suppose you might be right. The last one is keeping your brain active. I think that means it's important to do mental exercise as well as physical – reading, doing puzzles and crosswords, that sort of thing.
M: That's true. In fact, I think that's more important than physical exercise.
W: Yes, you're absolutely right. But then I love puzzles and I hate sport!

4.6

N = Narrator   L = Lecturer

N: You will hear a lecturer talking about animals and self-medication.
L: For most humans, a minor illness like a stomachache or a headache is easy to deal with – we just go to the chemist and buy some medicine. But animals in the wild haven't got that option; so what do they do?

Well, you may have seen domestic animals like dogs and cats eating grass sometimes. Why do they do it? As most pet owners know, they do this when they've eaten something bad and they feel sick. It seems that animals have a natural ability to find a solution in their surroundings to treat their symptoms. The technical term for this is 'self-medication' and there are plenty of examples of it in the animal world.

Domestic pets are not the only animals to eat something to relieve an illness. We know that some animals eat clay or soil because it helps them destroy germs in their stomach, which can take away the stomachache. The Amazon bird, the Macaw, has a diet high in seeds, which means they sometimes also eat poisonous berries. However, the clay and soil that they eat can help kill anything poisonous they eat by accident.

So how do we know if an animal is eating something for self-medication or if it is just part of their normal diet? Well, one sign that the animal is self-medicating is if it only eats something at certain times. For example, some animals self-medicate because they suffer from fleas or other insects, which are usually worse at certain times of year. We know that chimpanzees eat the leaves of a particular plant, which help them get rid of a worm living inside them. The South American Tamarin monkey eats very large seeds for the same purpose.

Another interesting example of self-medication is something we see in pregnant elephant mothers shortly before they have their babies. The animal eats leaves from a particular tree, which is not part of their regular diet. Scientists believe that the tree contains a substance which encourages the baby to arrive. Interestingly, local Kenyan women make a drink from the same tree to encourage their babies to arrive – a clear example of how humans can learn from animal behaviour.

But self-medication doesn't have to involve eating. More than two hundred species of bird pick up insects, usually ants, and rub them on their bodies. Scientists think that the ants produce a substance – called formic acid – which helps kill unwelcome creatures living in the birds' feathers. Capuchin monkeys also put ants as well as plants, leaves and fruit on their fur for the same purpose, especially during the rainy season, when there are more insects around. Brown bears also rub plants on their fur to keep insects away. The plants may also help with the pain from insect bites.

So what can we learn from self-medication in the animal world? Are any of these treatments suitable for human illnesses? Well, one thing that scientists are looking at …

4.7

E = Examiner   C = Candidate

E: So let's now talk about the natural world. Why do people like visiting natural attractions?
C: For many reasons, I think. For instance, in my country one of the most popular natural attractions is a lake in the mountains, and people go there on holiday to relax or do activities like fishing or water sports like sailing. They like to enjoy the clean air and peace and quiet of the place. They can also see wildlife such as birds and trees or plants. So there are lots of reasons.
E: How can people who live in the city enjoy the natural world?
C: I think even if you live in a city, you can still enjoy nature. For instance, many cities have lots of green spaces like parks or rivers where people can go for walks and enjoy nature. An example of this is in my city, where there is a big park just on the edge of the city and many people go there at weekends to walk and cycle.
E: What can we teach children about the natural world?
C: Lots of things. We should teach them to respect the world they live in and show them how to take care of it. For example, we should teach them to protect animals that are endangered, like tigers and pandas. We also need to show them how to keep the countryside clean and tidy – for instance, by picking up rubbish or cleaning up after themselves. This is especially important if children live in towns or cities because they don't have much contact with nature and perhaps don't understand it.

Module 5

5.1

N = Narrator   TG = Tour guide

N: You will hear a tour guide talking to a group of tourists.
TG: Good evening, everyone, and on behalf of World Adventure Tours, welcome to Borneo. I will try to keep this meeting very short so that you can go off and relax and enjoy the rest of the evening. So you have the first day free here in Kota Kinabalu, and I have a few suggestions of activities you might like to do.

One very popular trip is to the Mari-Mari Cultural Village. It's a chance to see the lifestyle of the local people. You will see inside the native long houses and meet local hunters and fishermen who will show you their traditions and customs. If you decide to go on this trip, I suggest you don't have a big breakfast as there will be a large lunch of local dishes.

If you're feeling active after your long flight, you might like to take part in the jungle trek on Gaya Island. It's a short boat trip from here and a local guide will lead you on a two-hour walk through

Audio scripts

the forest with a chance to spot birds and other wildlife. It's a good idea to take plenty of sunscreen and a swimsuit as there will be a chance for a swim afterwards.

Finally, if you prefer to stay in the city, we are offering you a chance to explore the city with a local guide. You will visit all the major sites in the city, including the state mosque. The cost of this tour includes entrance to the Sabah museum, which is really interesting. There is quite a lot of walking on this trip, so wear suitable shoes and take plenty of water as it will be hot. If you're interested in any of these trips, please let me know after this meeting as we need to confirm numbers tonight.

5.2

N = Narrator   TG = Tour guide

N: You will hear a tour guide talking to a group of tourists.
TG: So, we've got a busy few days planned for you once we leave the city on day 2. We start bright and early on Tuesday and head straight to Kinabalu National Park. After arrival, there will be a chance for you to enjoy a guided walk in the park, including a visit to the mountain garden. Your guide will show you some of the rare species of plant that grow there, including the famous pitcher plant. The rest of the day is free but I would strongly advise you to go to the evening talk by one of the local mountain guides – it gives an excellent background into the history, geography and ecology of the site.

Days 3 and 4 are devoted to your climb of Mount Kinabalu, which I'm sure will be the highlight of the trip for many of you. Remember you'll be staying overnight on the mountain and the aim is to reach the top as the sun is coming up. I'm not going to talk in detail about the climb but I would like to remind you now about the equipment you need. I have a list here that I would like everyone to check. In particular, a couple of things that people often forget: make sure you take snacks for energy and a torch for the final climb to the top on the morning of day 3 – remember you'll be doing this in the dark. So, by the afternoon of day 4 you'll be back down the mountain and we will go back to our hotel for some rest.

On day 5 we have another early start when we head to Kuala Abai for a forty-five-minute boat ride to Mantanani, a group of three islands where you'll stay for two nights. This is where you have a chance to relax on the beautiful beaches, but I do recommend you to do some of the activities on offer. Of course, the biggest attractions are the diving and snorkelling trips. The water is crystal clear and you should be able to see all sorts of marine life. For these activities, we will provide all the equipment and there will be experts to guide you. One thing to remember for this part of your trip is that it is sometimes difficult and expensive to buy things like sunscreen on the islands, so it's a good idea to buy it before you go, and take it with you. So, now, before I hand over to your local guide, are there any questions …

5.3

For my holidays I <u>generally</u> go to different places because I enjoy seeing different countries and finding out about their history. <u>On the whole</u>, I prefer taking trips to cities and this is for a number of reasons. <u>To start with</u>, there is always so much to do in a city. <u>First of all</u>, there are all the museums and art galleries to visit – this is probably my favourite thing to do because I love history. And the good thing about cities is that it doesn't matter if the weather is bad because there is always something to do inside. Um, but you can <u>also</u> just walk around seeing the sights and there are usually parks and places where you can relax <u>as well</u>. And then there's the shopping – I really enjoy looking around local shops and buying gifts for my family and friends. <u>Another thing I love about city holidays is</u> there is always a good choice of places to eat. Um, <u>one more point is</u> there are usually plenty of things to do in the evening, like going to the theatre or cinema. And <u>lastly</u>, it's usually easy to travel to cities because there are good transport links so you can fly or get a train easily. And when you arrive, it's easy to get around by bus or tram, which I think is important. So, <u>overall</u>, even though you can get very tired because you are so busy all the time, I really prefer this type of holiday.

5.4

N = Narrator   S = Speaker

N: You will hear a radio talk about the effects of the weather and seasons on how we feel and behave.
S: Do you ever feel that the weather affects your mood and feelings, and even your behaviour? I know I usually feel happier when the sun is out and I can feel miserable when the skies are grey, so I decided to find out a little bit more about how the weather can affect us.

Like me, many people suffer from low mood during the winter months, but for some people, it's a little more serious and they have quite serious symptoms of depression, including sleep problems and lack of energy. This is known as Seasonal Affective Disorder, or SAD for short, and it affects people living in places with short days, such as Scandinavia or Canada where there is not much daylight during the winter. Although there are many ideas about what causes SAD, some believe that it could be to do with a chemical produced in the brain which is affected by sunlight.

You might not think that the season in which you were born can influence you when you grow up, but a study found that it can affect things like your temperament and mood. This study found that winter babies are less likely to be bad-tempered as adults and autumn babies show fewer signs of depression when they grow up. Now, I was born in May, and the same study shows that people who were born at that time of year and in summer are more likely to have very positive feelings than those born at other times of year.

So what about hurricanes, floods and other extreme weather events? Well, scientists believe that worry about extreme weather conditions can cause stress and mental health issues. Those who suffer most include people who depend on the natural environment – for example, farmers and fishermen – and those who live in areas which frequently suffer such events, such as people living near a river.

However, the effects of extreme weather are not necessarily always negative – often after a weather disaster, people feel less selfish and experience kind and generous feelings towards people within and outside their community. We could see this when a severe hurricane hit New Orleans in the southern United States in 2005: more than a million volunteers came to the city to help clear up and rebuild homes and thousands of people offered their homes to strangers who had lost everything.

For many people, higher temperatures produce positive and happy feelings but research also shows that there may be a link between high temperatures and higher levels of crime. Studies in Chicago found that antisocial behaviour increases in late spring, when temperatures start to rise. However, this could be because during the summer, days are longer and people stay outside in the streets, where there are more opportunities for crime. In fact, another study found that when temperatures rise above a certain level, there are fewer crimes because people generally stay inside to keep cool.

It seems clear that weather and seasons can affect us, so what can we do if we …

5.5

E = Examiner   C = Candidate

E: Can you start speaking now, please?
C: Well, there are quite a few environmental problems in my country at the moment. But I'm going to talk about a place near my home which has a serious problem with pollution. It's a beach a few kilometres from where I live and it's one of the most popular places in the area for families and young people. But a few years ago it started having a big problem with people leaving rubbish on the beach and there are a number of reasons for this. First of all, I think the beach is becoming more and more popular nowadays with tourists and also with groups of young people who go there to have picnics. The problem is that there aren't many litter bins on the beach, so some people just leave their rubbish lying around instead of taking it with them. The last time I was there, you could see litter everywhere – food, plastic bags, bottles … It's a shame because when I was younger, I often went there with my friends and I know it was much cleaner. At that time I think somebody cleaned the beach

Audio scripts

every morning and picked up all the litter. But that doesn't happen often these days and it really looks quite dirty and not as attractive as it was in the past. Another problem with the beach right now is that the sea is so polluted you can't swim in it; I think this is because of industrial waste from factories. This problem is a lot worse now than in the past – I remember the sea was much cleaner when I swam in it as a child. Overall, water pollution is a serious issue in my country and swimming is not safe in many beaches and rivers, which is very sad.

Module 6

6.2

N = Narrator   SA = Sales assistant   C = Customer

N: You will hear a conversation between a customer and sales assistant in a health food shop.
SA: Hello, can I help you?
C: Yes, I spoke to you on the phone earlier.
SA: Oh yes, I remember. You run a health and fitness company, don't you?
C: Yes, that right. I'd like to find out a bit more about the products you have on offer.
SA: OK, we have a good range of products for sports nutrition, for weight loss, for vegetarians … What are you interested in?
C: Umm … did you say weight loss? Can you tell me more about that?
SA: Well, we have a selection of nutrition drinks – they come in three flavours and each drink only has two hundred calories; so they're great as a meal replacement if you're trying to lose weight. They are very nutritious and contain all the vitamins and minerals you need. We also have these snack bars which contain fruit, cereals and nuts.
C: OK. Have you got any of those for people who are allergic to nuts?
SA: Yes, we have a special range of products for people who can't eat certain things, including nuts, eggs and dairy. Look – here's a list.
C: Ah yes, that's the sort of thing. Now, I'm not so interested in vegetarian products, but I do have a few clients who do a lot of sport.
SA: OK, so we have a range of energy drinks, which are very popular with sportspeople. We have a number of different flavours and they're all totally organic, which I think your customers will like.
C: Yes, I think you're right. Now, what about protein food – you know, for building up strength and muscle?
SA: We have this protein powder which contains milk and egg protein, as well as vitamins and minerals.
C: I'm not sure I like the sound of that – it sounds disgusting!
A: Actually, you use it to make a drink – it's just like drinking a strawberry or vanilla milkshake. And we are selling it at half price at the moment, so you can get two tins for the price of one.
C: Oh, that sounds good. Umm … one more thing: I notice on your website that you sell vitamin and mineral supplements?
SA: Yes, actually we sell more of those than anything else. What are you interested in?
C: Well, have you got any special offers on these?
SA: No special offers at the moment, but one of our most popular products are these multi-vitamin pills – they contain all the essential vitamins and minerals plus added energy.
C: That's exactly the sort of thing I was looking for. OK, so if I want to place an order, can I do that online or shall I …

6.3

A: This meal is delicious, Yannis. I didn't realise you were such a good cook.
B: Thank you. Yes, I love cooking, especially traditional Greek dishes like this.
A: So is this dish from a particular region?
B: I'm not sure, but I think it's from the north of the country originally – although it's popular everywhere now. My region is very famous for its olives and its olive oil. I'm from the Peloponnese – that's in the south. We produce a lot of olive oil and we use it in all our cooking. I suppose it's what we're best-known for, along with feta cheese and Greek salad.
A: Oh yes. Is that Kalamata olive oil? I've heard of that. I could be wrong, but isn't that why people say you have one of healthiest diets? Because of all the olive oil you use?
B: It's difficult to say, but I know many people say that olive oil is very good for you. But we also eat a lot of fruit and vegetables – lots of people grow them in their gardens and we usually have salad with every meal. And I live very near the coast, so we have fish four or five times a week. I suppose our diet is quite balanced and we don't have much junk food – at least not where I come from.
A: Do you think that will change in the future?
B: Perhaps. I can't say for sure, but I think people in the cities are eating more fast food nowadays. I know that in some of the tourist areas there are more fast food restaurants now than in the past – you know, burgers and pizza, things like that. But Greek restaurants are still very popular with local people and with the tourists, so I hope that continues.

6.6

N = Narrator   M = Manager   E = Employee

N: You will hear the manager of a shop talking to a new member of staff.
M: Hello, Martin. Welcome! How are you feeling?
E: A little nervous. But excited, too.
M: Good. So, I think the first thing to do is to show you around the store and tell you a little about each department.
E: OK.
M: You probably know we have five main departments: books, greetings cards, DVDs, newspapers and magazines and finally, stationery. That is probably our most important department and what most people come in here for; and that's why we put it at the back of the shop.
E: Why's that?
M: Well, it's so that customers wanting to buy pens and notebooks will have to walk through the other departments first, so we hope they will pick up a book or magazine on the way. Apart from the usual pens and pencils, we have computer and printer accessories here too and these are also very popular.
E: I thought that papers and magazines were your most popular items?
M: Second most popular. That's why they go at the front of the shop. We need something that makes an attractive display, and people who come into the shop to buy them generally don't stop to browse other items – they just want to be in and out very quickly.
E: Hmm … You've done a lot of research into where you put things in the store.
M: Yes, it's quite scientific but very interesting; obviously, we want to make best use of the space and make the most profit. OK, so over here we always have a temporary display. Now this might be a special offer – sometimes we have those on books – or it could be something that's particularly relevant for the time of year. So for example, at the moment we've got a display of Father's Day cards here because that's coming up soon.
E: I see. So you said on the phone that I'm going to be working in the book department.
M: Yes, that's right. We'll start you off there and perhaps move you to another department in a couple of months. You'll be starting in our quietest department, so it'll give you a chance to get to know how things work before you move somewhere a bit busier. So moving on, over here by the books we have the DVDs. Now as you can see, all the products in this section are half price because we're in the process of removing them altogether by the end of the month.
E: I suppose that's because they don't sell as well now.
M: That's right – there's too much competition from online stores. OK, so you've seen the store. I'll take you upstairs now – that's where the staff room is and then we'll go to the stock room to see …

6.7

E = Examiner   C = Candidate

E: Do you think there is too much advertising around us?
C: Absolutely. Nowadays we get advertising everywhere we look, really. In my country, it's all over the place – in magazines, on TV, at the cinema, online. I certainly think it's impossible to avoid some adverts, like the ones that pop up on your phone or on websites. There seems to be advertising in every place you look. It's definitely too much.

Audio scripts

E: Do you think we often buy things we don't need because of advertising?
C: Hmm ... <u>maybe</u> – it's difficult to say. Adverts can make you think you need things that are <u>probably</u> not really necessary. And adverts <u>clearly</u> are very good at persuading us that our lives will be different if we buy a certain product – and lots of people believe them. So, yes, we <u>possibly</u> buy things that we can do without.
E: Do you think the amount of advertising we have should be controlled?
C: Well, <u>perhaps</u> – I'm not really sure. Erm ... <u>Of course</u>, some countries already have controls to stop some advertising. I could be wrong, but I think in Sao Paolo there are laws to say you cannot put advertisements up on the streets and highways. But I also think that with internet and multi-media advertising it's <u>probably</u> going to be very difficult to have many restrictions over this type of advertising in the future.

Module 7

7.1

1
A: So what sort of problems are you experiencing?
B: Well, there were a lot of thefts recently, particularly of laptops and mobile phones and other electronic equipment; and last week we also had some vandalism.

2
A: Is there a lot of crime each year?
B: Quite a lot, yes. Let's see, I've got some figures here ... Over the last few years the average is three hundred, so yes, I think that is quite a lot.

3
A: Do you know who is committing these crimes? It's not students, is it?
B: No, no. The police say it's mainly local teenagers – there are a few groups in the area and the university is just one of the places they have targeted.

4
A: So is everywhere on campus affected or is there one particular area where the crimes take place?
B: Well, there have been incidents in many places, but it's the library that is most badly affected, maybe because students often leave their laptops and phones lying around.

5
A: And do these crimes happen during the day?
B: Sometimes. But it's usually in the evening, when there are fewer people around.

6
A: So, is there anything we can do to protect the campus and make it a safer place?
B: There are a number of things we are considering in the future, including more security guards. But something we're already doing is installing more CCTV, especially in and around the library.

7.2

N = Narrator   S1 = Student 1   S2 = Student 2

N: You will hear a conversation between two students about crime on a university campus.
S1: Hi, Claude. Are you OK? You look tired.
S2: Yes, I am a bit. I'm working on this assignment and it's hard work but I've nearly finished now.
S1: What's it about?
S2: I'm looking into crime on the university campus.
S1: Crime? What sort of crime? I thought the campus was a fairly safe place.
S2: Well, it is, actually. We don't get any really serious crimes here, thankfully, so it's still a safe place, really – much safer than most cities. In fact, all the crimes recorded by the police in the last year, they say are minor.
S1: Well, that's good to know, I suppose.
S2: Yes, but we do get a surprising number of these minor crimes. And some types of crime are currently on the rise – especially shoplifting and vandalism.
S1: Yes, I remember hearing something about vandalism in the science block recently.
S2: Yes, there was a more serious incident of vandalism recently, which caused a lot of damage. So that's very worrying. But actually, vandalism is still quite rare compared to theft – that's what we see most of.
S1: How common is it then?
S2: Well, for my research I've spoken to the campus security team as well as the local police – they've been great in helping me out with this project. I've recorded all incidents over the last six months. In that time there was a total of eighty-eight criminal incidents on campus. And of those, only nine percent were reports of vandalism, whereas sixty-seven percent were reports of stolen items.
S1: That's quite a lot. What sort of things are stolen?
S2: Anything and everything – you'd be surprised, actually, by some of the things that they steal. We've had bikes, keys, briefcases, bags, laptops, mobile phones, books ... Someone even stole some exam papers from one of the professors in the psychology department!
S1: Really? What happened?
S2: Well, they were in a briefcase and I suppose the thief thought there was something valuable in it. They were returned a few days later.
S1: So, is this sort of thing happening all over the campus?
S2: Well, there are incidents in most areas, but the place which seems to be most badly affected is the sports centre.
S1: Hmm ... the security's not very good there. And people just leave their stuff lying around when they're in the gym or in the pool.
S2: Yes, you're right – lots of things are stolen from the changing rooms. But the problem is there's nowhere safe to leave anything because of all the broken lockers. That's one of my recommendations – that they repair these as soon as possible.
S1: So, what other suggestions do you make?
S2: There's already plenty of CCTV and security guards. I think the main issue is most people do not expect crime on campus, so they are not very aware of what's going on around them. I think we will see a fall in crime if there is better awareness and people are more careful.
S1: I think you're right. When you live in this close community, it's easy to forget the real world sometimes but crime still happens, unfortunately. Well, I think your assignment sounds really interesting. Why don't you publish it in the student newspaper? That would get everyone thinking ...

7.3

A   Oh actually, it's very small. I live in a village where everyone knows each other. Some people complain that our village is too small and nothing ever happens, but I like living there. It's true that we haven't got many facilities in the village but there is always something going on and we have lots of social events.

B   Well, I think it's easier to feel part of the community and know that there are always people around you who can help you, although sometimes that means everyone knows what your problems are. We have lots of community events in the village and almost everyone takes part. However, village life is not for everyone and some people prefer to keep themselves to themselves.

C   Erm, quite a lot, actually. I'm in the local football team and I also help coach some of the younger players. It takes up a lot of my free time but at the same time it's really good fun and I enjoy doing it because it makes you feel part of what's going on. It's not true that small villages can be boring. On the contrary, our football team is really active and we have matches and other events two or three times a week.

D   Well, on the one hand, it can be more difficult to hold the community together nowadays because many young people prefer to move to the city, where there are more job opportunities. On the other hand, I think technology is making it easier for communities to stay in touch with the people who move away. For example, I have some friends from my village who live abroad, but they still get involved with community projects by keeping in touch online.

7.4

N = Narrator   T = Tutor   S = Student

N: You will hear a conversation between a student and her tutor about an assignment she is working on.
T: So Marion, how are you getting on with your assignment? What subject did you choose in the end?

Audio scripts

S: It's going OK, thanks, Dr Foulkes. It had to involve a survey of people in the local community, so I decided to ask about public services and facilities in the town. It's been really interesting but hard work, and not as easy as I thought it would be.
T: What did you find difficult then?
S: Nothing major and it wasn't difficult finding people to ask, which I thought it would be. Lots of people wanted to talk to me, but they were all retired people – and I needed to ask a variety of people.
T: So what did you do?
S: I had to go out again at different times of day and to different places and make sure I found a wider range of people. I went to a number of places, including the train station, a supermarket, a health centre outside the leisure centre – there were plenty of places to choose from.
T: So what did you ask them? Sometimes it's difficult thinking of suitable questions.
S: I think I had some good questions – that wasn't too hard, actually. I wanted to see what services and facilities people use, which ones they're happy with and which ones they're not so happy with and why. And what they would like to see improve in the future. I got some interesting findings. And that's where I'm a bit stuck – I'm not really sure what to do with these and I wondered if you could help.
T: Of course. So what did you find?
S: The interesting thing was the difference between the age groups, so it's good I did ask some younger people! There were eight different facilities in town that I asked people about. I wanted to find out whether they used them and if so, to rate their satisfaction. I was surprised that some of the facilities are so little used. The under-twenty-five-year-olds hardly use the town library at all! Even the students don't because they prefer to use the one on campus.
T: So this is the sort of thing you can talk about in your report – things that are particularly surprising or unexpected. There's no need to describe every single result – just pick the most relevant or interesting ones.
S: I see.
T: Try to start with some overall findings – the most popular and least popular facility, that sort of thing.
S: OK, well, overall, the place people use most was the shopping centre – I suppose that's not surprising, really, but there was a big difference in opinion about that. Older people were much happier with it than younger ones and it was the same for eating places – older people seemed more easily satisfied than the young!
T: That doesn't surprise me! What else did you find?
S: I was disappointed that not more people use the community centre. Some people didn't really know what it's there for, which is a pity because there's all sorts of classes and groups that meet there. It was interesting to see that all the parents knew about it as there are three different toddler groups that meet there and there's also a youth club. And lots of dance classes for kids too; these are very popular, actually – kids love them.
T: So it's a popular place?
S: Well, no not exactly. People weren't very happy with the centre's security. They say vandals are always breaking in and damaging things. Another place people generally weren't satisfied with was the new leisure centre.
T: But that only opened last year. What's the matter with it?
S: The facilities there are fantastic and it's much better than the old one, but the problem is the prices they charge. Many people say they can't afford to use it – especially young people.
T: That's a shame. Well, I think you've got more than enough material here, Marion. What you need to do now is think about any recommendations you might have …

7.5

1   Um, most towns and cities in my country have, um, a town hall, um, yes, a town hall – that's where there are government offices and, err … where people go to get married. Um, and they have other important events there. And I think many town halls … err, inside many town halls you can often, um, find the city museum or art gallery as well.

2   Let me see … Well, I think all towns and cities in my country have a public space. How can I describe it? It's like a main square in the centre of the city. This is where they often have a market once or twice a week and it's also where they have important public events.

For example, in my town we have a festival every summer and most of the events take place in the main square.

7.6

E = Examiner   C = Candidate
E: How important are public places like these?
C: Are they important? Well, I suppose they are very important because people need a place where they can all meet and … how can I explain? I think this gives them a sense of community. For example, when we celebrate our National Day, we have a parade and everyone goes to the main square. I guess it's like a tradition to go there and it connects us to history as well. So yes, I think they're very important.
E: Is there any difference between the appearance of public buildings today and those in the past?
C: Let me see. Well, most public buildings in my town are very old and have a lot of history. It's true that inside they usually have modern technology but the buildings themselves are very old and have beautiful architecture. When they build new public buildings today, I don't think they look very attractive. On the contrary, they just design them to be practical and useful.
E: Are public buildings for everyone or just some people?
C: To be honest, I haven't thought about that before. I suppose they're meant to be for everyone and that's why they are called public buildings. Most people use places like hospitals and libraries at some point in their lives. However, people use some public buildings more than others. For example, I don't think many people go to the town hall much, except for weddings and important official events. Public buildings like museums and art galleries are for everyone and I think they should always be free.

Module 8

8.1

Good evening, everyone. Thank you for asking me here today to talk to you. The question people most often ask me, particularly after I won my gold medal at the last Olympics, is, 'What is the reason for your success?' So I have thought about this a great deal and I believe there are a number of factors involved. However, today I'm going to tell you what I think are the three key reasons behind my achievement.

The first factor is the funding I have received from various sources. This meant I could afford to give up my job and concentrate on my training full-time. It also meant I could afford to go to special training camps, get the best equipment and hire a really good coach.

The second reason I think I've had so much success is my coach, Graham. He has trained me for six years now and we have worked really hard together. We get on really well, which is important, and he always gives me really good advice about every aspect of my training, including things like my diet, so I feel so much better prepared for each competition with him.

The final factor is I've spent a lot of time in the last three years working with a sports psychologist. One of the areas I think I've really worked hard on with her help is my mental strength. She has helped me deal with failure in a much more positive way and has taught me to believe in myself, even when things go wrong. I know this helped me enormously when I went to the Olympics.

So, to sum up, the three factors which I consider have contributed most to my success are my financial backing, my coach Graham and the work I've done with a sports psychologist.

8.2

N = Narrator   L = Lecturer
N: You will hear a lecturer giving a talk to a group of sports students about what is important for success at a sport.
L: I'm very grateful to the university for inviting me here today to talk to you. I'm delighted to have this opportunity to discuss one of the key things that I think affects how successful people are at sport.

This is that there seems to be a belief that you either are or aren't naturally talented at sports. What is worrying is that this type of thinking begins early, so even young children start to think, 'Oh, I'm

Audio scripts

good at – or bad at – sport,' whether it's true or not. So what you notice is that students, by the time they reach their mid-teens, are either very involved in sports or, more typically, they don't do sport any more at all. It's such a shame because, in fact, anyone can be good at sport. And this is something I especially want you to think about if you are planning to be coaches in school.

Of course, to be successful at any sport, you need to devote a lot of time to training and this is very important, but there is more to success than this. Now, I have done research into this subject by speaking to many professional athletes, including some national and world champions, and I think we can see some other common features in all of these successful people.

The first thing I noticed in all the successful sportspeople I spoke to is the strong desire to succeed. These athletes are extremely motivated and set their goals very high. Even those at the top of their sport have goals, so whether it is achieving a personal best time, winning a world championship or breaking a new world record, there is always a goal in sight. Importantly, because they have such a clear focus on what they want to achieve, they don't allow problems to get in the way. On the contrary, it seems that dealing with problems makes them stronger and more successful.

We've talked about the desire to succeed, so let's now consider how athletes cope with failure. Although all sportspeople dream of winning, all of them lose at some point in their careers. And it seems that how they manage their failure can play a key role in their future success. The most successful athletes are able to learn lessons and become stronger.

This links to my next point, which is to do with strength. Now we usually associate sport with physical strength, but to be really successful, it's often equally important to be mentally strong. This is so you can deal with the competition, which can be extremely tough mentally, and so that you can come back stronger when you lose. This requires great self-belief – believing in yourself – something that all these sportspeople seem to have in common.

The next feature might sound a little obvious, but what I found really interesting about all the athletes I interviewed was their in-depth knowledge of all aspects of their sport. As well as all the time they spend training, many of them also spend hours watching the sport and studying the technique of the great champions, as well as the strengths and weaknesses of their competitors.

Finally, I want to point out that it is important to remember that natural talent is, of course, an important factor in sporting success, as is hard work and training, but it is difficult to succeed with these alone. The other factors that I have talked about today also contribute greatly to a person's sporting achievement. Many of you will find that the people you are going to teach can achieve far more if you help them with these things. Thank you.

8.3

E = Examiner   C = Candidate

E: Can you start speaking now, please?
C: Yes. One very popular sport in my country is basketball. It's a good team game. I have lots of friends who play and I know they really enjoy it although I don't actually play myself any more. The reason I don't play now is because you have to be tall to be good, and I'm too short. In fact, I did learn how to play at school, but I haven't played since then. I gave it up because I didn't grow tall enough and I didn't think any team would want me! One of the good things about basketball is you can play it inside or outside, so people play it all year round. Most schools have a basketball court and children usually learn to play at school. You also see basketball courts in every city and town. I think even very small towns and villages have at least one court. For instance, in my town we have a sports centre with two outdoor courts and one indoor court.

One of the reasons why basketball is popular in my country is that we have some really good professional teams and some of the top players are very famous. Most people follow a team and when there is an important match on, everyone watches it on TV. I think it's also a good sport to watch live and although I don't go to see games myself, I have friends who go and they say it's really exciting and there's a great atmosphere. I think the tickets are quite cheap as well, especially compared to other sports like football. Another reason why it's popular is that both men and women can play it, although I think the big competitions are the men's ones.

8.6

N = Narrator   L = Lecturer

N: You will hear a sports lecturer talking about how football clubs make money.
L: So, I'm now going to talk a little about how top English football clubs make their money and how the source of their income has changed in the last thirty or so years. In today's world of advertising and sponsorship deals, it's difficult to imagine that thirty years ago things were very different. Nearly all of football clubs' income came from ticket sales and, to a lesser extent, from food and drink sold inside their grounds on match days. Even today, match day ticket sales bring in a large amount of cash. For example, ticket sales for Arsenal home matches brought in £101.84 million in the 2014–2015 season, and Manchester United matches raised £87.96 million. But things started to change in 1992, when the top twenty clubs broke away from the Football League, to create the Premier League. The primary reason for this, of course, was financial. Specifically, the clubs wanted to make a very profitable deal with media companies which would give them the rights to broadcast live Premier League matches.

So the first of a number of changes to football club income was this important agreement with TV companies. Today the TV deal is worth £81 million a season for each Premier League Club. So as you can see, it brings in almost as much as tickets sales for clubs like Arsenal and Manchester United, and quite a bit more for clubs like Liverpool, where tickets sales generate £57 million.

A second major source of income is directly linked to the TV rights deal. Broadcasting Premier League matches around the world to millions of viewers is very attractive to key sponsors, and I'm sure you have noticed that all sports stars around the world, including Premier League football teams, wear shirts carrying the name or logo of the company that sponsors them. In addition to the shirts, the company uses advertising within the stadium, which millions of people see on TV. The sponsorship deals are very profitable for the club. Take Arsenal as an example again. They have a major deal with the airline Emirates, worth £150 million. Apart from the shirt sponsorship, the deal included a change of name for the Arsenal ground, which is now known as the Emirates Stadium. In total, the deal brings in £30 million a season for the club.

Now let's consider product sales: the selling of shirts and scarves and other products to the fans. These have grown significantly in recent years, and this is mainly due to a growing number of fans and an increasing TV audience from around the world.

The final major money-maker for clubs is perhaps one that receives the most publicity in the media, and that is 'the transfer deal' – that is when one club sells a player to another club – and I'll give you a good example. In 2007 London club Tottenham Hotspur signed Welsh player Gareth Bale for £7 million. That might sound like a lot of money, but when you consider that six years later they sold him to Real Madrid for £85.3 million, you can see that clubs can really make a huge profit from the deal.

So, as you can see, Premier League football clubs make their money from a variety of sources, including TV broadcasting rights, sponsorship deals, transfer deals, as well as sales of tickets and products. Now let's move on to consider what the clubs spend their money on. We've already seen …

8.7

E = Examiner   C = Candidate

E: Can you start speaking now, please?
C: OK, well, I'm going to talk about when I learned to play tennis. This was about seven years ago and the reason I decided to take it up was because I moved to a new town. What I mean is I wanted to make new friends and the only person I knew there was a girl who was a member of the tennis club. She was always playing in tennis matches and organising social events for the club – such as quiz nights and fundraising events – and she encouraged me to join. In other words, it was my friend who got me into playing tennis. For

219

Audio scripts

me, it was a really good chance to meet new people. So I joined the club and although I already knew quite a bit about tennis, I started having proper lessons. What I'm trying to say is I always followed tennis tournaments on TV and I knew the rules, but I didn't have the skills – so I needed the lessons. I didn't find it very difficult to learn, really. To put it another way, I suppose it was quite easy for me because I already knew the rules. Tennis is a cheap and easy sport to take up. What I mean by that is you don't need much equipment – just a racquet and some trainers. I had two lessons a week to start with, and my tennis coach was really good and patient. I suppose I have been quite successful because I still play regularly now. What I want to say is I'm good enough to play in club matches against other clubs and sometimes I win.

Module 9

9.1

E = Editor   S = Student

E: Good morning. Can I help you?
S: Oh, yes, hello. I spoke to one of your colleagues last week about the possibility of getting some work experience with you.
E: Oh yes, Paul mentioned it. Yes, come in and take a seat. It's James, isn't it?
S: Yes, that's right.
E: Well, we don't often take work experience students on but actually, we may have a post available in the next few weeks. So, I'll take a few details from you and then we can contact you later in the summer, when we know for sure what we have available.
S: That would be great, thank you.

9.2

E = Editor   S = Student

E: So, Paul tells me you've just finished your second year at university. What subject are you doing?
S: My course is in media and communications, but one of the modules I'm doing is journalism and I'm really enjoying it – I think that's the route I'd like go down.
E: Great. And where is it that you're studying? I thought they'd closed the media department at Midlands University?
S: Yes, you're right – it closed last year. No, I'm at Central College. It's quite a new course, but it's very good and I'm really enjoying it.

9.3

N = Narrator   E = Editor   S = Student

N: You will hear a newspaper editor talking to a student about work experience.
E: Well, as you know, James, we're only a local newspaper, but our print sales are actually growing at the moment and we have a strong website and social media presence. Do any of those areas interest you?
S: Well, I do like traditional print media, but I have to admit my real interest definitely lies in new media.
E: OK. Well, I can't promise anything but I'll note it down and we'll see what we can do. So have you got any practical journalism experience?
S: Yes, I've been very involved in our campus newsletter for the past couple of years and I've just been made deputy editor, so I'll have a bit more responsibility there.
E: That's good experience. We probably can't give you any writing work, at least to begin with, but keeping social media updated is a full-time job, so there may be something there for you. Would you be prepared to work unsocial hours – you know, weekends, nights, early mornings?
S: Yes. In fact, weekends or evenings would suit me best. I can't do early mornings because I have a nine o'clock lecture on most days.
E: Right. Now, do you have your own transport – you know, in case we need to send you out on a job?
S: Well, I haven't got a car at the moment. But I'm going to have use of my brother's motorbike next term as he's just gone to work in Canada for a year and he's agreed to lend it to me.
E: Well, that would be handy. It's much better if you have your own transport. OK, now I just need a few personal details. So what's your surname, James?
S: Fernandes. That's F-E-R-N-A-N-D-E-S.
E: Thank you – that sounds Spanish?
S: Actually, it's Portuguese – my dad is Brazilian but my mum's from Birmingham and that's where I was born and brought up, so I'm British.
E: OK. Now, as I said, I'll probably contact you in a couple of weeks or so, once I know if we have any openings. So I'll take your email address if that's OK.
S: Yes, it's jas96@bmail.com – that's J-A-S-9-6.
E: Got that. OK, I think that's all I need for now. Have you got any questions?
S: No, I don't think so. Just one thing, in case you try to contact me: I'm going on holiday for two weeks and I don't know how easy it'll be to pick up emails. I'll be away for the last two weeks of July. But I'll be back on the second of August.
E: OK, thanks for letting me know. I'll just make a note of that.
S: Thank you for seeing me today.
E: My pleasure. I'll be in touch soon.

9.5

E = Examiner   C = Candidate

E: How has the way we get news changed in the last few years?
C: Well, clearly, it has changed a lot. In the past people got news from traditional media like print newspapers, radio and TV and you usually got news once or twice a day. But now we have constant updates on the internet and on social media, so naturally, everyone expects to get news quickly and news soon becomes old. As a result, I don't think people read about the news in as much detail as they did in the past. Sadly, it's also easier now to get inaccurate news because people get a lot of information from social media, which is usually less reliable than traditional media.
E: Do you think famous people should have privacy in the media?
C: Hmm … well, people are naturally interested in finding out about the lives of celebrities and looking at their photos. Obviously, if you are in the public eye, you have to accept that people want to take your photograph and write stories about you. However, in my view, some newspapers and paparazzi go too far and unfortunately, there have been cases where they write stories that are untrue or publish photos that really invade their privacy. So there definitely should be laws to stop that.
E: And how easy is it to control the stories that the media publish?
C: Well, this is a difficult question because it depends on the type of media. I know some famous people have tried to stop newspapers or magazines publishing stories about them but apparently, people on social media were discussing the same stories. So I think it's easier to control stories on traditional media, but obviously, it's more difficult to control social media. People can say anything they like on social media, whether it is true or not.

9.6

N = Narrator   A = Advisor   W = Woman

N: You will hear a conversation between a woman and a college advisor.
A: Good morning, Central College. How can I help you?
W: Oh hello. Yes, I've recently set up my own business and I've noticed on your website that you offer some computing courses that might help me with some aspects of my business.
A: That's right. We have a number of courses that might be of interest. What is it you need help with in particular?
W: Well, my IT skills are not very good at all, really.
A: Well, we do have some beginners' courses. There's Introduction to Email and the Internet. The next one starts next week, but it's not held here – it's at our Sydney Street centre, on the other side of town.
W: Actually, those are the things I'm not too bad at. No, I was thinking of something that would help me more with my business. For instance, I need to set up a website and I also need to produce some flyers to advertise my business.
A: Well, we do cover website design and desktop publishing in our Computing Level 1 course, but I'm not sure if you want to study full-time if you've got your own business?
W: No, I can only do part-time. I can only spare a few hours a week.

A: I think the best thing for you would be to do a couple of our part-time evening courses. We have an Introduction to Website Design course starting next week. It's on Tuesday evening for ten weeks. But it's at our Eastgate campus, so it might be too far for you. Where do you live?
W: Well, it's quite far for me – I live in Newhampton. But I'm happy to travel. Have you got any desktop publishing courses starting soon?
A: Let's see. Yes, there's one starting here on the tenth. Let's see … it's Thursday evenings, so you could do both at the same time. No, wait – it says it's for people with some previous knowledge of the application.
W: Are there any lower level courses?
A: Not until next term.
W: OK. Can I sign up for the website design course now and then I can think about starting the other next term.
A: Of course. I just need to take a few personal details. Can I take your name?
W: Yes it's Maria Wilenska. That's W-I-L-E-N-S-K-A.
A: OK. And what's your nationality – are you Polish?
W: A lot of people think I'm Polish but actually, I'm Russian.
A: So that's your first language?
W: Actually, no. It's French! I lived in Paris for the first twenty years of my life and that's where my husband's from, so it's the language I use most.
A: And can I take either an email or a daytime phone number?
W: Yes. It's probably easier to get me on my mobile, so I'll give you that. It's 077 64 6453 991.
A: Right. Now, just a couple more questions. Can you just let me know what your previous education is – what's the highest level you've achieved: high school, college, university?
W: University. My first degree was in art and I also have a postgraduate diploma.
A: Oh what's that in?
W: Jewellery design – that's what my business is.
A: Sounds interesting. Now have you got any special needs that we need to know about – any health issues or learning difficulties?
W: Not unless you count my terrible computer skills!
A: OK, so I'll put 'None'. Finally, I just need to know how you're going to pay. You can either pay a twenty-five-percent deposit now – that's thirty-five pounds – and then the balance of one hundred and five pounds on the first day of the course, or you can pay the whole amount now if you prefer – the total is one hundred and forty pounds.
W: Yes, I think I'll pay in full now. Do you take credit cards?
A: Yes, of course. I'll just …

9.7

E = Examiner   C = Candidate

1

E: Do you think we rely too much on technology nowadays?
C: When you say 'technology', do you mean computers and mobile phones?

2

E: Do you think technology has improved education?
C: Could you repeat the question, please?

3

E: Why do people always want to have the latest gadget?
C: Sorry, I'm not sure what 'gadget' means. Could you explain it in another way, please?

4

E: Do you think the recent rate of technological development will continue in the future?
C: Could you please explain what 'rate' means?

5

E: What are the differences in attitude between older and younger people towards technology?
C: Sorry, I don't understand the question. Could you explain?

6

E: What are some of the benefits of technology in the workplace?
C: Sorry, would you mind repeating the question?

9.8

E = Examiner   C = Candidate

E: Do you think we rely too much on technology nowadays?
C: When you say 'technology', do you mean computers and mobile phones?
E: All types of technology, not just computers and phones.
C: Well, obviously, we do rely a lot on technology for everything we do, particularly for communication, and I think that's the area that we would find it difficult to live without. Worryingly, I think some people would struggle even a few hours without their mobile phones. In my view, technology stops us thinking for ourselves. For example, we use it to find our way in the car instead of looking at a map and working out a route. Some people say that's a good thing and it makes life easier, but I'm not sure I entirely agree.
E: Why do people always want to have the latest gadget?
C: Sorry, I'm not sure what 'gadget' means. Could you explain it in another way, please?
E: A gadget is a device.
C: Thank you. Well, naturally, people always want to have the best gadget, which is usually the latest one because it has all the new features. For instance, everyone wants to get the latest smartphone as soon as it comes out. In my view, it's a bit like fashion – you want to be fashionable and have what other people have. Personally, I don't mind not having the latest gadget but I know a lot of people who do.
E: What are the differences in attitude between older and younger people towards technology?
C: Sorry, I don't understand the question. Could you explain?
E: Do older and younger people have different attitudes to technology?
C: Oh I see. Yes, some of them do. Obviously, it's easier for young people because they have grown up with technology and they don't know what it's like to not have it. But older people have to learn a new skill, such as using the internet, which can be difficult for them. They can remember a time when they didn't have computers and mobile phones and some of them think that was a better time. However, I think many older people are very good with technology and use it just as much as young people do.

Module 10

10.1

Now, if you could all look at this slide, you'll see that we can divide the features of effective communication into three different parts. Surprisingly, the most obvious communication tool is represented by the smallest section of the chart and that is the words that we use when we speak – our verbal communication. This means that what we actually say when we speak only contributes a tiny seven percent to our overall message. So, what is more important in getting our message across are all the features in the other two sections. You can see the largest section of the chart relates to features that we can group together as non-verbal communication. In other words, they do not relate to the language we use but as you will see, they still have an extremely important role to play. And the third section of the chart represents a really fascinating area, which accounts for thirty-eight percent of communication, and that is how we use our voice. It is these two areas that I'm going to concentrate on in this talk.

10.2

N = Narrator   L = Lecturer

N: You will hear a lecturer talking to a group of students about effective communication.
L: So let's talk first about non-verbal communication and what I feel is one of its most important features: this one in the middle here, and that's our facial expression. An important point to remember here is we're talking about communication, so it's not just about what the speaker does but also what the listener does. So you can see that if you're in a conversation with someone, a smile or a frown can show interest or boredom in the conversation.

Audio scripts

And it's not just our face that shows emotion, of course. If we move over and look at the features of voice, down the bottom here, we can see 'Tone'. This is perhaps the most important of the vocal features, as we use it to show a range of attitudes and emotions, and it also plays an important role in managing a conversation.

Moving back to non-verbal communication, we can see that another area of body language that can show our mood or attitude are the movements or gestures we make with our hands, head or other parts of our body. So, for example, we can show we are getting impatient by tapping our fingers on a table; and arms crossed across our body can be a sign of disagreement. However, it's important to remember that gestures and their meanings can vary between cultures and can often lead to misunderstandings.

So moving down to the next feature which is eye contact – well, the same sort of cultural misunderstandings can be linked to this, actually. Although making eye contact is a key feature in building trust with someone in many cultures, staring at someone for a long time can be a sign of disrespect or even aggression in others.

So let me now go back and take you through the rest of the features of voice which can contribute to effective communication. We've already discussed tone. Similar to this is how high or low we speak – and we call this pitch. This can affect the message we are giving and how other people understand that message because it can vary depending on our emotions. We tend to use a high pitch when we feel strongly about something but a low pitch can indicate calm. Similarly, the volume of our voice can affect the message: if we speak too loudly, we can sound angry and aggressive; but a quiet voice can make us appear shy, uncertain or under-confident. One piece of advice people often give to public speakers is to slow down and this is because when we speak quickly, we can sound nervous. On the other hand, if the speed of delivery is too slow, the listener may find it hard to follow the message. So with this feature, the key to successful communication is to use variety, which can add interest and can help get our message across more effectively.

Moving back to non-verbal communication, let's look at my final two points, which both concern the overall impression people give when they are communicating. The first of these is posture, and by that I'm referring to how you stand or sit, whether you cross your arms or legs, etc. For example, we can lean forward to show our interest in the conversation. Or we can show we feel confident about something by standing straight. Finally, our physical appearance is essential in communicating our message to others as it plays an important role in creating first impressions. Therefore, attention to this is particularly important for public speaking as audiences will concentrate their attention on strange clothing, hairstyles or even choice of colour, which can mean the message the speakers are trying to give becomes unclear.

So you can see that to communicate effectively, although words are important, we also need to pay attention to all of these other features. I'd now like to talk to you about …

10.3

E = Examiner   C = Candidate

E: Can you start speaking now, please?
C: OK, well, first I want to stress that I don't really want to learn another foreign language because I'm already learning two – English and Japanese – and that's enough for me, I think. But if I had to learn another language, I would choose Spanish. The important thing about Spanish is it is the most spoken language after Chinese because they speak it in Spain and most of South and Central America. So in that respect, it's very useful and opens up more job opportunities. I don't think I would find it very easy to learn, although I understand it's easier than some languages. I think for me, the pronunciation would be difficult. Also, Spanish speakers always seem to speak very quickly, so I'm sure understanding would be difficult too. I expect the writing and reading would be OK for me. I already know English and I think English and Spanish have the same alphabet, so I wouldn't have to learn a new one. That's why I think it would be easier than, say, Arabic or Russian. I'm not sure about the grammar but I usually enjoy learning grammar rules and so I hope that would not be too difficult for me. I think when you're learning a language, you should always try to visit a country where it is spoken. I've always wanted to go to Peru and so that is a very good reason to learn the language. Of course, if you want to use a language for work, it's better if you try to get a qualification in it, so I would probably want to take an exam to show that I have a good level. But that can take a long time, I'm afraid.

10.4

1 Well, I suppose the essential point is that written communication is much more permanent than spoken communication. You can keep a written document for hundreds of years but with speaking, once you've said it, it's gone forever.
2 One of the differences I'd like to highlight is that when we speak, we are usually quite informal compared to some of the things we write. Although some of the language we use on social media is very informal, letters and things like that are much more formal.
3 Actually, there are quite a few differences but the important thing is that when we write something, we take time to think about it and we can edit and rewrite it if necessary. You can't do that when you're speaking.

10.7

N = Narrator   L = Lecturer

N: You will hear a lecturer talking about the concept of the cultural iceberg.
L: So I'm going to start today's lecture by talking a little about the concept of the cultural iceberg. This idea was proposed by Edward T. Hall in 1976 and what he did was compare culture to an iceberg. Now I'm sure you know that the part of the iceberg that we see above the surface of the water is only a tiny proportion of the total area, and that most of the iceberg is much deeper beneath the surface of the water. Well, Hall used the iceberg to show that culture can be divided into two distinct parts.

So what we have here is the visible tip of the iceberg, which represents the external, or surface, culture, which as you can see is only about ten percent of the total. This contains the behaviour and traditions of a culture that are visible to the outside world. So what does this mean? Well, we're talking here about the things that you naturally associate with a particular culture, like the food and language, the dress, the music and literature. So examples would be sushi for Japanese culture or Flamenco music for Spanish or Shakespeare for British. These are the things that the tourists see when they visit. But they don't really tell us much about the internal, or deep, culture. That's this large area below the surface of the water – the invisible values and beliefs of the culture, the parts that are hidden; and as you can see, it's a much bigger area, making up about ninety percent of the total. It's also a much more complex part of the culture and is much more related to who we really are.

So here at the top we have different types of non-verbal communication – so that's the way we express ourselves without words, like body language, eye contact and tone of voice, which as I'm sure you know can often lead to inter-cultural misunderstandings. A bit lower down, we have rules on how to behave in different situations. So this is things like what is considered polite or rude, what the culture views as good or bad manners and so on. Then as we go lower, we come to some really important features of culture like its attitudes towards major life events like how to raise children, marriage and even death. Then right at the bottom we have the culture's opinions about the roles of different groups of people in society – for instance, old people, teenagers and women. So as you can see, these different areas of culture are not the sort of things you could pick up from a short visit.

So how do we understand the core values of our culture? And how do they survive through the ages? Well, there are a number of factors which guide and influence us here. Obviously, our parents and other family members are key factors in teaching us, but our education system plays an important part, too. Then there are factors like our history and religion, and economics also plays a part. And nowadays the media has an enormous influence on our ideas and opinions. All of these come together to shape the core values and allow them to carry on to the next generation. And this is why a culture's core values don't really change much over time – at least not quickly or easily.

So how can we learn about another culture? As I've already said, if we visit as a tourist, we only really see the external visible aspects of the culture and we do not really come into contact with what lies beneath. Well, obviously, we need to spend time in that culture but that clearly isn't enough. The only way to truly learn about another culture is to actively participate in that culture by interacting with others. So that could be living, working or studying with members of the culture. If we do this, then we start to understand some of the other, hidden aspects of the culture. So you can compare living in another culture to the Titanic. It feels a little like being on a sinking ship: as you go deeper into the ocean, you will understand the culture that's around you better.

10.8

E = Examiner   C = Candidate

E: Can you start speaking now, please?

C: Yes. The place I'm going to talk about is an area of New York that I've visited recently and that is Chinatown. I was on holiday in New York last summer and one evening we went to Chinatown in order to get a Chinese meal. The meal was fantastic and the whole area looked really interesting, so we decided to return the next day to explore the area more carefully and find out about Chinese culture in New York. We decided the best way to find out about the history was by visiting the museum there. It's small but it explains the whole history of Chinese immigration into America. The museum has lots of pictures and videos and it's done in such a way that you really get a good idea of what it was like to be a Chinese immigrant arriving in America. After the museum we walked around Chinatown and looked at some of the shops. We wanted to eat there again, so we asked the people in the museum for a recommendation so as not to miss the best food and they told us where to go. We only found the place with great difficulty because it was in a little back street but it was worth it because the food was delicious. We spent a long time talking to the owner of the restaurant and we learned a lot about their culture. Actually, I think that you can often find out more about a culture just by talking to someone. It was such an enjoyable day and it has really made me interested in Chinese culture so that now I'd like to visit China too.

10.9–10.10

It was such an enjoyable day and it has really made me interested in Chinese culture so that now I'd like to visit China too.

Pearson Education Limited
Edinburgh Gate, Harlow, Essex. CM20 2JE and Associated Companies throughout the world

www.english.com/expertielts

© Pearson Education Limited 2017

The right Elaine Boyd to be identified as author of this Work has been asserted by them in accordance with the Copyright, Designs and Patents Act 1988.

All rights reserved. No part of this publication may be reproduced, stored in a retrieval system, or transmitted in any form or by any means, electronic, mechanical, photocopying, recording or otherwise, without the prior written permission of the copyright holders.

First published 2017
ISBN 978-1-292-12519-0
Set in Amasis and Mundo Sans
Printed and bound in Slovakia by Neografia

Acknowledgements

The publishers and authors would like to thank the following people and institutions for their contribution to the development of the material:

Carole Allsop, Sarah Emsden-Bonfanti, Felicity O'Dell, Joanna Preshous, the teachers at the English Centre at The American University of Sharjah

Souha Adlouni, Nouf Al-Salem (video), Rasheed Al-Siddiq, Fiona Aish, Marine Andre (video), Asmaa Awad, Jan Ball, Jason Bednarz, Freya Beesely, Ludmilla Boysan, Edward Burnham, Yuka Chibioni (video), Andrew Condor, Jude Conroy, Brendan Cox, Natalia Donmez, Tim Edwards, Nick Falkinder, Filippo Geraci (video), Mark Gillespie, Rebecca Gilligan, Nazli Gonca (video), Douglas Greig, Niva Gunasegaran, Rita Hanlon, Mark Hanson, Ramin Hashemian, Deborah Hobbs, Dr. Paul Hudson, Alexander Ingle, Daphne-Ann Kelly, Brian John Knight, David Knowles, Carl Lam, Jill Landry, Christien Lee, Sydney Liu, Sally Lloyds, Andrew Loader, Mark Long, Daniel Meager, Claire Murphy, Tom O'Brien, Sheila Parrott, Gonzalo Pastrana (video), Olivia Qin, Abdelghani A. Remache, Louis Rogers, Amber Roshay, Abdelhameed Safa, Kareen Sharawy, Li Shengyue, Kelly Smith, Helen Stobie, Jo Tomlinson, Amira Traish, Richard Vile, Joseph Vitta, Claire Wallis, Clare Walsh (video), Ian Watson, Liu Weili, Elaine Wilson, Mehtap Yavuzdogan, Yulia Yarmolinsky, Eden Zhange, Cee Zhao

We are grateful to the following for permission to reproduce copyright material:

Figures

Figure on page 80 adapted from Defra National Statistics Release: Air quality statistics in the UK 1987 to 2015 (Line graph: Days with moderate or higher air pollution), Department for Environment, Food and Rural Affairs, Contains public sector information licensed under the Open Government Licence v3.0

Text

Extract 1.2 adapted from Seven Characteristics of Good Learners, Weimer, M. 22/01/ 2014, Magna Publications © by Faculty Focus, a division of Magna Publications. Reproduced with permission of Magna Publications in the format Republish in a book via Copyright Clearance Center; Article 5.13 adapted from Seven things you learn when you cycle around the world, *Telegraph*, 11/02/2016 (Bailey,M.),Telegraph Media Group Ltd 2016; Article on page 121 adapted from Mind games: how footballers use sports psychology *Telegraph*, 19/02/2014 (Bailey,M.), Telegraph Media Group Ltd 2016; Article on page 153 from Better Technology = Better Communication? Not Necessarily DeHart & Co. 27/09/2013, Copyright © 2016 by the ACM. All rights reserved. DeHart & Co/Geoffrey Tumlin with permission.

Illustration Acknowledgements

Illustrated by ROARR Design

Photo Acknowledgements

The publisher would like to thank the following for their kind permission to reproduce their photographs:

(Key: b-bottom; c-centre; l-left; r-right; t-top)

123RF.com: 103tl, Jakub Cejpek 119b, Oleg Dudko 43t, Alexander Raths 66cr, Wavebreakmediamicro 23tl; **Alamy Stock Photo:** 60tr, 83, 87br, 96, 104b, Stephen Barnes / Society 44t, Simon Belcher 87tl, Rafael Ben-Ari 41b, Anna Berkut 44b, Jeffrey Blackler 127, Ian Canham 17, Chronicle 105, Cultura Creative 131, Peter Devlin 73, Katie Edwards 27, Folio Images 77, Andrew Fox 11, Ted Foxx 20bl, Hero Images 43b, Hero Images Inc. 15, 23br, 71b, Robert Holland 125, Image navi - QxQ images 20tr, Image navi - Sozaijiten 90, Image Source 53, Image Source Plus 25b, Imagemore Co 25t, Juice Images 39b, 113, 121, Robert Kneschke 101, Yadid Levy 71tr, Artur Marciniec 98, Marrakeshh 67, MBI 54, Sergey Nivens 146, Photo Researchers, Inc 60bl, Purestock 20br, Reuters 123, 128, Manuel Ribeiro 111, Robert Harding 115, SERDAR 102, Michael Simons 160, Jochen Tack 89, Colin Underhill 20tl, Wavebreak Media ltd 153, World History Archive 35, ZUMA Press, Inc. 41t; **Buffer Inc.:** Todd Balsley 51t, Andrew Yates 51b; **Fotolia.com:** Gianluca Ciro Tancredi 143, esmehelit 103tr, JJAVA 36, Monkey Business 61, 151tl, Andrei Nekrassov 22, rh2010 71tr; **Getty Images:** DigitalVision 137; **MIXA Co., Ltd:** 119tl; **Pearson Education Ltd:** 194-199, Jon Barlow 13; **PhotoDisc:** 70, Photolink 119tr; **Science Photo Library Ltd:** 60br; **Shutterstock.com:** 12, Arogant 135tl, ArtisticPhoto 36r, ArtWell 14, baranq 23tr, bikeriderlondon 106, 162, Bikeworldtravel 129, Jon Bilous 114, Grisha Bruev 23bl, Sam DCruz 63, Falconia 10t, Melinda Fawver 122, g-stockstudio 135b, Rostislav Glinsky 87bl, Kaspars Grinvalds 135tr, Halfpoint 55cr, imagedb.com 99, Matej Kastelic 19, LDprod 151b, Lopolo 130, Jacob Lund 9t, Viktar Malyshchyts 66cl, Maxx-Studio 157, Anastasia Mdivanian 155, Monkey Business Images 136b, Nadezda Murmakova 132, Nejron Photo 92, nenetus 151tr, Sergey Novikov 103b, Andrea Obzerova 33, Cantemir Olaru 97, Steven Paine 31, Pavel L Photo and Video 87tr, Phase4Studios 55bl, PhotoRoman 82, Pressmaster 28, Alexander Raths 39tr, Rawpixel.com 50, 57, RIRF Stock 64, Robnroll 145, RTimages 134, Science Photo Library 39tl, StudioSmart 66r, Timmary 66l, Aleksandar Todorovic 94, Tzido Sun 108, Elya Vatel 133, Dani Vincek 55tl, Wellphoto 141, Yurchyks 68; **Wellcome Library, London:** 60tl

All other images © Pearson Education

Video produced by Silversun Media Group for Pearson Education

Every effort has been made to trace the copyright holders and we apologise in advance for any unintentional omissions. We would be pleased to insert the appropriate acknowledgement in any subsequent edition of this publication.

CARD

John Lancaster

Consultant: Henry Pluckrose

Photography: Chris Fairclough

FRANKLIN WATTS
London/New York/Sydney/Toronto

Copyright © 1989
Franklin Watts

Franklin Watts
12a Golden Square
London W1R 4BA

Franklin Watts Australia
14 Mars Road
Lane Cove
N.S.W. 2066

UK ISBN: 0 86313 806 3

Design: Edward Kinsey

Editor: Jenny Wood

Printed in Belgium

Contents

Equipment and materials 4
Getting ready 5
Trying out some scraps of card 6
A simple curving sculpture 11
A tubular model 16
A relief model 19
A peep-hole theatre 22
A rolled newspaper model 25
Newspaper tower blocks 30
A standing animal 33
A rolled-paper relief model 34
Card zig-zags 37
Five-sided units 39
On your own 41
Further information 47
Index 48

Equipment and materials

This book describes activities which use the following:

Card – household waste materials such as used food cartons and packets, the cardboard centres of paper towel rolls, pieces of card used in packaging new shirts, card supports from tights packets, 35mm film packets, toilet roll centres, the card backings from used writing pads, old calendars, used Christmas cards and old shoe boxes
– card bought from artists' materials shops

Cardboard boxes of varying shapes and sizes (available from your local greengrocer or supermarket, and useful for large-scale models)

Corrugated card

Cutting board (an offcut of hardboard or formica) – always use this when cutting card

Cutting knife (a 'Stanley' knife, or sharp craft knife)

Glue (UHU or similar)

Paintbrush (a watercolour brush, size 4 or 5)

Paints (powder paints, acrylic PVA, household paint, spray paint or lacquer)

Paper – old magazines
– old newspapers
– used wrapping paper

Paper clips

Pencil (H or HB)

Rubber bands

Ruler (must be metal)

Saw (a junior hacksaw, coping saw or fretsaw)

Scissors

Sticky tape

Thread

Torch

Wood – hardboard or plywood offcuts (available from a DIY store)

Getting ready

When I went to school I can't remember ever doing any three-dimensional card models. But making card models is easy, as well as being fun.

Drawing and painting are done on flat surfaces, but when you make things with card you will be constructing 'in the round' or in what is referred to as 'three dimensions'. Artists who do this are called sculptors. You may call yourself a 'card sculptor'!

If you read the list of equipment and materials on page 4, you will see that you will need to spend very little money indeed. Most of the card materials I suggest you use are household scraps which would normally be thrown away. So you will probably spend no money at all on card – unless you decide that you need one or two sheets of good, strong card for a particular model.

Some hints

When you are working, wear some kind of smock or apron. An old jacket or shirt will do nicely, though a sack – folded over and tied round your waist with strong string – is a good substitute.

You will need a workspace – an area of floor, or a table which is covered with hardboard or formica. If you are lucky, you might be able to use a workbench in a garage or garden shed.

Store your equipment and materials in a large cardboard box. This will help to keep your workspace tidy.

When you have been working for a period of time, stop and have a short break. This will give you a chance to look at the object you are making. Look at it from the front, from the sides, from the back, and possibly from above and below. Think carefully about its three-dimensional form and how you intend to proceed.

Make a quick drawing of your model as you see it from the front. Now do another drawing of it as you wish it to look when completed.

One important point to remember is that you will need a sharp cutting knife. Be very careful when you use it and always work on your cutting board. When you are cutting card you must always cut downwards through the card. Never point your knife at anyone!

Trying out some scraps of card

Like all other artists, sculptors experiment with materials to find out what each different material will do and what can be achieved with it. Now see what *you* can do with pieces of card. You will need card, scissors, glue and paperclips.

1 Cut a strip of card and try bending it to form a curve...

2 ... then try bending it further to form a ring. Glue the ends of the ring together then fasten them with a paper clip until the glue sets. Make sure you select a flexible piece of card. If your card is too thick, you will have difficulty bending it.

3 Take another piece of card and try tearing it. (Make sure that it is possible to tear the type of card you have chosen!) Continue to tear it into a number of small pieces of different shapes and sizes.

In order to bend a piece of card so that the bent edge is straight and crisp, you will need to practise scoring and cutting card. Use your cutting board, cutting knife and metal ruler. If you follow the step-by-step instructions in pictures **4–8**, you should develop a good, safe cutting technique.

4 Place the card flat on the cutting board.

5 Take your knife in your 'work' hand, with the blade pointing downwards.

6 Place the metal ruler flat on the card. One of its long, straight edges should be placed exactly where you wish to cut into the card.

7 Hold the ruler down firmly with your other hand and make a gentle but firm cut. (If you try to cut through the card all at once, you will either tear it or the knife will slip. If you cut into the card gently, you will make a slight channel in the surface of the card and this will then help to guide your knife blade when you cut again.)

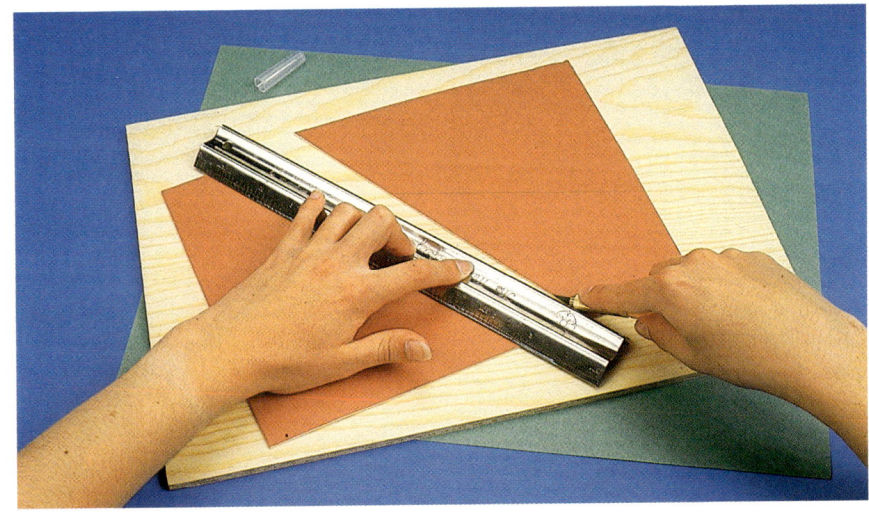

8 Make a series of gentle cuts, increasing the pressure slightly each time until you cut right through the card.

9 Practise making a few cuts into a piece of scrap card. Make some shallow cuts, as well as some which go right through the card.

10 Now score and bend some pieces of card to form right-angles.

A simple curving sculpture

This first simple but effective model is constructed from strips of thin card. Cut a number of strips of varying widths (between 1 cm and 4 cm) and varying lengths (between 15 cm and 40 cm). (The strips in pictures **1–3** are 1 cm wide.) Use coloured card, or scrap card from food packets. You will also need a base of strong card, hardboard or plywood (approximately 10 cm square, or a rectangle 8 cm × 12 cm), and glue.

1 Take your first long, thin strip of card. Glue one end on to the base and hold it in place until it is fixed.

2 Now bend the strip into a graceful curve or loop and glue the loose end down on to the base to join up with the end that is already stuck down.

3 Add more loops in the same way.

4 You can make your model more interesting by varying the size of your loops.

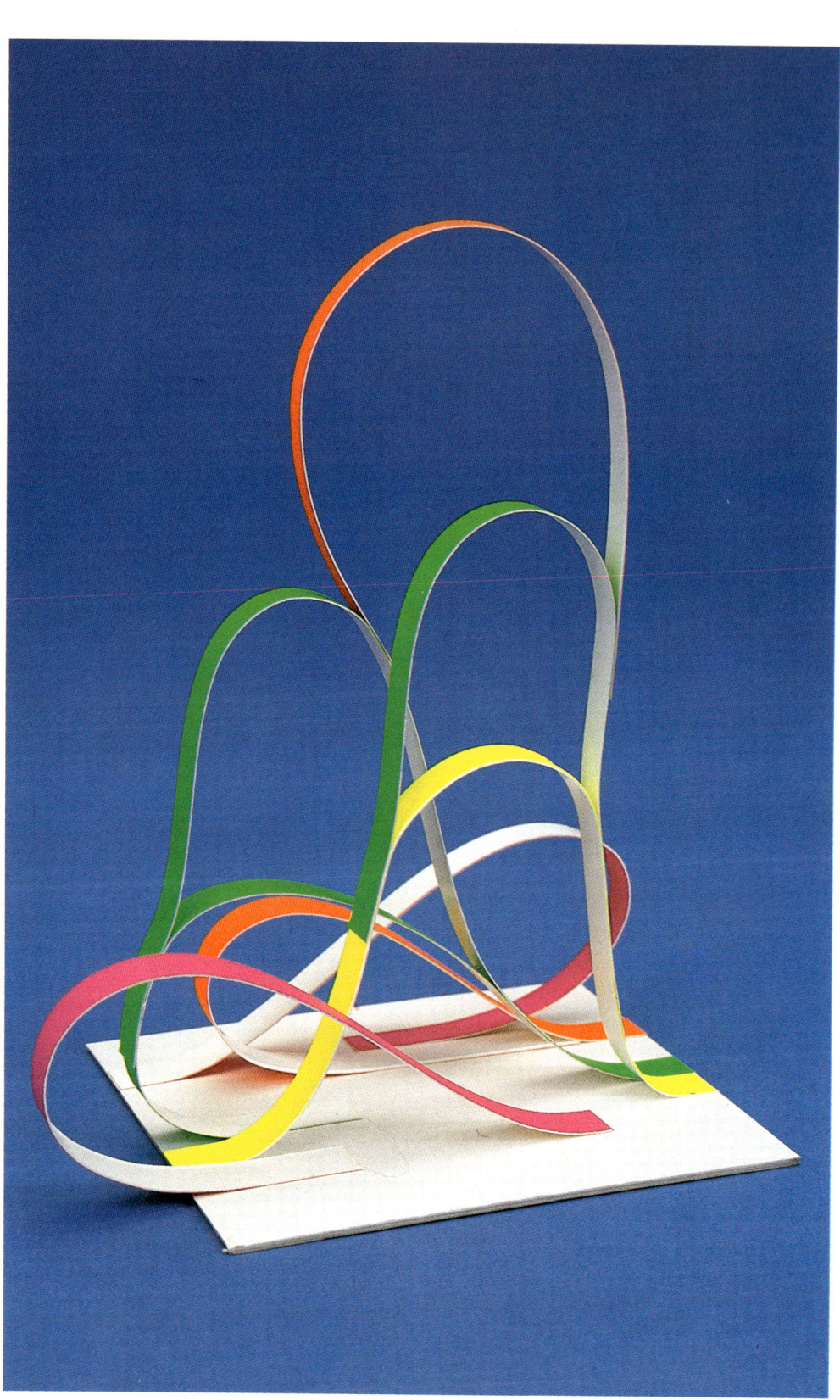

Add interesting effects to your model by using one or more of the following ideas:

1 Try *twisting* some of the loops before sticking their free ends to the base.

2 Add cobwebs of glue to your model.

3 Add lengths of thin nylon thread or coloured cotton to your model, gluing them in place carefully.

5 This sculpture was made from a small cardboard box, curving strips of card, and scrap pieces of card for the towers. UHU glue was dripped over it carefully to add cobweb threads and then it was sprayed red.

6 An effective, unpainted model on a base of scrap corrugated card. It uses both curved and angular card strips.

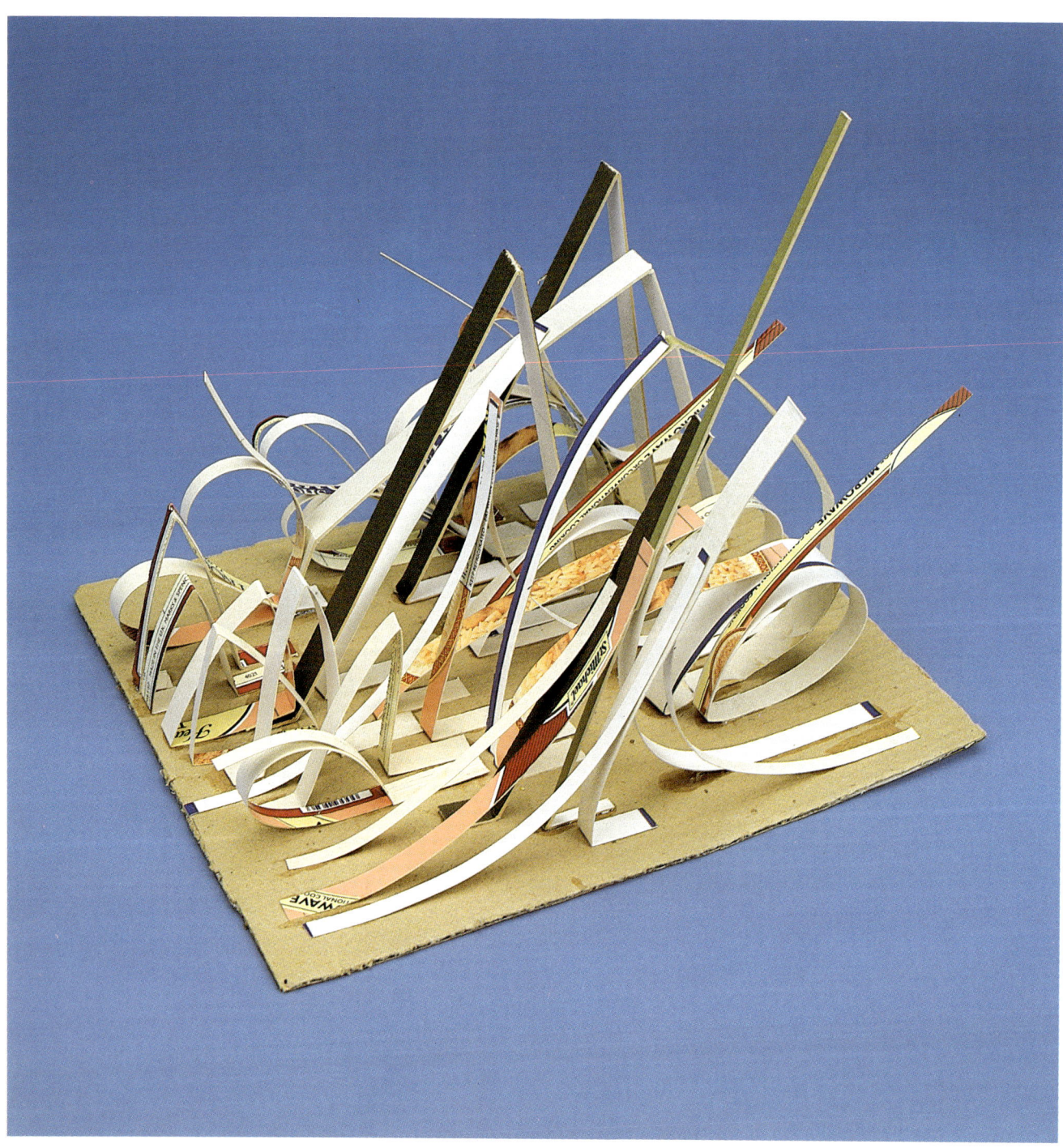

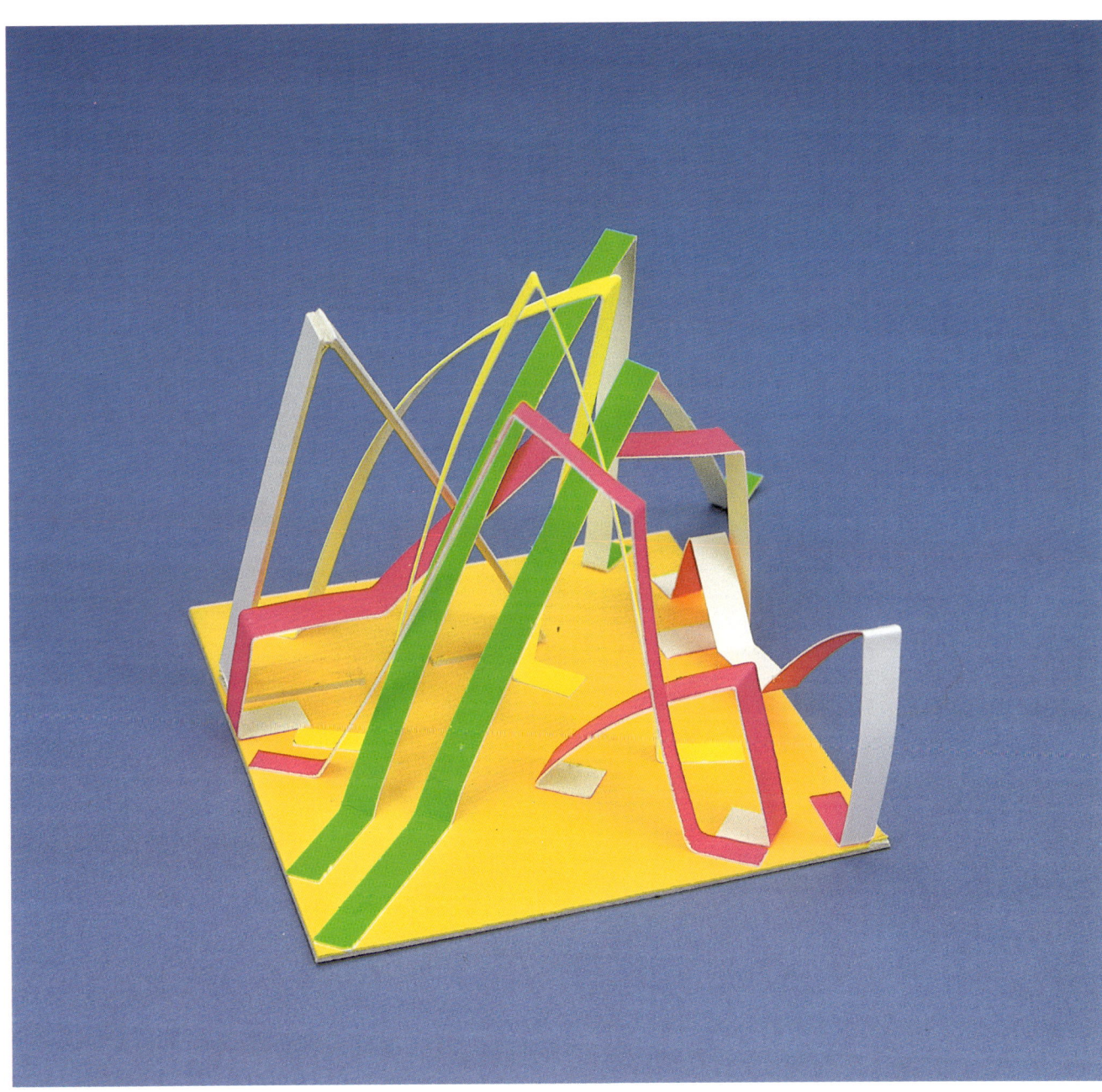

7 A colourful model made with gently curving and angular strips of card.

A tubular model

You will need a strong cardboard base for this model, although plywood or hardboard would also do quite nicely. Your base should be approximately 16 cm × 15 cm in size.

You will also need four or five toilet roll centres, one or two other cardboard tubes of different sizes and thicknesses, a cutting knife or saw, glue, paint and a paintbrush.

1 Cut through one of the cardboard tubes. (Remember to take great care when using your cutting tool.) You will now have three or four rings of card. Do the same again, but this time make sloping cuts to obtain two or three pointed rings.

2 Arrange the rings on the base. Some will stick up further than others, and this will add interest. Make some of the rings touch each other, and use half rings to add to the effect.

3 Look at the model from above to see if the rings make an interesting pattern. If they do not, reposition them until they do. Glue each ring to the base. Where rings touch, glue them to each other to make your model stronger.

Complete your model by painting it. One suggestion is to paint the whole model white. The inside and outside shapes, as well as the shadows, will make it look interesting. Pictures **4** and **5** offer other ideas.

4 Paint the whole of one shape in one colour. Add black to the top edges of two or three rings and a third colour inside two or three other rings.

5 Paint the whole of your sculpture in bright colours, with black inside one or two rings for added effect.

A relief model

A relief model is a three-dimensional model which rests on a base. When finished, it can be placed on a flat surface such as a table top or mantlepiece, or hung like a picture, projecting or sticking out from a wall.

You will need a piece of strong card, hardboard or plywood as your base. This could be about 30 cm square, although you should choose the size of base to suit the size you intend to make your model. You will also need two or three toilet roll centres, scissors, glue, paint and a paintbrush, and card or paper.

1 Cut through the toilet roll tubes, lengthwise. This will give you a number of semi-circular half tubes.

2 Place these on to the base to form a line of small, cardboard hills. Leave spaces between them. Glue their bottom edges to the base. Paint the base.

3 Cut up some thin strips of card or paper, about 1 cm wide. Position the strips to go up and over the mounds formed by the half toilet roll tubes, and glue them in place. Paint your model, or parts of it, carefully.

4 This model is made from cardboard tubes of different sizes. Strips of newspaper and small painted designs add to the effect.

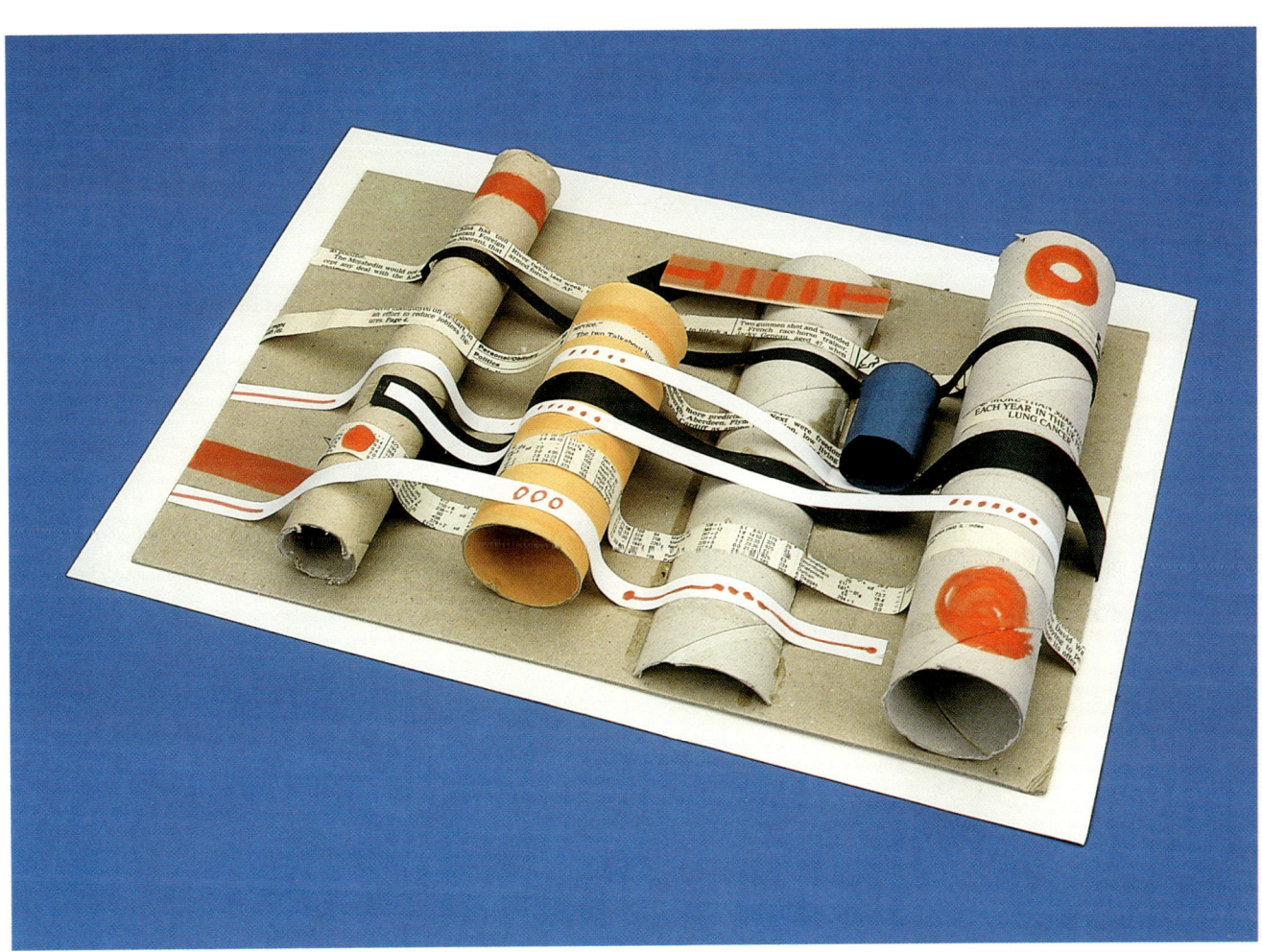

A peep-hole theatre

Your peep-hole theatre will be exciting and fun to play with.

You will need a cardboard box. A shoe box with a lid is ideal, though if you wish to make a large peep-hole theatre then a large cardboard box from your local grocer's shop or supermarket will be required.

You will also need a cutting knife, scrap pieces of card and other materials to make models, and a torch.

1 Make a small hole in one of the short sides of the box, just below the lid. This is the peep-hole.

2 Now make two window flaps in the box lid, each approximately 3 cm × 5 cm, with a space of approximately 1 cm in between. Position these on the end of the lid away from the peep-hole. Start the first flap approximately 3 cm in from the short edge of the lid. With your cutting knife, cut through three sides of each rectangle.

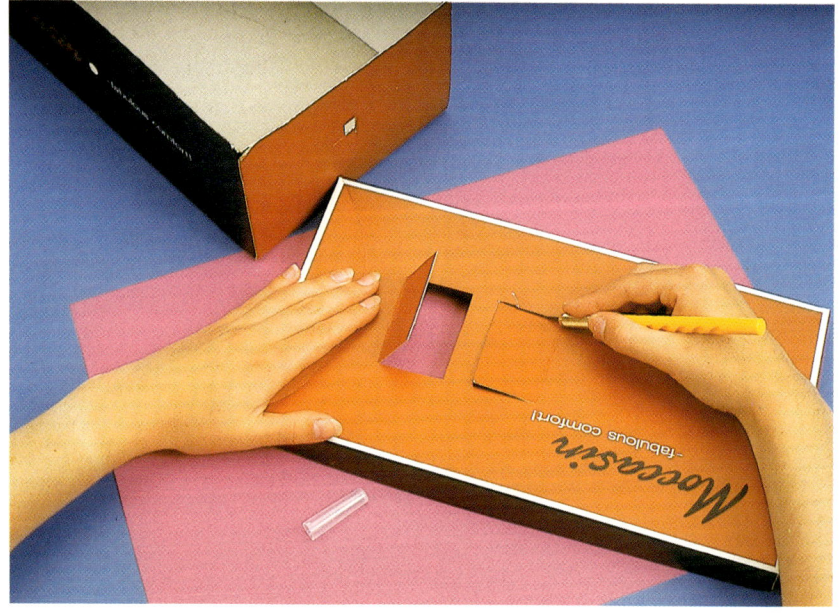

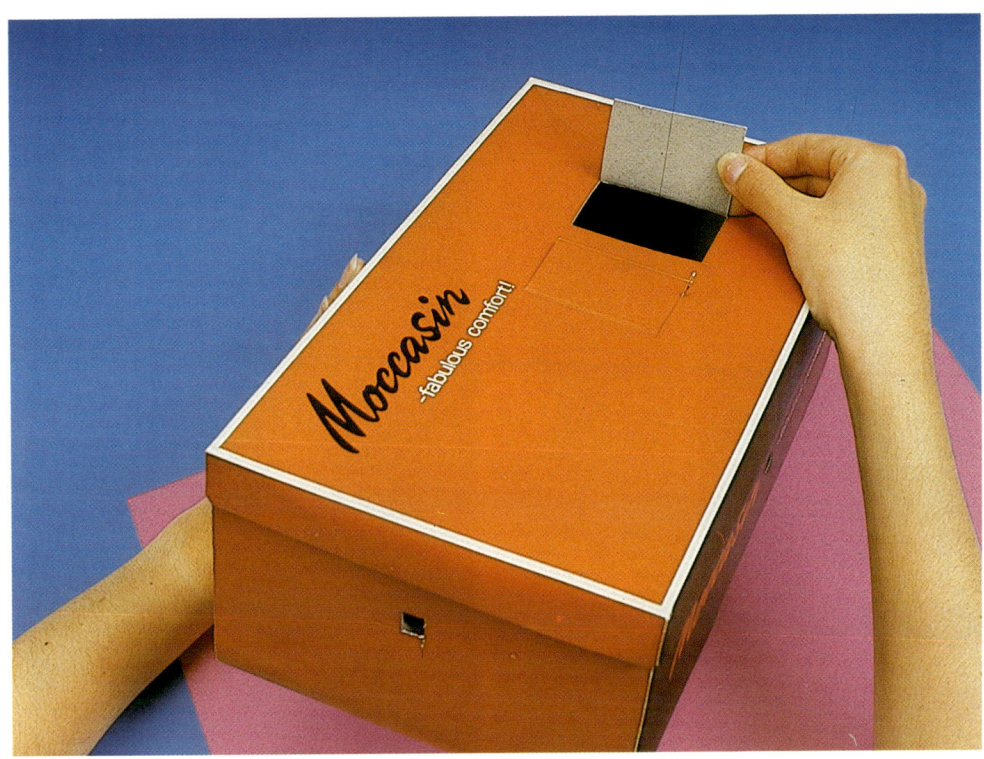

3 The window flaps can be bent upwards to allow light into the far end of the box. Look through the peep-hole and experiment with lighting effects by lifting up the flaps to different extents, to allow different amounts of light into the box.

Now make an interesting theatre set inside the box by adding card models and other objects.

4 Use scrap pieces of card and other materials to make models that you can place inside the box. Stand them on the floor of the box. You could make trees, animals, soldiers and toilet-roll pillars (painted brightly). You could also add flowers, twigs and grass.

5 Shine a small torch through one of the window flaps. If you want to be more adventurous, use coloured tissue paper or coloured cellophane to change the lighting effects.

Some more ideas

Take off the box lid. Place two or three lengths of strong card across the open top and tape them into place. Hang small objects such as shells, paper clips, keys and feathers from these card struts with fine cotton thread. Close the lid and peep into your theatre. The objects will move and create an interesting effect.

Here are some theme ideas for your theatre: Under The Sea; Space Invaders; Fairyland; The Jungle. Try to think of more.

A rolled newspaper model

Rolled newspaper models are made with old newspapers. Smaller models can be made with magazine pages.

This standing model is based on triangles – three-sided figures.

You will need old newspapers or magazines, scissors, sticky tape, paint and a paintbrush, glue, and a base of strong card, hardboard or plywood.

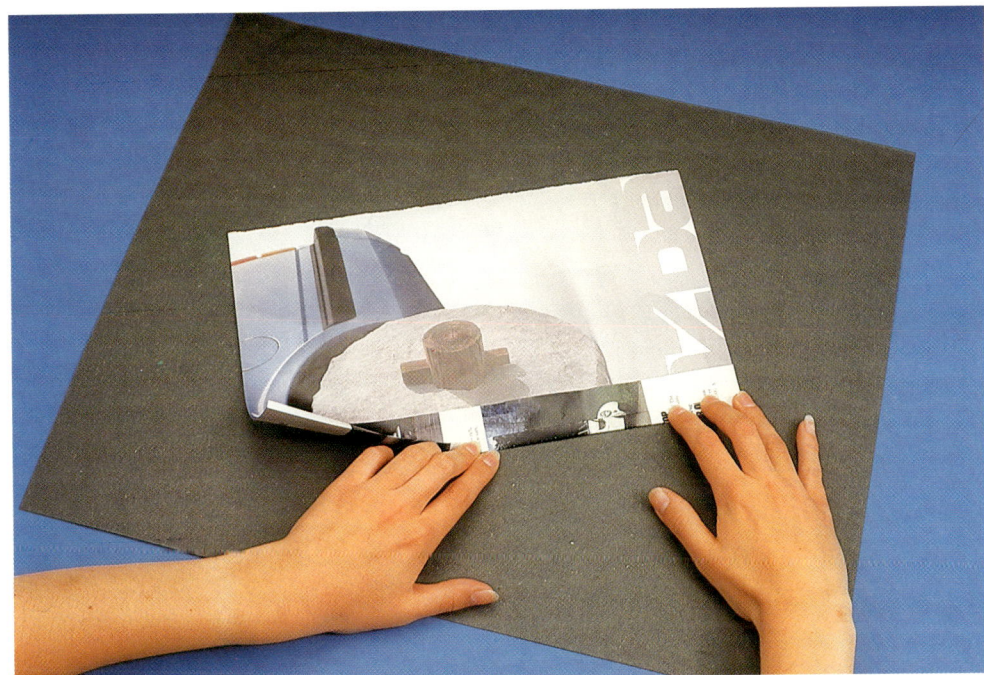

1 Take a sheet of newspaper or magazine paper and make it into a tight roll.

2 To stop the paper unrolling, fasten one or two small pieces of sticky tape round it. Go on to make a number of paper rolls.

3 Fold each of your paper rolls into an equilateral triangle (an equilateral triangle is one which has three equal sides).

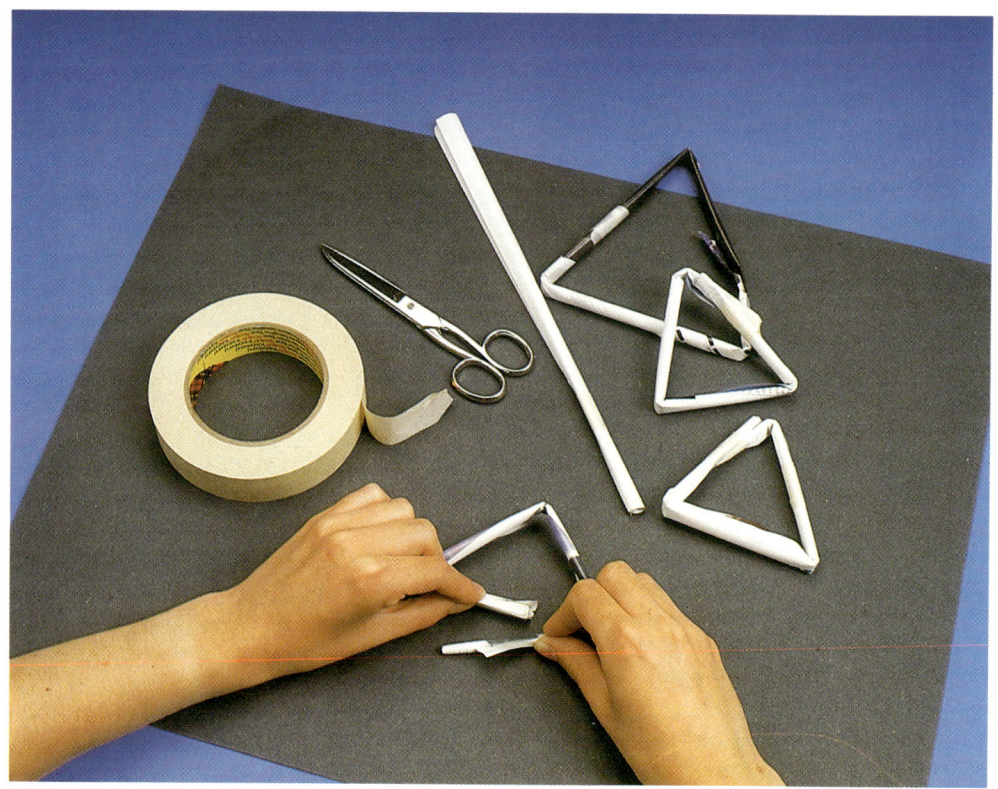

4 Firmly tape the ends of each triangle.

5 Make ten or more triangles then paint them in bright colours.

6 Glue one triangle firmly to your base to make your model strong. Add more triangles.

In pictures **7–10** we see paper triangles being used in an inventive way to form different models.

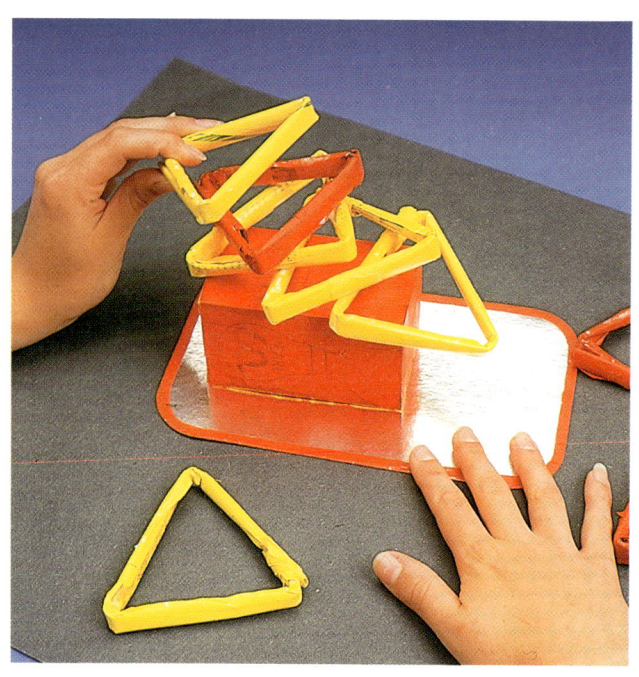

7

8

9

10

Now invent some more models. Design and build a structure up to 40 cm high by standing each triangle on end, side-by-side with other triangles. Tape or glue them to each other. Finish off your sculpture by painting it.

Useful tips

1 If you use paper from magazines instead of newspaper you will produce shorter but stronger rolls.

2 A dowel rod about 60 cm long is a useful 'rolling aid'. Simply place a half-folded newspaper on the floor or on a table top then roll it around the wooden dowel rod.

3 Instead of waiting until your sculpture is finished before painting it, try painting the paper rolls *before* you start to construct models with them.

Newspaper tower blocks

Once again you need to make a number of paper rolls, as shown on page 25. You will need old newspapers or magazines, scissors, sticky tape, and a base of strong card, hardboard or plywood, about 30 cm square. The idea is to build three tower blocks of different heights.

1 Fold each paper roll to form a square. It doesn't matter if the lengths of each side of the square vary a little. Some of your rolled paper squares may be smaller than others to give variety.

2 Tape the squares together.

3 Decide how you want to position the tower blocks on the base then glue three of the tightly rolled paper squares in place. Each of these squares will act as the base of a tower block. Build up your tower blocks by gluing rolled paper squares one on top of the other.

4 Keep going until you have formed three skyscraper constructions. The tallest should be about 60 cm high.

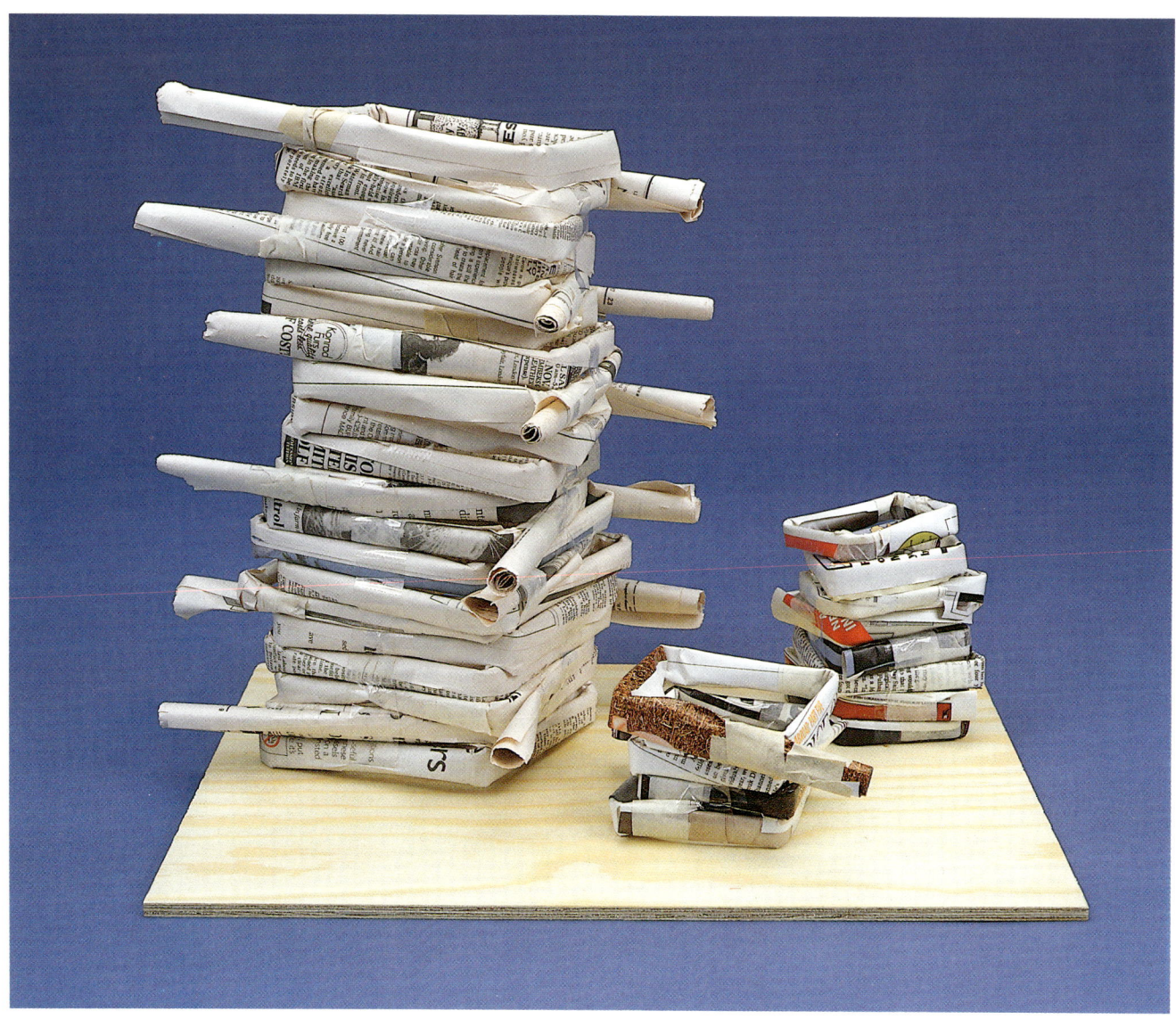

5 This model has three strong, unpainted towers.

Some more ideas

1 Let some of the rolled paper squares twist slightly as you build each tower, to produce a spiral effect.

2 Complete your model by spray-painting it in one colour *or* by painting each tower in a different colour.

A standing animal

To make a standing animal you will need a box for the body. This could be an old chocolate box, toothpaste packet, cereal packet or soap packet. If you want to make a very big animal you will need a large cardboard box and a friend to help you!

Give your animal four or more legs. These can be made from cardboard tubes or folded lengths of card. Stick them to the body with tape or glue.

Add a neck and a head. Use small boxes or folded card shapes for these and glue them to the animal's body.

Add ears, horns and a tail. Pattern your animal's body by adding coloured shapes of sticky paper or by painting it. Small pieces of corrugated paper or small balls of screwed-up paper look very effective when stuck all over the body. Finish your animal by adding more colour and texture.

Be adventurous and make a zoo, with animals of different sizes, shapes and colours.

A brightly-coloured standing animal.

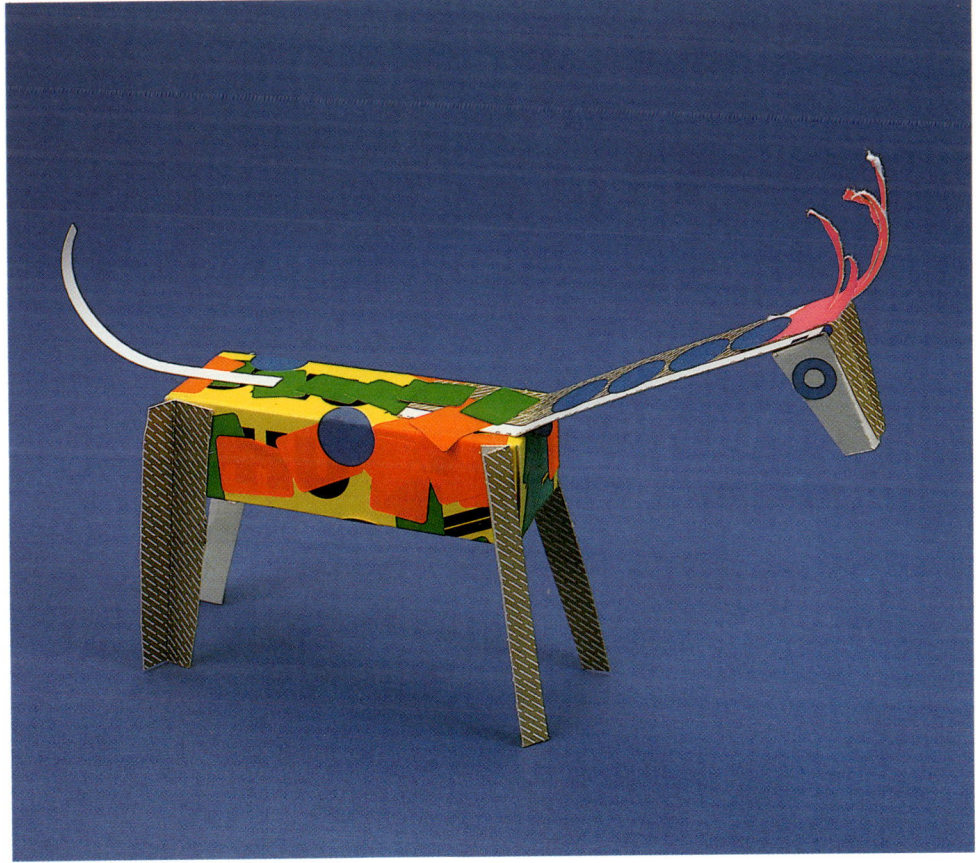

A rolled-paper relief model

You will need a long strip of card aproximately 60 cm long and between 5 cm and 8 cm wide (or two strips, each approximately 30 cm long), a cutting knife, a metal ruler, glue, paper clips, strips of scrap card and paper, and rubber bands or sticky tape.

1 Using the cutting knife and ruler, score and cut the long strip of card into two pieces of equal length. Leave a small tab at the end of each piece.

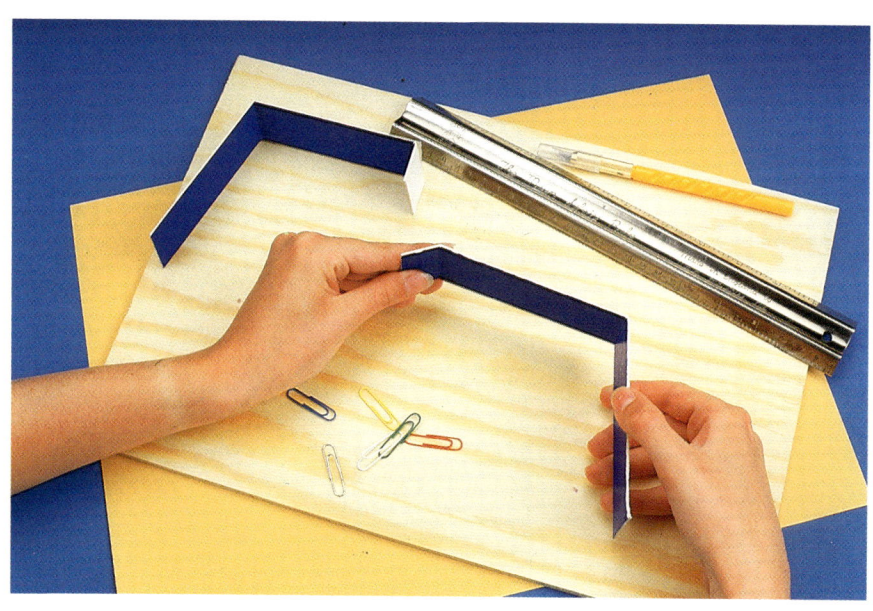

2 Bend each strip in the middle to form a right-angled corner. Bend the tab lines too.

3 Glue the strips together to make an open box shape.

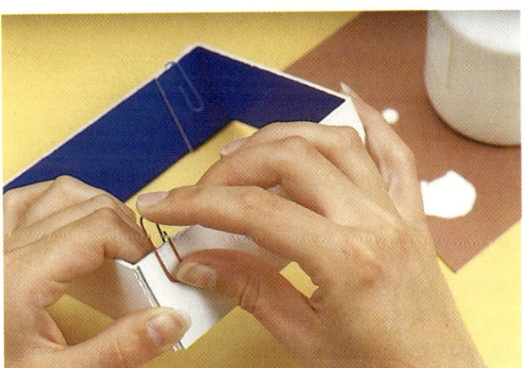

4 Hold the strips in place with paper clips until the glue sets.

5 Make tight paper rolls from the scrap card and paper strips. (These can vary in width from, say, 1 cm to 5 cm and be of different lengths.) Rubber bands or sticky tape will prevent the strips from unrolling. Starting at one corner of the open box, glue the paper rolls in position.

6 Continue to add more rolls – some smaller and others bigger – until you completely fill the box shape.

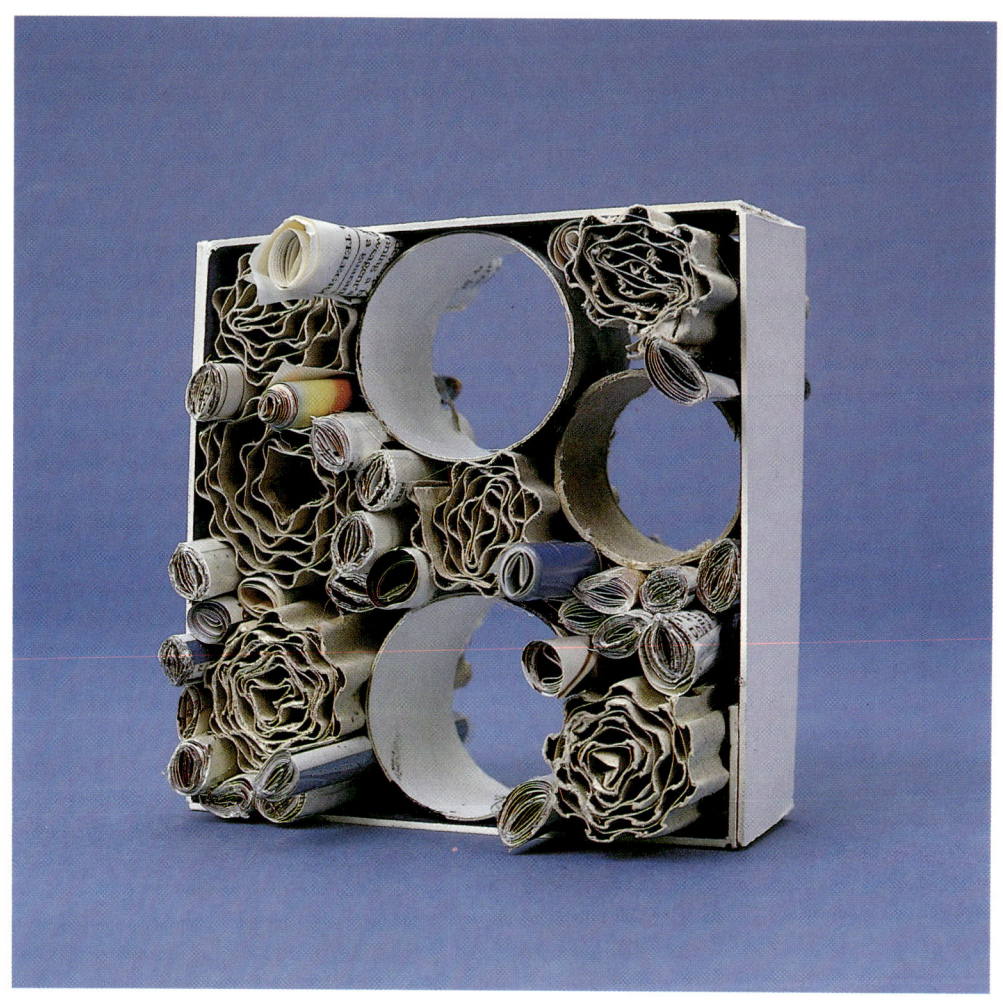

Some more ideas
1 Allow some paper rolls to stick out further than others.
2 Try painting the ends of some of the rolls, using a small brush and thick, bright colours.
3 Think of this model as a two-sided sculpture. Paint both sides.

Stand your sculpture on a sideboard or hang it from a ceiling hook like a mobile.

Card zig-zags

It is possible to cut card so that you can bend it both backwards and forwards.

1 Place a strip of card flat on your cutting board. Draw pencil lines on both sides of the card using a ruler. These should be spaced out at regular intervals (for example, 2 cm, 3 cm or 5 cm). Use your ruler and cutting knife to make gentle scoring cuts on both sides of the card strip. Make cut number one on the top side, number two on the underside, number three on the top side, and so on.

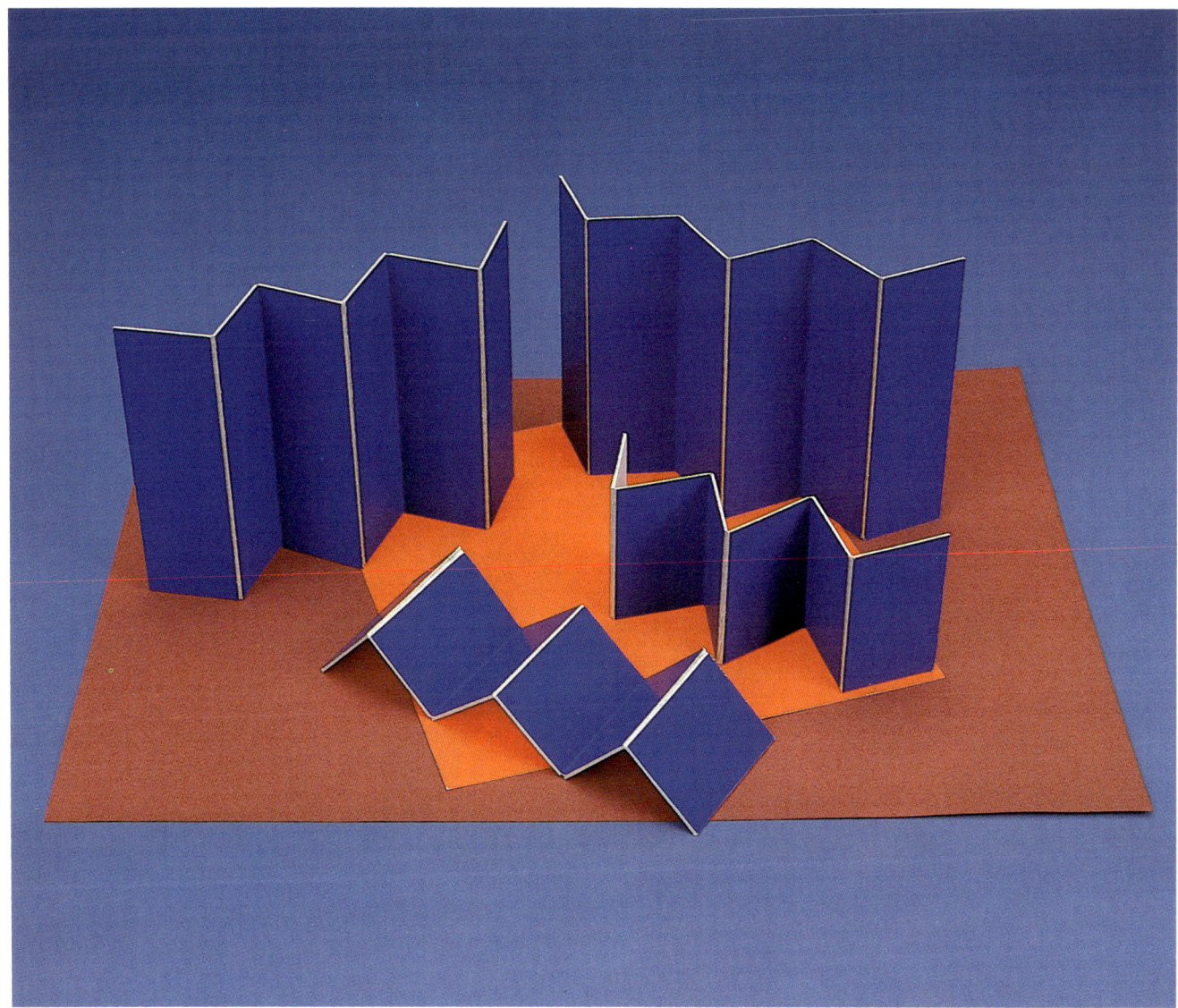

2 Now bend your card strip – first one way and then the other. This will give you a zig-zag. Construct models from these zig-zag units. The lines of crisp white where this strong blue card was scored with the cutting knife are an effective addition.

Five-sided units

Once again you need strips of card. This time make five gentle scoring cuts in each length of card, but on one side of the card only. The distances between the cuts should be the same each time. Before you start cutting, measure these distances carefully and draw in guidelines with your pencil and ruler. At the end of each card strip leave a small tab. This tab will be stuck to the inside of the unit.

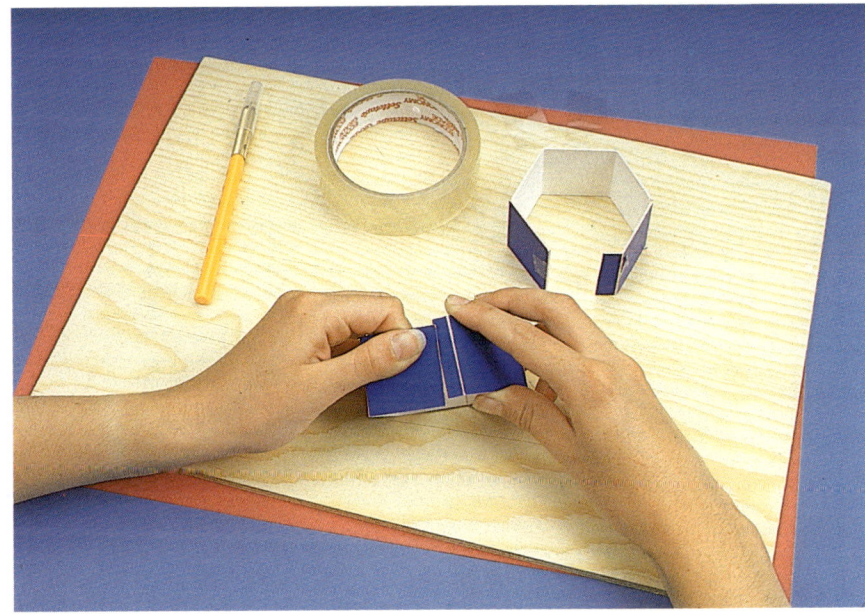

1 Bend each unit to form a five-sided figure. Put a little glue on the tab and use a paper clip to hold it securely while the glue sets.

2 When you have made a number of units, use them to invent mathematical models.

3 Try making other mathematical shapes.

On your own

This book has attempted to start you off making simple card sculptures. In following the various instructions you should have produced a number of different pieces. Now develop your own versions of some of the ideas, or try new ones. Here are some suggestions to help you.

1 Try making a card model which combines two ideas in this book – for example, one with curved card strips and a tube (see pages 12–18).

1 This model has a card ring for a base. Scrap pieces of coloured card seem to grow from it. Make a crown based on this idea, to wear to a fancy dress party.

1 Make an open box shape (see pages 34–35). Develop this as a relief model with odd strips of card instead of paper rolls.

2 This relief model is designed to stand on a sideboard or table. It consists of curved and straight strips of card.

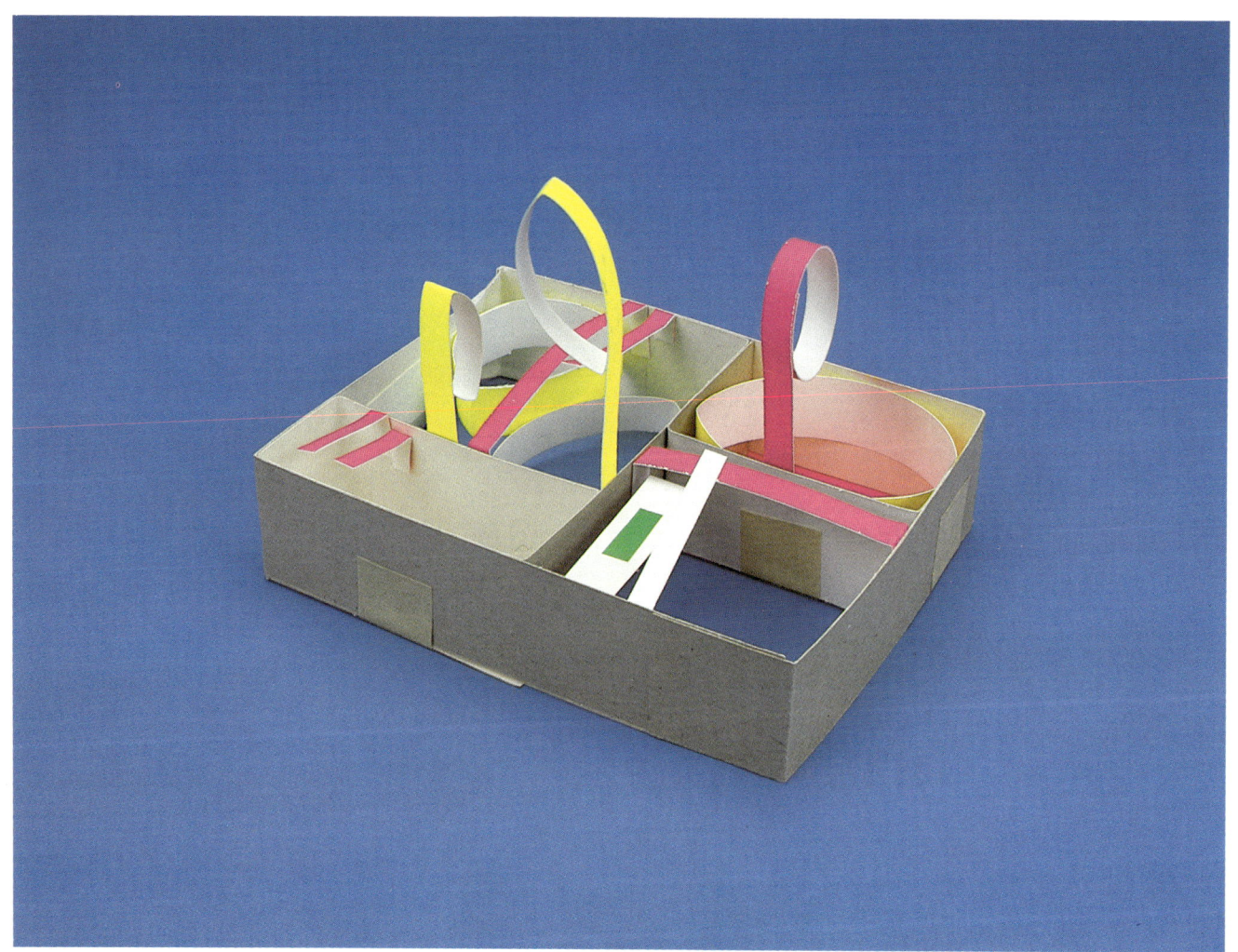

3 Construct a tall card tower. You will need some small boxes – matchboxes, old soap boxes or tea packets will do very well. Use scrap pieces of card left over from some of your model-making and cut them into smaller pieces and different shapes. Stick some of your boxes and card pieces together – one on top of another – until you have a tall tower. Remember to start off with a strong base. Can you make a tower which is as tall as yourself?

4 An interesting way to make other rolled newspaper models is to bend some rolls to form letters. Limit yourself to straight letters (A, E, F, H, I, K, L, M, N, T, V, W, X, Y, Z), as this will make your sculpture easier to construct.

You could use ten or more of one letter to make a sculpture. Another model could be made from only two or three letters.

Use a base of strong card, hardboard or plywood. Glue one letter to it and then add more. The letters could lie flat or stand upright, or you could use a mixture of both.

Paint the letters in different colours before you start.

3 Here, letters made from newspaper rolls have been used to make a clock face.

4 Make some simple sculptures with card or wooden bases like those in pictures **4** and **5**. Oddly-shaped card pieces were used but these have been arranged nicely.

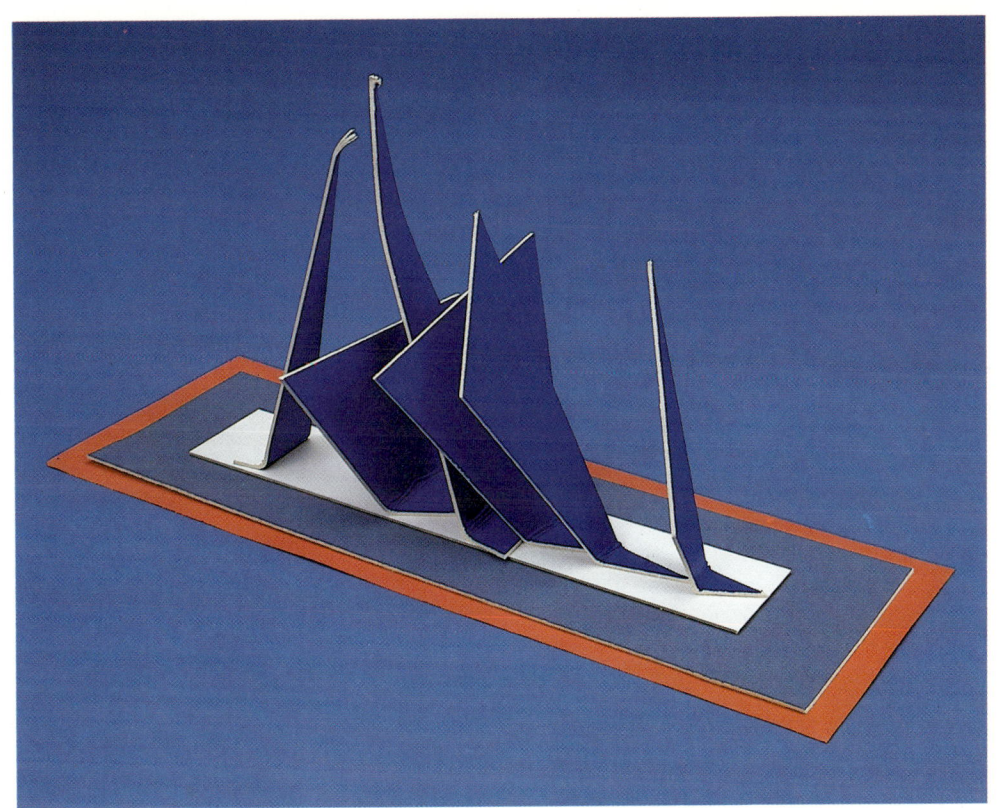

5

6 This model was made on a small, wooden door panel bought in a DIY store. Scrap card and toilet rolls were used in its construction and then it was painted.

7 Construct a model with a cardboard tube and torn pieces of paper. Simply tear leaf-like shapes from colourful magazine pages and stick them on to the tube until you have covered all of it.

8 Think of other ideas. Make an oil-rig, a bridge or a castle.

Further information

Most of the materials mentioned in this book are scrap materials which would usually be thrown into the dustbin. Once you start looking, you will find all sorts of interestingly shaped cardboard packets and tubes! Keep an assortment of these scrap materials in a large cardboard box.

If you are working on a special project, you may decide that you would like to use good card rather than an old food packet or similar. Many stationers such as W.H. SMITH LTD carry a wide range of card, but you will find an even larger choice in a shop specialising in artists' materials. The kind of card stocked in artists' materials shops comes in different colours and can be very effective. The colours you can purchase will include white (both sides), black (white on the reverse side), and a whole range of different colours (usually coloured on one side with the reverse white). To start with, buy one sheet of each of the following colours: white, black, red, blue and green. Later on, if you can afford to, go on to buy other colours, depending on the number and kinds of models you intend to make.

Artists' materials stockists should also be able to supply many of the other items you need such as paints, paintbrushes, glue, a metal ruler and a cutting knife.

Specialist materials (or materials in large quantities) can be purchased through one of the following suppliers:

DRYAD, Northgates, Leicester LE1 9BU

WINSOR & NEWTON LTD, 51 Rathbone Place, London W1

E.J. ARNOLD, Parkside, Dewsbury Road, Leeds LS11 5TD

Index

Card 4, 5, 6, 7, 8, 9, 10, 11, 13, 16, 19, 22, 23, 24, 25, 30, 33, 34, 37, 38, 41, 42, 43, 44, 45, 47
    Bending card 6, 7, 8, 10, 11, 34, 37, 38
    Scoring and cutting card 8–10, 34, 37, 38, 39
    Tearing card 7
    Twisting card 13
Card rings 7, 16–18, 41
Card strips 6, 11, 13, 14, 15, 20, 34, 35, 37, 38, 39, 41, 42
Cardboard box(es) 4, 5, 13, 22, 33, 47
Cardboard tubes 16, 21, 32, 33, 41, 46, 47
Corrugated card 4, 14
Curving sculpture 11–15
Cutting board 4, 5, 8, 37
Cutting knife 4, 5, 8, 9, 16, 22, 34, 37, 38, 47

Five-sided units 39–40
Food cartons 4, 11, 33, 47
Formica 4, 5

Glue 4, 6, 7, 11, 13, 16, 19, 20, 25, 27, 29, 31, 33, 34, 35, 39, 43, 47

Hardboard 4, 5, 11, 16, 19, 25, 30, 43

Magazine(s) 4, 25, 29, 30, 46
Mathematical models 39–40

Newspaper(s) 4, 21, 25, 29, 30
Newspaper tower blocks 30–32

Paintbrush 4, 16, 19, 25, 36, 47
Paint(s) 4, 16, 17, 18, 19, 20, 25, 27, 29, 32, 36, 43, 45, 47
Paper 4, 19, 20, 33, 34, 35, 46
Paper clips 4, 6, 7, 24, 34, 35, 39
Paper rolls 25, 26, 29, 30, 35, 36, 42, 43
Paper squares 30–31, 32
Paper triangles 26, 27, 28, 29
Peep-hole theatre 22–24
Plywood 4, 11, 16, 19, 25, 30, 43

Relief model 19–21, 42
Rolled newspaper model 25–29, 43
Rolled-paper relief model 34–36
Rubber bands 4, 34, 35
Ruler 4, 8, 9, 34, 37, 38

Saw 4, 16
Scissors 4, 6, 19, 25, 30
Shoe box 4, 22
Standing animal 33
Sticky tape 4, 24, 25, 26, 29, 30, 33, 34, 35

Thread 4, 13, 24
Toilet roll centres 4, 16, 19, 20, 45
Torch 4, 22, 24
Tubular model 16–18

Zig-zags 37–38